THE
Golden Hands
COMPLETE
BOOK
OF
Knitting & Crochet

RANDOM HOUSE
NEW YORK

Knitting

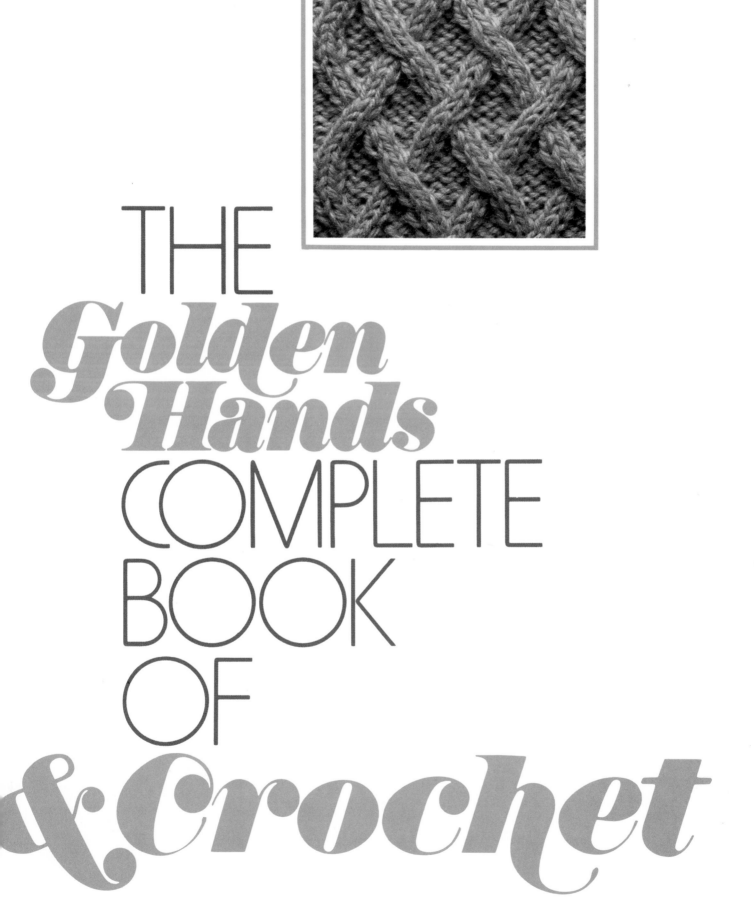

THE Golden Hands COMPLETE BOOK OF & Crochet

First Printing
© Marshall Cavendish Limited 1973
All rights reserved under International and
Pan-American Copyright Conventions. Published in
the United States by Random House, Inc., New York,
and simultaneously in Canada by Random House
of Canada Limited, Toronto.

The greater part of the material published in this
book was first published by Marshall Cavendish Ltd.
in "Golden Hands." The British edition entitled
*Golden Hands Encyclopedia of Knitting and
Crochet* was published by William Collins Sons &
Co. Ltd.

Library of Congress Card Catalog Number 73-5012
ISBN 0-394-48569-6

Manufactured in the United States of America

CONTENTS

Knitting Know-how

Basic Wardrobe

CONTENTS *(continued)*

Crochet Know-how

Basic Wardrobe

Collector's Pieces

ACKNOWLEDGEMENTS

Photographers:

John Adriaan, Malcolm Aird, Adèle Baker, Michael Barrington-Martin, Stephen Wicknell, Clive Bearsnell, John Carter, Clive Corless, Bob Croxford, Richard Dormer, Leslie Emms, Michael Harvey, Michael Harwood, Chris Lewis, Patrick Lichfield, Dawn Marsden, David Newsome, Peter Rand, Paul Redman, Bruce Scott, M. Stuart, Chris Thomson, Peter Watkins, Jim Williams.

Illustrators:

Annette Critten, M. Edwards, Elizabeth Embleton, Barbara Firth, Sally Foy, Susan France, Diane Groves, Isobel Hollowood, Andrei Pearman, Margaret Power, Renee Robinson, Posy Simmonds, Paul Williams.

Designers:

Diana Chabot, Rae Compton, Marjorie Finbow, Bairnswear, J. & P. Coats Ltd, Jaeger Hand Knitting Ltd, Lister & Co. Ltd, Martin Mahony Ltd, R. V. Marriner Ltd, Patons & Baldwins Ltd, Robin yarns, Sirdar Ltd, Pingouin yarns, J. Templeton & Son Ltd, H. G. Twilley Ltd, Wendy yarns.

Text:

Rae Compton, Pam Dawson, Marjorie Finbow, Ina Milton.

Credits:

W. Bill Ltd, Camera Press, London: GMN

We would like to thank the following for their help and co-operation:

Abel Ferrall Ltd; Mary Coleman, Dixon & Partners Ltd, The Felt and Hessian Shop, London; Highland Home Industries, Edinburgh; Patons & Baldwins Ltd.

Introduction

Knitting and crochet are still as popular as ever and the increasing range of yarns and designs means endless possibilities for making beautiful garments and household articles. So whether you want to experiment with new ideas or whether you are a traditionalist at heart, the Golden Hands Complete Book of Knitting and Crochet will please you.

The step-by-step instructions, clearly illustrated with diagrams and color photographs at each stage, could not be simpler to follow, and beginners will be encouraged to find that they can create garments right from the start—from a cozy knitted scarf to a multi-colored vest in crocheted squares.

A professional-looking finish is vital to the success of a piece of work, and this book is full of tips to help you achieve this, covering such techniques as buttonholes, hems, pockets and necklines.

For all those who have a favorite pattern but would like to experiment with different effects, Golden Hands includes a wide variety of stitch patterns from the most delicate of lacy looks to the bulkiest of fabric weaves, and from the boldest of jacquard motifs to the most subtle of toning stripes. As you become more skillful, try the superb traditional designs of Aran and Shetland knitting or Irish crochet lace.

The Basic Wardrobe patterns after each section are related closely to the techniques described in the Know-how chapters, and are the ideal way of putting your newly-acquired skills into practice. There are garments for the whole family— pretty, practical play clothes for children, chunky casuals for men and boys and a whole range of fashion garments for yourself, including sweaters, shawls, dresses and pants for every occasion from a country weekend to a special evening out.

Once you have mastered the techniques and experimented with the stitches, you can learn to create designs of your own, combining new styles, colors and patterns to make truly original garments.

Anyone excited by all the possibilities of hand knitting and crochet today will find this book a constant source of inspiration—so begin right away. You will be delighted by the results.

Chapter 1

Introduction to fashion knitting

Hand knitting is one of the most popular fashion crafts these days. New dyes, fibers, metallic yarns, mixed yarns and beautiful nubby textures all lend themselves well to the fluid, flexible quality of hand knitting. What is more, techniques from different countries are now circulating internationally, so that there is a wealth of new information available. For beginners, these Knitting Know-how chapters present a clear guide to the basic techniques. For more experienced knitters, there are many clever, little-known techniques like the invisible casting-on method in Knitting Know-how Chapter 3, a range of garments in the Basic Wardrobe chapters and hints on how to do your own designing.

The Tools of the Trade

☐ A metal or wooden ruler
☐ Scissors
☐ Darning needles
☐ Rustless steel pins
☐ Stitch holder (like a large safety pin, to hold stitches not in use)
☐ Row counter
☐ Knitting needle gauge to check correct needle size
☐ Cloth or plastic bag in which to keep knitting clean
☐ Iron and ironing board with pad
☐ Cotton cloths suitable for use when pressing

Know your needles
Modern knitting needles are usually made of lightweight coated metal or of plastic, and should always be kept in good condition. Bent, scratched or uneven needles will spoil the evenness of your knitting, and should be discarded.

For "straight" knitting—that is, knitting worked backwards and forwards on two needles—needles with knobs at one end are advisable, as they lessen the possibility of dropped stitches, which is frustrating to the most even-tempered knitter.

For socks, gloves, certain types of sweaters, and any garment which is knitted "around"—that is, in a circle instead of straight —a set of four or more needles is used, pointed at both ends. A flexible circular needle is used for some designs for seamless circular garments, like skirts. The effect is the same as dividing the work among three or more needles, but the work is much easier to handle and one avoids having loose stitches where the needles join.

Needle sizes
With any knitted design, you will need a specified number in a knitting needle. Here is a chart of American, British and metric sizes. As you will see, with American sizes the lower the number, the smaller the diameter of the needle, whereas with the British sizes the reverse is true.

Knitting Needle Sizes		
American	**British**	**Metric**
15	000	9
13	00	$8\frac{1}{2}$
12	0	8
11	1	$7\frac{1}{2}$
$10\frac{1}{2}$	2	7
10	3	$6\frac{1}{2}$
9	4	6
8	5	$5\frac{1}{2}$
7	6	5
6	7	$4\frac{1}{2}$
5	8	4
4	9	$3\frac{1}{2}$
3	10	$3\frac{1}{4}$
2	11	3
1	12	$2\frac{1}{2}$
0	13	$2\frac{1}{4}$
00	14	2

Yarns and ply

Yarn is the word used to describe any spun thread, whether it is fine or thick. It may be a natural fiber like wool, cotton, linen, silk, angora, or mohair—or a man-made fiber like Acrilan, Orlon, nylon or rayon.

When choosing a yarn, you will come across the word ply. This indicates the number of spun single threads that have been twisted together. Each single thread can be spun to any thickness so that a simple reference to the ply does not necessarily determine the thickness of the finished yarn, although the terms 2-ply, 3-ply and 4-ply are often used to mean yarn of a recognized thickness. The following ply classification is broadly applicable to the majority of hand-knitting yarns whether made from wool, man-made fibers or blends of both.

Baby yarns are usually made from the higher quality yarns, and are available in 3-ply and 4-ply.

2-ply, 3-ply and 4-ply yarns may consist of wool, wool and man-made fiber blends, or 100% man-made fiber.

Sport Weight yarns are usually 4-ply yarns about $\frac{1}{2}$ the thickness of knitting worsted.

Knitting Worsted yarns are the most widely used of all yarns, and are usually made from four spun single threads (although there are exceptions to this), twisted together to produce hard-wearing yarns.

Bulky yarns can either be 2-ply, 3-ply or 4-ply. They are spun like any other basic yarn but each strand is of a heavier weight.

Dress yarns are usually novelty yarns, spun in a completely different manner to the basic yarns in order to create more interesting and unusual textures. They are generally not designated according to ply.

Very important!
Since there is no official standardization, yarns marketed by different firms often vary in thickness and in yardage.

If you cannot obtain the yarn suggested in the directions, or have set your heart on something else, it is possible to use other yarn, provided you can obtain the same gauge as given in the pattern. The Great Yarn Chart on pages 10 and 11 will help you here. Always buy sufficient yarn at one time so that all the yarn used is from the same dye lot. Yarn from a different dye lot may vary very slightly, but even the slightest difference can cause an unsightly line across your work, marring the whole garment.

Yarn weights — ounces and grams

When buying yarn, it is advisable to check with the salesperson as to the weight of the balls. You may find that some brands, especially if they have been imported from Europe, will give the weight in grams instead of ounces, which is the normal practice and the way the yarn requirements for the Basic Wardrobe patterns have been stated. Below is a table to help you convert grams to ounces. If you are at all worried, remember, it is wiser to buy too much than to run short.

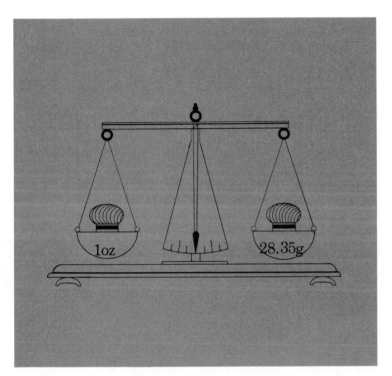

A 1 oz ball of wool weighs just a little more than a 25g ball.

Useful weights—in grams (g) and kilograms (kg)	
1oz	= 28·35g
4oz	= 113·4g
8oz	= 226·8g
1lb	= 454g
25g	= 0·9oz
50g	= 1·8oz
1kg/1000g	= 2·2lb

Knitting yarn quantities (to convert either way)

1oz=25g+3·35g
For 3oz buy 4 balls of 25g

7oz buy 8 balls of 25g	16oz buy 18 balls of 25g
12oz buy 14 balls of 25g	20oz buy 23 balls of 25g

Your success depends on gauge

To make any design successfully it is absolutely vital that you obtain the same gauge as given in the directions. This point cannot be overemphasized!

This means that you must obtain the same number of stitches to the inch and *also* the same number of rows to the inch as the designer obtained.

To test your knit gauge, cast on 20 sts with the needles that are specified. Work even for 3 inches in given pattern. Bind off and press swatch lightly. Pin down on paper. With a ruler, measure across one inch, then down one inch, counting the number of stitches and rows to the inch. If you have more stitches to the inch than given in the directions, use a larger needle. If you have fewer stitches and rows to the inch than given, use a smaller needle. Continue to work up swatches until the gauge is correct. Testing the gauge not only applies to the beginner but also to the experienced knitter.

A few minutes spent on this preparation lays the foundation for a successful garment. If it is overlooked, a great deal of work may be undertaken before the error in size is realized. Even half a stitch too many or too few, although seemingly little, amounts to nine stitches too many or too few on the back of a 34 inch sweater. This can mean the completed sweater is 2 inches too large or too small. Once you have worked your gauge swatch, lay it on a flat surface and pin it down. Place a tape measure on your knitting and mark out one inch with pins. Count the number of stitches between the two pins very carefully.

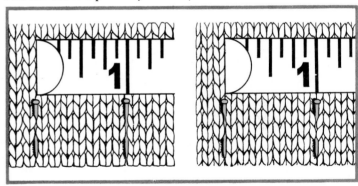

▲ *The inches are marked out with pins, left, showing 7 stitches to the inch: right, measuring between the pins gives 7½ stitches to the inch*
▼ *The gauge swatch is pinned into a perfect square, ready to measure*

The Great Yarn Chart

How to use your favorite yarns for all the garments in the Golden Hands wardrobe of knitting and crochet

We're going to let you in on a trade secret. If you've fallen in love with a particular color or yarn, or find it impossible to obtain the yarn featured in any of the photographs in Golden Hands, it is possible to use an equivalent yarn.

This does not mean that you will automatically be able to substitute one yarn for another, but if you test the gauge carefully with the help of this chart, you should be able to use an alternative.

It may not necessarily look quite the same as in the photograph, but it will knit up to the same size in your hands as the original yarn would have. Start by knitting a small gauge square, for example 4 inches by 4 inches, in the yarn of your choice, to see that you can get the same number of stitches to the inch as given in the pattern. Pat Boyle, our knitting and crochet expert, has tested every yarn and has based this chart on her results. To make your number of stitches to the inch equal hers you may need to use a size smaller or larger needle than suggested. Don't worry, some people knit very loosely, others knit very tightly. The important point is for you to have exactly the same number of stitches to one inch as given in the pattern.

This chart shows the yarns (with approximate yardage in each ball of yarn given in parentheses) listed under the number of stitches to one inch, worked on a given needle size and measured over stockinette stitch.

However, it is difficult to judge how to count, say, $3\frac{1}{2}$ stitches or $4\frac{1}{2}$ stitches to the inch! Therefore it is always wise to count stitches over 4 inches and then divide by 4. (For example, $3\frac{1}{2}$ sts x 4 over 1in = 14sts over 4in.) If you are working with even half a stitch to the inch too few or too many, the finished garment will be too small or too big.

Those of you who have had problems of conversion for crochet yarn will be happy to know that these yarn equivalents apply also to crochet.

Information in this table has been checked at the time of publishing, but brands and standards can change. To avoid disappointment, we suggest you take particular care to knit up a gauge square before you begin.

$2\frac{1}{2}$ sts on No.13 needles

Bernat
Scandia (55)
Columbia-Minerva
Bulky Nantuk (75)
Nantuk Cascade (96)
Spinnerin
Homespun (85)
Homespun Heathertones (85)

$2\frac{1}{2}$ sts on No.15 needles

Bear Brand or Fleisher
Go-Go (44)
Gigantic (44)
Botany
Colossal (44)

3sts on No.10½ needles

Bear Brand or Fleisher
Supra Mohair 2 strands (80)
Bernat
Shakerspun (50)
Reynolds
Lopi (120)
Unger
Bim Bam (40)

3sts on No.11 needles

Bear Brand or Fleisher
Supra Mohair (80)
Gigantic (44)
Botany
Colossal (44)
Columbia-Minerva
Bulky Nantuk (75)
Nantuk Cascade (96)

3½ sts on No.10 needles

Brunswick
Lochwind Orlon Sayelle (100)
Aspen (60)
Reynolds
Lopi (120)

3½ sts on No.10½ needles

Bear Brand or Fleisher
Supra Mohair (80)
Four Seasons (71)
Botany
Jiffy (71)
Columbia-Minerva
Bulky Nantuk (75)
Nantuk Cascade (96)
Reynolds
Grizzli (80)
Spinnerin
Misty (90)

4sts on No.8 needles

Bernat
Mohair Plus (103)
Reynolds
Mohair No.1 (140)
Unger
Les Bouquets (125)
Traditional Fleck (108)
Renata (112)

4sts on No.9 needles

Reynolds
Trocadero (87)
Unger
Flair (88)

4sts on No.10 needles

Bear Brand or Fleisher
Supra Mohair (80)
Highlight (115)
Four Seasons (71)
Columbia-Minerva
Knitting Worsted (280)
Nantuk 4-ply Yarn (300)
Reynolds
Grizzli (80)
Spinnerin
Topflight (80)
Peppi (85)
Unger
Regatta (83)

4½ sts on No.6 needles

Bernat
Sunlin-Spun (49)
Reynolds
Mohair No.1 (140)
Unger
Les Bouquets (125)

4½ sts on No.8 needles

American Thread
Dawn Knitting
  Worsted (252)
Dawn Sayelle (258)
Bear Brand or Fleisher
Ever-Match Futura (100)
Twin-Pak Win-Knit (280)
Columbia-Minerva
Knitting Worsted (280)
Nantuk Dimension (87)
Reynolds
Irish Fisherman (75)
Versailles (145)
Unger
Nanette (150)
Domino (150)

4½ sts on No.9 needles

Bear Brand or Fleisher
Win-tot (90)
Winsom (180)
Bernat
Super Angora (27)

5sts on No.5 needles

Bear Brand or Fleisher
Soufflé (175)
Reynolds
Mohair No.1 (140)
Spinnerin
Charisma (100)
Unger
Les Coraux (170)
Les Bouquets (125)

5sts on No.6 needles

Bear Brand or Fleisher
Shamrock (135)
Ever-Match Futura (100)
Twin-Pak Knitting
  Worsted (270)
Bernat
Cott'n Silk (137)
Blarney Spun (104)
Columbia-Minerva
Nantuk Sports Yarn (210)
Reynolds
Alpaca & Wool (165)
Baby Orlon (115)
Cascatelle (77)
Unger
Rygja (280)
Nanette (150)
Mimosa (148)
Firebird (88)

5sts on No.7 needles

Bear Brand, Fleisher or Botany
Supra Mohair (80)
Bucilla
Melody (100)
Spinnerin
Deluxe Knitting
  Worsted (215)
Frostlon Petite (88)
Irish Fisherman Yarn (275)
Unger
Natté Sport (104)

5sts on No.8 needles

Bear Brand, Fleisher or Botany
Win-tot (90)
Winsom (180)
Totem (125)
Bernat
Berella 4 (286)
Berella Germantown (133)
Venetian Bouclé (75)
Brunswick
Germantown Worsted (255)
Windrush Wintuk (265)

5½sts on No.4 needles

Unger
Les Coraux (170)

5½sts on No.5 needles

Bernat
Baby Germantown (100)
Berella Sportspun (193)
Columbia-Minerva
Nantuk Sports Yarn (210)
Precious Quick Knitting
  Nantuk (105)
Reynolds
Danskyarn (115)

5½sts on No.6 needles

Reynolds
Alpaca & Wool (165)
Unger
Tosca (210)

5½sts on No.7 needles

Bear Brand or Fleisher
Win-tot (90)
Winsom (180)
Botany
Scottie (170)

6sts on No.3 needles

American Thread
Dawn Orlon (143)
Reynolds
Kalimousse (125)
Unger
Les Coraux (170)

6sts on No.4 needles

Bear Brand or Fleisher
Shamrock (135)
Botany
Twin-Pak Win-Knit (280)
Reynolds
Novita (230)
Parfait (134)
Unger
Erica (73)
Gardone (92)
Carlotta (80)

6sts on No.5 needles

American Thread
Dawn Wintuk Sports (195)
Bernat
Berella Baby Bulky (100)
Nylo Sports (275)
Bucilla
Paradise (88)
Paradise Puff (88)
Brocade (100)
Brunswick
Pomfret Sport Yarn (200)
Fore-'n-Aft Sport (200)
Columbia-Minerva
Featherweight Worsted (230)
Scamper (135)
Reynolds
Classique (175)
Kermesse (170)
Spinnerin
Wintuk Sport (224)
Wintuk Sport Print (224)
Mona (170)
Mystique (105)
Unger
Musette (200)

6sts on No.6 needles

Reynolds
Feu d'Artifice (135)
Unger
Roxanne (170)
English Crepe (104)

6½sts on No.3 needles

American Thread
Dawn Orlon Pompadour (123)
Reynolds
Angora/Lurex (60)
Audacious (125)
Angelina (22)

6½sts on No.4 needles

Bear Brand or Fleisher
Baby Germantown (115)
Columbia-Minerva
Featherweight Worsted (230)
Camelot Metallic Yarn (130)

7sts on No.3 needles

American Thread
Dawn Nylon (166)
Dawn Wintuk Baby Yarn (166)
Bernat
Berella Fingering (143)
Meadowspun (185)
Nylo Baby Yarn (220)
Brunswick
Fairhaven Fingering Yarn (175)
Reynolds
Cotillion (125)
Grand Cotillion (165)
Spinnerin
Sayelle Baby (185)
Sayelle Baby Print (185)

7sts on No.4 needles

Bear Brand or Fleisher
Win-Sport (235)
Ever-Match Sport &
  Sweater (116)
Botany
Classic Sport No-Dye-
  Lot (116)
Columbia-Minerva
Baby Nantuk (185)
Nantuk Fingering Yarn (185)
Reynolds
Cashmere/Lamb (145)
Natté Fin (190)
Firefly (210)

7½sts on No.3 needles

American Thread
Dawn Nylon Pompadour (133)
Bear Brand or Fleisher
Win-Sport (235)
Ever-Match Sport &
  Sweater (116)
Botany
Classic Sport No-Dye-Lot (116)
Reynolds
Gleneagles (210)

8sts on No.2 needles

Bear Brand or Fleisher
Win-Sport (235)
Botany
Classic Sport No-Dye-Lot (116)

8sts on No.3 needles

Bear Brand or Botany
Win-Spin (175)
Winfant (175)
Columbia-Minerva
Baby Nantuk (185)
Nantuk Fingering Yarn (185)
Reynolds
Baby Supra (Unique) (220)
Spinnerin
Wintuk Fingering (185)

8½sts on No.2 needles

Bear Brand or Fleisher
Winfant (175)
Ever-Match Baby Zephyr (170)

9sts on No.1 needles

Bear Brand or Fleisher
Win-Spin (175)
Winfant (175)
Botany
Baby Zephyr No-Dye-Lot (170)
Saxatones No-Dye-Lot (170)

9sts on No.2 needles

Columbia-Minerva
Baby Nantuk (185)
Nantuk Fingering Yarn (185)

When you use a different
yarn you may find that the
number of ounces or balls
is slightly different.

11

Yarn manufacturers' addresses

In case of difficulty in obtaining any yarns featured in this book, please write directly to the following manufacturers' addresses to find out the location of your nearest retailer.

American Thread and **Dawn** yarns by—
American Thread, High Ridge Park, Stamford, Connecticut 06905.

Bear Brand, Botany, Bucilla and **Fleisher** yarns by–
Bernhard Ulmann Co., Division of Indian Head, 30-20 Thomson Avenue, Long Island City, New York 11101.

Bernat yarns by—
Emile Bernat & Sons Co., Uxbridge, Massachusetts 01569.

Brunswick yarns by—
Brunswick Worsted Mills Inc., Pickens, South Carolina 29671.

Coats & Clark's yarns by—
Coats & Clark's, 430 Park Avenue, New York, New York 10022.

Columbia-Minerva yarns by—
Columbia-Minerva Corp., 295 Fifth Avenue, New York, New York 10016.

Reynolds yarn by—
Reynolds Yarns Inc., 215 Central Avenue, East Farmingdale, New York 11735.

Spinnerin yarns by—
Spinnerin Yarn Co. Inc., 230 Fifth Avenue, New York, New York 10001.

Unger yarns by—
William Unger & Co., 230 Fifth Avenue, New York, New York 10001.

Abbreviations

Here is a list of knitting terms which are usually printed in a shortened form.

In some designs it is necessary to use a special abbreviation applicable to that design only. In such a case the abbreviation will be explained at the point where it is first used, or placed in a clear note before the beginning of the instructions.

alt	=**alternate(ly)**
approx	=**approximate(ly)**
beg	=**begin(ning)**
cont	=**continu(e)(ing)**
dbl	=**double**
dec	=**decreas(e)(ing) by working two stitches together**
dp	=**double-pointed**
foll	=**follow(ing)**
g st	=**garter stitch (every row knit)**
in	=**inch(es)**
inc	=**increas(e)(ing) by working into front and back of stitch**
K	=**knit**
KB	=**knit into back of stitch**
K1B	=**knit one through loop below next stitch**
K up	=**pick up and knit**
K-wise	=**knitwise**
LH	=**left-hand**
M1K	=**make one knitwise by picking up loop that lies between stitch just worked and following stitch, and knitting into back of it**
M1P	=**make one purlwise by picking up loop that lies between stitch just worked and following stitch, and purling into back of it**
No	=**number**
P	=**purl**
patt	=**pattern**
PB	=**purl into back of stitch**
psso	=**pass slip stitch over**
P up	=**pick up and purl**
P-wise	=**purlwise**

rem	=**remain(ing)**
rep	=**repeat**
RH	=**right-hand**
RS	=**right side**
Sl 1K	=**slip 1 knitwise**
Sl 1P	=**slip 1 purlwise**
st(s)	=**stitch(es)**
st st	=**stockinette stitch (one row knit, one row purl)**
tbl	=**through back of loop of stitch**
tog	=**together**
TW2B	=**twist 2 in back by knitting into back of 2nd stitch then back of first stitch on left-hand needle and slipping 2 stitches off needle together**
TW2F	=**twist 2 in front by knitting into front of 2nd stitch then front of first stitch on left-hand needle and slipping 2 stitches off needle together**
WS	=**wrong side**
yo	=**yarn over**
yo as to K	=**bring yarn under right-hand needle to front, then over needle to back, then you are ready to knit the next st**
yo as to P	=**wind yarn around right-hand needle once and yarn is then in position to P the next st**
yon	=**yarn over needle**
yrn	=**yarn around needle**
ytb	=**yarn to back**
ytf	=**yarn to front**
*****	=**(asterisk) repeat directions following * as many extra times as indicated**
[]	=**(brackets) numbers set in brackets refer to alternate sizes**
()	=**(parentheses) when parentheses are used to show repeats, work the directions as many times as specified. "(K1, P1) 3 times" means to do what is inside ( ) 3 times in all**
multiple	=**multiple in pattern stitches means the number of stitches necessary to complete one whole pattern. If the pattern given is 4 sts, the number of stitches on needle should be evenly divisible by 4. If the pattern reads "multiple of 4 sts, plus 1" then 1 extra stitch is required in addition to the multiple of 4 (for example, 29).**

Chapter 2

Knitting Know-how

The secret of knitting success

Your finished garment can and should look just as attractive and well-fitting as it does in the photograph which catches your eye. The secret of knitting success lies in remembering to read through all the directions before you even consider putting needles to yarn. Otherwise it is all too easy to end up with a garment which is so small that you can't squeeze into it or so enormous that you have room to spare. Don't allow yourself to be carried away by that first rush of enthusiasm to cast on and start knitting. Make sure before you start that you completely understand everything, from buying the yarn to the final pressing. Publication styles vary, but basically directions fall into three sections:
1. Materials required and finished sizes
2. Working directions
3. Finishing details
The first section is often the most neglected, but all three are of vital importance to the success of your garment.

Sizes

Check that the pattern actually provides you with the size you want. If it is one size smaller or larger than required, the results will be unsatisfactory. If the skirt or sleeve length needs alteration, read through the working instructions to see if the design allows for this adjustment. It is usually only where a large, intricate repeat is used that alterations in length may be difficult.

After the actual measurements of the design are stated, you will generally find that the smallest size is given first throughout the directions. Any alterations for other sizes follow in order in either square brackets [] or parentheses (). If you find that only one figure is given, then you can be sure that this applies to all sizes.

Gauge

Although it is often ignored completely, the section on gauge is the key to your success. If you don't get the same number of stitches and rows to the inch as the designer, then no amount of careful knitting and finishing will give you a perfect garment.

To obtain the correct gauge, you may have to change the size needles that you use. If you have too many stitches to the inch, you will need to try a size larger pair of needles. If you have too few stitches to the inch, you will need to use a size smaller pair. (The fact that you may have to use a different needle size is of no importance at all. What is of the greatest importance is that you obtain the same number of stitches and rows as the designer.) When knitting a gauge square, never try to measure over only one inch. It is much easier to measure over not less than 4 inches. If there is even a quarter of a stitch too many or too few, it will begin to show over 4 inches, whereas over an inch it is too easy to feel that it is not enough of a difference to matter. Measure on a flat surface and don't be tempted to pull the sample to the right size!

Ignoring notes on gauge or yarn may lead to garments like these!

Materials

Each design has been worked out for the knitting yarn which is stated; therefore, you should try to use this brand if you want your garment to look like the picture. If for any reason it is just impossible for you to obtain the recommended yarn, then you can substitute something else. But again, you must make absolutely sure that you can achieve the gauge stated. Even if the pattern just calls for a simple knitting worsted, don't assume that every other knitting worsted yarn will automatically knit up to the same gauge. You can only be certain by working sample squares until you find a yarn which works up identically.

If you use a different yarn from the brand given, you may find that you have to use a slightly different quantity. The quantity given only applies to the stated brand.

Always buy or reserve enough yarn to complete the garment. If you fail to do this, you may have to buy extra balls of a different dye lot. This means that it will be the same yarn, but it will have been dyed at a different time. The color can vary enough to cause an unsightly stripe across your work where the two different dyes meet. Each ball of yarn is marked not only with the shade number but also with a dye lot number, so you can always tell whether or not all the balls are the same.

Do not overlook the fact that needles and stitch holders should be in good condition. Bent, twisted or roughened needles or holders will spoil the yarn and make the best knitting irregular. If it has been many years since you bought new needles, perhaps now is the time to treat yourself to some new tools.

Measuring knitting

When measuring knitting, lay it on a flat surface. It is very tempting to try to measure with your work lying along your knee or on the arm of your chair, but you must be accurate and not just hope that it is correct. Always measure with a rigid ruler, not a tape, and don't be tempted to stretch it "just a little" so that you can avoid having to work those extra few rows before reaching the next stage. It will really take you longer if you do this, because you will find that the sections don't fit together when you try to finish the garment. Also, never measure around a curve. If you want to measure an armhole, then you must measure the depth on a straight line. In the same way, to measure a sleeve don't measure up the sloping side, but up the center of the work (unless stated).

Points to note

The main sections of a garment are usually given first in the directions (although sometimes a small section such as a pocket lining must be worked before beginning the main section, so that it is ready to join in when required). Where an asterisk* occurs, it means repeat and is used in two different ways. It may appear in the directions for one particular row, where it means repeat from that point as directed. Or you may find it before the beginning of a sentence, and sometimes after a paragraph, to show a part which is repeated later in the directions. The section(s) to be repeated will always be made clear.

In some designs, the rows which form the pattern to be repeated throughout the garment are given in a note on their own before the directions begin. If you read through the directions before starting, you will spot these notes and know to refer back to them when you read "continue in pattern".

Where there is only brief mention about casting on and binding off or increasing and decreasing, you may find it helpful to look back to the specific chapters for details on these points.

Marker threads

Occasionally you are directed in a design to place a marker thread at one or both ends of a row. This acts as a visual guide so that this point can be identified easily later in the directions, either as a point for measuring to or from, or in order to assist when it comes to finishing. All that is required is that a short length of any contrasting yarn is threaded through the stitch and tied in place so that it does not accidentally come out while you are working. It is always removed after it has served its purpose.

Finishing

Details are always given in the order in which the sections are to be assembled along with directions for edges and finishing. Also in this part of the instructions you will find a guide to whether or not you should press the yarn. Again, remember that the directions refer to the most suitable yarn for the particular pattern. It is most important to ascertain whether or not the yarn can stand pressing. Some man-made fibers can be completely spoiled by pressing and it would be too bad to ruin your garment.

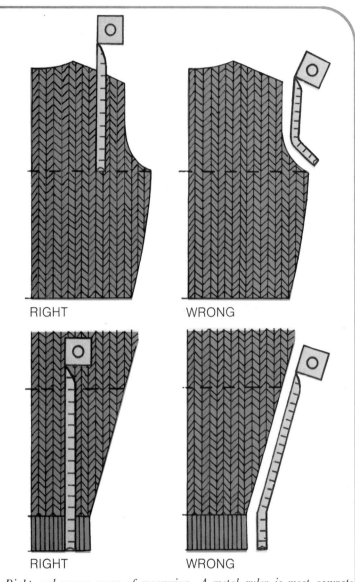

RIGHT　　　　WRONG

RIGHT　　　　WRONG

Right and wrong ways of measuring. A metal ruler is most accurate

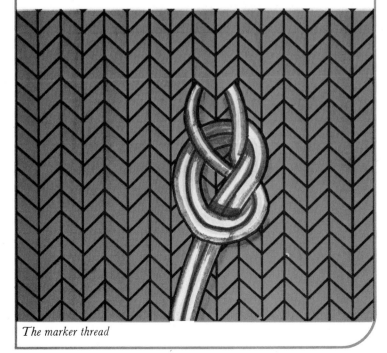

The marker thread

Chapter 3

Casting on methods

The first step in knitting is casting on, which provides the first row of loops, or stitches, on the needle. There are various ways of casting on, each with its own appropriate use, and here, the two most popular methods are outlined. Also, the intriguing "invisible" European method, which may be new to many experienced knitters, is introduced.

The Thumb method (using only one needle) is an excellent way to begin most garments, since it gives an elastic and therefore hard-wearing edge. On the other hand, the Two needle (or English cable) version is necessary when you want to cast on extra stitches during the knitting itself, for instance for a buttonhole or a pocket.

The "invisible" European method of casting on gives the fashionably flat-hemmed effect of a machine-made garment. It is a flexible, strong finish which can hold ribbon or elastic and is very useful for designs which need casings.

The scarf on this page uses the Thumb method and in Knitting Know-how Chapters 4 and 5 are further instructions for completing your scarf.

Pick your own scarf color, then follow instructions on the facing page

Thumb method— using one needle

To cast on make a slip loop in the yarn about a yard from the end. (This length varies with the number of stitches to be cast on—allow about $\frac{1}{2}$in for each stitch in medium and about 1in for each stitch in heavier yarn. A guide to the length required is—the width of the piece of knitting to be cast on, multiplied by three.)

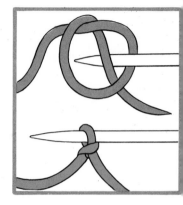

1. Slip loop on to needle which should be held in the right hand.

Two needle method— or English cable

To cast on make a slip loop in the yarn as given for the Thumb method, at least three inches from the end. It is not necessary to try and estimate the length of yarn required to cast on the number of stitches with this method, as you will be working from the ball of yarn. Slip this loop onto the left-hand knitting needle.

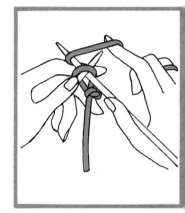

1. Insert right-hand needle into loop holding yarn in right hand and wind yarn under and over the needle.

Invisible casting-on method

Even if you are an experienced knitter, you'll be delighted to discover the many uses to which this marvelous new technique lends itself.

1. Using a contrast yarn, which is later removed, and the Thumb method, cast on half the number of stitches required, plus one. Now using the correct yarn for the garment, begin the ribbing.

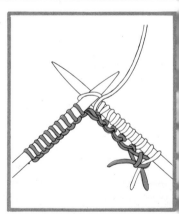

1st row. K1, *ytf, K1, rep from * to end.
2nd row. K1, *ytf, sl 1, ytb, K1, rep from * to end.
3rd row. Sl 1, *ytb, K1, ytf, sl 1, rep from * to end.

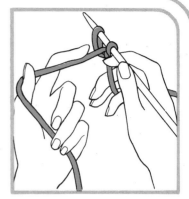

Working with the short length of yarn in the left hand, pass this around the left thumb.

3. Insert the point of the needle under the loop on the thumb, and hook forward the long end of yarn from the ball.

4. Wind yarn under and over the needle and draw through loop, leaving stitch on needle.

5. Tighten stitch on needle, noting that yarn is around thumb ready for next stitch.

6. Repeat steps 3-5 for required number of stitches.

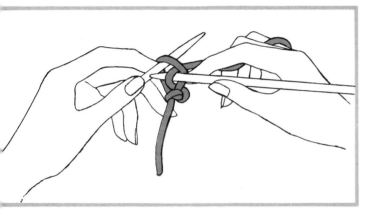

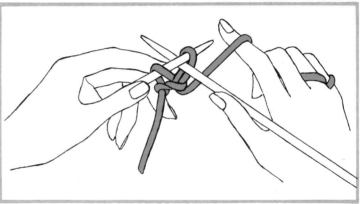

Draw the new loop through the first loop on left-hand needle thus forming a second loop. Pass newly made loop onto the left-hand needle.

3. Place point of right-hand needle between two loops on left-hand needle and wind yarn under and over the right-hand needle point and draw this new loop through between the two stitches on the left-hand needle. Slip this loop onto left-hand needle.

4. Repeat steps described in paragraph 3 between last 2 stitches on left-hand needle until the required number of stitches have been cast on.

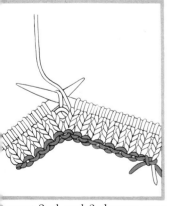

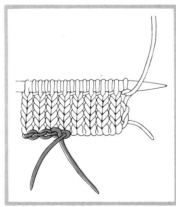

Repeat 2nd and 3rd rows once more.

th row. K1, *P1, K1, rep from * to end.

th row. P1, *K1, P1, rep from * to end.

2. Repeating rows 6 and 7, continue in ribbing for the required depth. Pick out the contrasting yarn. The ribbing should appear to be running under the edge.

Beginners — knit yourself a scarf

If you have never knitted before start with one of the scarves on the opposite page. After Chapter 5 it will be ready to wear.

Sizes: Woman's is 12½in × 72 in; Child's is 7½in × 50in. Directions are given for the woman's scarf. Changes for the child's are in parentheses.

Materials: Columbia-Minerva Nantuk 4-Ply Knitting Yarn, or any other yarn that gives the same gauge, 4-oz skeins, 3 for woman's; 2 for child's. No. 10 knitting needles.

Gauge: 4 stitches = 1in.

To begin: Using the Thumb method of casting on, cast on 50 (30) stitches.

(For directions on how to knit these scarves, see Knitting Know-how Chapter 4.)

Chapter 4

The basic stitches

In knitting, there are only two basic stitches—knit and purl. A wide variety of patterns is possible using just one or a combination of both these stitches. And depending on the needles and yarn you choose, the texture of these patterns can range from smooth to heavy, or even be as light as lace!

How to join yarn

Always join yarn at the beginning of a row, never in the center, or it will spoil the continuity of the stitches. The only exception is when you are using circular or double-pointed needles, which are featured in Chapter 19. Leave a short length of yarn at the end of the row; begin the next row with the new yarn, again leaving a short end for darning in. Tie these ends together in a square knot. You can then darn these ends neatly into the edge when your knitting is finished.

How to measure

Never try to lay the work to be measured over your knee or along the arm of a chair. Be certain that you lay the knitting on a flat surface and that you measure with a non-stretch ruler rather than a tape. Do not include the cast-on edge in your measurement, but begin with the base of the first row. When measuring an armhole or sleeve, do not measure around the curve or up the sloping edge, but measure straight up the center of the fabric.

Every time you meet a new stitch, it's wise to make a 4in gauge swatch. When you've enough swatches, sew them up into a bright patchwork quilt!

Knit stitch

1. Take the needle with the cast-on stitches in your left hand, and the other needle in your right hand. Insert the right-hand needle point through the first stitch on the left-hand needle from front to back.
Keeping the yarn away from you behind the needles, pass the yarn around the point of the right-hand needle so that you form a loop.
2. Draw this loop through the stitch on the left-hand needle, thus forming a new loop on the right-hand needle.
3. Allow the stitch on the left-hand needle to slip off.
Repeat these steps until you have drawn loops through all the stitches on the left-hand needle to the right-hand one. You have now knitted one row. To work the next row, change the needle holding the stitches to your left hand and the free needle to your right hand, and work this row in exactly the same manner as the first row.

Purl stitch

1. Take the needle with the cast-on stitches in your left hand, and the other needle in your right hand. Insert the right-hand needle point through the first stitch on the left-hand needle from back to front. Keeping the yarn toward you in front of the needles, pass yarn around point of right-hand needle to form a loop.
2. Draw this loop through the stitch on the left-hand needle, thus forming a new loop on the right-hand needle.
3. Allow the stitch on the left-hand needle to slip off.
Repeat these steps with the next stitch, until you have drawn loops through all the stitches on the left-hand needle and passed them onto the right-hand needle.
You have now purled one row. Change the needles, and work other rows in the same way. If you practice knitting and purling, you will find that you become faster and that your work becomes much more even and regular.

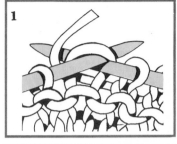
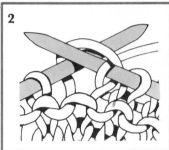
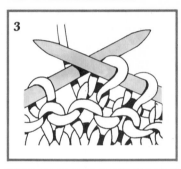
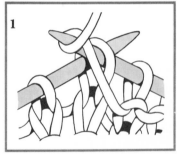
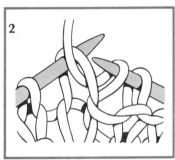
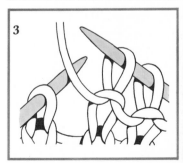

Garter stitch

This is the simplest of all the knitting patterns, formed by working every row in the same stitch, either knit or purl.

If you purl every row, however, you will not get as smooth or even a surface as when you knit every row. This is because all knitters knit more evenly than they purl. So, whenever you come across directions referring to garter stitch, it is intended that you knit every row, unless otherwise specified.

▲ *Knitted garter stitch*

Stockinette stitch

This is the smoothest of all the patterns in knitting and is made by alternately knitting one row and purling the next. The knit side of the work in stockinette stitch is usually called the right side. If the pattern uses the purl side as the right side, it is then called reversed stockinette stitch.

▲ *Stockinette stitch*

▼ *Reversed stockinette stitch*

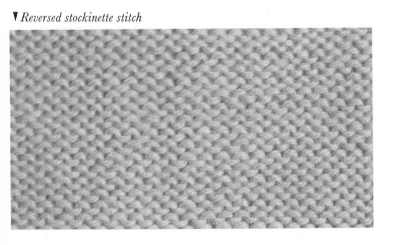

When the scarf is completed, you can muffle up against the weather

Beginners — continuing your scarves

Having cast on 50 sts for the woman's scarf or 30 sts for the child's scarf, you are now ready to start knitting.

To make: Work in garter stitch (knit every row) until 70in (50in) from beg, or desired length.

You can, of course, make either scarf shorter or longer if you like. Remember, you will need to buy more yarn if you want to make the scarf longer.

Don't be tempted to press your scarf at any stage. Garter stitch should always be treated like velvet—never pressed or flattened. If by any chance this warning is too late and the harm is already done, it can quite easily be repaired. Hold the scarf in the steam from a steadily boiling kettle, and the damp heat will rapidly raise the flattened wool fibers back to their original springiness.

Chapter 5

Binding off and the slipped stitch

This chapter starts with binding off. Gauge control is very important for this, as it must be done in exactly the same gauge as the knitting. If it is not, the edge will be too tight or too loose, and either will spoil the finished appearance of the garment. Slipped stitch is so called because it is slipped from the left-hand to the right-hand needle without being worked, the yarn being carried either behind or in front of the stitch. Slipped stitches can be used in several different ways in forming part of a pattern, in decreasing and shaping, in producing a neat edge for making up a garment, or in making a fold for a pleat or facing.

If you are working a pattern and the strand is passed behind the work, the stitch itself forms the pattern. If the strand is carried across the front of the stitch, then it can be used to build up the design, in much the same way as a woven design is made. You can also make fascinating herringbone textured effects using slipped stitches.

Binding off

To bind off on a knit row, knit the first two stitches. Then * with the left-hand needle point, lift the first stitch over the second stitch, leaving one stitch on right-hand needle. Knit the next stitch, repeat from * until all stitches but one have been worked off. Cut the yarn, draw through the last stitch and pull the stitch tight.

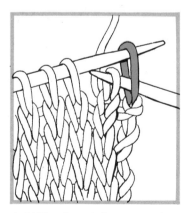

▲ *Lifting first stitch over second*

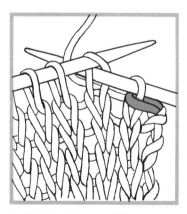

▲ *Knitting the next stitch*

When working a purl row, each stitch is purled before it is bound off. To bind off in pattern or ribbing, lift each stitch over the next stitch following the pattern of the knitting.

Care should always be taken that the binding off is not too tight or too slack, but is similar to the gauge of the work itself. If you always bind off too tightly, then use a needle one size larger for binding off. If, on the other hand, you bind off too loosely, use a needle one size smaller to obtain the best results.

Slip stitch purlwise on a knit row

Slipped stitches

Slip stitch knitwise on a knit row

Hold the yarn behind the work as if to knit the stitch. Insert the right-hand needle point into the stitch from front to back, as you would to knit, and slip it onto the right-hand needle.

Slip stitch purlwise on a knit row

Hold the yarn behind the work as if to knit the stitch. Insert the right-hand needle point into the stitch from back to front, as you would to purl, and slip it onto the right-hand needle.

Slip stitch purlwise on a purl row

Hold the yarn at the front of the work as if to purl the stitch. Insert the right-hand needle point from back to front as you would to purl, and slip it onto the right-hand needle.

It is most important to remember that when a slip stitch forms part of a decrease on a knit row, the stitch must be slipped knitwise, otherwise it will become twisted. On a purl row, make sure you slip the stitch purlwise.

In working a pattern, however, when the slip stitch is not part of a decrease, it must be slipped purlwise on a knit row to prevent it from becoming twisted when purled in the following row. Don't forget to check which position you need for the best results.

▲ *Slip stitch purlwise on a purl row*

Fringe making

Take six strands of yarn and fold them in half. Draw the loop through the edge of the knitting, then draw the ends of yarn through the loop and pull tight. Repeat evenly all the way along the cast-on and bound-off edges of the scarf.

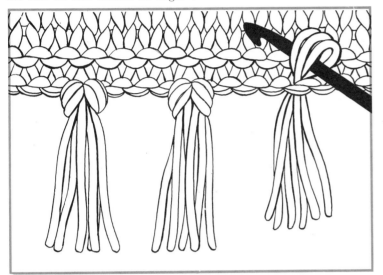

Drawing the loop through the edge of the knitting

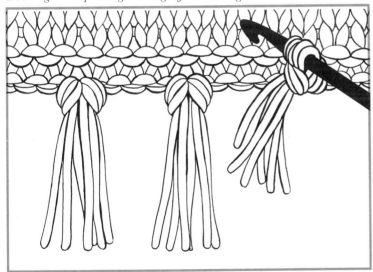

Drawing the ends of yarn through the loop

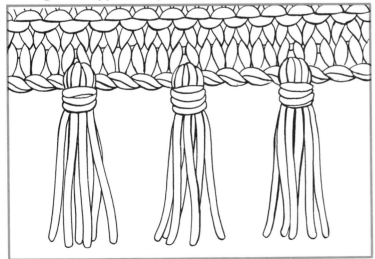

The fringe seen from the other side (usually called the right side)

The fringed scarves when they are finished

Scarves for mother and child (continued)

You've just learned how to bind off—so now you can put it into practice. When you have finished binding off your scarf you are ready to start working the fringe.

The garter stitch scarf in itself has no right or wrong side, but the first tassel dictates the pattern the rest must follow. Continue to work on the same side along the first end, and make sure that the other end matches the first.

To make the fringe: cut lengths of yarn 20in long for the mother's scarf, or 16in long for the child's scarf. You will need six strands for each tassel, and 16 tassels at each end of the mother's scarf, or 10 tassels at each end of the child's scarf. Use a crochet hook to pull the tassel loops through the edge of the scarf.

Chapter 6

Binding off invisibly

Experienced knitters and beginners alike have probably experimented with the special invisible casting on method shown in Knitting Know-how Chapter 3. Now Golden Hands introduces you to an equally marvelous technique for invisible binding off. You will also see how to work double casting on, and with both methods you can fashion a ready-made hem with built-in casing for elastic or cords. The depth of the hems can be varied by the number of rows worked.

Although the invisible technique may be a little slower than your usual method at first, don't let this discourage you. For once you have mastered it, you will find that the very professional results are well worth the extra time.

The drawing on the opposite page shows some of the uses for which these invisible binding off methods are most appropriate. For example, you can use them for neck edging, belts and hems; for rib collars, V-necks and round necks.

Invisible binding off

Directions are given for binding off when K1, P1 rib over an odd number of stitches has been used, the first row beginning with K1.

Work the ribbing normally until only 2 more rows are required to give the finished depth or, if a hem casing is required, less the depth of this hem, ending with a wrong side row.

1st row. K1, *ytf, sl 1, ytb, K1, rep from * to end.
2nd row. Sl 1, *ytb, K1, ytf, sl 1, rep from * to end.

Repeat these 2 rows once more, or required number of times to give correct depth of hem.

Break yarn, leaving a length at least three times the length of the edge to be bound off. Thread this into a darning needle. Holding the darning needle in the right hand and the needle with the stitches in the left hand, work throughout from right to left along the stitches on the needle.

1. Insert the darning needle in the first knit stitch as if to purl it and pull the yarn through, then into the next purl stitch as if to knit it and pull the yarn through, leaving both of these stitches on the left-hand needle.

2. *First work 2 of the knit stitches.

Insert the darning needle into the first knit stitch as if to knit it, pull the yarn through it and slip off the needle.

Pass the darning needle in front of the next purl stitch and into the following knit stitch as if to purl it. Pull the yarn through.

3. Now work 2 of the purl stitches.

Insert the darning needle into the purl stitch at the end of the row as if to purl and slip it off the needle.

Pass the darning needle behind the next stitch and into the following purl stitch as if to knit it. Pull yarn through.

Repeat from * until all stitches have been worked off. Fasten off.

1. *Invisible binding off, working the first two stitches on the row*

2. *Invisible binding off, working the 2nd knit stitch*

3. *Invisible binding off, working the 2nd purl stitch*

Double casting on

When a less elastic cast-on edge is required at the lower edge of a jacket or sweater, the double casting on method is more suitable. Use a short length of contrasting yarn for casting on. This does not become part of the finished work. Using the one needle method, cast on half the number of stitches required.

Using the yarn in which the garment is to be made, begin with a knit row and work 6 rows of stockinette stitch, or the required number of rows to give correct depth of hem casing.

1. Slip the first row of loops which show in the contrast yarn onto a spare needle and pick off the contrast yarn because it is no longer required.

2. Fold the work in half, holding the spare needle behind the other needle, and work both sets of stitches onto one needle in the following way: *K1 from front needle, P1 from back needle, rep from * until all stitches are on one needle.

Continue in rib for required length. If you want to use this edge for a pattern which does not give detailed directions, simply cast on half the number of stitches given. The total number will be made up when the stitches are worked onto one needle.

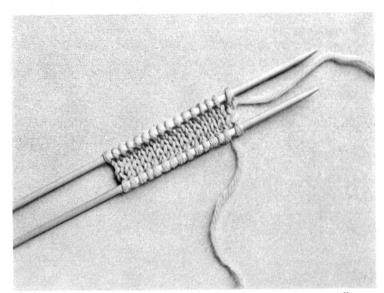

1. *Double casting on—the garment yarn loops put onto a spare needle*

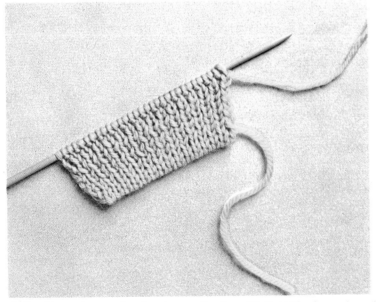

2. *Double casting on, showing the smooth edge with its hidden inner channel*

Chapter 7

Patterns from purl and knit

Once you have learned to knit and purl, these stitches can be combined to make a wide variety of decorative patterns, as you can see from the illustrations on the opposite page. The best way to try out these simple stitches is by knitting squares. If you don't have any left-over scraps of yarn, buy several colors in the same ply—knitting worsted is best. A good size for the squares is 4 inches, but you can make them larger or smaller as long as they all measure the same. Besides giving you experience, squares have a number of practical uses. For example, you can sew them up into a pillow case or decorative afghan. Or use them to make any garment where you want a patchwork effect. This chapter will show you how to make a smooth edge on a piece of knitting, so your squares will be neat and easier to sew together.

1. Edge stitch

You'll find that the edges of your work are neater, and therefore more easily sewn together, if you slip the first stitch and knit the last stitch of each row. This is particularly the case in stockinette stitch, where the ends of rows tend to be loose. Knitting the last stitch of every row tightens this edge and gives a smooth finish.

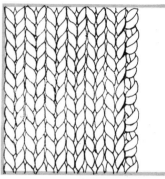

▲ *Sl st edge at the end of row*

Another means of making a neat edge for stockinette stitch is by knitting the first and last stitch on every purl row. This is particularly good for finishing using backstitch or invisible seaming (see Knitting Know-how Chapter 11).

K st edge at the end of row ►

2. Rib (1 and 1 rib, or single rib)
Cast on an even number of stitches.
1st row. *K1, P1, rep from * to end.
Rep this row for length required.

3. Rib (2 and 2 rib, or double rib)
Cast on a number of stitches divisible by 4.
1st row. *K2, P2, rep from * to end.
Rep this row for length required.

4. Seed (or moss) stitch
Cast on an odd number of stitches.
1st row. K1, *P1, K1, rep from * to end.
Rep this row for length required.

5. Twisted stockinette stitch
This looks much like stockinette stitch, but has an added twist, made by knitting into the back of the stitch on all K rows.
Cast on any number of stitches.
1st row. K into back of all stitches.
2nd row. P.
Rep these 2 rows for length required.

6. Double seed (or moss) stitch
Cast on a number of stitches divisible by 4, plus 2.
1st row. K2, *P2, K2, rep from * to end.
Rep this row for length required.

7. Basket stitch
Cast on a number of stitches divisible by 8.
1st row. *K4, P4, rep from * to end.
2nd, 3rd, and 4th rows. As first row.
5th row. *P4, K4, rep from * to end.
6th, 7th, and 8th rows. As 5th row.
These 8 rows form the pattern, and are repeated as required.

Single rib ▲

Seed (or moss) stitch ▲

Double rib ▲   Twisted stockinette stitch ▼

Double seed (or moss) stitch ▲   Basket stitch ▼

Chapter 8

Knitting Know-how

Increasing step by step

Knitting can be straight or shapely and it is by increasing or decreasing that we give garments the shape they need. Putting it simply, knitting is made wider by increasing the number of stitches in a row and made narrower by reducing the number of stitches. Interest is added in more ambitious designs by using these two processes to form patterns in lace knitting. These step-by-step pictures show all the techniques from plain increasing to openwork lace effects.

How to increase

The simplest way is to make an extra stitch at the beginning or the end of a row depending on the shape you're making.
Do this by knitting or purling the stitch in the usual way, but do not slip it off the needle. Instead, place the point of the right-hand needle into the back of the stitch and knit or purl into the stitch again. Slip both these stitches onto your right-hand needle. You have now made two stitches out of one.

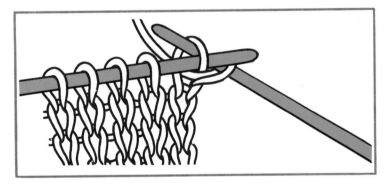

Invisible increasing

Insert the right-hand needle into the front of the stitch below that on the left-hand needle and knit a new stitch. If the increase is on purl work, then purl the new stitch. As it's almost invisible, this method is particularly good when the increase is not at the end of a row, or doesn't form part of a pattern.

Increasing between stitches knitwise (M1K)

1. With right-hand needle, pick up the yarn which lies between the stitch just worked and the next stitch, and place it on the left-hand needle.
2. Knit into back of this loop. This twists and tightens the loop so that no hole is formed.
3. Slip the loop off the left-hand needle, so making one stitch.

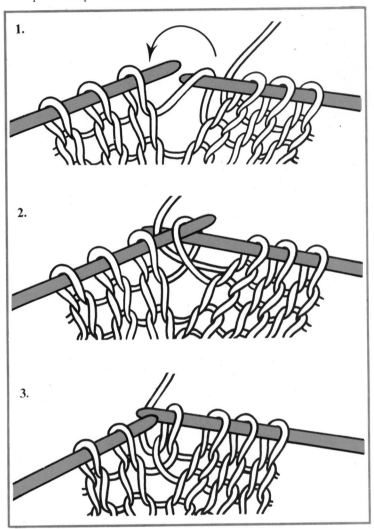

Increasing between stitches purlwise (M1P)

This is worked in the same way as for M1K, but the loop picked up is purled into from the back.

Multiple increasing

You will need this technique when you make a dolman sleeve. Cast on the required number of stitches at the beginning of the side edge, using the two needle method. At the end of the row, reverse the work and cast on.

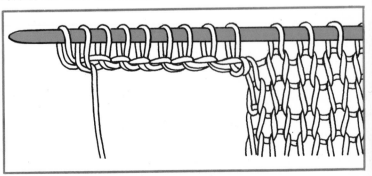

To make a stitch between two knit stitches
Bring the yarn forward (ytf) as if to purl, then back over the right-hand needle ready to knit the next stitch.

To make a stitch between a purl and a knit stitch
The yarn is already in position to the front, and the next stitch is knitted in the usual way, the yarn taken over the needle (yon).

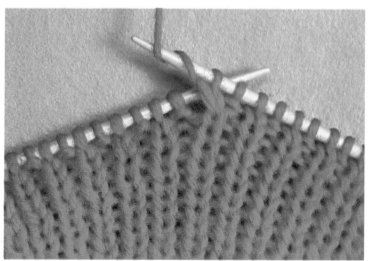

To make a stitch between two purl stitches
Take the yarn over and around the needle (yrn).

To make a stitch between a knit and a purl stitch
Bring the yarn forward and once around the needle (yrn).

Decorative increasing

Increasing can be used not only to shape a garment, but also to be decorative at the same time. This way of increasing is usually made one or more stitches in from the edge, the number of edge stitches being determined by the pattern you are using or by your own preference. In the illustrations, three stitches are used for the edge.

The simplest lace effect may be obtained by lifting the yarn immediately after the edge stitches and then knitting into it. The end of the row is worked in the same way, lifting the yarn before the edge stitches.

A more openwork effect, shown in the illustrations, is made by knitting the edge stitches, knitting into the stitch below the next stitch on the left-hand needle, then increasing by knitting into the stitch immediately above.

To reverse this for the left-hand side of the work, knit to one stitch before the edge stitches. Knit the next stitch, increase by knitting into stitch immediately below this stitch, then knit edge stitches.

▼ *Increase at beginning of row* ▼ *Increase at end of row*

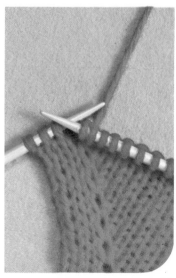

Chapter 9

Methods of decreasing

Passing a slipped stitch over a knitted stitch (Sl1, K1, psso)

Decreasing simply means shaping a piece of work to reduce the size, whether it is at the side-seams of a garment or for darts, tucks or forming gussets. It can be worked so that it is almost invisible and may be hidden by seaming when you are finishing the garment. Decreasing can be decorative as well as practical and a good example of this is when it is used on the raglan shaping of a sweater or cardigan. If the decreasing is worked on the end stitches a neat, hidden-shaping effect will be achieved when seamed or, alternatively, by working the decreasing inside, say, two or three stitches, a fully-fashioned effect is produced.

The way to make a simple decrease is by working two stitches together, either at the ends of the row or at any other given point.

To decrease one stitch knitwise (K2 tog)
Insert the right-hand needle point through two stitches instead of one, and knit together. This will slant to the right.

Knit two stitches together (K2 tog)   *Purl two stitches together (P2 tog)*

To decrease one stitch purlwise (P2 tog)
Insert right-hand needle point through two stitches, and purl together as if they were one stitch. This will slant to the left.
A simple decrease can also be made by knitting or purling through the back loops of the stitches and is then referred to as K2 tog tbl, or P2 tog tbl. This reverses the slant of the stitches.

To decrease using a slipped stitch (sl 1, K1, psso)
This method is most commonly used where decreases are paired, one slanting left and one slanting right as on a raglan sleeve. Slip the first stitch from left to right-hand needle, knit the next stitch. With left-hand needle point, lift the slipped stitch over the knitted one and off the needle. This will slant to the left.
On a purl row the decrease, slanting to the right, is normally made by purling 2 together through back loop of the stitch (P2

tog tbl). You can also achieve the same effect by purling one stitch and returning it to the left-hand needle. With the right-hand needle point lift the next stitch over and off the needle. Return the purled stitch to the right-hand needle.

Decreasing in pairs on alternate rows
When you are decreasing at both ends of a row and forming a line that will be seen in the finished garment, the lines should be paired so that they slant in opposite directions.
When decreasing on knit rows of stockinette stitch on the right-hand side of the work slip 1, knit 1, pass slip stitch over (sl1, K1, psso). These stitches will slant to the left.
For the other end of the row use a knit 2 together (K2 tog) decrease. These stitches will slant to the right.
When used at opposite ends on alternate rows, they will then give you the inward sloping chain effect shown in the illustration.

Right-hand side (Sl1, K1, psso) ▲   *Left-hand side (K2 tog)* ▼

Lines formed by slanting decreases on alternative rows

Decreasing in pairs on every row

When decreasing on the purl side of the work as well as on the knit side, you should decrease in pairs to keep the slant correct. On the knit side use a slipped stitch at the beginning of the row and a knit 2 together (K2 tog) decrease at the end.

On the following row, use a purl 2 together (P2 tog) decrease at the beginning and purl 2 together through the back of the stitch (P2 tog tbl) at the end.

The alternative to purling 2 together through the back of the stitch (P2 tog tbl) is to purl the stitch and return it to the left-hand needle. With the right-hand needle point lift the second stitch on left-hand needle over the purled stitch. Return the purled stitch to right-hand needle.

To make use of the chain effect, and so that it is not lost in the seam when finishing, the decreases are often worked inside two or more edge stitches, the number of which can vary.

Purling 2 tog on purl side ▲ *Lifting st over st already purled* ▼

Beginning to forget your abbreviations? Then look back to Knitting Know-how Chapter 1.

Twisted Decorative Decreasing

Sometimes the decorative use of decreasing is accentuated by twisting the stitches around the decrease to give them emphasis. This can also be given by incorporating a lace or eyelet effect into the decreasing.

The illustration below shows a decrease which is accentuated by having been twisted as well as lying in the opposite direction to the line of the seam.

This decrease is worked at the end of right side or knit rows for the left-hand side, and at the end of the wrong side or purl rows for the right-hand side.

Knit to last 6 stitches, pass right-hand needle behind first stitch on the left-hand needle and knit next 2 stitches together through the backs of the loops, then knit the first stitch and slip both stitches off left-hand needle. Knit the last 3 stitches in the usual way.

On the next row purl to the last 6 stitches, pass right-hand needle across front of first stitch on left-hand needle and purl the next 2 stitches together, then purl the first stitch and slip both stitches off left-hand needle. Purl the last 3 stitches as usual.

▲ *Left-hand side decorative decrease* ▼ *Right-hand side decorative decrease*

Chapter 10

Double increasing & decreasing

Double increasing in knitting is where two stitches are made as a pair, usually at either side of a central point. Double decreasing is where two stitches are taken out of the work. While both double increasing and decreasing may be used just for shaping, they may also have very stunning decorative uses. They are essential, for example, if you want to make a lacy pattern or create the zigzag designs and stripes which produce the chevron effect illustrated below.

Double increasing

Purled double increase

This method uses a central stitch and is worked on stockinette stitch. Knit up to one stitch before the center stitch. Knit into that

Striped chevron pattern using double increases and decreases

stitch, but before slipping it off the needle purl into the yarn in the row immediately below from the back of the work. Slip the original stitches off the left-hand needle. Knit the center stitch. Knit the next stitch, but again purl into the back of the stitch below before slipping the stitch off the needle. Purl all the stitches on the next row.

Twisted double increase

Again a central stitch is used and the increased stitches are on either side of it.
Work to one stitch before the center stitch. Knit into the front and then into the back of this stitch. Knit the center stitch. Knit into the front and then the back of the next stitch. Purl all stitches on the next row.

Crossed double increase

With this method, both stitches to be increased are worked into the center stitch.
Knit to the center stitch. Knit into the row below the center stitch, knit the center stitch and knit again into the row below the center stitch. Purl all the stitches on the next row.

Double decreasing

The simple double decrease

Probably the most commonly used pair of double decreases are those made by working three stitches together.
Knitting three stitches together (K3tog) gives you a right-slanting decrease.
Knitting three stitches together through the back of the loops (K3tog tbl) gives you a left-slanting decrease.
A neater form of this left-slanting decrease is to slip the first stitch and then the second stitch from left- to right-hand needle. Knit the next stitch. With the left-hand needle point, lift both slipped stitches over the knitted stitch.

The slipped decrease

This decrease is worked over three stitches. Slip the first stitch onto the right-hand needle. Knit the next two stitches together and, with the left-hand needle, lift the slipped stitch over the stitch made by knitting two together. This slants to the left.
The right-slanting version of this decrease is used much less frequently and directions for working it are usually given in full when it does occur.
Slip the first stitch onto the right-hand needle. Knit the next stitch and, with left-hand needle point, lift the slipped stitch over the knitted stitch and off the needle. Put the knitted stitch back onto the left-hand needle and lift the next stitch over it with the right-hand needle point. Return the knitted stitch to the right-hand needle.

A double decrease worked on the purl side of the work

This decrease is worked on the purl, or wrong side, of stockinette stitch and slants to the left on the knit side of the work. Purl two together (P2tog) and return to the left-hand needle. With the right-hand needle point, lift the second stitch on the left-hand needle over the first and then return the first stitch to the right-hand needle.
The reverse of this (slanting to the right on the knit side of the work) is worked by slipping one stitch onto the right-hand needle. Knit the next stitch, then twist the following one by reversing it on the needle, leaving it on the left-hand needle. Return the knitted stitch to the left-hand needle with the right-hand needle point and lift the twisted stitch over it. Return the knitted stitch to the right-hand needle.

Purled double increase

Twisted double increase

Crossed double increase

Simple double decrease : K3tog ▲ K3 tog tbl ▼

Slipped decrease : slip stitch over K2tog ▲ lift second slip stitch over ▼

31

Chapter 11

Finishing, blocking and pressing

The finishing of a garment is very important. If you have followed the directions and made each piece with great care, it would be a pity to spoil all your work by being in too much of a hurry to give proper attention to the finishing.

Always check whether or not the directions tell you to press the pieces before you begin to finish them. It will be too late to realize that you must not press after you have already done so and certain man-made fibers can be completely ruined by contact with heat. So read first and be safe!

Blocking

If pressing is required, prepare the pieces by running in any yarn ends. To do this, darn the ends up the edges of the work which are to be seamed so that the ends are secure and cannot eventually work themselves loose.

Next, place each piece of knitting, right side down, on an ironing pad and pin evenly around the edges. If in doubt, always use too many pins rather than too few. Also, they should be the stainless steel variety, like tailor's pins, that won't leave rust marks. Never stretch the knitting or the pins will make a fluted edge. The shape you obtain when pinning should be the perfect finished shape which you seam. When the pieces are pinned, check with a ruler that the width and length are the same as those in the directions.

Pressing

Since an ironing board is too narrow for most knitted pieces, the knitter who wants a perfectly finished garment would be well advised to make herself an ironing pad. This can be done easily. First decide on the size and shape you want: It should be large enough to take a dress length and may be either square or oblong. To back the ironing pad use a piece of felt or wool, lay three or four pieces of blanket on top (old blanket pieces are ideal), then two layers of white sheet material. Bind all the edges together with wide bias tape. You now have a pressing pad which can be used on an unpolished hard surface like a kitchen table or even on the floor.

Rinse a clean, white, cotton cloth or piece of an old sheet in warm water, wring it out, and place it over the knitted work to be pressed. Do not allow the damp cloth to extend over any of the ribbed edges: These do not require pressing. With a warm iron, press the surface of the knitting evenly but not too heavily. You could spoil your work by pressing too hard, either by flattening the stitches beyond recognition or by leaving tell-tale iron marks. The iron should be pressed down and lifted up again, not moved along the surface as it would be in actual ironing. If you do use the ordinary ironing method, you will stretch and crease the

knitting, and thus spoil the perfect shape you have obtained by pinning the garment so carefully when you started. If any garter stitch or ribbing becomes pressed in error, it can be steamed back into shape (this applies only to wool and not to man-made fibers). But do, of course, be very careful not to direct the steam onto yourself as you hold the knitting in the jet of steam from a boiling kettle! The damp heat will soon make the over-flattened strands spring back into shape again.

Of course, this can become a tedious job if the area to be revived is very large. In this case, lay the piece to be treated on your ironing pad. Do not pin, simply pat it flat. Rinse and wring out your cloth in warm water again, place it flat over the knitting and leave until the ribbing, garter stitch or pattern springs back into life.

Knitting pinned in place for pressing with warm iron through damp cloth

Seams

To sew knitting, use a blunt-pointed needle as it is less likely to split the stitches and spoil the effect of a neat seam.

If the garment has been made in a fairly thick yarn, it is best to split the yarn for sewing or buy a thinner one in the same shade: Your work will be far easier and your result neater.

Backstitch seam

The backstitch seam is worked in very much the same way as in dressmaking except that it is important to keep looking at the other side of the seam to check that you are not splitting any of the stitches and are working along a straight line. Whether you

32

work half or one stitch in from the edge is a matter of personal choice and may be determined by the thickness of the garment which is to be seamed.

Start seaming by working two small stitches, one on top of the other. *Now, with the needle at the back of the work, move along to the left, bringing the needle through to the front of the work the width of one stitch away from the last stitch. Take the needle back to the left-hand end of the last stitch and take it through to the back of the work. Repeat from * until the seam is complete. Care must be taken to pull the stitches firmly through the knitting so that they do not show an untidy line on the right side when finished. Do not stretch the seam by pulling it over your fingers, or draw it too tight so that it becomes a different length from the knitting around it.

Backstitch seaming

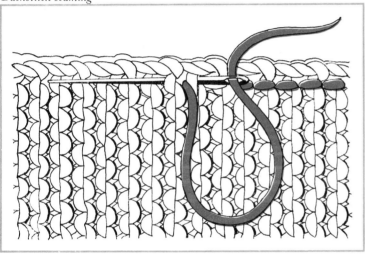

Invisible seam

The diagram shows the seam being worked on the right side of the work.

Begin by securing the sewing yarn to one side. Pass the needle directly across to the other side of the work, picking up one stitch. Pass the needle directly back to the first side of the work, picking up one loop. Continue working in this way as if you were making rungs of a ladder but pull the stitches tight so that they are not seen on the right side when finished.

All seams should be pressed on the wrong side after completion.

Invisible seaming

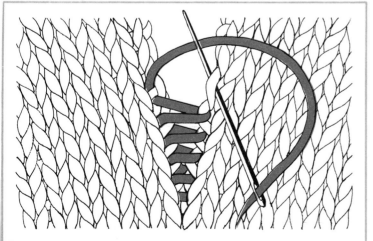

Flat seam

This is the best seam to use when two edges are to be drawn together such as in ribbing.

This method can also be worked on the wrong side working through the extreme edge stitches as seen in the diagram on the right. Pass the threaded darning needle through the edge stitch on the right-hand side directly across to the edge stitch on the left-hand side and pull the yarn through. Turn the needle and work through the next stitch on the left-hand side directly across to the edge stitch on the right-hand side, again pulling the yarn through. Continue up the seam in this manner.

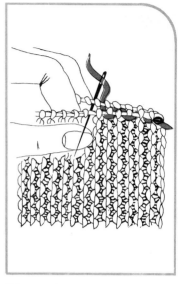

Flat seaming

Sewing in a pocket

Pockets

When sewing either patch or inserted pockets, they must be absolutely in line with the knitted stitches and rows. The best way is to run a fine knitting needle up the line of the stitches to be followed, picking up alternate loops; the edge is slip stitched to these loops. It is very important that the cast-on lower edge lies straight along a row.

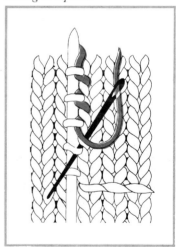

Casing stitch

Casing stitch is often referred to in finishing instructions where a waist edge requires a non-bulky hem to carry elastic, as on a skirt. This is usually worked like herringbone stitch, using a needle, but the strongest method of working is to crochet a zigzag chain using the same yarn as used for the garment. The number of chains used to form the sloping sides of the zigzag will depend on the width of the elastic which you plan to use for a particular garment.

Casing stitch

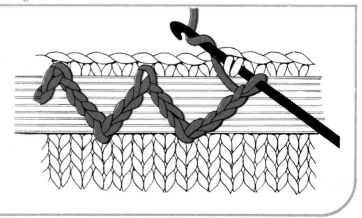

Chapter 12

Picking up stitches and weaving

The yarn color and texture you've chosen are perfect, the needles are right, the gauge is correct and all your knitted pieces look immaculate. If you're asking yourself, "now what?" the answer is that still more care is required. The finishing stages must be done well if your garment is to look really professional. Knitted borders, collars, cuffs or contrasting edgings, for example, can be ruined if stitched on by hand with thick, lumpy seams which are impossible to press. Picking up stitches instead is really a very simple job if it's done methodically, but it can completely mar the finished effect if it is worked carelessly or without very cautious regard for regularity.

Weaving, also, is often overlooked as a method of finishing. The directions on these pages give weaving for stockinette stitch (which is used most frequently) and also for joining purl fabrics, garter stitch and ribbing.

Picking up stitches

This method of finishing a neckline or other edge will save you the trouble of casting on a separate collar, cuff, or edging and sewing it on when completing the garment. Picking up stitches is not difficult, but you must be sure to work very carefully if you want to save time and avoid disappointment.

It is usual to begin to pick up stitches with the right side of the work facing you. The directions will always specify if this is not the case in a particular pattern.

Lifting stitches onto the needle with a crochet hook

Lifting stitches with an afghan hook—very practical for this purpose

The most widely known method involves using the same knitting needle which you will use to knit the edging. Hold the yarn behind the work and insert the tip of the needle through the stitch, drawing through a loop of yarn to the right side and forming one loop on the needle. Continue until all the required stitches are on the needle.

Some knitters prefer to draw the loop of yarn through with a crochet hook, then slip the loop onto the needle to be used. There is, however, a tool on the market which makes the entire process much easier. It is the Bernat afghan hook, which looks like a long slender knitting needle with a hook on one end. The hook end is used just as the crochet hook to draw the loop through. It is then on the needle and does not need to be transferred to another one. Once the stitches have been picked up, you can then knit them off the pointed end with the correct size needle.

In order to have the yarn end up already attached at the pointed end for knitting, measure in from the end of the ball about three times the length of the row to be picked up and then work from this point back toward the end as you pick up the loops. If you don't feel you can judge the length required, then use a separate length of yarn for picking up the stitches and join in the ball of yarn in the normal way when you begin to knit the stitches onto the correct size needle.

You will only need the size A afghan hook. The fineness of this size is a great help in drawing loops through firmer fabrics and there is no chance of the loop slipping off and staying on the wrong side as happens only too often when using a knitting needle. If you are picking up stitches around a neck, or on a long edge, it is always easier to mark the edge into sections than to use the trial and error method. Some directions will give you detailed information as to exactly how many stitches should be on the back neck, side neck and the center front of the neck; but sooner or later you will be confronted with a pattern which states that you have to pick up 124 stitches evenly around the neck. If you always make it a practice to divide the edge by putting in marker pins, then you will have no trouble and will not have to try again and again to get the correct number of stitches. Mark the center back and front with pins, then fold this in half again and insert two more pins. Now you will know that between pins you have a quarter of the total number of stitches to pick up. If you treat every edge in this way, dividing it as often as you like, it is easy to pick up the correct number of stitches at once.

Weaving

Weaving is a method of joining two rows of stitches invisibly. It is used in knitting mittens and at the toes of socks where the ridge formed by a seamed bound-off edge would be uncomfortable. It is also most useful for joining buttonhole and button strips where they are not continuous but meet at the center back of the neck. The bulkiness of underarm seams can be completely avoided by leaving the stitches normally bound off at armholes and sleeve cap shapings unworked and by weaving them together before the remainder of the sleeve and side seams are worked. Weaving is usually worked on stockinette, purled or garter stitch surfaces, but, if worked with care, can also be used for joining ribbing.

Weaving off needles

When the edges are ready for weaving, cut off the ball of yarn, leaving an end about three to four times the length of the row to be woven, and thread this into a darning needle. The illustrations below show a contrast colored yarn being threaded through the stitches so that you can see it clearly. As the weave is to be invisible, you would naturally use the same yarn as the garment. The illustrations also show the stitches slipped off the needles. Some knitters do weave in this way, but there is always the danger of dropping one or more of the stitches.

Weaving on needles

To weave two stockinette stitch edges together, have the stitches on two knitting needles, one behind the other, length of yarn threaded into the darning needle and needle points, all at the right-hand side of the work with the wrong sides of work touching.
Insert the threaded darning needle into the first stitch on the front knitting needle as if to purl it and draw the yarn through, leaving the stitch on the knitting needle. *Insert the darning needle into the first stitch on the back knitting needle as if to purl it and slip it off the knitting needle, then insert the darning needle into the next stitch on the back needle as if to knit it and leave it on the knitting needle, but draw the yarn through. Insert the darning needle into the first stitch on the front knitting needle as if to knit it and slip it off the knitting needle, then insert the darning needle into the next stitch on the front needle as if to purl it, leaving it on the knitting needle, but pulling the yarn through. Now repeat from * until all the stitches have been worked off. When you draw the yarn through, don't pull it too tight or leave it too slack. The row of weaving stitches should be the same size as the knitted ones, thus making them invisible. If they are not even, use the darning needle to work the yarn along the row before finishing off the end, pulling wide stitches smaller or working extra yarn along the row if the stitches are too tight. When you are weaving hold the needles with the stitches on them in your left hand, keeping the stitches near the tips of the needles so that you do not need to tug at them to slip them off the points.

To weave two edges of purl fabric together, work in the same way as for stockinette stitch, reading knit for purl and purl for knit. It is, however, possible to turn the knitting to the wrong side and work as for stockinette stitch, turning to the right side when the weaving is finished.

To weave ribbed edges together, just learn both of the above methods. If you do this, you will then be able to weave any type of ribbed edges together because you simply use both methods in combination. In other words, you will join stockinette stitch rib to stockinette stitch rib with the stockinette stitch method, and join purl rib to purl rib using the purl method.

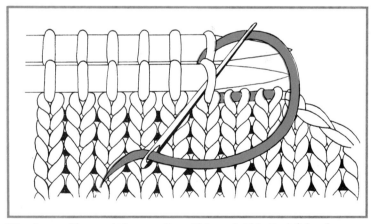

Weaving stockinette stitch on needles which are held in the left hand

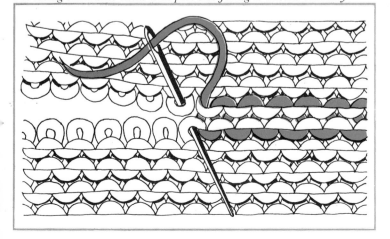

▲ *Weaving stockinette stitch, knit side facing (contrast yarn only for clarity)*
▼ *Weaving stockinette stitch with purl side facing is worked similarly*

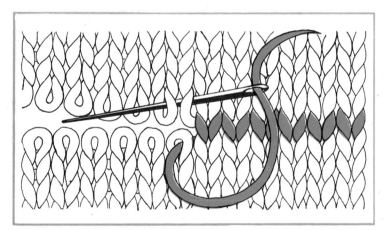

To weave garter stitch edges, you work as given for stockinette stitch, but you must first make certain that the last row knitted on the front needle left a ridge on the right side of the work and that the last row on the back needle formed a ridge on the wrong side or inside of the work. It may be necessary to add or take off a row on either side to obtain this before beginning to weave.
Weaving may seem involved the first time, but it is not difficult and there is one easy way to work it out. The yarn passes through each stitch twice. The first time it enters the stitch, it enters in the opposite way to the type of stitch. That is, into a knit stitch you must insert the needle purlwise and into a purl stitch you must insert the needle knitwise—the stitch is left on the knitting needle. The second time the stitch is slipped off the knitting needle after the darning needle has passed through it for the same type of stitch. This means that the second time you pass the darning needle knitwise into a knit stitch and purlwise into a purl stitch.

Chapter 13

"V"-neckbands

A well-knitted garment can be spoiled by a badly finished "V"-neck. Either the neckbands look frilly or the "V" doesn't lie flat. These simple variations will help you to achieve a professional-looking neckline every time.

These neckbands are added to a garment by picking up stitches around the neck as shown in Knitting Know-how Chapter 12. One shoulder should be left unseamed, so that the neckband can be worked in rows on two needles.

For an even more attractive finish on the single rib examples shown here, bind off by the invisible method (see Knitting Know-how Chapter 6.)

Count the number of rows on the right and left fronts from the center "V" point and allow one stitch for every row and one stitch for every stitch of the back neck bound-off stitches. Note the multiples of stitches, plus extra stitches, which are required to keep the rib correct on either side of the center point. For example, the double rib neckband requires two center stitches and multiples of four stitches plus two extra stitches.

Single rib neckband with center stitch using slip stitch decreasing

With RS facing, pick up the required number of stitches, noting that the center stitch must be a knit stitch for the right side of the work. Mark the center stitch with colored thread. Rib 1 row.

1st row (right side). Work in K1, P1 rib to within 2 sts of center st ending with P1, K next 2 sts tog tbl, K center st, K next 2 sts tog, beg with P1, work in rib to end.

2nd row. Rib to 2 sts before center st, P2 tog, P center st, P2 tog, beg with P1, work in rib to end.

Rep these 2 rows for required depth of neckband. Bind off in rib, still decreasing at center point, or bind off invisibly.

Single rib neckband with center stitch combining two methods of decreasing

With RS facing, pick up the required number of stitches, noting that the center stitch must be a knit stitch for the right side of the work. Mark the center stitch with colored thread. Rib 1 row.

1st row (right side). Work in K1, P1 rib to within 2 sts of center st ending with P1, sl 1, K1, psso, K center st, K2 tog, beg with P1, work in rib to end.

2nd row. Rib to 2 sts before center st, sl 1, K1, psso, P center st, K2 tog, beg with P1, work in rib to end.

Rep these 2 rows for required depth of neckband. Bind off in rib, still decreasing at center point, or bind off invisibly.

A "V"-neckband for a man's sweater ▶

▲ *Single rib neckband with center stitch using slip stitch decreasing method*

▼ *Single rib neckband with center stitch combining two methods of decreasing*

▲ *Double rib neckband with two center stitches combining two methods of decreasing*

▼ *An example of a single rib neckband, the "V"-neck stitches picked up and bound off by the invisible method*

Double rib neckband with two center stitches combining two methods of decreasing

With RS facing, pick up the required number of stitches, noting that the 2 center stitches must be knit stitches for the right side of the work. Mark the 2 center stitches with colored thread. Rib 1 row.

1st row (right side). Work in K2, P2 rib to within one st of center 2 sts ending P1, K tog next st and first of 2 center sts, sl second center st, K next st, psso, beg with P1, work in rib to end.

2nd row. Rib to one st before 2 center sts, P next st and replace it on left-hand needle, sl first of 2 center sts over this st and re-place st on right-hand needle, P tog second center st and next st, rib to end.

3rd row. Rib to one st before 2 center sts, K tog next st and first of 2 center sts, sl second center st, K next st, psso, rib to end.

Rep 2nd and 3rd rows for required depth of neckband. Bind off in rib, still decreasing at center point.

Neat corners on borders

Where front and hem borders or collars are to be worked for a knitted garment, it is extremely effective to use a mitered corner to obtain a neat look. These edges can be worked separately from the outside edge and sewed on when the garment is completed, or stitches can be picked up for the required length of the border.

As an alternative, by the clever use of a contrasting stitch, a border can be easily worked at the same time as the main fabric of the garment. This method is particularly useful when making square or rectangular shawls and crib blankets.

The child's coat illustrated shows how a contrasting stitch can be used effectively as an edging. The hem and front borders are in seed stitch against a stockinette stitch background. The collar is cleverly shaped inside the seed stitch edge to give a very neat fit and—to continue the theme—the sleeves are edged with a seed stitch cuff.

Seed stitch border

Cast on an odd number of sts, allowing 10 sts for each side border.

1st row. *K1, P1, rep from * to last st, K1.

Rep 1st row 9 times more for lower seed stitch edge.

11th row. (K1, P1) 5 times, K to last 10 sts, (P1, K1) 5 times.

12th row. (K1, P1) 5 times, P to last 10 sts, (P1, K1) 5 times. Rep 11th and 12th rows until work is required length, less 10 rows. Rep 1st row 10 times more for top seed stitch edge. Bind off.

Ribbed edge

Work collar or pocket over an odd number of sts with double-pointed needles for required depth of K1, P1 rib, ending with a right side row. Slip sts on holder. Break off yarn.

1st row. WS is reversed to become RS of work so that first st on needle is P1. Use second needle and pick up required number of sts along one side edge, ending with K1 (mark this corner st with colored thread). Work in rib across sts on holder and beg with K1, pick up same number of sts along second side (mark this corner with colored thread).

2nd row. Work in K1, P1 rib to end, keeping corner sts correct.

3rd row. Work in K1, P1 rib to corner st, inc 1 by working into loop between sts, K corner st, inc 1 as before, work in rib to next corner st, inc 1 as before, K corner st, inc 1 as before, rib to end.

Rep 2nd and 3rd rows for required depth, ending with a 3rd row. Bind off in rib.

Garter stitch edge—method 1

Cast on required number of sts and mark corner st with colored thread.

1st row (right side). K to within 2 sts of corner st, K2 tog, K corner st, K2 tog tbl, K to end.

2nd row. K to corner st, P corner st, K to end.

Rep these 2 rows until edge is required depth. Bind off still decreasing on either side of corner st.

Garter stitch edge—method 2

Cast on as for first garter st edge.

1st row (right side). K to within 2 sts of corner st, K2 tog, ytf, K corner st, ytf, K2 tog tbl, K to end.

2nd row. K to within 2 sts of corner st, K next st and yo tog, P corner st, K yo and next st tog, K to end.

Rep these 2 rows until edge is required depth, ending with a 1st row. Bind off still decreasing on either side of corner st.

▼ *Contrasting stitch borders worked on the main fabric of a child's coat*

▲ *Garter stitch border worked from outside edge with simple decreasing at either side to achieve the miter, method 1.*

▲ *Seed stitch border worked with stockinette stitch*

▲ *Garter stitch border worked from outside edge, method 2*

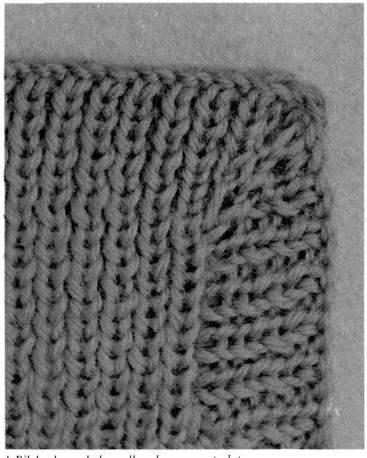

▲ *Rib border worked on collar edges or on a pocket*

Chapter 15

Knitting Know-how

Neatly finished buttonholes

Unless buttonholes are worked very neatly, they can spoil the appearance of an otherwise perfectly made garment.
Depending on the size of the button and the width of the buttonhole border, one of several different methods can be applied. The holes can be worked horizontally when the buttonhole band is fairly wide, whereas on a narrow band it is neater to work them vertically. Buttonholes on baby garments are worked as eyelet holes.

Horizontal buttonholes

Simple buttonhole

When the buttonhole is to be made as part of the main section of a cardigan, finish at the center front edge. On the next row, work a few stitches to the position for the buttonhole, then bind off the number of stitches needed for the size of the button and work to the end of the row. On the following row, work to the bound-off stitches in the previous row, turn the work and cast on the same number of stitches, turn the work again and continue to the end of the row. Always remember to work the stitch immediately after the last cast-on stitch fairly tightly in order to make the buttonhole look even.

A perfect buttonhole

Often a horizontal cast-on and bound-off buttonhole is spoiled by a loose loop of yarn across one end. To avoid this, work as follows:
Work the first row as given, binding off the full number of stitches. On the second row work to the last stitch before the bound-off stitches and increase in this stitch by working into the front and back of it. Then cast on one stitch fewer than you bound off so that you retain the correct number of stitches.

Tailored buttonhole

When the position for the buttonhole is reached, work the stitches required for the size of the button in a different colored yarn, then slip these stitches back onto the left-hand needle and work them again in the original yarn being used. When the work is finished, pull out the different colored yarn, being careful not to drop the stitches. Now complete the buttonhole by threading a length of the correct yarn through these stitches. Oversew, or buttonhole stitch, around the edges to hold the buttonhole and make it neat.

Vertical buttonholes

Work until the point for the buttonhole is reached. On the next row work a few stitches to the position for the buttonhole, then work the required number of rows over these stitches for the size of the button. Break off the yarn and return to the remaining stitches. Attach the yarn and work the same number of rows over these stitches, then continue across all the stitches in the usual manner.

Layette buttonhole

Work until the point for the buttonhole is reached. On the next row work a few stitches into the position for the buttonhole, pass the yarn over or around the needle to make an eyelet hole and work the next two stitches together. On the next row work across all the stitches in the usual way, including the yarn over stitch.

Reinforcing buttonholes

All buttonholes, except possibly those on baby garments, require reinforcing before they are complete to prevent fraying. Vertical and horizontal buttonholes require buttonhole stitching in matching silk along both edges with one straight stitch and two slanted stitches at each end. Small round eyelets require several evenly spaced buttonhole stitches around the hole, the loops lying toward the center.
Be careful not to work too many stitches around the hole (this would stretch the edges) or too few stitches (this would make the buttonhole smaller than intended).

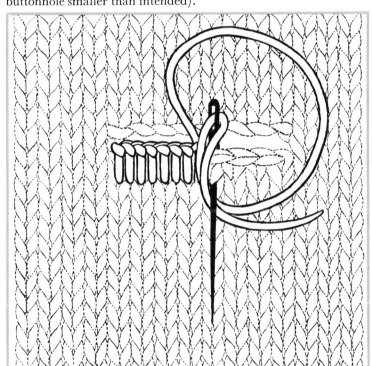

▲ *Working buttonhole stitch to strengthen a knitted buttonhole*
▼ *Correctly reinforced buttonhole with straight stitches at each end*

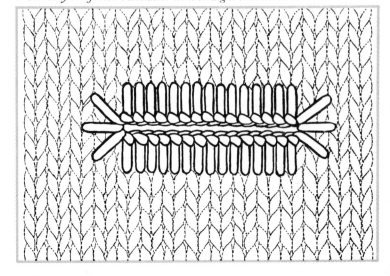

▲ *Simple buttonhole binding off*

▲ *Simple buttonhole casting on*

▲ *Simple buttonhole completed*

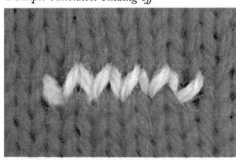

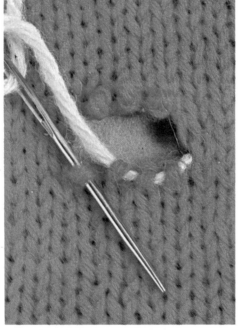

▲ *Method for tailored buttonhole, contrast yarn used for clarity throughout*
▼ *Vertical buttonhole, one side completed*

▲ *Tailored buttonhole completed*
▼ *Layette eyelet buttonhole*

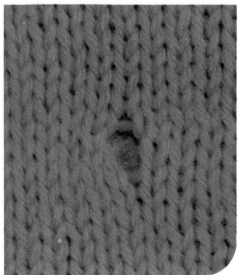

Chapter 16

Hem techniques

Most knitted garments look neater when finished with a knitted hem or border. The hem will have a better appearance if the rows which are to form the under layer are worked on needles which are one size smaller than those used for the main part of the garment.

Stockinette stitch hem for sweater hem
Cast on the required number of stitches and, beginning with a knit row, work an odd number of rows. Knit the next row instead of purling it to mark the foldline; then, beginning with a knit row, work the same number of rows as were worked initially to complete the hem. When the garment is finished, turn the hem to the wrong side of the work at the foldline and slip stitch in place. This hem is ideal for the bottom of a sweater where a certain amount of elasticity is needed.

Knitted-in hem for coats and jackets
Cast on and work as given for the stockinette stitch hem, working one row less after the foldline to end with a purl row. Before continuing with the garment, pick up the stitches of the cast-on row with an extra needle and hold these stitches behind the stitches already on the left-hand needle. Knit to the end of the next row by working one stitch from the left-hand needle together with one stitch from the extra needle. Beginning with a purl row, continue

▲ *Stockinette stitch hem*   ▼ *Stockinette stitch hem sewed to wrong side*

▲ *Knitted-in hem*   ▼ *Knitted-in hem from right side*

in stockinette stitch. This forms a very firm hemline and is excellent for use on a coat or jacket.

Picot hem for lacy patterns
Cast on an odd number of stitches and, beginning with a knit row, work an even number of rows in stockinette stitch. On the next row, or right side of the work, make a row of picot eyelets by *K2 tog, ytf, and repeat from * to last stitch, K1. Beginning with a purl row, work the same number of rows as were worked initially to complete the hem. When the garment is finished, turn the hem to the wrong side of the work at the picot row and slip stitch in place. This method forms an attractive scalloped edge, suitable for trimming baby garments or for giving a dainty edge to lace patterns.

Reversed stockinette stitch hem for necklines and sleeve edges
When the edging is completed, leave the stitches on the needle instead of binding off and fold the required depth of hem onto the right side of the work, so that the purl side forms the hem. Sew along the edge, taking one stitch from the needle and one stitch from right side. This method is ideal for finishing necklines and for completing skirts which are worked from the waist down. It can also be made by folding the hem to the wrong side to form a plain stockinette stitch edge.

Slip stitch vertical edge for jacket edges
Cast on the required number of stitches, allowing six extra stitches for the border. Work in stockinette stitch across the full width of stitches, but on every knit row slip the sixth stitch in from the required edge of the row knitwise to form a foldline. When the garment is finished, turn the border to the wrong side at the foldline and slip stitch down. This edge is suitable for the front edges of a jacket or a coat which is unbuttoned.

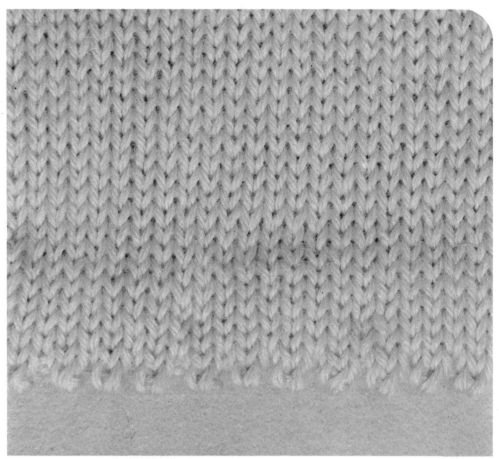

◄ *Picot hem before finishing* ▲ *Picot hem completed*
◄ *Slip stitch border for cardigans*
▼ *Reversed stockinette stitch hem picking up one stitch from needle and one from fabric*

Chapter 17

Placing pockets

Most inserted pockets can be worked along with the main section of a garment, and knitting patterns usually include directions for working pockets. This chapter includes the know-how for the placing of pockets, and by following these simple, step-by-step directions you can easily add them to a plain dress, pullover or cardigan.

Patch pockets, as shown on the illustrated jacket, are made to the required size and then simply sewed onto the outside of the finished garment. They can be bulky and for details of applying them neatly see Knitting Know-how Chapter 11.

Inserted pocket with garter stitch edge

When working an inserted pocket, make the inside flap first and leave these stitches on a holder until they are required. Calculate the number of stitches you need to make the pocket size you want. Cast on this number plus an extra two stitches. Work in stockinette stitch for the required length of the pocket, knitting two stitches together at each end of the last row, and slip stitches on a holder to be worked later. Now work the front of the pullover or cardigan in stockinette stitch until the position for the pocket is reached, less four rows, ending with a right side row and making sure that you allow for the depth of the inside pocket flap. With the wrong side of the work facing, purl until the pocket opening stitches are reached, knit across these stitches, then purl to the end of the row. Work a further three rows, working in garter stitch across the pocket opening stitches, then bind off the pocket opening stitches knitwise. Place the needle holding the inside flap stitches behind the main section with the right side facing, knit to the bound-off opening stitches, then knit across inside flap stitches in place of those bound off and knit to the end of the row (see Figure 1). Continue in stockinette stitch, working three more rows in garter stitch across pocket opening stitches (see Figure 2). When work is completed, stitch down inside flap neatly to wrong side of work (see Figure 3).

Flap pocket

Work inside pocket flap as given for pocket with garter stitch edge, but do not knit two together at each end of last row, and bind off stitches instead of leaving them on a holder. Work outside pocket flap in the size and pattern desired and slip these stitches on a holder. Now work in stockinette stitch on the front of the pullover or cardigan until the position for the pocket is reached, ending with a right side row. On the next row, purl until the pocket opening stitches are reached, bind off the pocket opening stitches knitwise and purl to the end of the row. Place the needle holding the outside pocket flap stitches in front of the main section with the right side facing you, knit to the bound-off opening stitches, then knit across the pocket flap stitches in place of those bound off and knit to the end of the remaining stitches. Place the inside pocket flap behind the pocket opening on the wrong side and stitch neatly in place.

1. *Inserting the inside of a pocket*

2. *The completed garter stitch pocket opening*

3. *Stitch down the inside of the pocket*

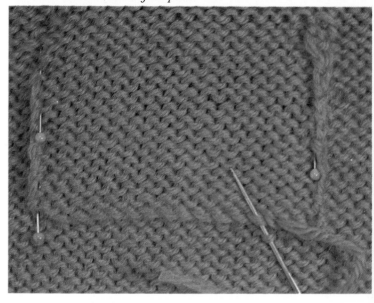

▲ **4.** *Pocket with an outside flap*

▼ **5.** *Stitching down the inside of a flap pocket*

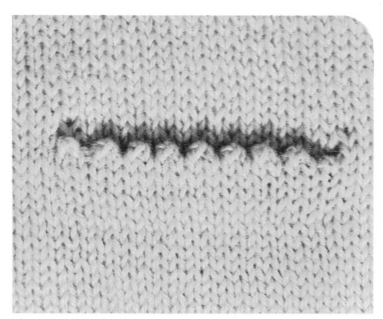

▲ **6.** *Pocket edge with picots*

▼ **7.** *Patch pockets on a smart jacket*

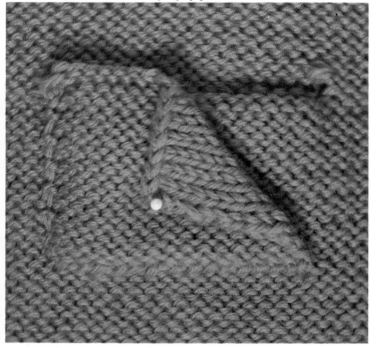

Inserted pocket with picot edge

Work inside pocket flap as given for pocket with garter stitch edge. Now work the front of pullover or cardigan in stockinette stitch until the pocket position is reached, allowing an odd number of stitches for opening, ending with a wrong side row. With right side of work facing, knit until the pocket opening stitches are reached, then work across opening stitches as follows: K1, *ytf, K2 tog, rep from * to the end of these stitches, turn. Work 5 more rows stockinette stitch across pocket opening stitches only. Bind off these stitches knitwise. Break yarn. With right side of work facing, attach yarn to remaining stitches and knit to end. Place the needle holding the inside flap stitches in front of main section, with purl side facing you, purl to the bound-off opening stitches, then purl across inside flap stitches in place of those bound off and purl to end of row. Continue in stockinette stitch. When work is completed, stitch down pocket opening stitches at picot row to wrong side. Stitch down inside pocket flap neatly to wrong side of work.

Chapter 18

Knitting Know-how

Knitted pleats

A knitted pleated skirt is a smart and useful addition to any wardrobe, and because it is casual and easy to wear also makes a useful garment for little girls. Made in pure wool, knitted skirts will hold their shape and the pleats will keep their swing. Pleats can be knitted on two needles, but for a woman's skirt requiring more stitches a circular needle is useful (see page 52).

Mock pleats

Decide on the full hem width required and use this measurement, plus the gauge per inch in the yarn you have selected, to arrive at the number of stitches you will need. Cast on a number of stitches divisible by 8, using two needles or a circular needle. For example, a hem width of 42 inches and a gauge of 7 stitches to the inch gives 294 stitches, so cast on either 288 or 296 stitches (both divisible by 8).

Two-needle pattern
1st row. *K7, P1, rep from * to end.
2nd row. K4, *P1, K7, rep from * to last 4 sts, P1, K3. These two rows form pattern and are repeated for the desired length.

Circular pattern
1st round. *K7, P1, rep from * to end of round.
2nd round. P3, K1, *P7, K1, rep from * to last 4 sts, P4. These 2 rounds form pattern and are repeated for required length.

To complete skirt
Join center back seam if worked on two needles. Cut a waist length of 1in wide elastic and join into a circle. Sew inside waistband using casing stitch (see Knitting Know-how Chapter 11).

▲ *Finished effect of the full pleating stitch*
▼ *Dividing stitches to close a full pleat*

▼ *Finished effect of the mock pleating stitch*

▼ *Knitting stitches together to close a full pleat*

▲ *A full pleated skirt for a little girl*

Full pleats

Work out the full hem width as for mock pleating, based on 3 times the waist measurement required plus an extra 1½in. Cast on a number of stitches divisible by 12, plus 8, using two needles. This gives a pleat fold of 4 stitches.

1st row. *K8, P1, K2, sl 1P, rep from * to last 8 sts, K8
2nd row. *P11, K1, rep from * to last 8 sts, P8.
These 2 rows form pattern and are repeated for the required length, less 1¼in for the waistband.

To close pleats

Two extra needles of the same size are required to close the pleats.
Next row. K4, *slip next 4 sts onto first extra needle, slip next 4 sts onto 2nd extra needle, place first extra needle behind 2nd extra needle and hold both extra needles behind left-hand needle,

(K tog one st from all 3 needles) 4 times, rep from * to last 4 sts, K4. Bind off.

To complete skirt

Join center back seam and overlap 4 stitches at the beginning of the row over 4 stitches at the end of the row to complete pleating. Cast on required number of stitches for the waistband, adding 2–3 inches extra for ease in dressing and undressing, and work 2½in in stockinette stitch. Bind off.
With RS of waistband facing RS of top of skirt, sew band to skirt. Cut a waist length of 1in wide elastic and join the ends. Fold waistband in half to WS and stitch down over elastic. This elasticated waistband means that a side opening is not necessary and does away with the need for an inserted zipper. The seam can be worn on either the side or back.

Chapter 19

Introduction to knitting in the round

Sweaters, socks, stockings, gloves, mittens, skirts and many other garments can be worked on sets of needles, producing a tubular, seamless piece of work. This does not mean that there cannot be shaping with carefully planned increasing and decreasing calculated to give the required shape.

Knitting in rounds also aids the knitter because the right side of the work is always facing, which helps when working complicated or multi-colored patterns. It is for this reason, in fact, that Fair Isle knitters use the method, even in sweaters with long sleeves. Instead of stopping at armhole level, a tube is worked the whole length of the sweater up to the shoulder. From the armhole level upward, the yarn is wound around the needle several times in a line where the armhole is required. On the next round, the previous loops are dropped and the process repeated. This gives a ladder of strands on either side which is cut when the work is completed, each end being darned back into the fabric. The stitches for the sleeves are then picked up around the armhole and the sleeves knitted in rounds down to the wrist.

This method is both quick and practical, since it is a simple matter to add or lengthen cuffs at any time.

Casting on with more than two needles

The actual casting on of each stitch is exactly as normal, but because there are more needles to be considered there are two methods of working. When using a set of four needles, one is used for knitting and the total number of stitches is divided between the remaining three needles. You can either cast on the number of stitches required on the first needle, then proceed to the second and so on, or you can cast on the total number onto one needle and then slip them onto the other needles. The second method is perhaps the easier and is less likely to cause the cast-on edge to become twisted. Form the needles into a circle and slip the spare needle into the first stitch on the first needle. If you now knit this stitch, taking the yarn directly to it from the last stitch, the circle you require is formed. Continue to knit all the stitches on the first needle. Once the needle is free of stitches, knit along the second needle. Continue in this way. This is all there is to round knitting. Because the right side of the work is always facing you, every round produces stockinette stitch and not garter stitch, as would be the case when working back and forth in rows. Garter stitch is made by working one round knit and one round purl alternately.

Because it is easy to lose track of the beginning of a round, the simplest method of marking it is to slip a knotted loop of contrasting yarn onto the needle before the first stitch of a round. Simply slip this loop onto the right-hand needle, without knitting it, on every round, and the beginning of a round can be seen at a glance.

More than one marker may be required because the pattern may include shapings at either side of a point where a side seam would be placed, or down the back seam of a stocking. If you are working

a gored skirt, it may be easier to mark each gore with a loop of one color and use a second color to mark the actual round beginning.

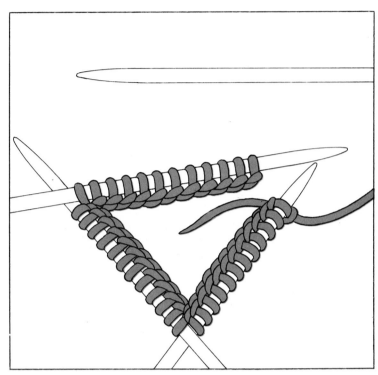

▲ *Casting on with four needles*

▼ *Joining casting on with 4 needles*

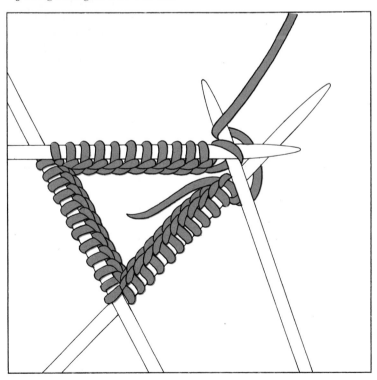

Socks and stockings

Socks and stockings, as well as being practical because of their longer life when handknitted, can be highly fashionable accessories if well made and well finished. The opposite page gives a few hints on the techniques involved—reinforcing, leg shaping, turning the heel and shaping the toe.

Shaping the leg

Leg shaping is necessary unless rib is used for the main part of the sock. Begin with 3 or 4 ins of ribbing, reinforcing if necessary with shirring elastic at the back. Change to pattern and shape the leg either side of a center st at the back forming a mock seam.

Dividing for the heel

On reaching the heel divide the sts into 2 sections, the instep and the heel itself. A well fitting sock has, if possible, an extra 2 sts in the instep section. The extra center sts forming the back seam should be included in the instep sts as shown. The heel flap is worked in rows backwards and forwards and can be reinforced by knitting a fine matching sewing thread in with the yarn. Work in st st as this gives a flat comfortable fit. Work until the heel section is square.

Turning the heel

The French heel and the Dutch heel are the most common methods, the Dutch heel giving a squarer look.

French heel—Divide heel flap sts into 2 sections either side of a center 2 or 3 sts. As the decs are worked on the side sections they must be divisible by 2. K across 1st section and center sts, make 1st dec in side section thus—sl 1, K1, psso, turn, P dec st and center sts, P tog first 2 sts of other side section, turn. Cont in this way until all heel flap sts have been worked.

Dutch heel—Divide heel flap sts into 3 sections. Work as for French heel but the decs should begin by using the last st of the center section as the sl st plus 1 st from the side section and the same on the P 2 tog. Cont in this way until all heel flap sts have been worked.
Both heels should finish on a P row. Turn.

Forming the instep gusset

This is the triangle of decs either side of the instep and reduces the number of sts picked up for the heel. With 1st needle K half the heel sts, pick up and K sts evenly along side of heel flap, with 2nd needle K across all instep sts, with 3rd needle pick up and K same number of sts evenly along other side of heel flap. Work in rounds dec 1 st either side of instep sts, which would be at end of 1st needle and beginning of 3rd needle on alt rounds until heel sts are equal in number to instep sts. Continue in rounds for foot.

Shaping the toe

Begin about 2in before the end of the foot.

Flat toe—This is the most comfortable shape. Divide the sts equally onto 2 needles with sole sts on one needle and instep sts on the other. If the instep sts still include the extra st used for the back seam, dec by working 2 sts tog. Work across each needle as follows: K1, K2 tog, K to last 3 sts, K2 tog tbl, K1. Cont to dec on alternate rounds in this way until about half the sts have been decreased. Finish by binding 2 sets of sts off together or weaving together.

Round toe—Divide the sts into sections and work a dec in each section all around the toe ending with a few sts which are then pulled up on a thread (see top of mittens, page 50).

▲ *Shaping for flat toe*

▲ *Dividing stitches for heel showing center back stitch*

▲ *French heel*

Knitting
Know-how

Mittens and gloves

When gloves and mittens are worked on two needles, side and finger seams are necessary, but worked on sets of double-pointed needles they are smoothly seamless.

Choice of yarn

Select a yarn which is not too fine or too soft and will stand up to wear. Sports weight yarns are suitable and a yarn with a crepe finish would be an interesting texture choice. Needles should be finer than normal for the yarn you are using to give firm stitches which will not snag. A tight-fitting, weatherproof wrist ribbing is made by using needles one size smaller than used on the rest of the gloves or mittens. Remember that although the wrist must fit snugly, it must also be wide enough for the hand to be inserted easily.

▲ *Method of increasing for a thumb gusset, for both two and four needles*
▼ *Leaving the thumb gusset stitches on holder*

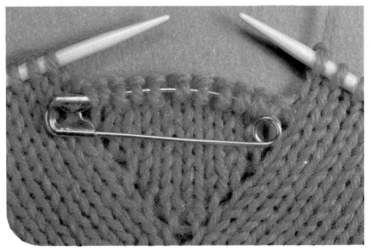

Calculating the number of stitches

As for any other garment, work a sample first so that you are satisfied that the pattern, the size of the needles and the type of yarn will together produce the surface you want. Measure the sample carefully to check how many stitches there are to the inch. The circumference of the hand just above the thumb division determines the number of inches you require. Multiply the number of inches needed by the number of stitches in one inch. For example, if your hand measures 7 inches around and the test sample of knitting produces 6 stitches to the inch, multiply 7 by 6, making 42, and cast on 42 stitches. This number of stitches appears to give a very loose wrist, but ribbing will draw in the extra width to make the wrist fit closely.

This number of stitches makes no allowance for the extra width below the thumb division, but this is usually worked as extra increasing in a triangular area between the wrist and thumb division. When sufficient stitches have been increased, they are slipped onto a stitch holder while extra stitches, to take their place, are cast on and then the remainder of the palm is worked.

Mittens on four needles

Size

To fit an average adult hand—the length is adjustable.

> **Gauge**
> 5½ sts and 7½ rows to 1in over stockinette stitch worked on No.5 needles.

Materials

Reynolds Danskyarn—2 balls
One set of No.5 double-pointed needles
Stitch holder

Mittens

Begin at wrist edge. Cast on 40 sts. Work 2in K2, P2 rib.

Continue in st st. Working K every round, work 6 rounds.

Shape for thumb

1st round K2, K up thread before next st to inc, K next st and mark with colored thread as a guide to center thumb st, K up thread before next st to inc, K to end of round.

K 1 round.

3rd round K2, K up 1, K3, K up 1, K to end.

K 1 round.

Continue in this way, inc at either side of thumb gusset until 5 sts at either side have been inc.

K 1 round.

Next round K2, sl 11 sts for thumb onto holder, turn work and using 2-needle method cast on to left-hand needle 7 sts to replace thumb sts, turn and K to end of round.

Next round K1, sl 1 K-wise, K1, psso, K5, K2 tog, K to end.

K 1 round.

Next round K1, sl 1 K-wise, K1, psso, K3, K2 tog, K to end.

K 1 round.

Next round K1, sl 1 K-wise, K1, psso, K1, K2 tog, K to end.

Continue in st st until work measures 1in less than desired length to finger tip, or approximately 3½in from thumb division.

Shape top

Dec 5 sts evenly on next round. K 1 round.
Rep last 2 rounds once.

Dec 5 sts evenly on next 5 rounds.

Break yarn, leaving an end long enough to thread through rem sts. Draw up and finish off.

Thumb

Attach yarn to thumb sts, K 6 sts from holder onto 1st needle, K rem 5 sts from holder onto 2nd needle and pick up and K7 sts along 7 cast-on sts.

Work in rounds of st st until 2in long, or 2 rounds less than desired length.

Next round *K1, K2 tog, rep from * to end.

Last round *K2 tog, rep from * to end.

Break off yarn and thread through rem sts. Draw up and finish off.

Make 2nd mitten in same way. This reversible design can be used for either hand.

Gloves on two needles

Size and gauge
As given for mittens.

Materials
Reynolds Danskyarn—2 balls
One pair No.5 needles

Right hand

Begin at wrist. Cast on 40 sts. Work 1¼in K1, P1 rib.

1st patt row (RS) P.

2nd patt row *K1, P1, rep from * to end.

These 2 rows form patt and are rep throughout.

Continue in patt until work measures 2½in from beg, ending with a WS row.

Shape thumb

1st row P21 sts, inc in next st by purling twice into same st, P1 marking this as center thumb st with colored thread, inc in next st, P rem 16 sts.

2nd row Patt to end.

3rd row P21 sts, inc 1, P3, inc 1, P to end.

4th row As 2nd.

Keeping patt correct, continue in this way, inc one st on either side of center thumb st on next and every other row until 6 incs at either side have been worked. (52 sts).

Next row Patt to last 22 sts, turn and work on thumb sts only.

Continue in patt across thumb sts, inc one st at each end of 1st row, until work measures 2¼in, or desired thumb length.

Last row *P2 tog, rep from * to end.

Break yarn and thread through rem sts. Draw up and seam side of thumb.

With WS facing, attach yarn

▲ *Simple and inexpensive accessories to make to coordinate with an outfit*

to 22 sts, work to end of row.

Next row Patt to thumb, pick up and K4 sts from base of thumb, patt to end of row. (42 sts). Continue in patt until work measures 5¼in from beg, or desired length to division for 1st finger ending with WS row. Break yarn.

Attach yarn to 12 central sts, leaving 15 sts on either side on holders.

Work 1st finger

Continue in patt on 12 sts, inc one st at each end of 1st row for 2½in or desired length, ending with a WS row.

Last row *P2 tog, rep from * to end.

Draw thread through rem sts and seam finger.

Work 2nd finger

With RS facing, work 5 sts from each holder and pick up and K4 sts along lower edge of 1st finger.

Continue in patt on 14 sts, inc one st at each end of 1st row for 2¾in or desired length, ending with a WS row. Complete as for 1st finger.

Work 3rd finger

Work as given for 2nd finger

until 2½in or desired length. Complete as before.

Work little finger

Work 5 rem sts from each holder and pick up and K4 sts from 3rd finger. Work as before for 2¼in or desired length. Complete as before. Join little finger and side seam.

Left hand

Work as given for right hand, reversing all shaping. 1st shaping row will read: P16, inc in next st, P1, inc in next st, P to end.

51

Bags in circular knitting

Circular knitting is a quick and simple way of making tubular, seamless fabrics. This method is used for the two handbags shown in the photograph, one a rather classic pocket bag, the other a pretty novelty shape. Either bag would make a useful fashion accessory.

Circular knitting

Knitting patterns often suggest using a circular needle for tubular work such as the lower part of a sweater. Circular needles have many advantages over pairs or sets of needles and they are made in the same sizes as ordinary needles in several different lengths. The two points of the circular needle are exactly like ordinary needles, but they are joined together in the center by a flexible nylon cord.

Using circular needles

A circular needle may be used to take the place of 4 or more needles to make a skirt or sweater in one piece without seams. The fact that there is only one needle in use naturally makes the knitting of a garment easier. The only type of garment where they cannot be used as substitutes for sets of needles is where there are only a small number of stitches, which would be insufficient to stretch around even the shortest needle length, such as gloves, mittens, socks or stockings. The use of circular needles is not limited, however, to working large tubular sections. They can also be used as a pair of needles by working along

a row in the usual way, turning and working back again. This is an additional advantage when working a sweater which has to be divided at the armholes.

Even distribution of weight

Because the work is held by both hands evenly, shoulders do not become strained or tired, even after many hours of knitting. Many handicapped knitters find that this makes circular needles ideal for all types of work.

New circular needles

If you have just purchased a circular needle which has not been used before, place it in hot water for a few seconds before use and then dry it. The heat will remove the twist which will have formed in the nylon cord during packing and storage.

Bellrope bag

Size

Approximately 11in by 11in.

Gauge
5 sts and 6½ rows to 1in over stockinette stitch worked on No.5 needles.

Materials

Unger Les Coraux
2 balls of main color A
1 additional ball of contrast color B for bell clappers
One No.5 circular needle
One No.F crochet hook
Buckram and lining material

Bag

Using No.5 circular needle and A, cast on 216 sts. Join into a circle (being careful that the sts are not twisted) by bringing end with last cast-on st around to join to first cast-on st. Work in rounds.
1st round *P2, K7, P2, K1 tbl, rep from * to end.
2nd, 3rd and 4th rounds As 1st.
5th round *P2, sl 1, K1, psso, K3, K2 tog, P2, K1 tbl, rep from * to end.
6th round *P2, K5, P2, K1 tbl, rep from * to end.
7th round *P2, sl 1, K1, psso, K1, K2 tog, P2, K1 tbl, rep from * to end.
8th round *P2, K3, P2, K1 tbl, rep from * to end.
9th round *P2, sl 1, K2 tog, psso, P2, K1 tbl, rep from * to end.
10th round *P2, K1 tbl, rep from * to end.
11th round *P2, K1 tbl, P2, (K1, P1, K1, P1, K1) all into next st—called 1 bell—rep from * to end.
12th round *P2, K1 tbl, P2, K5, rep from * to end.
13th and 14th rounds As 12th.
15th round *P2, K1 tbl, P2, sl 1, K1, psso, K1, K2 tog, rep from * to end.
16th round *P2, K1 tbl, P2, K3, rep from * to end.
17th round *P2, K1 tbl, P2, sl 1, K2 tog, psso, rep from * to end.
18th round *P2, 1 bell, P2, K1 tbl, rep from * to end.
19th round *P2, K5, P2, K1 tbl, rep from * to end.
20th and 21st rounds As 19th.
22nd round *P2, sl 1, K1, psso, K1, K2 tog, P2, K1 tbl, rep from * to end.
23rd round *P2, K3, P2, K1 tbl, rep from * to end.
24th round *P2, sl 1, K2 tog, psso, P2, K1 tbl, rep from * to end.
Rep from 11th-24th rounds twice more, then 11th-19th rounds once more.
Next round *P2, K1, K up 1, K3, K up 1, K1, P2, K1 tbl, rep from * to end.
Next round *P2, K7, P2, K1

tbl, rep from * to end.
Rep last round twice more.
Bind off.

Bells

Using No.5 circular needle and B, cast on 14 sts. Work in rows, turning the work at the end of every row.
1st row K.
2nd row P.
Rep these 2 rows once more.
5th row *K1, sl 1, K1, psso, K1, K2 tog, K1 rep from * once more.
6th row P.
7th row *K1, sl 1, K2 tog, psso, K1, rep from * once more.
8th row P.
9th row *Sl 1, K2 tog, psso, rep from * once more.
Break yarn and draw through rem sts, then seam two edges on WS to form bell.
Make 3 more bells in same way.

Bell clapper

Using No.F crochet hook and B, ch4. Join into a circle with ss into first ch.
1st round Ch2, 3sc into circle. Join with ss to 2nd of first 2ch.
2nd round Ch2, 1sc into same st, 2sc into each of rem 3sc. Join with ss to 2nd of first 2ch.
3rd round Ch2, *skip 1sc, 1sc into next sc, rep from * to end. Join with ss to 2nd of first 2ch.
4th round Ch2, work 1sc into each st leaving last loop of each sc on hook, yoh and draw through all loops on hook, ch4.
Fasten off.
Work 12 more bell clappers in same way.

Finishing

Press bell sections lightly, if required.
Sew one bell clapper inside each bell flute along half of cast-on edge. Fold work in half so that the other side of each bell flute along cast-on edge completes the bells. Sew ribs together between bells. Join bottom of bag by sewing

▲ *On the right, the bellrope bag with drawstring handle. On the left, the pocket bag with a tab and buckle fastening*

firmly between stitches just above bells.

Cut buckram and lining to fit bag and join side edges on WS. Place buckram and lining inside bag and sl st in place around lower edge of bells at bound-off edge.

Using 18 strands of yarn, allowing 6 strands for each section, make a braid the required handle length and sew to either side of bound-off edge of bag.

Trim each end of braid with 2 bells on each side.

Pocketbook bag

Size

Approximately 9in by 7in.

Gauge

6 sts and 8 rows to 1in over stockinette stitch worked on No.5 needles.

Materials

Spinnerin Wintuk Sport
2 balls
One No.5 circular needle
One cable needle
Buckram and lining material
One buckle

Bag

Using No.5 circular needle, cast on 53 sts for base of bag. Beg with a P row, work 7 rows st st, turning work at end of each row.

Turn so that K side is facing and cast on 67 sts.

With P side facing, join for circular knitting as given for bell-trimmed bag.

1st round P53 sts for front, K1, (P1, K1) 3 times for side, P53 sts for back, K1, (P1, K1) 3 times for other side. Place marker after last st worked to mark beg of round.

Rep 1st round until circular section measures 7in or desired depth, ending last round 6 sts before marker.

Divide for flap

Next round Bind off 6 sts from side, bind off 53 sts from front, bind off 6 sts from other side, K1, P53 sts across back, K1. Continue for flap on these 55 sts, working in rows of cluster patt.

1st row K.

2nd row K1, *P1, P3, sl last 3 P sts onto cable needle and wind yarn around all 3 sts 6 times ending with yarn at front of work, sl 3 sts from cable needle to right-hand needle—called cl 3—rep from * to last 2 sts, P1, K1.

3rd row K.

4th row K1, P3, *cl 3, P1, rep from * to last 3 sts, P2, K1.

Rep last 4 rows 3 times more.

Divide for tab fastening

Bind off 20 sts, K to last 20 sts, bind off 20 sts.

With RS facing, attach yarn to rem 15 center sts and work in cluster patt for 11 rows. Bind off.

Handle

Using No.5 circular needle, cast on 16 sts.

Work back and forth in K1, P1 rib until handle measures 20in or desired length. Bind off.

Finishing

Do not press.

Cut buckram and lining to fit bag, allowing turning on lining around flap and opening edges. Join side seams. Seam cast-on edge of base to cast-on edge of back. Seam cast-on edges of sides to sides of base.

Insert buckram and sl st in place. Insert lining and sew around all edges, turning in hem.

Seam long side edges of handle and insert buckram through center of handle. Join short ends and stitch in place on side panels.

Sew buckle in position on front for tab fastening.

Chapter 20

Introduction to lace stitches

Knitting lace patterns will bring you compliments because they look so difficult. But most of them are straight-forward. The designs often build up from an arrangement of open-work patterns made by increasing one stitch and decreasing another, either next to the increase or in another part of the design, so that the number of stitches is constant. If you are a beginner you can use these patterns to make squares for ponchos, strips for scarves and oblongs for shawls which will not involve the shaping needed for a garment.

Shawls, ponchos, pillows and scarves are easy ways to use lacy stitches

Open-work ladder stitch

Open-work ladder stitch

Worked over a number of stitches divisible by 10, plus 6. (For example, 36, 46 and so on.)

1st row (wrong side). P6, *K2 tog tbl, wind yarn twice around needle, K2 tog, P6, rep from * to end.
2nd row. K6, *P1, P into first yarn over and K into the second yarn over, P1, K6, rep from * to end.
These 2 rows form the pattern and are repeated throughout.

Oblique open-work stitch

Worked over a number of stitches divisible by 9.

1st row. *K4, K up horizontal thread before next st to inc 1 st, K2 tog, lift inc st over sts knitted tog, K up horizontal thread before next st, K3, rep from * to end.
2nd row. P.
3rd row. *K3, K up horizontal thread before next st, K2 tog, lift inc st over sts knitted tog, K up horizontal thread before next st, K4, rep from * to end.
4th row. P.
These rows are repeated working one K st less at the beginning of each K row to move the crossed stitches to the right and so maintain the diagonal line. The extra stitches at the end of the row are worked into the pattern when possible.

Oblique open-work stitch

Ridged lace stitch

Worked over a number of stitches divisible by 6, plus 1.
1st row. *P1, P2 tog, yon, K1, yrn, P2 tog, rep from * to last st, P1.
2nd row. P.
3rd row. K.
4th row. P.
These 4 rows form the pattern and are repeated throughout.

Ridged lace stitch ▲

Old shale stitch

Worked over a number of stitches divisible by 11, plus 2.
1st row. K.
2nd row. P.
3rd row. K1, *(P2 tog) twice, (yon, K1) 3 times, yrn, (P2 tog) twice, rep from * to last st, K1.
4th row. P.
These 4 rows form the pattern and are repeated throughout.

▲ *Old shale stitch*   ▼ *Crisscross ladder stitch*

Crisscross ladder stitch

Worked over a number of stitches divisible by 8, plus 4.
1st row (wrong side). *P6, yrn, sl 1 purlwise, P1, psso, rep from * to last 4sts, P4.
2nd row. *K6, ytf, sl 1 knitwise, K1, psso, rep from * to last 4 sts, K4.
These 2 rows form the pattern and are repeated throughout.

Forgotten the abbreviations? Refer to Knitting Know-how Chapter 1 for how to work 'ytf', 'yon' and 'yrn'.

More lace stitches

Because of the lovely look they produce, lace stitches have always been among the most popular forms of knitting. Some of the most beautiful examples originated in the north of Scotland more than one hundred years ago. Many of these old stitches have charming names evoking their history and are recognized by knitters all over the world. Three of the most popular are given here, along with an ascot pattern which will help you practice candlelight stitch.

No matter how intricate these stitches may look, the patterns are really very simple to work. The principle is exactly the same as that shown on pages 54 and 55, that is, making an extra stitch by means of a loop and compensating for the extra stitch by working two stitches together somewhere in the pattern sequence. The decreased stitches may not necessarily be worked in the same row as the extra stitches, which means that on subsequent rows you will have more stitches than you started with. However, by the end of the number of rows needed to complete one whole pattern, you will have reverted to the correct number of stitches and will be ready to start the next repeat.

Traveling vine stitch

Cast on a number of stitches divisible by 8, plus 4.
1st row. Sl 1, K1, *ytf, K1 tbl, ytf, sl 1, K1, psso, K5, rep from * to last 2 sts, K2.
2nd row. Sl 1, P1, *P4, P2 tog tbl, P3, rep from * to last 2 sts, P1, K1.
3rd row. Sl 1, K1, *ytf, K1 tbl, ytf, K2, sl 1, K1, psso, K3, rep from * to last 2 sts, K2.
4th row. Sl 1, P1, * P2, P2 tog tbl, P5, rep from * to last 2 sts,

▼ *Traveling vine knitted lace stitch*

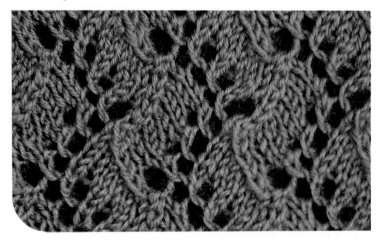

P1, K1.
5th row. Sl 1, K1, *K1 tbl, ytf, K4, sl 1, K1, psso, K1, ytf, rep from * to last 2 sts, K2.
6th row. Sl 1, P1, *P1, P2 tog tbl, P6, rep from * to last 2 sts, P1, K1.
7th row. Sl 1, K1, *K5, K2 tog, ytf, K1 tbl, ytf, rep from * to last 2 sts, K2.
8th row. Sl 1, P1, *P3, P2 tog, P4, rep from * to last 2 sts, P1, K1.
9th row. Sl 1, K1, *K3, K2 tog, K2, ytf, K1 tbl, ytf, rep from * to last 2 sts, K2.
10th row. Sl 1, P1, *P5, P2 tog, P2, rep from * to last 2 sts, P1, K1.
11th row. Sl 1, K1, *ytf, K1, K2 tog, K4, ytf, K1 tbl, rep from * to last 2 sts, K2.
12th row. Sl 1, P1, *P6, K2 tog, P1, rep from * to last 2 sts, P1, K1.
These 12 rows form pattern and are repeated throughout.

Fern stitch

Cast on a number of stitches divisible by 29, plus 2.
1st row. K1, *K1, sl 1, K2 tog, psso, K9, ytf, K1, yrn, P2, yon, K1, ytf, K9, sl 1, K2 tog, psso, rep from * to last st, K1.
2nd and every other row. P1, *P13, K2, P14, rep from * to last st, P1.
3rd row. K1, *K1, sl 1, K2 tog, psso, K8, ytf, K1, ytf, K1, P2, K1, ytf, K1, ytf, K8, sl 1, K2 tog, psso, rep from * to last st, K1.
5th row. K1, *K1, sl 1, K2 tog, psso, K7, ytf, K1, ytf, K2, P2, K2, ytf, K1, ytf, K7, sl 1, K2 tog, psso, rep from * to last st, K1.
7th row. K1, *K1, sl 1, K2 tog, psso, K6, ytf, K1, ytf, K3, P2, K3, ytf, K1, ytf, K6, sl 1, K2 tog, psso, rep from * to last st, K1.
9th row. K1, *K1, sl 1, K2 tog, psso, K5, ytf, K1, ytf, K4, P2, K4, ytf, K1, ytf, K5, sl 1, K2 tog, psso, rep from * to last st, K1.
10th row. As 2nd.
These 10 rows form pattern and are repeated throughout. Note that when this pattern is completed it forms zigzag edges.

Candlelight stitch

Cast on a number of stitches divisible by 12, plus 1.
1st row. *K1, ytf, sl 1, K1, psso, K7, K2 tog, ytf, rep from * to last st, K1.
2nd and every other row. P to end.
3rd row. *K1, ytf, K1, sl 1, K1, psso, K5, K2 tog, K1, ytf, rep from * to last st, K1.
5th row. *K1, ytf, K2, sl 1, K1, psso, K3, K2 tog, K2, ytf, rep from * to last st, K1.
7th row. *K1, ytf, K3, sl 1, K1, psso, K1, K2 tog, K3, ytf, rep from * to last st, K1.
9th row. *K1, ytf, K4, sl 1, K2 tog, psso, K4, ytf, rep from * to last st, K1.
11th row. *K4, K2 tog, ytf, K1, ytf, sl 1, K1, psso, K3, rep from * to last st, K1.
13th row. *K3, K2 tog, K1, ytf, K1, ytf, K1, sl 1, K1, psso, K2, rep from * to last st, K1.
15th row. *K2, K2 tog, K2, ytf, K1, ytf, K2, sl 1, K1, psso, K1, rep from * to last st, K1.
17th row. *K1, K2 tog, K3, ytf, K1, ytf, K3, sl 1, K1, psso, rep from * to last st, K1.
19th row. K2 tog, *K4, ytf, K1, ytf, K4, sl 1, K2 tog, psso, rep from * ending last rep sl 1, K1, psso.
20th row. As 2nd.
These 20 rows form pattern and are repeated throughout.

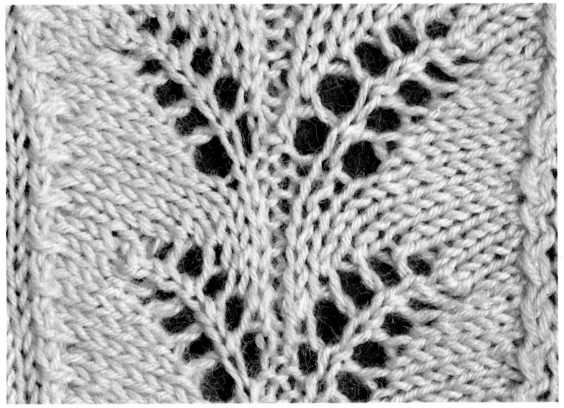

▲ *Fern stitch with a leafy look*

▼ *Candlelight stitch, used for the ascot*

▲ *Lacy ascot lined for crispness*

Ascot in lacy candlelight stitch

Size
8in wide by 30in long

Gauge
$8\frac{1}{2}$ sts and $10\frac{1}{2}$ rows to 1in over stockinette stitch worked on No.2 needles.

Materials
Bernat Super Baby Wool
7 1oz skeins
One pair No.2 needles
$\frac{1}{4}$yd of 36in wide lining material

Ascot
Using No.2 needles, cast on 73 sts.
Rep 20 patt rows given for candlelight stitch 16 times in all. Bind off.

Finishing
Press lightly on WS under a damp cloth with a warm iron. Cut lining to fit ascot. With RS of ascot facing RS of lining, seam one short and 2 long ends. Turn to RS and sl st rem short end.

Lacy eyelet patterns

Most traditional lace patterns are based on the technique for making eyelets described in this chapter. The method consists of using the yarn over or around the needle to form the eyelet hole, then decreasing a stitch elsewhere in the pattern to compensate. The eyelet holes are worked in regular and repeating groups and produce a variety of patterns.

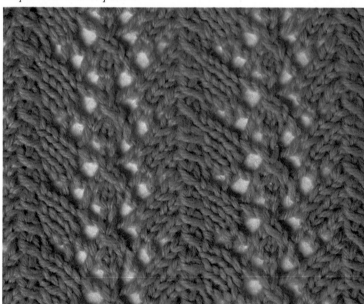

▲ *Spearhead lace rib pattern*

▲ *Diagonal eyelet rib (used above the ribbing on the pullover illustrated)*
▼ *Wavy eyelet rib pattern*

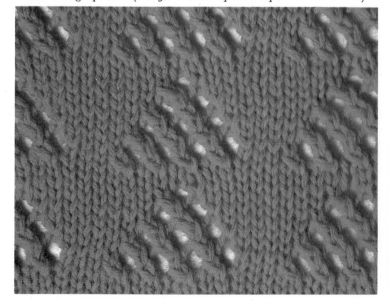

▲ *Arrowhead and diamond lace pattern*
▼ *Lace triangle pattern (used for a central panel on pullover illustrated)*

Diagonal eyelet rib

Cast on a number of stitches divisible by 5, plus 2. (For example, 27 stitches.)

1st row. (RS) K1, *K3, K2 tog, ytf, rep from * to last st, K1.
2nd and every other row. P.
3rd row. K1, *K2, K2 tog, ytf, K1, rep from * to last st, K1.
5th row. K1, *K1, K2 tog, ytf, K2, rep from * to last st, K1.
7th row. K1, *K2 tog, ytf, K3, rep from * to last st, K1.
9th row. K2 tog, *ytf, K3, K2 tog, rep from * ending last rep K2.
10th row. P.
These 10 rows form pattern and are repeated throughout.

Wavy eyelet rib

Cast on a number of stitches divisible by 4, plus 2. (For example, 26 stitches.)

1st row. (RS) K1, *K2, K2 tog, ytf, rep from * to last st, K1.
2nd and every other row. P.
3rd row. K1, *K1, K2 tog, ytf, K1, rep from * to last st, K1.
5th row. K1, *K2 tog, ytf, K2, rep from * to last st, K1.
7th row. K1, *K1, ytf, K2 tog, K1, rep from * to last st, K1.
9th row. K1, *K2, ytf, K2 tog, rep from * to last st, K1.
11th row. *K2 tog, K2, ytf, rep from * to last 2 sts, K2.
12th row. P.
Rows 3-12 form pattern and are repeated throughout.

Spearhead lace rib

Cast on a number of stitches divisible by 12, plus 2. (For example, 38 stitches.)

1st row. (RS) K1, *K3, ytf, sl 1, K1, psso, K2, K2 tog, ytf, K1, ytf, sl 1, K1, psso, rep from * to last st, K1.
2nd and every other row. P.
3rd row. K1, *K1, K2 tog, ytf, K1, ytf, sl 1, K1, psso, K1, K2 tog, ytf, K1, ytf, sl 1, K1, psso, rep from * to last st, K1.
5th row. K1, *K2 tog, ytf, K3, ytf, sl 1, K1, psso, K2 tog, ytf, K1, ytf, sl 1, K1, psso, rep from * to last st, K1.
6th row. P.
These 6 rows form pattern and are repeated throughout.

Arrowhead and diamond lace

Cast on a number of stitches divisible by 10, plus 2. (For example, 32 stitches.)

1st row. (RS) K1, ytf, *K3, sl 1, K2 tog, psso, K3, ytf, K1, ytf, rep from * to last 11 sts, K3, sl 1, K2 tog, psso, K3, ytf, K2.
2nd and every other row. P.
3rd row. K2, *ytf, K2, sl 1, K2 tog, psso, K2, ytf, K3, rep from * to end.
5th row. K2 tog, ytf, *K1, ytf, K1, sl 1, K2 tog, psso, K1, ytf, K1, ytf, sl 1, K2 tog, psso, ytf, rep from * to last 10 sts, K1, ytf, K1, sl 1, K2 tog, psso, K1, ytf, K1, ytf, sl 1, K1, psso, K1.
6th row. P.
These 6 rows form pattern and are repeated throughout.

Lace triangles

Cast on a number of stitches divisible by 11, plus 3. (For example, 36 stitches.)

1st row. (RS) *K3, (ytf, sl 1, K1, psso) 4 times, rep from * to last 3 sts, K3.
2nd and every other row. P.
3rd row. *K4, (ytf, sl 1, K1, psso) 3 times, K1, rep from * to last 3 sts, K3.
5th row. *K5, (ytf, sl 1, K1, psso) twice, K2, rep from * to last 3 sts, K3.
7th row. *K6, ytf, sl 1, K1, psso, K3, rep from * to last 3 sts, K3.
8th row. P. *9th row.* K. *10th row.* P.
These 10 rows form pattern and are repeated throughout.

▲ *Diagonal eyelet rib used for a band above the ribbing and lace triangles pattern used for a central panel on classic sleeveless pullovers*

Adapting a pattern

It is not difficult to adapt a simple classic stockinette stitch design to incorporate panels or bands of a patterned stitch which particularly appeals to you. Choose a stitch which is basically suitable. Don't select a pattern which has strong vertical lines, such as arrowhead and diamond or spearhead laces, for a horizontal band. Diagonal eyelet rib or wavy eyelet rib are much more suitable. Lace triangles would form an attractive border or panel, or are suitable to work as an all-over pattern.

Remember that most patterns using eyelet stitches alter the gauge slightly. This can usually be corrected by using one size smaller needles, as long as the pattern is going to be used over a fairly large area, such as a border or as an all-over fabric. Small inserted front panels are seldom large enough to affect the gauge of the whole garment.

It is always easier to use a set of directions which has the correct total number of stitches required for the repeating of the chosen pattern, but this is not always possible to find. Slight alterations can usually be made to overcome this point. For example, the lace stitches may require an even number of stitches, whereas the total number of stitches required for the pullover may be odd. If two lace panels were to be worked, one from each shoulder, the center panel could be worked over an odd number of stitches in stockinette stitch. If there is bust dart shaping, however, it is better to keep to just one central panel. This way, one extra stitch should be decreased after the ribbing. Where an alteration of this type is made, it is important to remember that it may affect other parts of the pattern. In this case, it is necessary to leave one stitch fewer on the center front stitches at the neck edge. If these are bound off instead of being slipped onto a holder, it will be simpler to pick up the correct total number of stitches required for the neckband.

Horizontal panel using diagonal eyelet rib

Work ribbing for back and front as given in your pattern. Work 8 rows stockinette stitch, or required depth before beginning of band. Knit 2 rows. Change to one size finer needles. Work in pattern as given for stitch, including edge stitches, and K or P any extra stitches at beginning and end of each row. Work 2½in in pattern, or required depth. Change to former needles. Knit 2 rows. Complete as given for pattern.

Chapter 21

Knitting Know-how

Techniques for looped effects

There are several different ways of working long looped stitches but usually their purpose is to form either an overlaid texture on a plain fabric background or to give a very lacy openwork appearance to the knitting.

Picking up a loop on the row below
This is a normal knitted stitch but the right-hand needle is inserted into the stitch directly below on the previous row, before the stitch is dropped from the left-hand needle (Figure **1**).

Picking up a loop 4 rows below
This is similar to knitting into a stitch on the previous row and is used in patterns with a stockinette stitch background. Insert the right-hand needle 4 or more rows below the stitch reached in the pattern, (Figure **2**), and knit one pulling up a long loop. Let the stitch drop from the left-hand needle until it reaches the row in which the loop stitch has been worked (Figure **3**).

Knitting a stitch with 3 loops
This stitch can be combined with stockinette stitch or garter stitch to form a band of lacy openwork but it can also be worked on its own to make soft, light stoles and evening tops. Begin with a knit row and wind the yarn 3 times around the right-hand needle for

▼ **1.** *Picking up a loop from the row below*

each stitch (Figure **4**). On the next row, knit or purl these stitches as required, unwinding the 3 loops of each stitch and letting them drop off the left-hand needle (Figure **5**).

Picking up a loop with a crochet hook
Some novelty patterns require extra loops which are worked with the aid of a crochet hook.

These loops are picked up knitwise several rows below. Knit to the position where the loop is required, leaving the yarn at the back of the work. Insert the crochet hook from the front of the work 4 or more rows below and pull a long loop of yarn through to the right side of the work, making one extra long, loose stitch

▲ **2.** *Picking up a loop from 4 rows below*
▼ **3.** *Pulling up long loop from 4 rows below*

(Figure **6**). Slip this extra stitch onto the left-hand needle and knit into the back of it together with the next stitch on the left-hand needle.

To transfer this extra loop diagonally across the front of the work, leave it on the crochet hook and work 3 or more stitches onto the right-hand needle in the usual way. Then knit the extra loop together with the next stitch on the left-hand needle.

▲ **4.** *Winding yarn 3 times around needle*
▼ **5.** *Forming long openwork loops*

▲ **6.** *Dainty bedjacket with a looped effect*
▼ **7.** *Picking up a loop with a crochet hook*

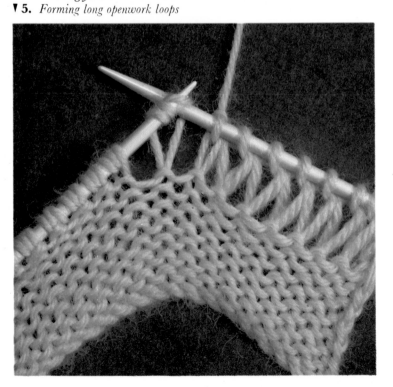

Cap and collar set in loop stitch

Loop stitch knitting produces a warm-looking fabric which can be used to make fashion garments, accessories and pretty trims.

Working loop stitch
The loop lies on the right side, or outside, of the fabric but is formed when working a wrong side row. For a sample swatch, cast on 21 sts and K3 rows.

4th row (WS) K1, *insert needle into next st on left-hand needle as if to knit it, wind yarn over needle point and around first and second fingers of left hand twice, then over and around needle point once. Draw all 3 loops through stitch and slip onto the left-hand needle, insert right-hand needle through back of these 3 loops and through the original stitch and knit all together—called ML—K1, rep from * to end of row.

5th row K.

6th row K2, *ML, K1, rep from * to last st, K1.

7th row K.

Rep the last 4 rows four times to see the effect of the design. Bind off.

Variations of loop stitch
Loop stitch can be worked quickly if care is taken not to wind the yarn so tightly around the fingers that it becomes difficult to free the loops when completing the stitch.

Different effects can be obtained by altering the number of stitches between loops and also by changing the number of rows between loop rows. The length of the loops can be varied by working over only two fingers for a short loop or

Cap and matching collar

by working over 3 or even 4 fingers for a longer loop. Bulky yarns, or two or more strands of yarn used together, worked over two fingers with loops close together and worked on alternate rows will give a close, deep, bulky pile. A softer effect can be achieved for an evening stole or poncho by using a fine yarn wound around all 4 fingers and worked on every 4th stitch, with 3 plain rows between loop rows.

Caps and Collar

Size
Caps. To fit average adult head
Collar. Depth 14in or as desired

> **Gauge**
> 4 sts and 7 rows to 1in over garter st worked with double yarn on No.7 needles.

Materials
Unger Les Coraux
Caps. 2 balls for one-color version
1 ball A and 1 ball B for two-color version
Collar. 2 balls A
One pair No.7 needles
Three buttons for collar
One No.F crochet hook

Caps
Using No.7 needles and A, double, cast on 25 sts.
1st row (WS) K1, *insert needle into next st as if to K, wind yarn over needle point and first finger loosely 3 times then over and around needle point once, draw loops through st and return to left-hand needle, insert right-hand needle through back of loops and st and K tog—called ML—K1, rep from * to end.
2nd row K.

3rd row K2, *ML, K1, rep from * to last 3 sts, ytf to avoid making a hole, sl 1. Turn.
4th row Ytf, sl 1, ytb, K to end.
5th row As 1st.
6th row Change to color B if more than 1 color is being used, K.
7th row K20, ytf, sl 1. Turn.
8th row Ytf, sl 1, ytb, K20.
9th row K18, ytf, sl 1. Turn.
10th row Ytf, sl 1, ytb, K18.
11th row K15, ytf, sl 1. Turn.
12th row Ytf, sl 1, ytb, K15.
13th row K12, ytf, sl 1. Turn.
14th row Ytf, sl 1, ytb, K12.
Work 11th, 12th, 9th, 10th, 7th and 8th rows once more.
21st row K all sts.
22nd row Change to color A, K to end.
Rep 1st—22nd rows 4 times more, then 1st—21st rows once.
Bind off.

Finishing
Draw short top edge up and join back seam. Fasten off all ends.

Collar
Using No.7 needles and A double, cast on 15 sts.
Work first 2 rows as given for caps.
3rd row K2, *ML, K1, rep from * to last st, K1.
4th row K.
These 4 rows form patt. Continue in patt until work measures 14in or desired length. Bind off.

Finishing
Using No.F crochet hook and one strand of A, work in sc along one short end, work 2nd row sc, making 3 button loops at regular intervals by working ch3 and skipping 2sc. Fasten off.
Sew on buttons to correspond.

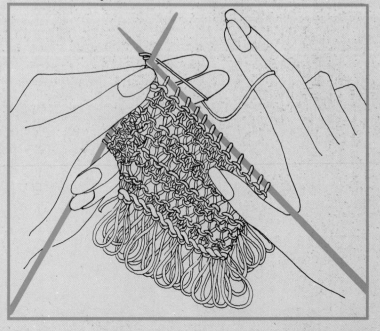

◄ *Winding yarn around two fingers
One-color version of looped cap*

Chapter 22

Crochet look knitting stitches

There are many attractive knitting stitches which give a similar impression to lacy work done with a crochet hook. They are formed by using the same principle as for long loop stitches, shown in Knitting Know-how Chapter 21. These stitches are very quick and simple to knit, and in this chapter you can try patterns for two of the most attractive ones. If you work them in bands, alternating with stockinette stitch or garter stitch, you will produce a firm but lacy finish which can be used for a variety of garments.

Dimple stitch and seashell stitch are effective in both sports weight and knitting worsted, although sports weight may be more suitable for light summer garments, a lacy top or a little girl's party dress. You might try a delicate baby's jacket in a finer yarn. And a knitting worsted could make a pretty and unusual cot cover, or a dress with an openwork effect for summer or evening as shown in the illustration.

Dimple stitch

Cast on a number of stitches divisible by 3, plus 2.

1st row. P to end.

2nd row. P1, *yarn around right-hand needle twice—called y2rn— P1, rep from * to last st, P1.

3rd row. P1, *slip next 3 sts P-wise onto right-hand needle dropping extra loops, pull the loose loops gently upward and slip back onto left-hand needle, K3 tog tbl, bring yarn forward over right-hand needle and back, then K3 tog tbl again, rep from * to last st, P1.

4th row. P to end.

These 4 rows form pattern and are repeated throughout.

Seashell stitch

Cast on a number of stitches divisible by 6, plus 2.

1st row. K to end.

2nd row. P to end.

Rep 1st and 2nd rows once more.

5th row. K1, *y2rn, K1, rep from * to last st, K1.

6th row. P1, *holding yarn at back of work slip next 6 sts P-wise onto right-hand needle dropping extra loops, pull the loose stitches gently upward and slip back onto left-hand needle, yrn and P6 tog without slipping them off left-hand needle, yon and K1 into these 6 sts, then P1, K1 into same 6 sts in usual way, rep from * to last st, P1.

These 6 rows form pattern and are repeated throughout.

Knitted dress with a crochet look ▶

▲ *Dropping extra loops for dimple stitch*
▼ *Working loops together for dimple stitch*

▼ *Dropping extra loops for seashell stitch*

▼ *Working loops together for seashell stitch*

▼ *Seashell stitch*　　　　　　　　▲ *Dimple stitch*

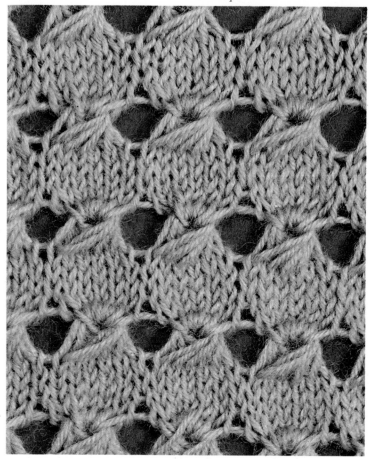

Chapter 23

Woven look stitches

Working with a favorite knitting pattern, interesting textures and a woven fabric effect can be achieved by substituting these simple "woven knitting" stitches for stockinette stitch and garter stitch. Because the stitches are based on multiples of two, they are easily adapted to patterns based on an even number of stitches. The gauge of these stitches is likely to be different from stockinette or garter stitch and you should work a test swatch and change the needle size if necessary until the gauge given in the pattern is obtained. Both sides of these woven knitting stitches can be used as the pattern. An unusual and interesting effect could be achieved by using both sides of a stitch in one design, such as a panel down the front of a sweater or dress.

Plain woven stitch
Worked over an even number of sts, plus 2 edge sts.
1st row. K.
2nd row. K1, *ytf, sl 1 knitwise, rep from * to last st, K1.
3rd row. K1, *K2 tog tbl, thus working together the slipped and the yo made on previous row, rep from * to last st, K1.
The 2nd and 3rd rows form pattern and are repeated throughout.

Woven vertical rib stitch
Worked over an even number of sts, plus 2 edge sts.
1st row. (WS) K1, *ytf, sl 1 knitwise, K1, rep from * to last st, K1.
2nd row. (RS) K1, *K1, K2 tog tbl, thus working together the slipped and the yo made on previous row, rep from * to last st, K1.
These 2 rows form the pattern and are repeated throughout.

Woven horizontal rib stitch
Worked over an even number of sts, plus 2 edge sts.
1st row. K.
2nd row. P.
3rd row. K1, *insert right-hand needle between next 2 sts on left-hand needle and draw st through, K first st on left-hand needle, rep from * to last st, K1.
4th row. K1, *P2 tog, rep from * to last st, K1.
These 4 rows form the pattern and are repeated throughout.

Woven herringbone stitch
Worked over an even number of sts.
1st row. K2 tog tbl, but drop only the first loop off the left-hand needle, *K the st rem on left-hand needle tog tbl with the next st on left-hand needle, again dropping only the first loop off the needle, rep from * until 1 loop rem on left-hand needle, K1 tbl.
2nd row. P2 tog, dropping only the first loop off the left-hand needle, *P the st rem on left-hand needle tog with the next st on left-hand needle, again dropping only the first loop off the needle, rep from * until 1 loop rem on left-hand needle, P1.
These 2 rows form the pattern and are repeated throughout.

Jumper with the woven look ▶

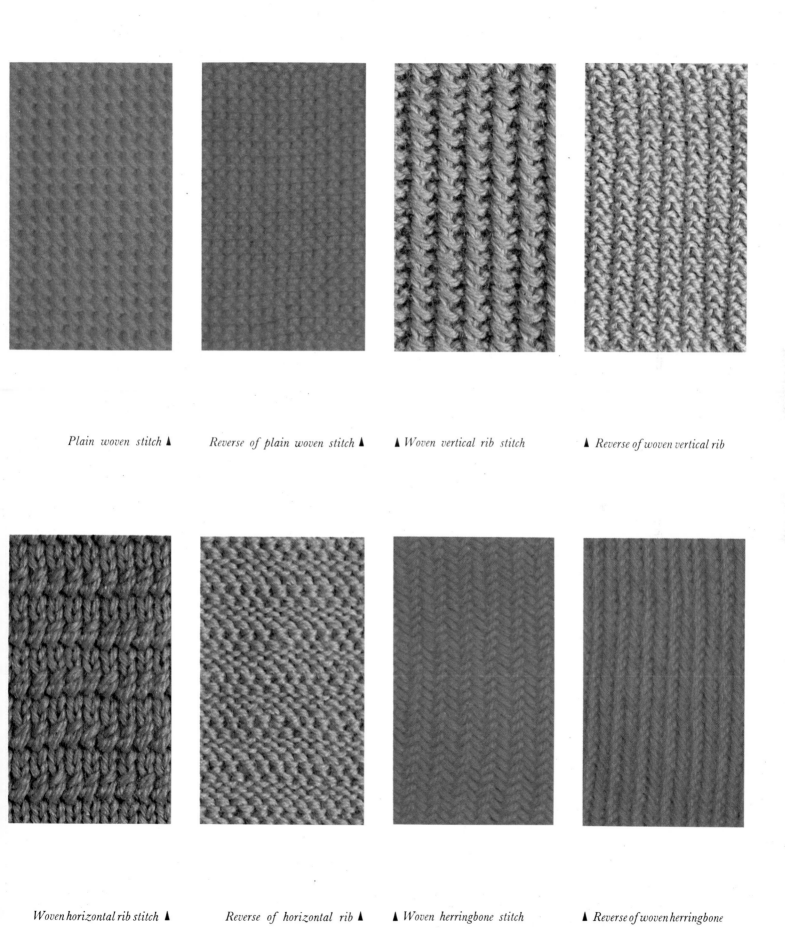

Plain woven stitch ▲   *Reverse of plain woven stitch* ▲   ▲ *Woven vertical rib stitch*   ▲ *Reverse of woven vertical rib*

Woven horizontal rib stitch ▲   *Reverse of horizontal rib* ▲   ▲ *Woven herringbone stitch*   ▲ *Reverse of woven herringbone*

Chapter 24

Knitting
Know-how

Mock cable stitches

You have already seen how you can alter the appearance of knitted stitches by working into the back of the stitch to produce a twisted effect (Knitting Know-how Chapter 7).

To give an even more twisted appearance, the method is to actually cross two or more stitches. This means that the second stitch on the left-hand needle is worked before the first, so that the stitches change place, producing an attractive miniature cable or twisted rib effect.

There are countless variations of cable patterns, of which six are described in this chapter, together with their standard abbreviations.

Knitted crossed stitch with back twist (Tw2B)

The twist lies to the left. Pass the right-hand needle behind the first stitch on the left-hand needle, knit into the back of the next stitch and leave on the needle. Then knit into the back of the first stitch and slip both stitches off the left-hand needle onto the right-hand needle. (This is used in twisted rib pattern and mock cable.)

Knitted crossed stitch with front twist (Tw2F)

The twist lies to the right. Pass the right-hand needle in front of the first stitch on the left-hand needle and knit the next stitch, leaving it on the needle. Then knit the first stitch and slip both stitches off the left-hand needle onto the right-hand needle.

Purled crossed stitch with front twist (Tw2PF)

This is often used on a purl row when the purled side is the wrong side. It produces a crossed thread lying to the right on the knit side of the work. Pass the right-hand needle in front of the first stitch on the left-hand needle and purl the next stitch, leaving it on the needle. Then purl the first stitch and slip both stitches off the left-hand needle onto the right-hand needle.

Purled crossed stitch with back twist (Tw2PB)

Because this is more difficult to work, it is less often used. It forms a cross lying to the left on the knit side of the work. Pass the right-hand needle behind the first stitch on the left-hand needle, purl the next stitch through the back of the loop and leave it on the needle. Then purl the first stitch and slip both stitches off the left-hand needle onto the right-hand needle.

Sometimes it is easier to use a cable needle to help with this stitch. Slip the first stitch from the left-hand needle onto the cable needle and hold at the front of the work, purl the next stitch through the back of the loop and purl the stitch from the cable needle.

A slightly different, or mock, twist can be given to the stitches if each stitch is lifted over the first one before the first one is worked. This is not usually referred to by any standard abbreviation, but will be described in detail in the directions for knitting garments in which the stitch appears.

Knitted crossed stitch with back twist (Tw2B)

Purled crossed stitch with front twist (Tw2PF)

Crossing two stitches to the right (Cross 2R)

Crossing two stitches to the right (Cross 2R)

Pass the right-hand needle in front of the first stitch on the left-hand needle and knit into back loop of second stitch. Lift it over the first stitch and off the needle point. Knit the first stitch on the left-hand needle. (This is used in crossed miniature cable.)

Crossing two stitches to the left (Cross 2L)

Slip the first stitch on the left-hand needle without knitting it. Knit the next stitch on the left-hand needle and slip it onto the right-hand needle. Using the left-hand needle point, pass the slipped stitch over the newly knitted stitch, knitting into the slipped stitch at the same time.

Twisted rib pattern

Worked over a number of stitches divisible by 14, plus 2.

1st row. P2, *Tw2B, P2, K4 all tbl, P2, Tw2B, P2, rep from * to end.

2nd row. K2, *P2, K2, P4, K2, P2, K2, rep from * to end.

Rep 1st and 2nd rows once.

5th row. P2, *Tw2B, P2, into 4th and 3rd sts on left-hand needle work Tw2B leaving sts on left-hand needle,

work Tw2B into 2nd and 1st sts on left-hand needle and slip all 4 sts from left to right-hand needle,

P2, Tw2B, P2, rep from * to end.

6th row. As 2nd.

These 6 rows form the pattern and are repeated throughout.

Mock cable

Worked over a number of stitches divisible by 5, plus 3.

1st row. P3, *K2, P3, rep from * to end.

2nd row. K3, *P2, K3, rep from * to end.

Rep 1st and 2nd rows once.

5th row. P3, *Tw2B, P3, rep from * to end.

6th row. As 2nd.

These 6 rows form the pattern and are repeated throughout.

Crossed miniature cable

Worked over a number of stitches divisible by 7, plus 3.

1st row. P3, *K4, P3, rep from * to end.

2nd row. K3, *P4, K3, rep from * to end.

3rd row. P3, *(cross 2R) twice, P3, rep from * to end.

4th row. As 2nd.

These 4 rows form the pattern and are repeated throughout.

Right: twisted rib pattern ►
Below left: mock cable ▼
Below right: crossed miniature cable ►

Chapter 25

Chunky "fabric" stitches

Here are four more patterns using twisted and crossed stitches. Basket weave may be worked using the yarn double throughout giving a very firm but light fabric which is suitable for jackets and clothes with a more tailored look.

Basket weave stitch
Worked over an even number of stitches.
1st row. *Tw2B, rep from * to end.
2nd row. P1, *Tw2PF, rep from * to last st, P1.
These 2 rows form the pattern and are repeated throughout.

Crossed basket weave stitch
Worked over an even number of stitches. This stitch is more easily and quickly worked than basket weave stitch but gives a similar effect.
1st row. *Holding yarn at back of work, sl 1 purlwise, K next st, yon, lift slipped stitch over both knitted stitch and yon, rep from * to end.
2nd row. P.
3rd row. K1, work from * as for 1st row to last st, K1.
4th row. P.
These 4 rows form the pattern and are repeated throughout.

Waffle stitch
Worked over a number of stitches divisible by 4.
1st row. *Tw2B, Tw2F, rep from * to end.
2nd row. P.
3rd row. *Tw2F, Tw2B, rep from * to end.
4th row. P.
These 4 rows form the pattern and are repeated throughout.

Twisted panel stitch
Worked over a number of stitches divisible by 8, plus 2.
1st row. K2, *(Tw2F) 3 times, K2, rep from * to end.
2nd row. P.
3rd row. K2, * (Tw3F) twice, K2, rep from * to end.
4th row. P.
These 4 rows form the pattern and are repeated throughout. Tw3F is worked in the same way as Tw2F, but is worked over 3 sts instead of 2. Work into the 3rd st on the left-hand needle, then into the 2nd and then into the 1st, slipping all 3 sts from left to right-hand needle.

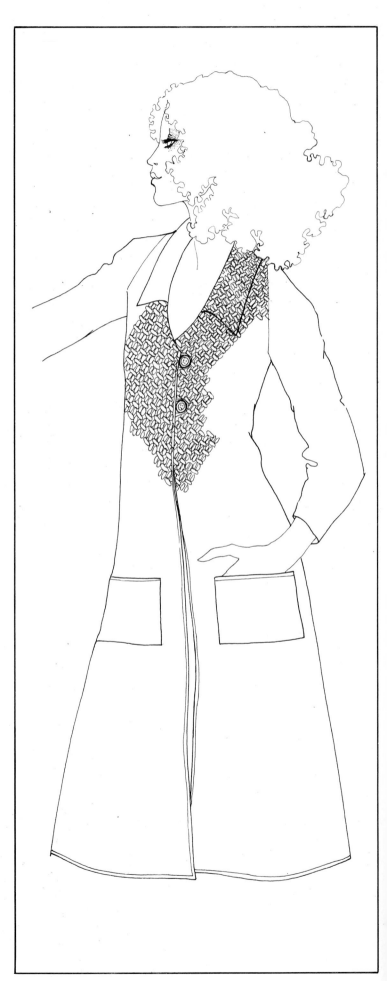

Coat in a firm fabric stitch ▶

▲ *Basket weave stitch*   ▼ *Crossed basket weave stitch*   ▲ *Waffle stitch*   ▼ *Twisted panel stitch*

71

Chapter 26

Introduction to cable stitch

Once you have mastered the principle of working cables, the possible stitch pattern variations are endless. The cable look is popular for the good reason that it is so easy to work and looks fantastic either in fine, lacy form or in thicker fabric for giving texture to sportswear.

Panels of cables can give a special twist to classic sweaters. For example, you could knit two separate bands on the front and back of a stockinette-stitch pattern, at the same time using the purl side of the fabric as the right side for a more interesting finish.

Be sure to keep your practice swatches! Joined together they can become a very effective afghan, or used singly they make handy pockets on plain cardigans or pullovers.

All cable designs are based on stitches being moved from one position to another by crossing over each other, which gives the effect of the twist you see in a rope.

In twisting two stitches it is possible to knit the second by passing the needle either behind or in front of the first, then working the first stitch. When altering the position of more than two stitches, it is easier to do so by means of a third needle. For this purpose a cable needle is best since it is very short and less likely to get in the way while you are working the other stitches. However, any double-pointed needle will do.

If the cable needle is not the same thickness as the needles being used for the garment, it should be finer, not thicker. A thicker needle is very difficult to use and will stretch the stitches and spoil the appearance of the finished work.

Simple twist from right to left

Try a simple cable of six knit stitches against a background of purl stitches, as follows:
Cast on 24 stitches.
1st row. P9, K6, P9.
2nd row. K9, P6, K9.
3rd row. As 1st.
4th row. As 2nd.
5th row. As 1st.
6th row. As 2nd.
7th row. P9, slip the next 3 knit stitches onto the cable needle and hold them at the front of the work; with the right-hand needle continue to knit the next 3 knit stitches from the left-hand needle, then knit the 3 stitches from the cable needle, P9.
8th row. As 2nd.
Repeat these 8 rows twice more. Bind off.
You will now have a swatch with a rope-like pattern in the center of the six knitted stitches, twisted three times. Each twist, or turn, lies in the same direction, from the right toward the left.

72

Simple twist from left to right

To twist the opposite way, that is from the left toward the right, the stitches on the cable needle are held behind the work instead of in front of it, as follows:
Cast on 24 stitches.
1st row. P9, K6, P9.
2nd row. K9, P6, K9.
Rep 1st and 2nd rows twice more.
7th row. P9, slip the next 3 knit stitches onto the cable needle and hold them at the back of the work; with the right-hand needle continue to knit the next 3 knit stitches from the left-hand needle, then knit the 3 stitches from the cable needle, P9.
8th row. As 2nd.
Repeat these 8 rows twice more. Bind off.
This second swatch will be similar to the first, but the turns will lie in the opposite direction.

 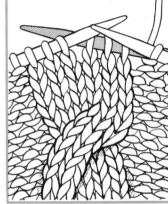

▲ *Cable six stitches to the front*　　▲ *Cable six stitches to the back*

Abbreviations

The abbreviations are usually given for cables in each set of directions. The letter C often stands for a cable and is then followed by the number of stitches to be cabled. It is also necessary to show whether the stitches are to be held at the front or the back of the work, so that the number may be followed by the letter F or B. In this way the abbreviation for the first swatch would read C6F, and for the second swatch, C6B.
Remember that the number of stitches held on the cable needle is half the number given for the cable.

Cable rope with row variations

The appearance of the cable is altered very much by the number of rows worked between each twist. The illustration shows a swatch worked in the same way as the first swatches, just altering the number of rows between each twist, as follows:
Cast on 24 stitches.
1st row. P9, K6, P9.
2nd row. K9, P6, K9.
Rep 1st and 2nd rows once more.
5th row. P9, C6F, P9.
6th row. As 2nd.
Repeat 1st and 2nd rows twice, then 5th and 6th rows once.
Repeat 1st and 2nd rows 4 times, then 5th and 6th rows once.
Repeat 1st and 2nd rows 6 times, then 5th and 6th rows once.
Repeat 1st and 2nd rows once. Bind off.
Twisting on every other row or even every 4th row gives the cable a very close, tight, rope look, whereas twisting on every 8th or 12th row gives a much softer look.

an interesting ballooning out of the rope between the twists. Another simple variation is an alternating cable, as follows:

Cast on 31 sts.

1st row. P1, *K4, P1, rep from * to end.

2nd row. K1, *P4, K1, rep from * to end.

3rd row. P1, *K4, P1, C4F, P1, rep from * to end.

4th row. As 2nd.

Repeat 1st and 2nd rows once more.

7th row. P1, *C4F, P1, K4, P1, rep from * to end.

8th row. As 2nd.

These 8 rows form the pattern and are repeated as required.

▲ *Alternating cables*

▼ *Pieces of test knitting joined together make a multicolored bedspread*

▲ *Cable rope with row variation*

Alternating cables

The number of stitches over which the cable is worked also alters the appearance. A simple cable is usually worked over 4 or 6 stitches. Very attractive variations can be made, however, by working over 10 or 12 stitches, using thick needles and a bulky yarn. In this type of variation, more rows worked between the twists gives

Knitting
Know-how

Variations of cable stitch

Cables give an interesting texture to almost any simple or casual garment, but the bulkiest patterns are perhaps shown to best effect on sports sweaters—men in particular admire heavily cabled cardigans and sweaters.
The interesting variations of cable stitches given here are made by combining twists to the right and to the left, forming more complicated-looking patterns or interwoven fabrics.

Bulky double cable

Dividing the number of stitches in a cabled panel and taking half to the right and half to the left gives the appearance of chain links, with each link appearing to come upward out of the one below.
Cast on 24 stitches.
1st row. P6, K12, P6.
2nd row. K6, P12, K6.
Repeat 1st and 2nd rows twice more.
7th row. P6, C6B (slip next 3 stitches onto cable needle and hold at back of work, K next 3 stitches from left-hand needle, K3 stitches from cable needle), C6F (slip next 3 stitches onto cable needle and hold at front of work, K next 3 stitches from left-hand needle, K3 stitches from cable needle), P6.
8th row. As 2nd.
These 8 rows form the pattern and are repeated as required.

Bulky double cable

Inverted bulky double cable

The opposite effect of one link joining and passing under the link above is given by reversing the order of the cable on the previous pattern, as follows:
Cast on 24 stitches.
1st row. P6, K12, P6.
2nd row. K6, P12, K6.
Repeat 1st and 2nd rows twice more.
7th row. P6, C6F, C6B, P6.
8th row. As 2nd.
These 8 rows form the pattern and are repeated as required.

Honeycomb cable

Both of the previous patterns worked alternately form a cable which appears to be superimposed on the fabric underneath. This is worked as follows:
Cast on 24 stitches.
1st row. P6, K12, P6.
2nd row. K6, P12, K6.
Repeat 1st and 2nd rows once more.
5th row. P6, C6B, C6F, P6.
6th row. As 2nd.
Repeat 1st and 2nd rows twice more.
11th row. P6, C6F, C6B, P6.
12th row. As 2nd.
These 12 rows form the pattern and are repeated as required.

Single plaited cable

A plaited effect can be achieved by dividing the group of stitches to be cabled into three instead of two and cabling each group alternately, as follows:
Cast on 30 stitches or a number of stitches divisible by 9, plus 3 (e.g. 39, 48, 57 etc.).
1st row. P3, *K6, P3, rep from * to end.
2nd row. K3, *P6, K3, rep from * to end.
3rd row. P3, *C4B (slip next 2 stitches onto cable needle and hold at back of work, K2 stitches from left-hand needle, K2 stitches from cable needle), K rem 2 stitches of K6 group, rep from * to end.
4th row. As 2nd.
5th row. P3, *K first 2 stitches of K6 group, C4F (slip next 2 stitches onto cable needle and hold at front of work, K2 stitches from left-hand needle, K2 stitches from cable needle), P3, rep from * to end.
6th row. As 2nd.
Repeat from 3rd–6th rows as required.

Double plaited cable

An even more textured and intricate appearance is given by a double plaited cable, as follows:
Cast on 30 stitches or a number of stitches divisible by 24, plus 6 (e.g. 54, 78, 102 etc.).
1st row. P6, *K18, P6, rep from * to end.
2nd row. K6, *P18, K6, rep from * to end.
3rd row. P6, *(C6B) 3 times, P6, rep from * to end.
4th row. As 2nd.
Repeat 1st and 2nd rows once more.
7th row. P6, *K3, (C6F) twice, K3, P6, rep from * to end.
8th row. As 2nd.
These 8 rows form the pattern and are repeated as required.

▲ *Inverted bulky double cable*   ▼ *Single plaited cable*   ▲ *Honeycomb cable*   ▼ *Double plaited cable*

Chapter 27

Knitting Know-how

Introduction to Aran knitting

The Aran islands of Inishmore, Inishmaan and Inisheer, off the west coast of Ireland, are the home of the popular and richly textured knitting known as Aran. The Irish name for the thick, homespun wool used for Aran knitting is bainin, pronounced "bawneen," meaning natural, or white. It is also known as fisherman yarn. The traditional patterns show to their best advantage on this light-colored wool, although it is sometimes tinted with seaweed or moss dyes to produce pale, subtle shades. Practice the stitches in this chapter (use knitting worsted and No.5 needles if fisherman yarn is difficult to obtain) by knitting panels which can then be joined together to make unique-looking furnishings such as pillow covers, bedspreads, or afghans.

Like all folk crafts, the traditional Aran designs derive their inspiration from the daily life of the islanders. The rocks and cliff paths are called to mind by the stitches of zigzag patterns, while chunky bobbles and the fishermen's ropes are depicted by a vast number of cable variations which play a major part in most designs. The life under the sea which surrounds the islands is acknowledged in such designs as Lobster claw cable. Religious symbolism appears in stitches such as Tree of Life, Trinity stitch and Ladder of Life, while everyday life is depicted in the ups and downs of Marriage lines and in several different seed stitches (see single and double seed stitches in Knitting Know-how Chapter 7). Even the industrious bee is remembered in Honeycomb stitch.

Honeycomb stitch
Worked over a number of stitches divisible by 8.
1st row. *Sl 2 sts onto cable needle and hold at back of work, K2, K2 from cable needle—called C4B—sl 2 sts onto cable needle and hold at front of work, K2, K2 from cable needle—called C4F—rep from * to end.
2nd row. P to end.
3rd row. K to end.
4th row. P to end.
5th row. *C4F, C4B, rep from * to end.
6th row. P to end.
7th row. K to end.
8th row. P to end.
These 8 rows form the pattern and are repeated throughout. A variation of Honeycomb stitch is made by working extra rows in stockinette stitch between the cable rows to elongate the design.

Ladder of Life
This is a simple design, depicting man's desire to do better and climb upward toward heaven. The rungs of the ladder are formed by purl rows worked on a stockinette stitch background.
Worked over a number of stitches divisible by 6, plus 1 (e.g. 37).
1st row. (RS) P1, *K5, P1, rep from * to end.

▲ *Honeycomb stitch*

▲ *Lobster claw cable*

2nd row. K1, *P5, K1, rep from * to end.
3rd row. P to end.
4th row. K1, *P5, K1, rep from * to end.
These 4 rows form the pattern and are repeated throughout. The number of stitches between the vertical purl lines may be altered to suit the area to be covered, as may the number of rows worked between the ladder rungs.

Trinity stitch
This stitch derives its name from the method of working, which is "3 in one and 1 in 3." In England it goes by the name of Blackberry stitch, while in Scotland it's called Bramble stitch.
Worked over a number of stitches divisible by 4.
1st row. P to end.
2nd row. *K1, P1, K1 all into same st making 3 sts from one st, P3 tog to make one st from 3 sts, rep from * to end.
3rd row. P to end.
4th row. *P3 tog, K1, P1, K1 all into one st, rep from * to end.
These 4 rows form the pattern and are repeated throughout.

Jacqueline Enthoven *is one of the country's lead-ing needlework authorities and author of* The Stitches of Creative Embroidery (*published by Van Nostrand Reinhold*). *Working with the editors of* Family Circle, *she has compiled this special 1971 Treasury with over 50 step-by-step illustrations of the most popular embroidery and needlepoint stitches, and a detailed description of the technique and suggested uses for each stitch. We're sure you will want to clip it out and save it as a handy reference.*

This valuable guide will serve as a primer for the beginner, a refresher for the more experienced needleworker and an inspiration to all to learn, to experiment, to try new combinations and to create your own designs. Try stitches that you have never worked before. Repeat several rows close together, for instance, and then adapt the pattern to interpret an idea you have developed. Try threading your stitches; it is one of the easiest ways to create something spontaneously. ❦ In this section, the embroidery stitches are grouped in five categories, according to the way they are made. The *flat-stitch* family, which is the largest, forms the first group. The stitches lie flat on the surface of the cloth, either close together or spaced. Flat stitches with a curve or loop become *looped stitches.* Closing the loop makes *chained stitches.* Twisting and tightening the loops make *knotted stitches.* The last section comprises some of the most popular *needlepoint* stitches. ❦ For materials, we suggest a No. 16, 17 or 18 tapestry needle (that is, a needle without a sharp point); a yarn in your favorite color (for a beginner, pearl cotton works well, as it does not separate or become fuzzy and gives a crisp definition). Or, use No. 3- or No. 4-ply worsted yarn. Choose a loosely woven fabric, such as homespun, linen or burlap. Use an embroidery hoop, if you wish, or spray the back of the fabric with spray starch for added stiffness. ❦ For needlepoint, use No. 10-mesh single- or double-thread needlepoint canvas, tapestry needle and tapestry wool. ❦ After you have become more confident you will want to try a variety of materials for texture and contrast, and very often the materials you use will determine the direction of your design. ❦ Raid your sewing basket for supplies and begin to work right now! Transfer your finished design to a pillow, a wall hanging, clothing, accessories, or make a decorative sampler of your favorite stitches—as we've done on the facing page.

FLAT STITCHES

1. Running Stitch—Runs in and out of the cloth at regular intervals.

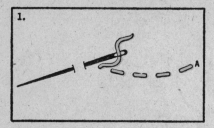

2. Darning Stitch—Picks up very little cloth with the needle. Most of the yarn stays on the front of the work.

These two simple stitches form the basis for countless exciting variations. Try as many as you can, varying the size of your stitches and the weight of the yarn.

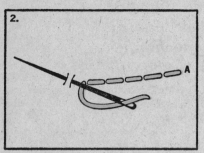

3. Double Running Stitch—Used for a solid line. After you have worked a row of regular *running stitches* (1) from right to left, turn your work around at the end of the row and stitch back, filling the gaps. You can use a different shade of the same color.

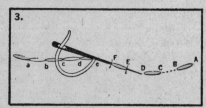

4. Pattern Darning—Another way to make borders and fill shapes. It is made up of rows of *darning stitches* (2) of varying lengths worked into definite patterns. We suggest a border made up of 3 to 5 rows of regular *darning stitches* worked very close together, checkerboard fashion.

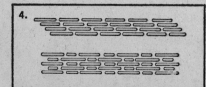

5. Back Stitch—A useful stitch for a crisp outline. It is good for stitchery lettering. Work from right to left. From A take a stitch backwards to B, coming out at C in front of A. Go back in at A, out at D, back to C, *etc.*

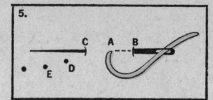

6. Seed or Dot Stitch—When you need a light airy effect, use small *back stitches* (5) placed in patterns or at random. To make a double seed stitch, make 2 *back stitches* in the same hole, neatly relaxed, side by side.
RUNNING, DARNING, BACK AND SEED STITCHES—Can be whipped, threaded and double-threaded. They are effective for outlines and produce interesting textures when several rows are close together. The same yarn can be used, or different weights or colors, to produce a variety of effects. Some of these can be worked quickly as a border on a table mat, a cushion, or around a skirt.

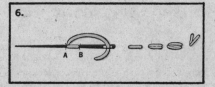

7. Whipped Running

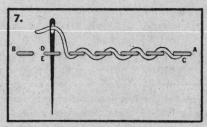

8. Double-threaded Running

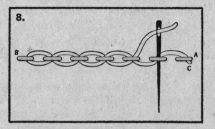

9. Threaded Checkerboard Running

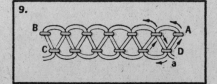

10. Threaded Zigzag Darning

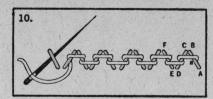

11. Satin Stitch—Made up of *back stitches* (5) worked side by side to cover a shape. It is sometimes difficult to work a neat edge. One remedy is to cover the edge with *stem* (21), *back* (5) or *chain* (34) stitches.

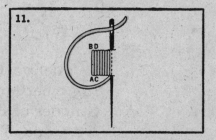

12. Surface Satin Stitch—This stitch has the same effect as the one above but requires less yarn. Instead of going to the back and around as for regular *satin stitch* (11), most of the yarn stays on the surface of the cloth; very small stitches are picked up on opposite edges.

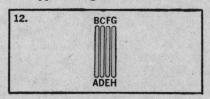

13. Straight (Stroke) Stitches—These are easy to work. They can be the same or different lengths going freely in any direction you want. They can also be worked in rows or geometric patterns. If they are too long, tie them down with *back stitches* (5).

14. Threaded Straight Stitches—One of the best ways to learn to create spontaneously with stitches is to thread *straight stitches* (13). It leads to many interesting designs such as growing forms, grasses, exciting circular shapes, quick and easy flowers. Start with a *straight stitch* from A to B. Come out at C and thread under AB, insert at D. Continue threading under either CB or DB.

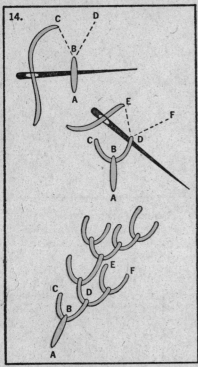

15. Cloud Filling—Another way of creating interesting effects by threading. First work a foundation of small, spaced, upright stitches. Thread the first and second rows together, then second and third rows, *etc.*

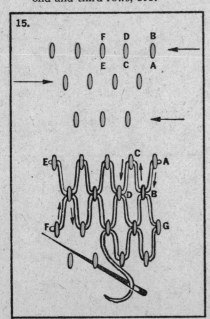

16. Wave Stitch—This is another threaded stitch which covers a shape quickly. Start with a row of small upright stitches worked across the top of the shape to be filled: AB—CD—EF. At the end of the row, from H go under to I and thread under HG, in at J, out at K under the next upright, *etc.*

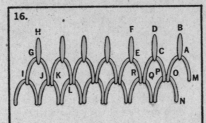

17. Cross Stitch—Made with 2 *straight stitches* (13) of equal size crossing each other diagonally. They can be worked individually going from D under, back to C to start another cross, or they can be worked in rows.

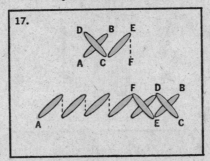

18. Upright Cross—This stitch makes a good filling.

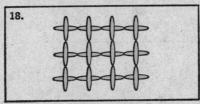

19. Star Stitch—A double *cross stitch*, that is, a regular *cross stitch* (17) with an *upright cross stitch* (18) worked over it, to which a small *cross stitch* is added on each side of the vertical stitch.

20. Cross Stitch Flower—A decorative *cross stitch* variation. It can be used in individual units or massed in groups. Work *2 cross stitches* (17) on top of each other, in the same holes. On the way back to D, with the point of the needle, and without picking up any cloth, go over the last stitch EF and under AB, or if AB presents itself first, under AB and over EF. You are weaving over and under, or under and over. Insert at D.

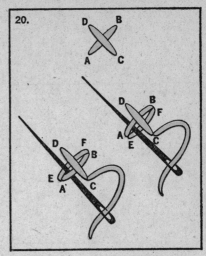

21. Stem or Crewel and Outline—Used for lines or as a filling by working rows closely side by side. Come out at A. Holding the thread down with your left thumb, insert the needle at B. Come out at C, halfway between AB. Over to D, still with the thread down, out at B, over to E and out at D, *etc.* When the yarn is kept *down,* the stitch is called a *stem* or *crewel.* When the yarn is kept *above* the line, it is called an *outline stitch,* the line looking straighter.

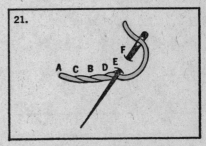

22. Alternating Stem Stitch—This stitch is worked like the *stem stitch* (21) from left to right. But instead of being held down for every stitch, the yarn is held alternately down for the first stitch from A to B, up for the second from C to D, down for the third, *etc.* A beautiful line is obtained by working 2 rows close to each other, the second reversing the first.

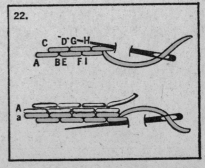

23. Herringbone—Once you master it, the herringbone is a stitch you can use in many different ways. Think in terms of a square with AB bisecting the square, going under to C, halfway back to the left. D is diagonally down, halfway across the next square as shown in the diagram.

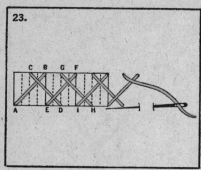

24. Threaded Herringbone—Threading a *herringbone stitch* (23) will surprise you. It is easy to do and very effective. Try using a contrasting color yarn. After you have worked a row of *herringbone*, bring the needle out at A. Lace over the crossed threads and under the slanting stitches without going through the cloth, except when you start and end.

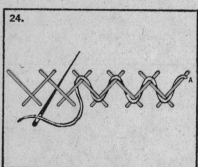

25. Double Herringbone—This stitch makes an effective border, especially if 2 colors are used. Two rows of *herringbone* (23) are worked over each other so that they interlace. The second color is laced under the first color on the way up, and over it on the way down.

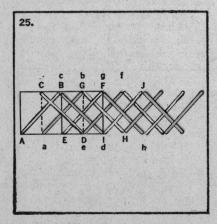

26. Buttonhole or Blanket Stitch—The only difference is that *buttonhole stitches* are closer together. Work from left to right. Come out at A. Hold the yarn down with your left thumb, insert the needle at B. Come out at C, just above and close to A, drawing the needle out over the yarn coming from A to form a loop. In at D, out at E, *etc.*

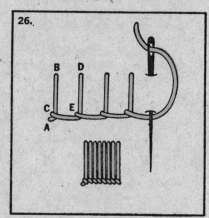

27. Closed Buttonhole Stitch—Made up of 2 *buttonhole stitches* (26) worked from the same hole, the first one from right to left, the second from left to right, making little triangles.

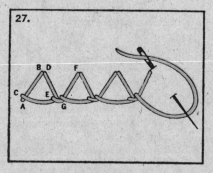

28. Double Buttonhole Stitch—For this effective border, work 2 rows of *blanket stitches* (26) facing each other. First work 1 row from left to right. At the end of the row, turn your work around and work the second row, fitting in between the arms of the first row.

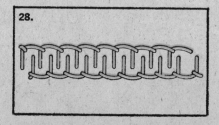

29. Single Feather Stitch—A good stitch for textured outlines. It is really a *blanket stitch* (26) with the stitches slanting instead of at right angles. Work from the top down, towards you.

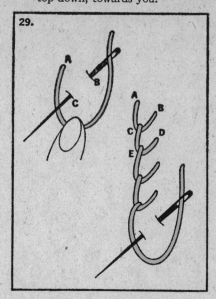

30. Slanting Feather Stitch—The best known of the feather stitch family. It is used for lines and for borders. Think in terms of working on 4 parallel lines and follow the diagram. Use it as a base for spontaneous stitching, adding stitches such as *detached chains* (35), *long stemmed knots* (42), or threading around each of the stitch ends.

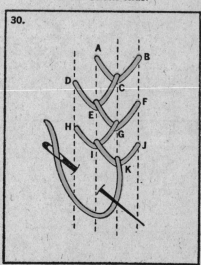

31. Cretan Stitch—Well worth the effort to learn and practice because it has many uses. It is a beautiful border stitch and is good for filling shapes as it adapts easily to various widths. It is a looped stitch, somewhat like a *blanket stitch* (26) worked first on one side then the other, except that instead of coming out on a center line, the stitches come out on 2 parallel lines. Note that the needle always points from outside in with the yarn under the needle.

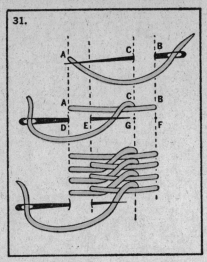

31.

32. Fly Stitch—Can be used in many ways. Make beautiful borders by having the stitches holding hands, back to back or facing each other. You can also overlap them. Bring the needle out at A. Hold the yarn down with the left thumb, looping it towards the right. Insert at B, coming out at C, below, halfway between A and B. The yarn is looped under the point of the needle from left to right. Pull it through over the loop. Anchor down by inserting at D. You can anchor it with a small stitch, or a long one, or with a *detached chain* (35).

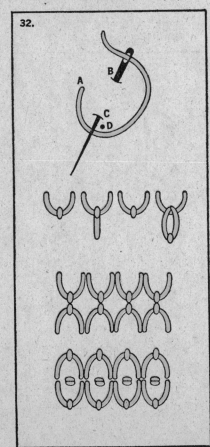

32.

33. Crown Stitch—A *fly stitch* (32) with an extra stitch on each side.

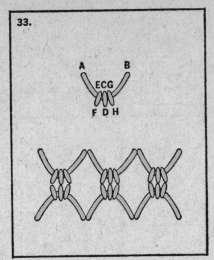

33.

CHAINED STITCHES

34. Chain Stitch—This is one of the most satisfying ways to follow an outline or to fill a shape. It also can be worked on canvas. Bring the needle out at A. Holding the yarn down with the left thumb, loop it towards the right. Insert the needle in the same hole at A and come out at B, with the yarn under the point of the needle from left to right. Draw the needle through. Repeat, inserting the needle at B inside the chain, in the same hole, keeping the yarn looped down from left to right. Come out at C, *etc.* At the end of the row, anchor the last chain down with a little stitch just below the last loop.

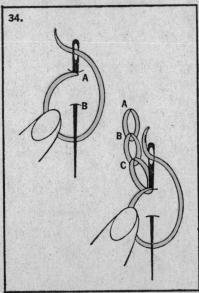

34.

35. Detached Chain—Instead of a row of chains, each chain can be

by itself, anchored with a small stitch at the bottom of the loop. It is also called "lazy daisy" and is useful for petals of flowers.

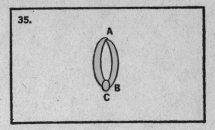

35.

36. Broad Chain or Threaded Chain—Many people, especially children, prefer this stitch to plain chain stitch. It is easier to work and follows curves beautifully. First take a small stitch from A to B. Come out at C. Now pass the needle behind the stitch AB from right to left "under the bridge" without picking up any cloth. Insert again at C, out at D. Pull through gently so that the stitches will be relaxed. Slide the needle behind the chain BC, insert at D, out at E, *etc.*

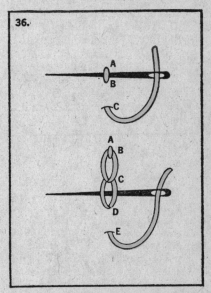

36.

Chain Stitch Variations—There are many ideas you can use to vary *chain stitches*. You can vary the length of the stitches. For some variations try introducing a different color or texture. Work *running* (1) or *back stitches* (5) in the middle or add a second row of chains on top of the first. Fill the chains with *seed stitches* (6), *French knots* (41), or work straight or slanting stitches over the sides. Chains can be whipped on one side or both sides, or the whole chain can be whipped.

37. Twisted Chain—This gives a different, somewhat knotted texture to a line. Work it as a *chain stitch* (34) but instead of always inserting the needle in the same hole, insert it to the left and take a slanting stitch from B to C.

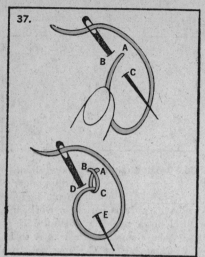

38. Threaded Square Chain—It makes interesting borders, can be increased and decreased with ease. It can also be used for *couching* (45) heavy yarns. Start with 2 parallel *straight stitches* (13), AB–CD like the top and bottom of a square. If you like, you can add a *straight stitch* from B to C. From D, go under to E. Slide the needle upward under the 2 bridges DC and AB, without picking up any cloth. Insert at F, come out at G; pull through gently, not tightly. Slide the needle upward under ED and FA, insert at H, out at I, *etc.*

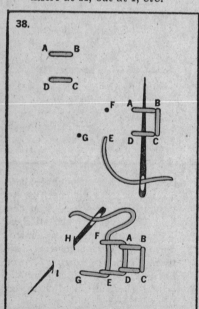

39. Vandyke Stitch—Very much like the *threaded square chain* (38), except that the stitches are crossed instead of straight. Work it relaxed or keep the cloth taut in a hoop or frame. The needle slides under the crossed stitches without picking up any cloth. Once you understand the rhythm of the stitch, it goes very quickly.

Try it first starting with a *cross stitch* (17), with stitches close together: You get a raised braid useful for heavy lines. Then try to work it freely with arms swinging to one side or the other, or both sides. The width can be varied to fill spaces. It is a good stitch to play with on your doodling cloth.

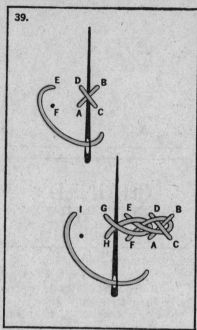

40. Chained Cross Stitch—A more interesting texture than plain *cross stitch* (17) and goes just as quickly. Bring the needle out at A, insert diagonally at B, coming out at C. From C make a *chain stitch* (34) to D. Start again from D to E.

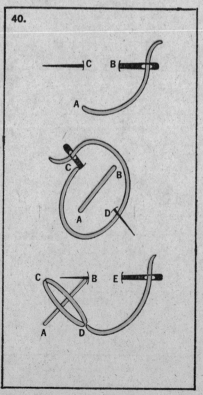

41. French Knot—The easiest way to learn to make a good *French knot* is to have the cloth stretched taut in a hoop or on a frame, and to use heavy yarns. Bring the needle out at A. Swing your yarn to the left of A, circle it down from left to right and hold it flat on the cloth with your left thumb at a place about an inch to the left of A. With your right hand, hold the needle by the eye and slide the point downward "under the bridge", without picking up any cloth. Now think of a clock: Your needle should be pointing to 6 o'clock. Still holding the needle by the eye, turn the point of the needle clockwise, over the yarn held by your left thumb, until it points to 12 o'clock. Continue to hold the yarn down with your left thumb. Insert the point of the needle very close to A but not in the same hole. Now gently pull the yarn with your left thumb and index finger to snug it around the needle. Push the needle straight down with your right hand and pull through gently. If you want bigger knots, use 2 or 3 yarns at the same time; try several shades of the same color in your needle.

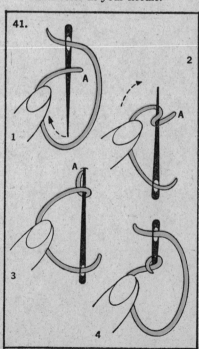

42. Long-stemmed Knot—Useful for small flowers and many designs. Start exactly as for a regular *French knot* (41). When your needle points at 12 o'clock, slide it sideways to where you want the knot to be and insert there, leaving a stem.

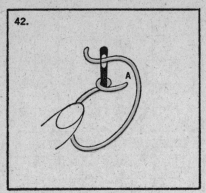

43. Coral Knot—Follows lines easily and gives them a decorative, nubby texture. The knots can be quite close together or spaced. Work from right to left. The yarn from A goes over the needle, then it is looped under the point, from left to right. *Coral knots* also can be worked in a zigzag.

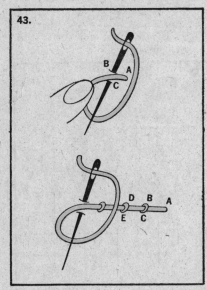

44. Palestrina Knot or Double Knot—This beautiful stitch produces a very decorative line. Use a heavy yarn and work the stitches close enough so they appear as a row of pearls. Work from left to right. Bring the needle out at A on the line to be covered. Take a small slanting stitch, inserting at B above the line, coming out at C below the line. The distance BC should equal AB for well-rounded knots close together. Slip the needle from above, under the AB stitch, without picking up any cloth. Pull through. Slip the needle from above under the first stitch again, to the right of the first slipped yarn which now goes under the needle, making a *buttonhole stitch* (26). Pull the yarn gently so that it encircles the first stitch. Start the next

slanting stitch to the right, inserting at D, coming out at E. DE equals BD.

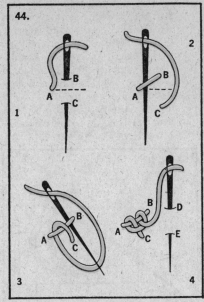

45. Couching—One of the oldest stitches in the world. It is very useful if you want to use yarns that are too thick or too fragile to go through the cloth easily. It is one of the best approaches to creating spontaneously with stitches, expressing a feeling or an idea. You will find it easiest if the cloth is held taut. Pull the beginning of the yarn you want to couch through to the back and lay it over the line you have in mind. Tack it down with another yarn. Besides the usual small even stitches, try couching with other stitches to vary the effect.

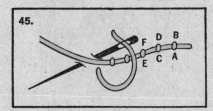

46. Roumanian Stitch—Good for broad lines and fillings. The same yarn is used for both couching and tying. Bring the needle out at A, go in at B, and come out at C just a little above AB, not quite half-way across. Pull through. Take a small diagonal stitch over AB to D. Start the next stitch coming out at E, over to F. The stitches are usually close together, but they also can be spaced.

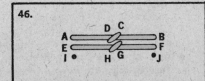

47. New England Laid—Good variation of the *Roumanian stitch* (46). It was used by pioneer women of New England to save yarns. The only difference is that the tacking down diagonal stitch CD is quite long, with C coming out near B, and D near A. The result is an interesting texture.

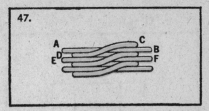

48. Bokhara Stitch—Uses the same principle. This time a long stitch AB is tacked down with small stitches CD, EF, using the same yarn.

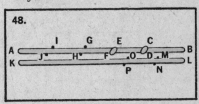

49. Spider Web Stitches—Very decorative and easy. There are several ways of working them. Try the Ribbed Spider Web: First work a number of *straight stitches* (13) from one center, pointing out, like the spokes of a wheel. You might try 6 spokes. To fill the web, bring the needle out at A between B and C. Take a step backwards and slide the needle under AB and AC. Pull through snugly. Continue taking a step backwards under AC and AD, backwards under AD and AE, and so on around as many times as necessary. Little ridges are formed on the spokes of the web. You can either fill it up or leave some of the spokes showing.

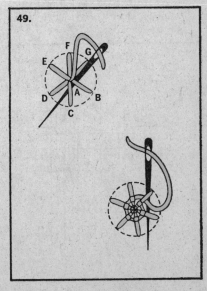

50. Couched Filling—Another form of couching. It is an easy way to fill large surfaces. A hoop or frame is essential to keep the work taut so that your pattern will be even. Yarn is laid across the shape, first vertically, then horizontally. Each intersection is tied down with a small diagonal *straight stitch* (13) or *cross stitch* (17).

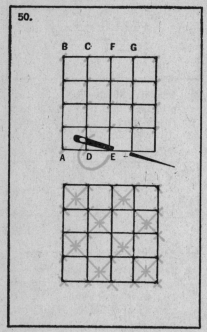

NEEDLEPOINT STITCHES

51. Half Cross Stitch—The simplest of canvas stitches. It must be worked on double-thread canvas, each row from left to right. When a row is completed, turn the work around to start again from left to right. It is good for pictures or pillows that are not subject to hard wear, and economical since there is little yarn on the back.

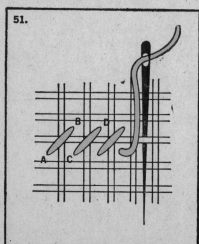

52. Continental or Tent Stitch—Considered the finest of canvas stitches, excellent for backgrounds as well as fine detail. It is good for pieces such as chairs and stools which need a hard-wearing surface. Worked from right to left on either single- or double-thread canvas. At the end of a row, turn work around and continue from right to left. A very fine *continental stitch* worked over only one thread of canvas is called Petit Point.

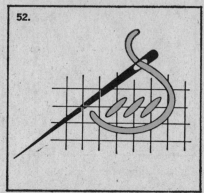

53. Basket Weave—Used mainly for backgrounds and filling shapes, can be worked on single- or double-thread canvas. It does not pull the canvas out of shape, looks smooth. It is hard wearing with a firm back which looks woven. Work on the diagonal with the needle horizontal as rows go up from right to left, then vertical as they go down from left to right.

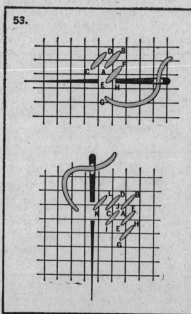

54. Straight or Upright Gobelin—Worked on single- or double-thread canvas. It is one of the oldest of canvas stitches used to imitate the woven Gobelin tapestries, giving a very effective texture. Stitches are worked vertically over 2 threads of the canvas.

If the yarn does not entirely cover the canvas, lay a strand over the row as a padding and work stitches over.

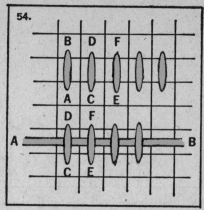

55. Encroaching Gobelin—Beautiful and effective for background and shading. It is worked over 2 horizontal rows and 1 vertical row over, slanting. Each new row starts 1 row lower and encroaches over the last canvas thread of the preceding row. The stitch can also be worked over 3, 4 or 5 horizontal rows, depending on the size of the canvas and yarn. It covers quickly.

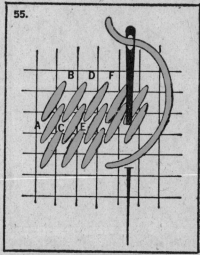

56. Bargello or Florentine Stitch—Is an *upright Gobelin* (54) usually worked in a zigzag or geometric pattern. The basic stitch is worked over 4 threads of canvas and under 2, rising and falling.   ##

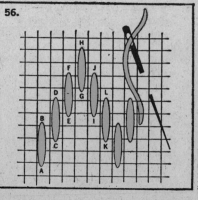

▲ *Ladder of Life*

▲ *Trinity stitch*

▲ *An unusual sampler of interlaced cable edged with a finishing panel of twisted stitches*

Lobster claw stitch

Worked over a number of stitches divisible by 9 (e.g. 45).

1st row. *P1, K7, P1, rep from * to end.

2nd row. *K1, P7, K1, rep from * to end.

3rd row. *P1, sl 2 sts onto cable needle and hold at back of work, K1, K2 from cable needle, K1, sl 1 st onto cable needle and hold at front of work, K2, K1 from cable needle, P1, rep from * to end.

4th row. *K1, P7, K1, rep from * to end.

These 4 rows form the pattern and are repeated throughout. The number of stitches over which the claw is worked and the number of rows between the cable rows may be altered but too much alteration changes the appearance of the claw-like look.

Sample of cable stitches

This sample is worked over 64 sts and includes two types of cables, which depict the fisherman's ropes, and is edged with a twisted stitch often used in Aran patterns.

1st row. (RS) K1, P1, K1y2rn, K2, P3, (K6, P3) twice, K12, (P3, K6) twice, P3, K1y2rn, K2, P1, K1.

2nd row. K2, P2, sl 1 keeping yarn on WS, K3, (P6, K3) twice, P12, K3, (P6, K3) twice, P2, sl 1 keeping yarn on WS, K2.

3rd row. K1, P1, sl long st onto cable needle and hold at front of work, K1y2rn, K1, K1 from cable needle—called CTw3—, P3, (K6, P3) twice, K12, (P3, K6) twice, P3, CTw3, P1, K1.

4th row. As 2nd.

5th row. K1, P1, CTw3, P3, (sl next 3 sts onto cable needle and hold at front of work, K3, K3 from cable needle—called C6F—, P3) twice, C6F twice, P3, (C6F, P3) twice, CTw3, P1, K1.

6th row. As 2nd.

7th row. As 1st, keeping CTw3 at each end.

8th row. As 2nd.

9th row. As 7th.

10th row. As 2nd.

11th row. K1, P1, CTw3, P3, (C6F, P3) twice, K3, sl next 3 sts onto cable needle and hold at back of work, K3, K3 from cable needle—called C6B—, K3, P3, (C6F, P3) twice, CTw3, P1, K1.

12th row. As 2nd. *13th row.* As 7th.

Rows 2-13 form the pattern and are repeated throughout.

Knitting
Know-how

More Aran
stitches

Stitches in cables and twisted panels which form many Aran patterns may change their position, but they usually return to their original place in the pattern sequence within a few rows. Traveling stitches, on the other hand, may move on every row or alternate row throughout the entire pattern repeat and form the basis of all trellis and lattice patterns, as well as being used in single motifs such as Tree of Life pattern and Marriage lines pattern.

A simplified form of trellis stitch, where only one ridge travels in a zigzag pattern within a panel, symbolizes the ups and downs of married life. Using a double ridge, a diamond pattern is formed (see the man's cardigan featured in Basic Wardrobe, page 178). This is often used as an all-over design and is reminiscent of the small walled fields of Ireland. The pattern also means "wealth." Extra texture may be added by filling the center of each diamond with seed stitch, Trinity stitch, or rock-like bobbles.

Narrow lines of traveling stitches branching out from a central stem form the famous Tree of Life design, sometimes used inverted with the branches drooping instead of rising upward.

Trellis sampler

The sampler is edged with a narrow panel of twisted stitches and is ideal for working in strips, which can then be joined together to make pillows, afghans or bedspreads.
Worked over 58 stitches.
1st row. K1, P1, K1 putting yarn twice around needle—called K1y2rn—K2, P2, K1, P3, *(sl 2 sts onto cable needle and hold at back of work, K2, K2 from cable needle—called C4B—P4) 4 times, C4B, P3, K1, P2, K1y2rn, K2, P1, K1.
2nd row. K2, P2, sl 1 dropping extra loop and keeping yarn on WS, K2, P1, K2, (P4, K4) 3 times, P4, K3, P1, K2, P2, sl 1 dropping extra loop and keeping yarn on WS, K2.
3rd row. K1, P1, sl next st onto cable needle and hold at front of work, K1y2rn, K1, K1 from cable needle—called CTw3—P2, K1, P2, (sl next st onto cable needle and hold at back of work, K2, P1 from cable needle—called C3PB—sl next 2 sts onto cable needle and hold at front of work, P1, K2 from cable needle—called C3PF—P2) 5 times, K1, P2, CTw3, P1, K1.
4th row. K2, P2, sl 1, K2, P1, K2, (P2, K2) 10 times, P1, K2, P2, sl 1, K2.
5th row. K1, P1, CTw3, P2, K1, P1, (C3PB, P2, C3PF) 5 times, P1, K1, P2, CTw3, P1, K1.
6th row. K2, P2, sl 1, K2, P1, K1, (P2, K4, P2) 5 times, K1, P1, K2, P2, sl 1, K2.
7th row. K1, P1, CTw3, P2, K1, P1, K2, P4, (sl next 2 sts onto cable needle and hold at front of work, K2, K2 from cable needle —called C4F—P4) 4 times, K2, P1, K1, P2, CTw3, P1, K1.
8th row. K2, P2, sl 1, K2, P1, K1, (P2, K4, P2) 5 times, K1, P1, K2, P2, sl 1, K2.

9th row. K1, P1, CTw3, P2, K1, P1, (C3PF, P2, C3PB) 5 times, P1, K1, P2, CTw3, P1, K1.
10th row. K2, P2, sl 1, K2, P1, K1, (K1, P2, K1) 10 times, K1, P1, K2, P2, sl 1, K2.
11th row. K1, P1, CTw3, P2, K1, P2, (C3PF, C3PB, P2) 5 times, K1, P2, CTw3, P1, K1.
12th row. K2, P2, sl 1, K2, P1, K1, (K2, P4, K2) 5 times, K1, P1, K2, P2, sl 1, K2.
13th row. K1, P1, CTw3, P2, K1, P3, (C4B, P4) 4 times, C4B P3, K1, P2, CTw3, K2, P1, K1.
Rows 2-13 form pattern and are repeated throughout.

Bobble sampler

This sampler is also edged and can be used in combination with the trellis sampler to produce a textured fabric.
Worked over 47 stitches.
1st row. (RS) K1, P1, K1y2rn, K2, P3, K1, P2, *into next st work K1, P1, K1, P1, K1 making 5 sts out of 1, turn and K these 5 sts, turn and P these 5 sts, lift 4th st over 5th and off needle and rep with 3rd, 2nd and 1st st until one st rems—called bobble 1—P5, rep from * to last 12 sts, bobble 1, P2, K1, P3, K1y2rn, K2, P1, K1.
2nd row. K2, P2, sl 1 dropping extra loop and keeping yarn on WS, K3, P1, K29, P1, K3, P2, sl 1, K2.
3rd row. K1, P1, sl next st onto cable needle and hold at front of work, K1y2rn, K1, K1 from cable needle—called CTw3—P3, K1, P29, K1, P3, CTw3, P1, K1.
4th row. As 2nd row.
5th row. K1, P1, CTw3, P3, K1, *P5, bobble 1, rep from * to last 14 sts, P5, K1, P3, CTw3, P1, K1.
6th row. As 2nd row.
7th row. As 3rd row.
8th row. As 2nd row.
9th row. K1, P1, CTw3, P3, K1, P2, *bobble 1, P5, rep from * to last 12 sts, bobble 1, P2, K1, P3, CTw3, P1, K1.
Rows 2-9 form pattern and are repeated throughout.

Tree of Life

Worked over a number of stitches divisible by 15.
1st row. (RS) *P7, K1, P7, rep from * to end.
2nd row. *K7, P1, K7, rep from * to end.
3rd row. *P5, slip next st onto cable needle and hold at back, K1, P1 from cable needle—called C2F—K1, slip next st onto cable needle and hold at front, P1, K1, from cable needle—called C2B—P5, rep from * to end.
4th row. *K5, sl 1 keeping yarn on WS, K1, P1, K1, sl 1, K5, rep from * to end.
5th row. *P4, C2F, P1, K1, P1, C2B, P4, rep from * to end.
6th row. *K4, sl 1, K2, P1, K2, sl 1, K4, rep from * to end.
7th row. *P3, C2F, P2, K1, P2, C2B, P3, rep from * to end.
8th row. *K3, sl 1, K3, P1, K3, sl 1, K3, rep from * to end.
9th row. *P2, C2F, P3, K1, P3, C2B, P2, rep from * to end.
10th row. *K2, sl 1, K4, P1, K4, sl 1, K2, rep from * to end.
These 10 rows form pattern and are repeated throughout.

Marriage lines

Worked over a number of stitches divisible by 20.
1st row. *P1, Tw2F, P6, K2, P2, K2, P2, Tw2B, P1, rep from * to end.
2nd row. *K1, P2, K2, P2, K2, P2, K6, P2, K1, rep from * to end.
3rd row. *P1, Tw2F, P5, sl next st onto cable needle and hold at back of work, K2, P1 from cable needle—called T3R—P1, T3R, P2, Tw2B, P1, rep from * to end.
4th row. *K1, P2, K3, P2, K2, P2, K5, P2, K1, rep from * to end.
5th row. *P1, Tw2F, P4, T3R, P1, T3R, P3, Tw2B, P1, rep from * to end.

▲ *Trellis sampler edged with twisted stitch panel*

▲ *Bobble sampler edged with twisted stitch panel*

▲ *Tree of Life pattern*

▲ *Marriage lines pattern with twisted stitch panels*

6th row. *K1, P2, K4, P2, K2, P2, K4, P2, K1, rep from * to end.
7th row. *P1, Tw2F, P3, T3R, P1, T3R, P4, Tw2B, P1, rep from * to end.
8th row. *K1, P2, K5, P2, K2, P2, K3, P2, K1, rep from * to end.
9th row. *P1, Tw2F, P2, T3R, P1, T3R, P5, Tw2B, P1, rep from * to end.
10th row. *K1, P2, K6, P2, K2, P2, K2, P2, K1, rep from * to end.
11th row. *P1, Tw2F, P2, sl next 2 sts onto cable needle and hold at front of work, P1, K2 from cable needle—called T3L—, P1, T3L, P5, Tw2B, P1, rep from * to end.

12th row. As 8th row.
13th row. *P1, Tw2F, P3, T3L, P1, T3L, P4, Tw2B, P1, rep from * to end.
14th row. As 6th row.
15th row. *P1, Tw2F, P4, T3L, P1, T3L, P3, Tw2B, P1, rep from * to end.
16th row. As 4th row.
17th row. *P1, Tw2F, P5, T3L, P1, T3L, P2, Tw2B, P1, rep from * to end.
Rows 2-17 form pattern and are repeated throughout.

79

Chapter 28

Traditional fisherman knitting

Try knitting a fisherman's traditional seamless pullover.
Around the coast of England and Scotland, wherever there are fishing fleets and fishermen, there can still be found examples of the traditional seamless pullover correctly called guernsey. While the guernseys are basically alike, each area has an individual style—some have distinctive yokes, others have vertical panel designs and some have horizontal patterns. Apart from regional styles each village, and even individual families, have their own designs. Some even have the initials of the owner worked into the pattern.

The designs are never haphazard, but use symbols to tell a story reflecting the fisherman's surroundings, family life and the tools of his trade.

Seamless knitting

The guernsey is knitted circularly, cast on with a set of four or five double pointed needles at the lower edge and worked in one up to the beginning of the armholes. The work then divides and the back and front are worked separately to the shoulders, which are bound off together.

This binding off is often on the right side to give a decorative ridge. The neckband is then worked circularly again, although in Scotland buttons and buttonholes would be added at the shoulder.

To give greater ease of movement, a gusset is often made just before the armhole division and carried on into the top of the sleeves, which are then picked up and knitted downward to the cuff. Although entirely seamless, a mock seam is often worked at either side. The gusset is increased in the center of the seam and the seam carried on down the sleeve once the gusset is completed.

Types of wool

The guernsey is not unlike a patterned brocade when finished and is always knitted on fine needles. The wool traditionally used is often as thick as knitting worsted or thicker, but it is made firm and weatherproof by the closeness of the stitches.

Anchor design

One of the many designs seen on guernseys on the coast of Fife in Scotland is the Anchor pattern, which can be worked as a repeat across the work or repeated upward in a vertical panel. It repeats over a number of stitches divisible by 21.

1st row. *P2, K1, P2, K11, P2, K1, P2, rep from * to end.
2nd row. *K2, P1, K2, P11, K2, P1, K2, rep from * to end.
Rep 1st and 2nd rows once more.
5th row. *P2, K1, P2, K5, P1, K5, P2, K1, P2, rep from * to end.
6th row. *K2, P1, K2, P4, K1, P1, K1, P4, K2, P1, K2, rep from * to end.
7th row. *P2, K1, P2, K3, (P1, K1) twice, P1, K3, P2, K1, P2, rep from * to end.
8th row. *K2, P1, K2, P2, K1, P5, K1, P2, K2, P1, K2, rep from * to end.
9th row. *P2, K1, P2, K1, P1, (K3, P1) twice, (K1, P2) twice, rep from * to end.

10th row. *(K2, P1) twice, K1, P7, K1, (P1, K2) twice, rep from * to end.
11th row. *P2, K1, P2, K5, P1, K5, P2, K1, P2, rep from * to end.
12th row. As 2nd.
13th row. As 11th.
14th row. As 2nd.
15th row. *P2, K1, P2, K3, P5, K3, P2, K1, P2, rep from * to end.
16th row. *K2, P1, K2, P3, K5, P3, K2, P1, K2, rep from * to end.
17th row. As 15th.
18th row. As 2nd.
19th row. As 11th.
20th row. As 2nd.
21st row. As 11th.
22nd row. *K2, P1, K2, P4, K1, P1, K1, P4, K2, P1, K2, rep from * to end.
23rd row. *P2, K1, P2, K3, (P1, K3) twice, P2, K1, P2, rep from * to end.
24th row. As 22nd.
25th row. As 11th.
26th row. As 2nd.
Rep 1st-26th rows for patt.

Sheringham design

This pattern was taken from a patterned yoke edged with ridged purl welts and shows patterning at its best. The pattern repeats over a number of stitches divisible by 24.
K2 rows. P2 rows.
Rep last 4 rows 3 times more.
Begin diamond pattern.
1st row. *K6, P1, K11, P1, K5, rep from * to end.
2nd row. *P4, K1, P1, K1, P9, K1, P1, K1, P5, rep from * to end.
3rd row. *K4, P1, K3, P1, K7, P1, (K1, P1) twice, K3, rep from * to end.
4th row. *P2, K1, (P1, K1) 3 times, (P5, K1) twice, P3, rep from * to end.
5th row. *K2, P1, K7, P1, K3, P1, (K1, P1) 4 times, K1, rep from * to end.
6th row. *K1, (P1, K1) 6 times, P9, K1, P1, rep from * to end.
7th row. *P1, K11, P12, rep from * to end.
8th row. *K11, P1, K1, P9, K1, P1, rep from * to end.
9th row. *K2, P1, K7, P1, K13, rep from * to end.
10th row. *P14, K1, P5, K1, P3,

rep from * to end.
11th row. *K4, P1, K3, P1 K15, rep from * to end.
12th row. *P16, K1, P1, K1, P5 rep from * to end.
Rep 1st—12th rows for patt.

Flag and cable design

This pattern is seen in designs from the Scottish and Yorkshire coastal areas, and can be used as an all over design or in narrow panels separated by seed stitch panels or cable panels.
Repeat the pattern over a number of stitches divisible by 26.
1st row (right side). *P2, K1, P2, slip next 3 sts onto cable needle and hold at back of work, K3, K3 from cable needle, P2, K1, P2, K2, P8, rep from * to end.
2nd row. *K7, P3, K5, P6, K5, rep from * to end.
3rd row. *P2, K1, P2, K6, P2, K1, P2, K4, P6, rep from * to end.
4th row. *K5, P5, K5, P6, K5 rep from * to end.
5th row. *P2, K1, P2, K6, P2, K1, P2, K6, P4, rep from * to end.
6th row. *K3, P7, K5, P6, K5, rep from * to end.
7th row. *P2, K1, P2, K6, P2, K1, P2, K8, P2, rep from * to end.
8th row. *K1, P9, K5, P6, K5, rep from * to end.
Rep 1st-8th rows for patt.

Pine tree design

This design is found in many variations, usually on guernseys belonging to Scottish fishermen. It can be used separately as a motif, or in conjunction with seed stitch borders and diamonds.
The pattern is worked over a number of stitches divisible by 15.
1st row (right side). K.
2nd row. P.
3rd row. *K7, P1, K7, rep from * to end.
4th row. *P6, K1, P1, K1, P6, rep from * to end.
5th row. *K5, P1, K3, P1, K5, rep from * to end.
6th row. *P4, (K1, P2) twice, K1, P4, rep from * to end.
7th row. *K3, P1, K2, P1, K1,

P1, K2, P1, K3, rep from * to end.
8th row. *(P2, K1) twice, P3, (K1, P2) twice, rep from * to end.
9th row. *K1, (P1, K2) twice, P1, (K2, P1) twice, K1, rep from * to end.
10th row. *P3, K1, P2, K1, P1, K1, P2, K1, P3, rep from * to end.
11th row. *K2, P1, K2, P1, K3, P1, K2, P1, K2, rep from * to end.
12th row. *P4, K1, P2, K1, P2, K1, P4, rep from * to end.
13th row. *K3, P1, K2, P1, K1, P1, K2, P1, K3, rep from * to end.
14th row. *P5, K1, P3, K1, P5, rep from * to end.
15th row. *K4, P1, (K2, P1) twice, K4, rep from * to end.
16th row. *P6, K1, P1, K1, P6, rep from * to end.
17th row. *K5, P1, K3, P1, K5, rep from * to end.
18th row. *P7, K1, P7, rep from * to end.
19th row. *K6, P1, K1, P1, K6, rep from * to end.
20th row. P.
21st row. As 3rd.
22nd row. P.
Rep 1st-22nd rows for patt.

▼ *Anchor design*

▲ *Sheringham fishermen wearing their guernseys, two in similar patterns*

▼ *Pine tree design*

▲ *Sheringham design*   ▼ *Flag and cable design*

Chapter 29

Shetland knitting

The most gossamer and the finest examples of lace knitting come from Unst, the most northerly of all the Shetland islands. In the early nineteenth century a visitor to the island brought with her a collection of fine Spanish lace. This delicate surface inspired the islanders to create knitted lace of similar beauty using their single ply homespun yarn. Although such very fine yarns are rarely used today, Shetland lace stitches can be used to make a variety of lovely garments in an average weight yarn.

Although Shetland lace stitches are adaptable, they are seen at their best if worked with reasonably fine yarns and needles. No.3 needles and fingering yarn are recommended for the stitches in this chapter to produce a fine, knitted lace.
Casting on for lace should be kept as loose as possible. Ideally use a simplified two-needle method. Cast on 2 stitches, insert the right-hand needle into the second stitch instead of between the stitches, draw one stitch through and transfer it to the left-hand needle. Wherever possible, weave edges together and bind off loosely so that the edges are soft and smooth.

Bead stitch

This is a simple lace to use for filling diamonds or hexagonal areas, or for working large areas such as shawl centers. The illustration uses it as an all-over pattern. It can easily be adapted to have a less open appearance by working 2, 3 or more knitted stitches between the panels.
It is worked over a number of stitches divisible by 7 (for example, 28).
1st row. (RS) *K1, K2 tog, ytf, K1, ytf, sl 1 knitwise, K1, psso, K1, rep from * to end.
2nd row. *P2 tog tbl, yrn, P3, yrn, P2 tog, rep from * to end.
3rd row. *K1, ytf, sl 1 knitwise, K1, psso, K1, K2 tog, ytf, K1, rep from * to end.
4th row. *P2, yrn, P3 tog, yrn, P2, rep from * to end.
These 4 rows form the pattern and are repeated as desired.

Crest of the wave stitch

Old shale stitch, reminiscent of the print left on sand by receding waves, is a simple design (see Knitting Know-how Chapter 20) which is also the basis for many equally simple but less often seen versions. Of these, crest of the wave stitch is perhaps the most effective.
It is worked over a number of stitches divisible by 12, plus 1 (for example, 37).
1st, 2nd, 3rd and 4th rows. K.
5th row. K1, *(K2 tog) twice, (ytf, K1) 3 times, ytf, (sl 1 knitwise, K1, psso) twice, K1, rep from * to end.
6th row. P.
Rep 5th and 6th rows 3 times more.

Knitting Know-how

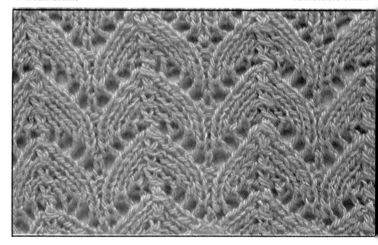

▲ *Bead stitch*   ▼ *Horseshoe stitch*

These 12 rows form the pattern and are repeated as desired.

Razor shell stitch

Another stitch which takes its name from a well known beach shell, this can be varied over 4, 6, 8, 10 or 12 stitches. Instructions are given for both 6 and 10 stitch variations.
The six stitch version is worked over a number of stitches divisible by 6, plus 1 (for example, 25).
1st row. (WS) P.
2nd row. K1, *ytf, K1, sl 1, K2 tog, psso, K1, ytf, K1, rep from * to end.
Repeat 1st and 2nd rows as desired.
The ten stitch version is worked over a number of stitches divisible by 10, plus 1 (for example, 31).
1st row. (WS) P.
2nd row. K1, *ytf, K3, sl 1, K2 tog, psso, K3, ytf, K1, rep from * to end.
These 2 rows form the pattern and are repeated as desired.

Horseshoe stitch

The imprint of horseshoes on damp sand is a familiar sight to the islanders and is used in this stitch to create a lace which has innumerable uses.
It is worked over a number of stitches divisible by 10, plus 1 (for example, 31).
1st row. (WS) P.
2nd row. K1, *ytf, K3, sl 1, K2 tog, psso, K3, ytf, K1, rep from * to end.
3rd row. As 1st.
4th row. P1, *K1, ytf, K2, sl 1, K2 tog, psso, K2, ytf, K1, P1, rep from * to end.

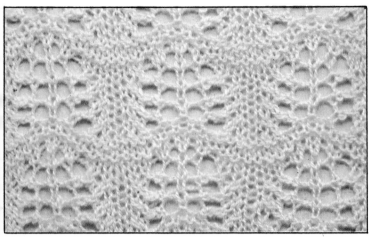

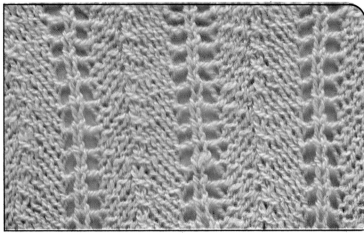

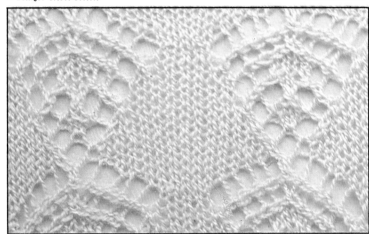

▲ *Crest of the wave stitch*　　　▼ *Faggoting cable stitch*　　　▲ *Razor shell stitch*　　　▼ *Fern stitch*

5th row. K1, *P9, K1, rep from * to end.

6th row. P1, *K2, ytf, K1, sl 1, K2 tog, psso, K1, ytf, K2, P1, rep from * to end.

7th row. As 5th.

8th row. P1, *K3, ytf, sl 1, K2 tog, psso, ytf, K3, P1, rep from * to end of the row.

These 8 rows form the pattern and are repeated as desired.

Faggoting cable stitch

Mainly a lace stitch, this gives an additional interest and texture to the lace by the introduction of the cable. The cable can be worked crossing in front or behind the work or can be alternated to incorporate both. It is often used as a single panel at either side of another motif or can form an all-over pattern as illustrated. It is worked over a number of stitches divisible by 12, plus 8 (for example, 32).

1st row. (WS) P2, *K2, ytf, K2 tog, P2, rep from * to end.

2nd row. K2, *P2, yrn, P2 tog, K2, rep from * to end.

3rd and 4th rows. As 1st and 2nd.

5th and 6th rows. As 1st and 2nd.

7th row. P2, K2, ytf, K2 tog, P2, *sl next 2 sts onto cable needle and hold at front of work, K2, K2 from cable needle—called C4F—P2, K2, ytf, K2 tog, P2, rep from * to end.

8th row. As 2nd.

9th and 10th rows. As 1st and 2nd.

11th and 12th rows. As 1st and 2nd.

13th and 14th rows. As 1st and 2nd.

15th row. P2, C4F, P2, *K2, ytf, K2 tog, P2, C4F, P2, rep from * to end.

16th row. As 2nd.

These 16 rows form the pattern and are repeated as desired.

Fern stitch

Often used as a shawl border, the shape of the motif allows for easy corner shaping. The size of the motif can vary from a miniature fern to a very large shape but the method of working remains the same, extra stitches being worked in. This is worked over a number of stitches divisible by 15 (for example, 45).

1st row. (RS) *K7, ytf, sl 1 knitwise, K1, psso, K6, rep from * to end.

2nd row. P.

3rd row. *K5, K2 tog, ytf, K1, ytf, sl 1 knitwise, K1, psso, K5.

4th row. P.

5th row. *K4, K2 tog, ytf, K3, ytf, sl 1 knitwise, K1, psso, K4, rep from * to end.

6th row. P.

7th row. *K4, ytf, sl 1 knitwise, K1, psso, ytf, sl 1, K2 tog, psso, ytf, K2 tog, ytf, K4, rep from * to end.

8th row. P.

9th row. *K2, K2 tog, ytf, K1, ytf, sl 1 knitwise, K1, psso, K1, K2 tog, ytf, K1, ytf, sl 1 knitwise, K1, psso, K2, rep from * to end.

10th row. P.

11th row. *K2, (ytf, sl 1 knitwise, K1, psso) twice, K3, (K2 tog, ytf) twice, K2, rep from * to end.

12th row. *P3, (yrn, P2 tog) twice, P1, (P2 tog tbl, yrn) twice, P3, rep from * to end.

13th row. *K4, ytf, sl 1 knitwise, K1, psso, ytf, sl 1, K2 tog, psso, ytf, K2 tog, ytf, K4, rep from * to end.

14th row. *P5, yrn, P2 tog, P1, P2 tog tbl, yrn, P5, rep from * to end.

15th row. *K6, ytf, sl 1, K2 tog, psso, ytf, K6, rep from * to end.

16th row. P. These 16 rows form patt and are repeated as desired.

Collector's Piece

Gossamer wool lace

This delicate wool lace shawl is probably one of the finest examples of handmade garments to be found today.

Knitted by a few skilled Shetland Islanders in their own homes, these ring shawls, as they are called, are in great demand and worth twice their weight in gold. The designs have been passed on by word of mouth from one generation to the next, but the instructions have never been written down.

Lace knitting developed in the Shetlands on the island of Unst in the early nineteenth century after Mrs Jessie Scanlon had visited the island to show the inhabitants a collection of fine Spanish lace. The islanders, inspired by its beauty, developed a technique of knitting lace fabrics. The yarn used to knit ring shawls is woven from the fine wool which grows around the sheep's neck. After being knitted on fine, steel needles, the shawls are washed and then hung on frames by an open fire to dry to their correct shape.

All the patterns have colorful names and represent objects which the knitters see around them—Horseshoe, Cat's Paw, Bird's Eye, Print of the Wave. When complete, ring shawls measure about six feet by six feet, but weigh only three ounces. They are so gossamer-fine that the entire shawl can be drawn literally through a wedding ring, hence their name. Traditionally made as christening robes, ring shawls also make beautiful winter wedding veils.

A beautiful example of a Shetland ring shawl ►
◄ *A tradition in knitting which still lives today*
▼ *Feather-light, a ring shawl slips through a ring*

Chapter 30

Introduction to knitted lace

Knitted lace is both simple to do and lovely to look at. This chapter gives some tips for suitable yarns, and casting-on methods which avoid unsightly seams. It also has two pretty edgings to work for handkerchief hems.

Suitable materials

The finer the cotton used the daintier and more gossamer the lace will be. Some really beautiful stoles are made in one ply wool, but for household linens and fine edgings Coats & Clark's cottons are some of the most successful materials. They have a neat finish and can be as fine as desired.

Edgings are usually made on a pair of needles and worked across the edging so that the desired length is obtained by repeating the pattern.

Table mats and larger areas of lace are worked on circular needles or sets of double-pointed needles to avoid seams.

If a mat is worked from the center outward, it is necessary to begin at the center with only a few stitches on each needle. As the work progresses and the stitches increase, it may be easier to transfer all the stitches onto a circular needle for the remainder of the work.

Needles must be fine. If too large a needle is used, perhaps in the mistaken hope of making the work grow more quickly, the solid areas will not be as regular as they should be and will not contrast as well against the openwork areas.

Casting on for lace

Hard, thick lines must be avoided whether caused by

seaming, or by casting on or binding off as they spoil the continuity of the lace.

The least noticeable cast-on edge is a two-needle method in which the right-hand needle is inserted into the last stitch on the left-hand needle, the yarn passed around the needle point and drawn through to form the new stitch. This is similar to the two-needle method normally used, except that the new stitch is drawn through the stitch instead of between the stitches.

For edgings which are to be worked lengthwise, normal cast-on and bound-off edges will spoil the look of the work, and it is

▼ *Method of casting on with the same thread*

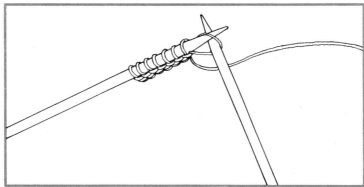

▼ *Method of casting on with separate thread to be removed later*

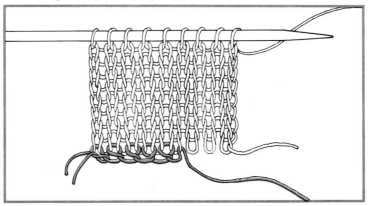

best to cast on using spare yarn which can later be removed, so that when the work is completed the first and last rows can be woven together for an invisible finish (see Knitting Know-how Chapter 12).

Begin with these two simple designs for beautiful handkerchief edgings.

Bird's eye edging

Size
It is possible to work any length desired.

Gauge
¾in wide.

Materials
J. & P. Coats Six Cord Mercerized No.20
1 ball
One pair No.1 needles
One handkerchief

To make the edging
Using No.1 needles, cast on 7 sts.

1st row K1, K2 tog, y2rn, K2 tog, y2rn, K2.
2nd row Sl 1, K2, P1, K2, P1, K2.
3rd row K1, K2 tog, y2rn, K2 tog, K4.
4th row Bind off 2 sts, K3, P1, K2.
Repeat these 4 rows for length desired, allowing a little fullness for corners. Bind off.

Leaf edging

Size
It is possible to work any length desired.

Gauge
1in wide.

Materials
J. & P. Coats Six Cord crochet No.50
1 ball
One pair No.3 needles
One handkerchief

To make the edging
Using No.3 needles, cast on 10 sts.

1st row K3, (ytf, K2 tog) twice, y2rn, K2 tog, K1.
2nd row K3, P1, K2, (ytf, K2 tog) twice, K1.
3rd row K3, (ytf, K2 tog) twice, K1, y2rn, K2 tog, K1.
4th row K3, P1, K3, (ytf, K2 tog) twice, K1.
5th row K3, (ytf, K2 tog) twice, K2, y2rn, K2 tog, K1.
6th row K3, P1, K4, (ytf, K2 tog) twice, K1.
7th row K3, (ytf, K2 tog) twice, K6.
8th row Bind off 3 sts, K4, (ytf, K2 tog) twice, K1.
Repeat these 8 rows until desired length. Bind off.

Finishing

Pin edging out in proper shape to correct measurements, WS up, and press with a damp cloth and a warm iron.
Slip stitch, neatly and securely, to handkerchief hem using fine sewing cotton. Seam cast-on and bound-off edges as invisibly as possible. Re-press.

Bird's eye edging (left) and leaf edging for handkerchief hems ▶

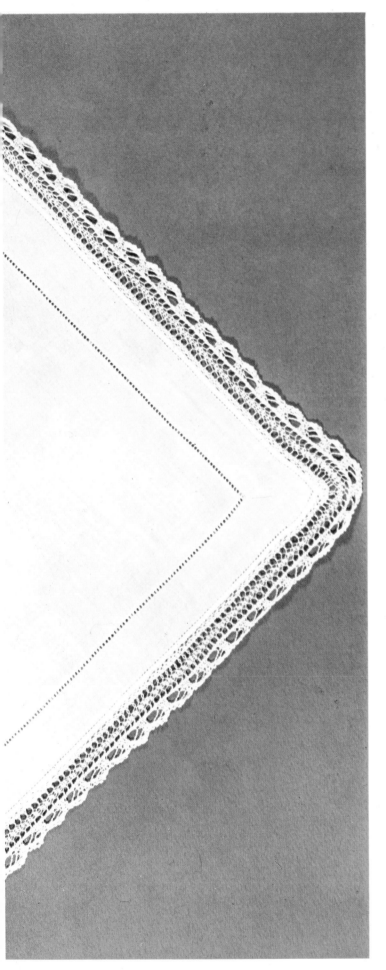

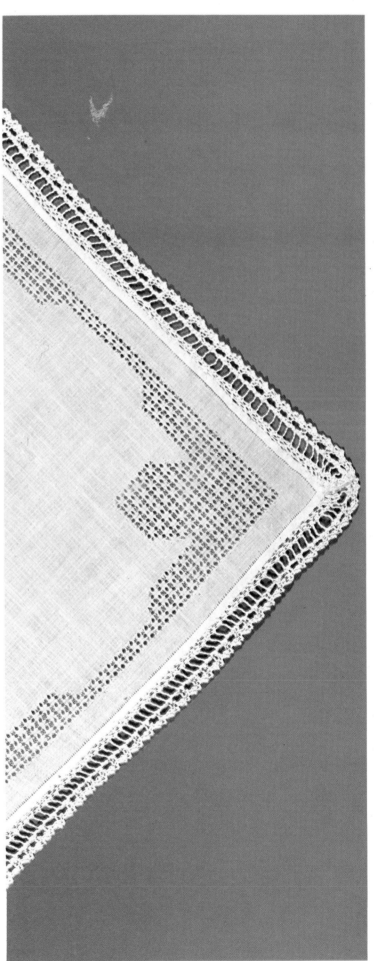

Lace edging for a pillowcase

Knitted lace can be used to give an individual finish to your household furnishings. This edging is not difficult to work and can be used to edge bed linen, table linen or lampshades.

The size is determined by the yarn and needles used. This table gives an approximate guide to the possibilities.
Using J. & P. Coats Knit-Cro-Sheen, work on No.1 needles.
Using Clark's Big Ball Mercerized Cotton No.30 work on No.0 needles.
The pillowcase edging can be worked on No.0 needles using Clark's Big Ball Mercerized Cotton No.30.
Each rep requires 16 sts plus 5 extra sts for the borders. The rep measures about 18in by 2½in deep. For the border 5 reps were worked, thus the required number to cast on was 5×16+5=85 sts.

Pillowcase edging

Length
18in.

Gauge
About 2½in deep

Materials
Clark's Big Ball Mercerized Cotton No.30
One pair No.0 needles
One No.10 steel crochet hook
One pillowcase

Edging
Using No.0 needles, cast on 85 sts.

Knitting Know-how

1st row K2, *ytf, K2 tog, ytf, sl 1, K1, psso, K1, (K1, ytf, K1, ytf, K2) twice, K2 tog, ytf, K1, rep from * to last 3 sts, ytf, K2 tog, K1.

2nd row K1, P1, *yon, P2 tog, P18, rep from * to last 3 sts, yon, P2 tog, K1.

3rd row K2, *ytf, K2 tog, ytf, K1, (ytf, sl 1, K2 tog, psso) 5 times, (ytf, K1) twice, rep from * to last 3 sts, ytf, K2 tog, K1.

4th row K1, P1, *yon, P2 tog, P16, rep from * to last 3 sts, yon, P2 tog, K1.

5th row K2,* ytf, K2 tog, K1, ytf, K2, ytf, sl 1, K1, psso, K2, ytf, K1, ytf, K2, K2 tog, (ytf, K2) twice, rep from * to last 3 sts, yft, K2 tog, K1.

6th row K1, P1, *yon, P2 tog, P20, rep from * to last 3 sts, yon, P2 tog, K1.

7th row K2, *ytf, K2 tog, K2, ytf, K3, (ytf, sl 1, K2 tog, psso) 3 times, (ytf, K3) twice, rep from * to last 3 sts, ytf, K2 tog, K1.

8th row K1, P1, *yon, P2 tog, P20, rep from * to last 3 sts, yon, P2 tog, K1.

9th row K2, *ytf, K2 tog, K7, ytf, sl 1, K1, psso, K1, K2 tog, ytf, K8, rep from * to last 3 sts, ytf, K2 tog, K1.

10th row K1, P1, *yon, P2 tog, P20, rep from * to last 3 sts, yon, P2 tog, K1.

11th row K2, *ytf, K2 tog, K8, ytf, sl 1, K2 tog, psso, ytf, K9, rep from * to last 3 sts, ytf, K2 tog, K1.

12th row As 10th.
13th row As 11th.
14th row As 10th.
15th row As 11th.

16th row As 10th.
17th row K2, *ytf, K2 tog, K6, K2 tog, ytf, K3, ytf, sl 1, K1, psso, K7, rep from * to last 3 sts, ytf, K2 tog, K1.

18th row As 10th.
19th row K2, *ytf, K2 tog, K5, K2 tog, ytf, K1, ytf, sl 1, K2 tog, psso, ytf, K1, ytf, sl 1, K1, psso, K6, rep from * to last 3 sts, ytf, K2 tog, K1.

20th row As 10th.
21st row K2, *ytf, K2 tog, K4, K2 tog, ytf, K3, ytf, K1, ytf, K3, ytf, sl 1, K1, psso, K5, rep from * to last 3 sts, ytf, K2 tog, K1.

22nd row K1, P1, *yon, P2 tog, P22, rep from * to last 3 sts, yon, P2 tog, K1.

23rd row K2, *ytf, K2 tog, K3, K2 tog, ytf, K1, (ytf, sl 1, K2 tog, psso) 3 times, ytf, K1, ytf, sl 1, K1, psso, K4, rep from * to last 3 sts, ytf, K2 tog, K1.

24th row As 10th.
25th row K2, *ytf, K2 tog, K2, K2 tog, ytf, K3, ytf, (K1, ytf, K3, ytf) twice, sl 1, K1, psso, K3, rep from * to last 3 sts, ytf, K2 tog, K1.

26th row K1, P1, *yon, P2 tog, P24, rep from * to last 3 sts, yon, P2 tog, K1.

27th row K2, *ytf, K2 tog, K1, K2 tog, ytf, K1, (ytf, sl 1, K2 tog, psso) 5 times, ytf, K1, ytf, sl 1, K1, psso, K2, rep from * to last 3 sts, ytf, K2 tog, K1.

28th row As 10th.
29th row K1, K3 tog, *K2 tog, ytf, K3, (ytf, K1, ytf, K3) 3 times, ytf, sl 1, K1, psso, K3 tog, rep from * to last st, K1.

30th row K1, P to last st, K1.
31st row K1, K2 tog, *ytf, K1, (ytf, sl 1, K2

tog, psso) 7 times, ytf, K1, ytf, sl 1, K2 tog, psso, rep from * to end.
Complete edging using crochet hook as follows:
Last row With WS of work facing, insert hook into first 2 sts and work 1sc, *ch7, 1sc into next st, ch7, insert hook into next 3 sts and work 1sc, rep from * until all sts have been worked off. Fasten off ends.

Finishing
Block to shape and press. Stitch securely to edge of pillowcase.

Finishing off lace
Lace is not usually starched, but hand-knitted lace in cotton or linen thread is made for everyday use and is better if lightly starched. Only table mats or articles which are to be fully supported by tray or table require stiff starching.

Washing lace
Wash lace when finished in warm, mild suds, rinsing carefully until the water is clear. Starch as required and leave aside wet until ready for blocking to size.

Blocking
The exact size of the article should be drawn out on brown or white paper which will not stain when damp. Whatever the shape of the article, the method is the same. Pin out to the correct size working on opposite corners. If the mat is rectangular, pin each corner and halfway along each side. Once the mat is positioned, divide each section by placing more pins to draw the mat to the desired size.
If the edging has tiny points of crochet or knitting, the final stage must be to pin each point separately so that the shape is perfect.
Leave pinned until completely dry. Remove pins and press carefully without pulling out of shape to give the final smooth finish.

▼ *Pinning out a piece of lace*

Knitted edging trims a pillowcase ►

Knitting lace in circles

This beautiful circular lace coffee table mat is achieved by graduating from a set of four needles to a set in a slightly larger size, and so on to a circular needle. In this way it is possible to cope with the ever increasing circumference.

Size
23in diameter.

Gauge
8 sts and 9 rows to 1in over st st worked on No.2 needles.

Materials
Clark's Big Ball Mercerized Cotton No.30
2 balls
One No.12 steel crochet hook
One No.2 circular needle 24in long
One set of 4 No.1 double-pointed needles 10in long
One set of 4 No.2 double-pointed needles 10in long

Using set of No.1 needles, cast on 10 sts, 3 sts on each of first and second needles and 4 sts on third needle.

1st round K.
2nd round *Ytf, K1, rep from * to end. 20 sts.
3rd, 4th and 5th rounds K.
6th round *Ytf, K2, rep from * to end. 30 sts.
7th round K.
8th round *Ytf, K3, rep from * to end. 40 sts.
9th, 11th, 13th, 15th, 17th, and 19th rounds K.
10th round *Ytf, K4, rep from * to end. 50 sts.
12th round *Ytf, K5,

![Knitting Know-how]

rep from * to end. 60 sts.
14th round *Ytf, K6, rep from * to end. 70 sts.
16th round *Ytf, K7, rep from * to end. 80 sts.
18th round *Ytf, K8, rep from * to end. 90 sts.
20th round *Ytf, K9, rep from * to end. 100 sts.
21st round *Ytf, K1, ytf, K8, K2 tog, K9, rep from * to end. 105 sts.
22nd round *Ytf, K3, ytf, sl 1, K1, psso, K16, rep from * to end. 110 sts.
23rd round *Ytf, K1, ytf, sl 1, K2 tog, psso, ytf, K1, ytf, K15, K2 tog, rep from * to end. 115 sts.
24th round *Ytf, K3, ytf, K1, ytf, K3, ytf, sl 1, K1, psso, K14, rep from * to end. 130 sts.
25th round *Ytf, sl 1, K1, psso, K1, K2 tog, ytf, K1, ytf, sl 1, K1, psso, K1, K2 tog, ytf, K15, rep from * to end. 130 sts.
26th round *Ytf, K1, ytf, sl 1, K2 tog, psso, ytf, K3, ytf, sl 1, K2 tog, psso, ytf, K1, ytf, sl 1, K1, psso, K11, K2 tog, rep from * to end. 130 sts.
27th round *Ytf, K3, ytf, K1, ytf, sl 1, K1, psso, K1, K2 tog, ytf, K1, ytf, K3, ytf, K13, rep from * to end. 150 sts.
28th round *Ytf, (sl 1, K1, psso, K1, K2 tog, ytf, K1, ytf) twice, sl 1, K1, psso, K1, K2 tog, ytf, sl 1, K1, psso, K9, K2 tog, rep from * to end. 140 sts.
29th round *Ytf, K1, (ytf, sl 1, K2 tog, psso, ytf, K3) twice, ytf, sl 1,

K2 tog, psso, ytf, K1, ytf, K11, rep from * to end. 150 sts.
30th round *Ytf, K3, (ytf, K1, ytf, sl 1, K1, psso, K1, K2 tog) twice, ytf, K1, ytf, K3, ytf, sl 1, K1, psso, K7, K2 tog, rep from * to end. 160 sts.
31st round *Ytf, K1, (ytf, sl 1, K2 tog, psso, ytf, K3) 3 times, ytf, sl 1, K2 tog, psso, ytf, K1, ytf, sl 1, K1, psso, K5, K2 tog, rep from * to end. 160 sts.
32nd round *Ytf, K3, (ytf, K1, ytf, sl 1, K1, psso, K1, K2 tog) 3 times, ytf, K1, ytf, K3, ytf, sl 1, K1, psso, K3, K2 tog, rep from * to end. 170 sts.
33rd round *Ytf, K1, (ytf, sl 1, K2 tog, psso, ytf, K3) 4 times, ytf, sl 1, K2 tog, psso, ytf, K1, ytf, sl 1, K1, psso, K1, K2 tog, rep from * to end. 170 sts.
34th round *K3, (ytf, K1, ytf, sl 1, K1, psso, K1, K2 tog) 4 times, ytf, K1, ytf, K3, ytf, sl 1, K1, psso, ytf, rep from * to end. 180 sts.
Change to set of No.2 needles.
35th round *Sl 1, K2 tog, psso, ytf, K3, ytf, rep from * to end.
36th round *Ytf, K1, ytf, sl 1, K1, psso, K1, K2 tog, rep from * to end.
37th round *Ytf, K3,

ytf, sl 1, K2 tog, psso, rep from * to end.
38th round *Sl 1, K1, psso, K1, K2 tog, ytf, K1, ytf, rep from * to end.
39th round As 35th.
40th round As 36th.
41st round As 37th. 180 sts.
42nd round *(K1 and P1 into each of next 2 sts, K1) twice, K1 and P1 into each of next 2 sts, K2, rep from * inc in last st. 289 sts.
Change to circular needle and place colored marker before first st to mark round beginning.
43rd round *Ytf, K15, K2 tog, rep from * to end.
44th round K.
Rep last 2 rounds 9 times more.
63rd round *Ytf, K1, ytf, sl 1, K1, psso, K12, K2 tog, rep from * to end.
64th round *Ytf, K3, ytf, sl 1, K1, psso, K10, K2 tog, rep from * to end.
65th round *Ytf, sl 1, K1, psso, K1, K2 tog, ytf, sl 1, K1, psso, K10, rep from * to end. 272 sts.
66th round *Ytf, K1, ytf, sl 1, K2 tog, psso, ytf, K1, ytf, sl 1, K1, psso, K7, K2 tog, rep from * to end.
67th round *Ytf, K3, ytf, K1, ytf, K3, ytf, sl 1, K1, psso, K7, rep from * to end. 323 sts.
68th round *Ytf, sl 1, K1,

▼ *Close-up detail of the lace stitch*

▲ *Circular lace cloth gives elegance to a coffee table*

psso, K1, K2 tog, ytf, K1, ytf, sl 1, K1, psso, K1, K2 tog, ytf, sl 1, K1, psso, K4, K2 tog, rep from * to end. 289 sts.

69th round *Ytf, K1, ytf, sl 1, K2 tog, psso, ytf, K3, ytf, sl 1, K2 tog, psso, ytf, K1, ytf, sl 1, K1, psso, K4, rep from * to end. 306 sts.

70th round *Ytf, K3, ytf, K1, ytf, sl 1, K1, psso, K1, K2 tog, ytf, K1, ytf, K3, ytf, sl 1, K1, psso, K1, K2 tog, rep from * to end. 340 sts.

71st round *(Sl 1, K1, psso, K1, K2 tog, ytf, K1, ytf) twice, sl 1, K1, psso, K1, K2 tog, ytf, sl 1, K2 tog, psso, ytf, rep from * to end. 306 sts.

72nd round *Sl 1, K2 tog, psso, ytf, K3, ytf, rep from * to end. 306 sts.

73rd round As 36th.

74th round As 37th.

75th round As 38th.

76th round As 35th.

77th-79th rounds As 36th to 38th. 306 sts.

80th round *K1, K1 and P1 into each of next 2 sts, rep from * to end. 510 sts.

81st round K inc 3 sts evenly in round. 513 sts.

82nd and 83rd rounds K.

84th round *Ytf, sl 1, K1, psso, rep from * to last st, K1.

85th round K.

86th round *Ytf, K7, K2 tog, rep from * to end.

87th round K.

88th round As 86th.

89th round K.

90th round As 86th.

91st round *Ytf, K1, ytf, sl 1, K1, psso, K4, K2 tog, rep from * to end.

92nd round *Ytf, K3, ytf, K6, rep from * to end. 627 sts.

93rd round *Ytf, sl 1, K1, psso, K1, K2 tog, ytf, sl 1, K1, psso, K2, K2 tog, rep from * to end. 513 sts.

94th round *Ytf, K1, ytf, sl 1, K2 tog, psso, ytf, K1, ytf, K4, rep from * to end. 627 sts.

95th round *Ytf, K3, ytf, K1, ytf, K3, ytf, sl 1, K1, psso, K2, rep from * to end. 798 sts.

96th round *Sl 1, K1, psso, K1, K2 tog, ytf, K1, ytf, sl 1, K1, psso, K1, K2 tog, ytf, K3, ytf, rep from * to end. 798 sts.

97th round *Sl 1, K2 tog, psso, ytf, K3, ytf, sl 1, K2 tog, psso, ytf, sl 1, K1, psso, K1, K2 tog, ytf, rep from * to end. 684 sts.

98th round *Ytf, K1, ytf, sl 1, K1, psso, K1, K2 tog, rep from * to end. 684 sts.

Edging

Using No.12 steel crochet hook, yoh, *work 1sc into next 3 sts tog, and slip off needle, ch10, rep from * ending with 1ss into first sc. Fasten off.

Finishing

Run in ends.
Damp evenly and pin out to size. Leave to dry.

Chapter 31

Striped effects in knitting

Stripes using one or more additional shades are the easiest way of achieving a colorful effect in knitting. As can be seen from the illustrations in this chapter, a wide variety of different results can be achieved by a simple change of color or clever combination of colors while using the most ordinary of stitch patterns.

Horizontal stripes

These are usually worked in stockinette stitch and are achieved by changing color at the beginning of a row. This gives an unbroken line of color on the RS of the fabric. Narrow stripes would need a color change every second or third row but interest is added if the distance between the stripes is varied. The example shown is worked on a repeating sequence of 8 rows using A, 4 rows using B, 2 rows using C.

Ribbed stripes

Stripes on ribbing, if required to show an unbroken line, need to have the color change row knitted throughout although the other rows are in ribbing, but an interesting effect is produced by working in rib or fancy rib irrespective of the color change thus giving a broken, random type of line to the pattern. The sample given shows this and can be worked as follows:

Cast on a number of stitches divisible by 10, plus 5.

1st row P5, *K1, ytf, sl 1P, ytb, K1, ytf, sl 1P, ytb, K1, P5, rep from * to end.

2nd row K1, ytf, sl 1P, ytb, K1, ytf, sl 1P, ytb, K1, *P5, K1, ytf, sl 1P, ytb, K1, ytf, sl 1P, ytb, K1, rep from * to end.

These 2 rows form the pattern and should be repeated throughout. The color sequence used is as follows:

2 rows using A, 10 rows using B, (2 rows using A, 6 rows using C) twice.

Chevron stripes

A zigzag striped effect can be made by the clever use of stitch added to color changes. The illustration shows simple stripes of four rows of each color, and the chevron shaping is formed by the vertical lines of increased and decreased stitches.

Cast on a number of stitches divisible by 14, using A.

1st row With A, *K1, inc by knitting into the loop below the next st on the left-hand needle and then K the stitch immediately above, K4, sl 1P, K2 tog, psso, K4, inc as before, rep from * to end.

2nd row With A, P.

3rd row With A, as 1st.

4th row With A, as 2nd.

Continue working four rows in this way in each of your chosen colors. A pretty effect can be achieved by using several shades of one or two colors, and graduating them from light to dark.

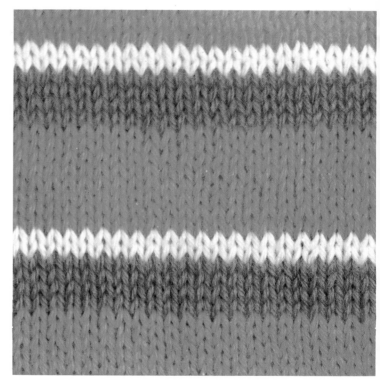

▲ *Horizontal striped pattern*

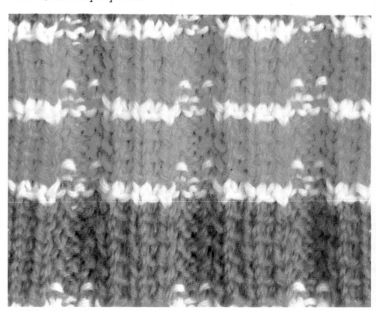

▲ *Ribbed striped pattern*

▲ *Chevron striped pattern*

Twisting yarns to change color

When working any form of horizontal stripe, there is no problem about joining in a different colored yarn, as one color is finished at the end of a row and the new one is brought in at the beginning of the next row. Vertical or diagonal stripes, however, present a different problem, as the colors must be changed at several points within the same row.

When working narrow vertical or diagonal stripes it is quite simple to twist the yarn and carry it across the back of the work and this method can be used in the example of narrow diagonal stripes illustrated. For wider stripes it would be most unsatisfactory to use this means of carrying the yarn. Apart from the waste of material, there is the chance of pulling too tight resulting in unsightly bunching of the fabric and loss of gauge. It is much better to divide the yarn into small quantities before beginning the pattern and this is done by winding the yarn into a small ball for each stripe and twisting the colors when the change is made. This is very simple to do as can be seen from the illustration.

When twisting the yarn, always cross it in the same direction, as this will prevent a gap appearing on the right side of the work, and will give a neat look at the back as shown.

It is important to remember that stripes worked by twisting the yarn on changing color give a fabric of normal thickness, while stripes worked by carrying the yarn along the back of the work give a fabric of double thickness.

Diagonal stripes

An unusual and striking effect can be achieved by knitting stripes diagonally across a garment. Although diagonal stripes may appear complicated to work, the method is in fact very simple.

Cast on a number of stitches divisible by 5, plus 3.

1st row K3A, *K2B, K3A, rep from * to end.
2nd row P1B, *P3A, P2B, rep from * to last 2 sts, P2A.
3rd row K1A, *K2B, K3A, rep from * to last 2 sts, K2B.
4th row P1A, P2B, *P3A, P2B, rep from * to end.

Continue to work in this way moving the stripe one stitch to the right on K rows and one stitch to the left on P rows.

Herringbone stripes

These stripes are worked in almost the same way as given for diagonal stripes, but instead of moving continuously to the right as shown, try moving the stripes to the left after six rows, then back again to the right.

This pattern is very effective when used, for example, on a knitted skirt.

Vertical stripes

This is a typical example of the wide stripe which needs to have the yarn divided into small quantities. In fact any stripe over 4 stitches in width would need to be worked in this manner.

Take, for example, a sweater with five wide stripes of 21 stitches in each stripe across the front. The first row is worked by knitting 21 stitches with the first ball of A, then 21 stitches with the first ball of B, 21 stitches with the second ball of A, 21 stitches with the second ball of B, and 21 stitches with the third ball of A. Continue working in stockinette stitch, as follows:

Next row (wrong side) P21 sts A, then carry yarn to the left at the front of the work, pick up the yarn B, and take it over A toward the right and P the next 21 sts with B, repeat in this way with each color to the end of the row.

Next row K21 sts A, hold the yarn over to the left at the back of the work, take up the yarn B and bring it toward the right under the A thread, which is no longer in use, and K the next 21 sts with B, repeat in this way with each color to the end of the row.

▲ *Diagonal striped pattern*

▲ *Joining in another color on right side of vertical stripes*

▲ *Joining in another color on wrong side of vertical stripes*

Chapter 32

Tweed effects in knitting

Striped designs are not the only way in which more than one color may be introduced into knitted fabrics. There are many simple variations where different colors may be used effectively to give all-over patterned or tweed effects.

In many of these patterns the work is simplified because only one color is needed in each row, thus avoiding the weaving in or carrying across of colors not in use. Where only a few rows are worked in one color, the other color or colors may be carried up the side of the work until required, although care must be taken not to pull them so tightly that the actual side length of the fabric is shortened. One pattern worked in two colors may take on a completely different appearance when worked in three or four colors, as illustrated.

Bobble tweed stitch
Worked over an even number of stitches.
1st row. Using 1st color, K.
2nd row. Using 1st color, K.
3rd row. Using 2nd color, *K1 double by inserting needle into row below next st and K1, return this st to left-hand needle and K tog with next st on left-hand needle, K1, rep from * to end.
4th row. Using 2nd color, K.
5th row. Using 1st color, *K1, K1 double, rep from * to end.
6th row. Using 1st color, K.
Continue repeating rows 3-6 as desired, working 2 rows of each color or 2 rows each of 3 or more colors.

Horizontal fabric stripe
Worked over an even number of stitches.
1st row. Using 1st color, K1, *ytf, K2, lift ytf over K2, rep from * to last st, K1.
2nd row. Using 1st color, P.
3rd row. Using 2nd color, work as given for 1st row.
4th row. Using 2nd color, P.
Continue repeating rows 1-4 as desired, working 2 rows of each color or 2 rows each of 3 or more colors.

Tweed stitch
Worked over a number of stitches divisible by 4, plus 3 (for example, 27 stitches).
1st row. (RS) Using 1st color, K3, *sl 1 P-wise keeping yarn on WS, K3, rep from * to end.
2nd row. Using 1st color, K3, *sl 1, P-wise keeping yarn on WS, K3, rep from * to end.
3rd row. Using 2nd color, K1, *sl 1, P-wise keeping yarn on WS, K3, rep from * to last 2 sts, sl 1 P-wise, K1.
4th row. Using 2nd color, K1, *sl 1, P-wise keeping yarn on WS, K3, rep from * to last 2 sts, sl 1 P-wise, K1.
Continue repeating rows 1-4 as desired.

94

▲ *Two-color bobble tweed stitch*   ▼ *Three-color bobble tweed stitch*

▼ *Four-color bobble tweed stitch*

Striped star stitch
Worked over a number of stitches divisible by 4, plus 3 (for example, 27 stitches).
1st row. Using 1st color, P.
2nd row. Using 1st color, *insert needle into next 3 sts as if to K3 tog and K1, K1 tbl, K1 all into these sts—called 1 star—K1, rep from * ending with 1 star.
3rd row. Using 2nd color, P.
4th row. Using 2nd color, K2, * 1 star, K1, rep from * ending K1.
Continue repeating rows 1-4 as desired.

▲ *Two-color horizontal fabric stripe*

▲ *Striped star stitch*

▲ *Three-color horizontal fabric stripe*   ▼ *Tweed stitch*

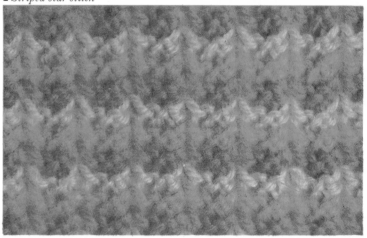

▲ *Striped fabric rib*   ▼ *Striped vertical rib*

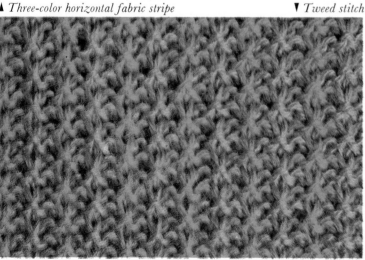

Striped fabric rib

Worked over a number of stitches divisible by 3 (for example, 27 stitches).

1st row. Using 1st color, *K1, ytf, K2 tog, repeat from * to end.

2nd row. Using 1st color, *K1, ytf, K2 tog, repeat from * to end.

Continue repeating rows 1 and 2 as desired, working 2 rows of each color and repeating color sequence. Try four or six colors to give a multi-tweed effect.

Striped vertical rib

Worked over a number of stitches divisible by 4, plus 2 (for example, 26 stitches).

1st row. Using 1st color, K1, *ytf, sl 2 carrying yarn across front of work, ytb, K2, rep from * to last st, K1.

2nd row. Using 1st color, K.

3rd row. Using 2nd color, K1, *K2, ytf, sl 2 carrying yarn across front of work, ytb, rep from * to last st, K1.

4th row. Using 2nd color, K.

Continue repeating rows 1-4 as desired.

Chapter 33
Jacquard knitting and border patterns

Knitting Know-how

Jacquard knitting is the name given to patterned fabrics where more than one color is used and where the pattern is knitted in at the same time as the background. It applies to the type of pattern which can be shown on a chart, in much the same way as cross-stitch in embroidery is indicated, but does not include all-over, multicolored patterns formed with different stitches. The usual feature is a bold repeating design in large blocks of color with the yarn being twisted at the back of the work to carry it along, giving a thick, woven fabric, particularly if worked in knitting worsted. Because of this jacquard designs are often used for outdoor wear. Made in a thinner yarn, they are attractive in skirts with one of the shades picked out for a plain matching sweater. A single jacquard motif makes a decorative patch pocket.

Two types of jacquard

There are two basic methods of knitting jacquard patterns. One is used where small motifs are being worked close together, such as on a border or on an all-over surface design. The other is used where larger motifs or stripes are being worked and the spaces between each motif are larger in proportion.

Small motifs
When the pattern is composed of small repeats with only a few stitches in any one color, the yarns not in use are carried across the back of the fabric until they are used again. If there are more than three stitches in a group, twist the thread not in use with the one being used in order to avoid loose loops on the wrong side of the garment. It is essential not to carry the yarn from one group of stitches to the next too tightly or the right side of the work will become puckered and uneven, spoiling the finished appearance.

If the garment is worked in bands of jacquard, separated by areas of stockinette stitch worked in one color only, it is advisable to use one size larger needle for the patterned bands than for the plain stockinette stitch to avoid a noticeable difference in gauge.

Large motifs and patterns
Vertical stripes, large diamonds and checks present a problem of their own. If they are worked in the same way as a small motif, they use a large amount of unnecessary yarn, causing bulk in the fabric. In this case, a great deal of care is required to keep the right side of the fabric smooth.

For this type of pattern it is best to use one ball of yarn for each area, twisting it with the next color when moving onto the next area, as described in vertical stripes in Chapter 31. If working a design of your own decide which method you will use before beginning, based on the thickness of fabric required and the distance between the blocks of color. In the case of published designs, the most appropriate method will almost certainly be given in the working instructions.

Working from a chart

It does not take long to learn to work from a chart and, indeed, it is often easier to read at a glance than trying to find your exact position in a maze of written instructions. Unless only two colors are used and it is obvious from the illustration which is the pattern and which is the background, you will usually find a key to the chart presented with it, describing which symbol stands for which color.

In the charts for the 1st and 2nd border patterns, a blank square denotes the background color A, which is worked with white; contrast color B is pink and is indicated with a slanting line and contrast color C, which is orange, is indicated by a dot.

The most important point in reading from a chart is to remember whether you are working in rows or in rounds. Working in rows of stockinette stitch the first row on the chart, which is usually shown at the lower edge, will be the right side or knitted row and will be read along the chart from right to left. The second row will be purled and is read from left to right because you have turned the work but cannot turn the chart. If you are working in rounds, then each round will begin on the chart at the right side and will, of course, be a knitted round and will be repeated to the end of the round.

To be certain that you understand these methods, try to work the border using the first chart. If you are in any doubt, you can check from the following row by row instructions repeating from A to B. The border is worked over a number of stitches divisible by 21 and over 15 rows of stockinette stitch, beginning and ending with a knitted row. Work 2 rows stockinette stitch in A before beginning the pattern.

1st patt row. *K1 A, 3C, 8A, 3B, 6A, rep from * to end.
2nd patt row. *P5 A, 5B, 6A, 5C, rep from * to end.
3rd patt row. *K6 C, 5A, 5B, 5A, rep from * to end.
4th patt row. *P2 A, 2B, 1A, 5B, 1A, 2B, 2A, 4C, 2A, rep from * to end.
5th patt row. *K3 A, 3C, 1A, 4B, 1A, 3B, 1A, 4B, 1A, rep from * to end.
6th patt row. *P1 A, 5B, 1A, 1C, 1A, 5B, 2A, 3C, 2A, rep from * to end.
7th patt row. *K1 A, 3C, 1A, 2B, 1A, 3B, (1A, 1B) twice, 1A, 3B, 1A, 1C, rep from * to end.
8th patt row. *P1 A, 1C, (3A, 1C) twice, 3A, 4B, 3A, 1C, rep from * to end.
9th patt row. *K1 A, 3C, 1A, 2B, 1A, 3B, (1A, 1C) twice, 1A, 3B, 1A, 1C, rep from * to end.
10th patt row. *P1 A, 5B, 1A, 1C, 1A, 5B, 2A, 3C, 2A, rep from * to end.
11th patt row. *K3 A, 3C, 1A, 4B, 1A, 3B, 1A, 4B, 1A, rep from * to end.
12th patt row. *P2 A, 2B, 1A, 5B, 1A, 2B, 2A, 4C, 2A, rep from * to end.
13th patt row. *K6 C, 5A, 5B, 5A, rep from * to end.
14th patt row. *P5 A, 5B, 6A, 5C, rep from * to end.
15th patt row. *K1 A, 3C, 8A, 3B, 6A, rep from * to end.

Beginning with a purl row, work 2 rows stockinette stitch with A only to complete this sample.

Now try the second jacquard border pattern, following the chart in the same way.

The third jacquard pattern, showing a carnation motif, is in two colors only. The cream background is indicated by a blank square on the chart and the pink contrast by a cross. This motif can be repeated as a border, worked for example along the hem of a cardigan, or used on its own. The arrangement of the motif depends on personal taste but the finished effect can give an original touch to even the simplest garment.

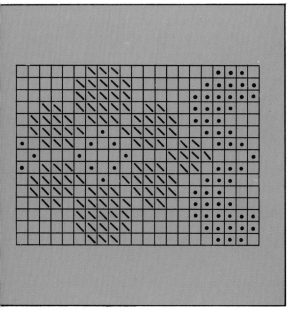

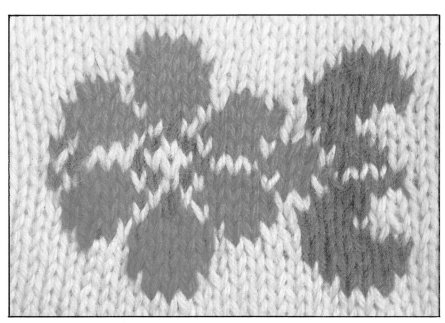

▲ *Chart for first jacquard border pattern*
▼ *Second jacquard border pattern*

▲ *First jacquard border pattern*
▼ *Work this jacquard border pattern from the chart on the left*

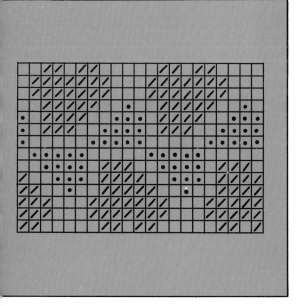

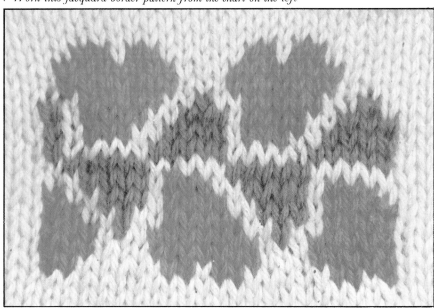

▼ *Chart for the carnation jacquard motif*

▼ *The carnation jacquard motif*

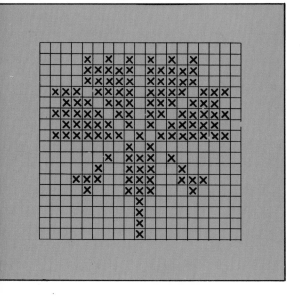

Chapter 34

Fair Isle techniques

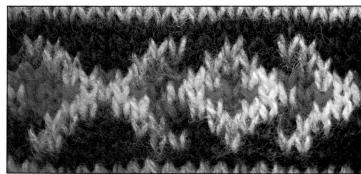

▲ *Fair Isle pattern based on a simple "O" and "X" design*

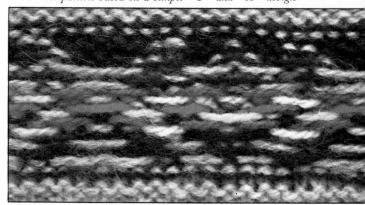

▲ *The "O" and "X" design viewed from the wrong side*
▼ *Working chart for the "O" and "X" design*

The bands of Fair Isle pattern were based on simple "O" and "X" shapes, often with the Spanish cross superimposed in the center, but were given an added subtlety by the changes of colors worked into the background in stripes, as well as the pattern itself. The softly twisted yarn was orginally "natural" in color, which could vary from white to a dark blackish brown, whatever the color of the sheep from which it came. These soft, natural tones gave the knitter a vast choice of shades to use in her pattern, but the many colors we know today were added much more recently, to cater to fashion demand.

The softness of the yarn is further enhanced by the seamlessness of the garment. Cardigans and pullovers are both knitted without seams. When the armholes are reached, the stitches are left unworked to be picked up or woven later, so that even below the arm there is no firm seam. Shoulders, too, are woven together, producing a softness and pliability of fabric which gives the garment an added charm and character.

Unlike most colored or jacquard patterns, Fair Isle designs do not have the yarns twisted on the wrong side of the fabric. Each area of color is small, and usually only two colors are used in any one row and they are carried directly from one stitch to the next to be worked in that color.

The greatest influence and change in Fair Isle work, apart from the addition of colors which the Shetlanders are so good at blending, came about during the war years of 1939-1945, when many Norwegians were stationed in Shetland. Their own colored knitting came from similar sources to those of the Shetlanders, but the motifs used were larger and more complicated. Many Fair Isle designs now incorporate these motifs most successfully. Traditionally, the patterns are handed on from mother to daughter, but where a design is written down for others to copy, the motifs are usually worked from a chart for ease of reading. Each color is marked on the chart with its own symbol. As most of the work is made by using circular or double-pointed needles to avoid seams, the right side of the work is toward the knitter who can follow the pattern visually far more quickly than attempting to read row by row instructions. Where openings are required, the work is cut later and the ends darned back in to secure them so that they do not ravel.

Simple O and X design

One of the very old, often used designs, this version repeats over 14 sts.

Flower motif

This motif is worked over 30 sts.
The colors for the motif are shown on the chart color key.
The background colors are changed on the following rows:
Rows 1 and 2 Beige.
Row 3 Light green.

98

Row 4	Lemon.
Rows 5-12	White.
Rows 13-15	Sand.
Rows 16-20	Lemon.
Row 21	Light green.
Rows 22-26	Lemon.
Rows 27-29	Sand.
Rows 30-37	White.
Row 38	Lemon.
Row 39	Light green.
Rows 40 & 41	Beige.

Star motif

This motif is worked over 36 sts. The colors used for the motif appear on the chart color key.
The background colors are as follows:
Rows 1-10 have beige background.
Rows 11-37 have off-white background.
Rows 38-40 have beige background.

The flower motif, worked on a changing background of rows of beige, reen, lemon, white and sand ▼ Working chart for the flower motif

▲ The star motif in tones of gray and brown on a background of beige and off-white ▼ Working chart for the star motif

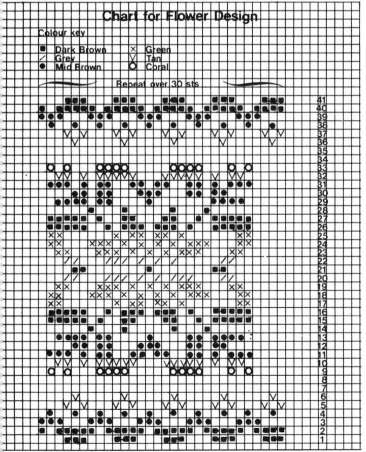

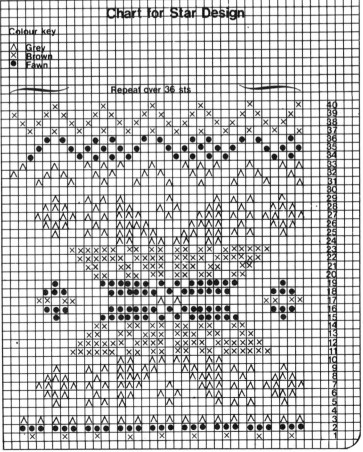

Chapter 35

Knitting with beads and sequins

Knitting Know-how

It is best to add beads or sequins to knitting while the fabric is being worked.

Choice of beads and sequins
Care when choosing beads and sequins for knitting will pay in the results obtained. Because large, heavy beads will drag the knitting out of shape, small beads are usually a better choice. If the beads are to be worked close together they should only cover a small area, because even with small beads a large area would soon become too heavy for the yarn.
It is always better to make sure that beads or sequins will not lose their color, and only those guaranteed suitable for dry cleaning are advisable. All beaded and sequined garments should be dry-cleaned, with the exception of those with small, lightweight plastic beads, which are usually washable.

Choice of stitch
Beads or sequins are decorative enough in themselves and should only be combined with fancy stitches if these genuinely contribute to the finished appearance.
Because of its smooth surface, stockinette stitch forms the most suitable background to show the decoration to best advantage.

Threading beads or sequins onto yarn
Occasionally it is possible to buy lightweight beads or sequins with large holes, in which case there is no problem threading them onto the yarn. However, the usual bead or sequin used for knitting has a

▼ *Placing a bead on a knit row*

▼ *Purling stitch after placing bead*

▼ *Placing a bead on a purl row*

▼ *Knitting stitch following bead*

relatively small hole which is not large enough to take a needle threaded with yarn.
In such a case, cut a length of sewing thread about 8 inches long and thread both ends into the eye of the needle. Slide the needle halfway along the doubled thread, thus forming a loop at one end. Smooth both the ends and the loop downward. Pass the end of the yarn into the loop for several inches and then smooth the double thickness of the yarn downward.
Slip the beads or sequins onto the needle, over the sewing thread and then the yarn.

Adding beads between stitches on a purl row
Purl along the row to the bead position, take the yarn behind the needle, slip a bead along next to the needle, knit the next stitch and return the yarn ready for purling.
Continue in purl until the next bead position. Work the next bead in exactly the same way.

Adding beads between stitches on a knit row
Work to the point where the bead is to be placed. Bring the yarn forward toward you and slip a bead up close to the needle, purl the next stitch, then continue knitting in the normal way until the next bead position is reached.

Adding beads (or sequins) in front of a stitch on a knit row
Knit to the desired position, bring the yarn forward and slip a bead close up to the fabric, slip the next stitch from the left-hand needle without knitting it and leaving the bead in front of the slipped stitch. Return the yarn to the knitting position and work to the next bead position.

Adding beads (or sequins) in front of a stitch on a purl row
Purl to the bead position. Take the yarn back to right side of work and slip bead up to the needle, slip next stitch, carry yarn across slipped stitch on

right side, bring yarn back an purl to next bead position

Alternative method of adding sequins
The type of sequin which has hole close to the edge must b able to hang. With either of the previous methods, the se quins would be distorted. In stead, use either of the follow ing methods after threadin the sequins onto the yarn.
Working a knit row. Knit t the point where the sequi is to be placed, knit the nex stitch through the back of th loop, pushing the sequi through the actual stitch fron back to front.
Working a purl row. Wor to the point where the sequi is to be placed, push the sequi close to the needle, purl th next stitch. This stitch hold the sequin in place withou having to push it through Once the sequin is in place continue along the row a usual on a purl row to th next sequin position.

Evening bag

Size
Top edge, approx 5in.
Depth including fringe, 7in.

Gauge
8 sts and 12 rows to 1in worked on No.3 needles.

Materials
Bucilla Brocade
1 ball
One pair No.3 needles
624 small pearl beads
One handbag frame
¼yd lining material

To work the bag
Thread beads onto ball of yarn.
Using No.3 needles, cast on 39 sts.
1st row K.
2nd and every other row K1, P to last st, K1.
3rd row K4, *ytf, slip bead close to work, slip next st keeping bead in front, ytb— called B1—, K5, rep from * t last 5 sts, B1, K4.

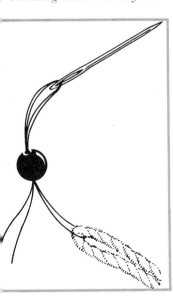

Threading beads onto the yarn   ▲ *Glitter yarn enhanced by pearl beads adds glamour to an evening bag*

5th row K3, *B1, K1, B1, K3, rep from * to end.
7th row K2, *B1, K3, B1, K1, rep from * to last st, K1.
9th row K1, *B1, K5, rep from * to last 2 sts, B1, K1.
11th row As 7th.
13th row As 5th.
14th row As 2nd.
Rows 3-14 form the patt and are repeated throughout, the continuity of the bead lines being kept and 1 st at either end of each row being knitted and kept free of beads.
Inc one st at each end of next 6 rows. Place marker thread at each end of last row.
Work 8 rows without shaping.

Dec 1 st at each end of next and every 4th row until 41 sts remain, every other row until 33 sts remain, then every row until 21 sts remain. Bind off 3 sts at beg of next 4 rows. Bind off.

Fringe
With RS facing, pick up and K72 sts between marker threads around the lower half of the bag (i.e. along one side, across bound-off sts and along other side).
Loop row *Insert needle into next st on left-hand needle, wind yarn over needle point and around 3 fingers of left

hand 3 times, then around needle point once, draw loops through and return to left-hand needle, K into back of loops and st (see Knitting Know-how Chapter 21), rep from * to end of row. Bind off. Work a second side in the same manner, omitting fringe.

Finishing
Cut lining slightly larger than knitted section.
Place 2 sections of knitting right sides together and join along bound-off edge of fringe. Seam lining along same edges. Stitch bag to frame. Insert lining and slip stitch in place.

101

Embroidery on knitting

Knitting provides an ideal fabric for embroidery. It can be used either as a plain background for working random patterns, or the structure of the fabric can be used for counted thread types of patterns.

When decorating knitting, single stitches can be outlined in a contrast color to build up small motifs, as in Swiss darning. Alternatively, embroidery may be used to highlight a knitted pattern, a technique found in Tyrolean designs.

Swiss darning

Knitting a motif into the actual garment inevitably slows the process of knitting, and may present difficulties if rounded shapes are required. In such a case, the quickest method is to knit the garment in stockinette stitch and then to darn in the motif, by outlining the stitches of the motif-area. Thread the yarn into a darning needle and pass the needle through to the right side of the work at the base of a stitch. Draw the yarn through, leaving a short end at the back to darn in once the work is completed. Insert the needle behind the threads at the top of the same stitch, taking the needle through to the wrong side at the right-hand side of the stitch and out to the right side of the work at the left of the stitch. Then insert the needle back into the base of the same stitch. This will now have outlined one complete stitch and the process is repeated over all the necessary stitches. Run in both ends invisibly on the wrong side.

102

Counted thread embroidery

In this technique, the upright and horizontal lines of the knitted stitch replace the canvas, and the spaces in the center of stitches or between stitches are used as holes.

It is best to use a darning needle with this method so that the knitted stitches are not spliced.

Tyrolean knitting

In these patterns the knitted stitches are used to create a self-colored pattern which is then highlighted by the addition of small, gay colored flowers, usually embroidered in wool. These are traditionally simple daisy shapes, sometimes formed by straight stitches like the spokes of a wheel, but more often with lazy-daisy stitch. These can be used to form leaves.

Tyrolean leaf pattern

The pattern is worked over 25 stitches and makes an attractive panel on either side of cardigan button panels.
(Not illustrated.)
1st row (RS) K6, P2 tog, P4, K up thread before next st tbl—called K up 1 tbl—, K1, K up 1 tbl, P4, P2 tog, K6.
2nd row K1, P4, K6, P3, K6, P4, K1.
3rd row K6, P2 tog, P3, (K1, ytf) twice, K1, P3, P2 tog, K6.
4th row K1, P4, K5, P5, K5, P4, K1.
5th row K1, sl next 2 sts onto cable needle and hold at back of work, K2, K2 from cable needle—called C4B—, K1, P2 tog, P2, K2, ytf, K1, ytf, K2, P2, P2 tog, K1, sl next 2 sts onto cable needle and hold

▲ *A simple embroidery motif to trim mother's and daughter's outfits*

at front of work, K2, K2 from cable needle—called C4F—, K1.
6th row K1, P4, K4, P7, K4, P4, K1.
7th row K6, P2 tog, P1, K3, ytf, K1, ytf, K3, P1, P2 tog, K6.
8th row K1, P4, K3, P9, K3, P4, K1.
9th row K6, P2 tog, K4, ytf, K1, ytf, K4, P2 tog, K6.
10th row K1, P4, K2, P11, K2, P4, K1.
11th row K1, C4B, K1, P1, K5, P into front and back of next st twice, turn, K4, turn, P4, turn, K4, turn, sl 2nd, 3rd and 4th sts over first st then sl first st onto right-hand needle—called Bobble 1—, K5, P1, K1, C4F, K1.
12th row As 10th.
13th row K6, inc by purling into front and back of next st, K4, sl 1, K2 tog, psso, K4, inc

in next st, K6.
14th row As 8th.
15th row K6, inc in next st, P1, K1, Bobble 1, K1, sl 1, K2 tog, psso, K1, Bobble 1, K1, P1, inc in next st, K6.
16th row As 6th.
17th row K1, C4B, K1, inc in next st, P2, K2, sl 1, K2 tog, psso, K2, P2, inc in next st, K1, C4F, K1.
18th row As 4th.
19th row K6, inc in next st, P3, K2 tog tbl, Bobble 1, K2 tog, P3, inc in next st, K6.
20th row As 2nd.
21st row K6, inc in next st, P4, sl 1, K2 tog, psso, P4, inc in next st, K6.
22nd row K1, P4, K7, P1, K7, P4, K1.
23rd row K1, C4B, K1, P13, K1, C4F, K1.
24th row K1, P4, K15, P4, K1.
These 24 rows form patt and are repeated as required.

--- Outline Stitch   ▬▬ Chain Stitch   ◉ ◉ ◉ Beads

▲ *Diagram for embroidery in chain and outline stitches with beads*

▲ *Embroidered mittens and alternative knitted trim on red mitten*

Decorated mittens

Size

To fit an average adult hand
Length, about 10in.

Gauge

6 sts and 8 rows to 1in
over st st worked on No.
3 needles.

Materials

Reynolds Danskyarn
Two 50grm balls
One set of 4 No.3 double-
pointed needles
Embroidery threads and beads

Left mitten

Using No.3 needles, cast on
48 sts and divide on 3 needles.
Cuff round *K1 tbl, P1, rep
from * to end.

Rep this round until cuff
measures 3in.
Change to st st.
1st round K22, lift thread
before next st and K into back
of it to M1 (this becomes
center st of thumb gusset), K26.
2nd round K.
3rd round K22, M1, K1,
M1, K26.
4th round As 2nd.
5th round K22, M1, K3,
M1, K26.
6th round As 2nd.
Continue in this way until
there are 19 sts on thumb
gusset. 67 sts.

Divide for thumb

1st round K22, sl next 19
sts onto thread or holder and
leave for thumb, K26.
Continue around on 48 sts
until work measures 9in from
cast-on edge or desired
length to top shaping.

Shape top

1st round *K2, K2 tog, K17,
sl 1, K1, psso, K1, rep from *
once more.
2nd round *K2, K2 tog,
K15, sl 1, K1, psso, K1, rep
from * once more.
Continue dec in this way on
every round until 4 sts rem.
Break yarn and draw through
rem sts and fasten off.

Thumb

Divide 19 sts from holder onto
3 needles. K 1 round.
2nd round K1, *K2 tog, K7,
rep from * once more. 17 sts.
Work for 2in without shaping.

Shape thumb top

1st round *K2, K2 tog, rep
from * to last st, K1.
2nd round *K1, K2 tog, rep
from * to last st, K1.
3rd round K1, *K2 tog, rep
from * to end. Break yarn and

draw through rem sts. Fasten
off.

Right mitten

Work as for left mitten, reversing position of thumb by working gusset after 26 sts instead
of 22 sts.

Finishing

Press mittens under a damp
cloth with a warm iron,
omitting ribbing.
Embroider back as in diagram.

Alternative knitted trim

Using No.3 needles, cast on
120 sts.
K 1 row. P 1 row. Bind off.
Allow strip to curl so cast-on
and bound-off edges touch.
Slip stitch together if preferred
to give a firm finish. Curl
strip to form a design.

Chapter 37

How to create your own designs

This chapter tells you in simple terms how to be your own designer. Once you have mastered one of the two possible techniques, you will be able to make patterns which are exactly what you want in style and fit. For both methods the first stages are the same. The yarn, stitch and gauge must all be chosen before you can begin. Whichever system you decide to try, don't be too ambitious to start with—progress gradually to more complicated ideas.

1. Graph paper planning method

The graph paper planning method, used by professional designers, involves planning on graph paper every stitch to be knitted—casting on and binding off, increasing, decreasing, and openings—and shows in diagram form what the written directions say in words. It is not worked to scale; one small square represents one stitch and each line of squares represents one row.

2. Paper pattern method

The paper pattern method involves making a paper shape from a garment which already exists in your wardrobe. You may prefer this method if you like to follow an existing outline.

Don't over-complicate what you are trying to do

Choosing the yarn (both methods)

Decide on a simple shape for a first attempt and then consider which yarn will be most suitable for the stitch you want to use. It may sound obvious, but don't choose a knitting yarn with a textured surface, such as bouclé or mohair, if you have already made up your mind to use a lace stitch. Alternatively, don't pick too fine a yarn if you want to make a bulky sports sweater. Once you have decided on the style, stitch and yarn, stick with it. At this stage it's very easy to become sidetracked by visions of all the beautiful garments that you can add to your wardrobe, but be content to work on one idea at a time. Don't try to combine too many ideas in one garment.

Don't just take any old yarn and start to knit

Gauge (both methods)

Make a sample square, using the stitch and the yarn you've chosen, so that you can find exactly how many stitches and rows there are to 1 inch. Make this test square at least 4 inches so that you can check the gauge for 1 inch over 4 inches. This way you stand less chance of being a half stitch off in your calculations.
Measure the square carefully with a ruler to see exactly how many stitches and rows there are to 1 inch. Write this down, because all your future work on this design must be based on this gauge.

Taking your measurements (both methods)

This is the moment to make a careful note of your own measurements, or those required for the garment.
Remember that in all garments an allowance is made for movement, which is called "ease." For a bust measurement the allowance is usually about 2 inches. A loose bulky jacket may have an "ease" of 4 inches added to the actual measurements.

Finding the right number of stitches to cast on (both methods)

A simple pullover in old shale stitch (see Knitting Know-how Chapter 20) is a good example to work from. On a sample using No. 3 needles and sports yarn, the gauge is 7 stitches and 9 rows to 1 inch.

If you are making this in the ordinary way, with back and front each being half of the work, then the number of stitches for the back will be half the bust measurement plus half the ease allowance, plus 2 stitches to allow for seaming. So, using the gauge given, for a 36in bust the sum will look like this: 18in at 7sts per in = 126 + 7 = 133 + 2 = 135.

Now it is essential to see if the stitch you have chosen will divide evenly into this total. You may have to decide whether you prefer to work with extra stitches or fewer stitches, altering the width slightly. In this case, old shale stitch requires a multiple of 11 + 2 edge stitches. The nearest to the required total of 135 is 134, and for a light pullover, one stitch less would be reasonable.

Having given the points which are common to both methods, it is now time to examine the differences.

Method 1 (graph paper planning)

The graph paper method is very much like making a map of what you are going to knit. Once you have calculated the number of stitches you are going to cast on, mark one square for each stitch along the first row of small squares. It is useful to develop your own code of marks, so that by glancing at the graph paper you can tell immediately whether the stitch is to be knitted or purled, decreased or bound off. For instance, a sloping line \ can be used to indicate a knit stitch and the reverse / for a purl stitch.

By now you have decided whether to have a hem or a ribbed edge and you know the number of rows to 1 inch. So, mark each line of small squares to represent one row until you have the correct number of squares marked to give you the required length of the side seam to the beginning of the armhole.

Continue working out each step—armhole shaping and depth, neck shaping and shoulder binding off—and mark out on the graph paper until you have completed the back and front.

Avoid circular yokes, seamless garments and any complicated decreasing and increasing. You will be able to work out more complicated designs when you have had experience.

Make sure each side of the garment is the same length

Method 2 (paper pattern)

Trace onto paper the exact shape of an existing garment, then simply knit each piece to the same shape. Before beginning to work, check carefully that the drawing of each piece is exact. If the shape is correct, the result will be much more satisfactory. Once you have begun to work, constantly check that your knitting is the same shape as the paper pattern. This is not always easy, as the unpressed knitting is, of course, not as flat as the paper pattern. However, if you are very careful to measure accurately, you will save yourself much disappointment and time spent in unraveling your work and re-knitting.

Don't try to combine too many ideas into one design

Pointers toward success

1. Choose a simple design to begin with. Don't put all your ideas into one design.
2. Choose the yarn and stitch carefully, so that both are suitable for the type of garment.
3. Make a large sample square before beginning the garment, using the yarn, needles and stitch you have chosen, so that you are certain about the number of stitches and rows to 1 inch.
4. Make a list of the required measurements for the garment you are going to make.
5. Decide which method you are going to use, and chart carefully or make the paper pattern with accuracy.
6. When making two similar parts, such as sleeves or fronts, use a row counter to be certain that they are exactly the same length—measuring is not sufficient.
7. The choice of materials is as much a part of designing as the actual working and finishing processes. Don't try to hurry any part or the result will suffer. The choice of trimmings, such as buttons or frog fastenings, is also important. Be sure that the color and size are correct for the type of design you want to make.

Collector's Piece

Painting with yarn

This beautiful sleeveless jacket is—believe it or not—hand knitted! Since it is the instinctive design of an experienced knitter, it is easily comparable to an original, one-of-a-kind painting: Reproductions are not available and, regrettably, explicit directions do not exist. For those who want to try to emulate it, the general technique is all that can be explained.

Every patch of color is knitted at random and every shape is different from the rest. Some patches are worked in stockinette stitch, others in seed stitch, broken rib or garter stitch. Even the yarns are mixed to include smooth and textured ones, with a few patches of mohair or angora.

The designer worked on the principle of first planning the outline shape of the garment. She next chose the colors and yarns and decided on the general outline of the pattern shapes—here they are irregular and angular, but they could be curved or geometric. Then, having cast on the number of stitches needed for the particular garment, the knitter made the hem in one color and then started working, say, 12 stitches of one color, 10 stitches of the next color in maybe a different wool, 15 stitches of the next and so on. The knitter sat surrounded by separate balls of the yarns in the colors selected—she didn't carry the strands across the inside of the work as in Fair Isle. If you look carefully, you will see that at least a dozen different balls of yarn were used across the back of this jerkin, but no one ball was worked twice in a single row. The knitter worked out the color and stitch patterns as she went along, being careful to follow the shaping. As one color was finished and the next introduced, the yarn was broken off.

The secret of the astonishingly tidy inside of the jerkin is that every tail was darned in meticulously along the color seamlines.

If you do try this method, keep in mind one vital point: Always use wools that knit up to the same gauge, otherwise your fabric will pucker. But if you can't resist including a yarn with a slightly different gauge, change onto a sock needle for the patch (as for cabling) while working this area so that you achieve the same number of stitches to the inch.

Baby bootees

Take your pick of these delightful baby bootees! The white moccasins, shown on the left, can be worn by both boys and girls, depending on the color of the lace trim. The slipper socks, shown center, are designed for a baby boy while the white lace bootees, shown on the extreme right, would be pretty for a baby girl.

Size
Length of foot, 4in.

Gauge
8sts and 10 rows to 1in over stockinette stitch worked on No.2 needles.

Materials
Bear Brand or Fleisher Ever Match Baby Zephyr
1 skein main color for each pair
1 skein contrast color for slipper socks
One pair No.2 needles
Two buttons for slipper socks
¾yd ribbon for moccasins and white lace boots
2yd lace for moccasins

Abbreviation
"y2rn" is the abbreviation for yarn twice around needle.

Slipper socks

Starting at upper edge with white, cast on 42sts.
Next row *K1, P1, rep from * to end.
Rep last row 3 times more.
Commence lace patt.
1st row K2, *P1, K4, P1, K2, rep from * to end.
2nd row P2, *K1, P4, K1,

P2, rep from * to end.
3rd row K2, *P1, K2 tog, y2rn, K2 tog tbl, P1, K2, rep from * to end.
4th row P2, *K1, P1, K first loop and then into back of 2nd loop, P1, K1, P2, rep from * to end.
Rep 1st-4th rows 7 times more. Break yarn.
With RS facing slip first 15sts on holder or spare needle.
Attach white to next st and work instep on center 12sts.
Work 17 rows keeping patt correct.
Next row K1, P2 tog, K1, P1, P2 tog, P1, K1, P2 tog, K1.
Break yarn.

Work foot
With contrast color, K 15sts from holder, pick up and K 15sts along side of instep, K 9sts from center, pick up and K 15sts along other side of instep, K rem 15sts (69sts).
K 15 rows.

Shape sole
1st row K6, K2 tog, K19, K2 tog, K11, K2 tog, K19, K2 tog, K6.
2nd, 4th, 6th, 8th and 10th rows K.
3rd row K5, K2 tog, K19, K2 tog, K9, K2 tog, K19, K2 tog, K5.
5th row K4, K2 tog, K19, K2 tog, K7, K2 tog, K19, K2 tog, K4.
7th row K3, K2 tog, K19, K2 tog, K5, K2 tog, K19, K2 tog, K3.
9th row K2, K2 tog, K19, K2 tog, K3, K2 tog, K19, K2 tog, K2.
11th row K1, K2 tog, K19,

K2 tog, K1, K2 tog, K19, K2 tog, K1.
12th row K2 tog, K19, K3 tog, K19, K2 tog. Bind off.

Strap

With contrast color, cast on 45sts.
K 2 rows.
3rd row K2, bind off 2sts, K to end.
4th row K to last 2sts, cast on 2sts, K2.
K 2 rows. Bind off.

Finishing

Join sole and back seams. Sew strap to center back. Sew button on strap end.

Moccasins

Instep
Cast on 11sts.
1st row K.
2nd row K1, *ytf, K2 tog, rep from * to end.
Rep 2nd row 10 times more. Break yarn and slip sts on holder.
Using 2 needle method, cast on 17sts.
Using same needle on which there are 17sts, pick up and K 13sts along side of instep, across center sts K2 tog, K7, K2 tog, pick up and K 13sts along other side of instep, turn and cast on 17sts (69sts).
1st row K1, *P1, K1, rep from * to end.
2nd row Sl 1, *K into st below next st (called K1d), P1, rep from * to end.
3rd row Sl 1, *P1, K1d, rep from * to last 2sts, P1, K1.
Rep 2nd and 3rd rows 5 times more.

Shape sole
Complete as given for slipper socks. Seam sole and back.

Cuff

With RS facing, pick up and K 35sts around ankle.
K 3 rows.
Next row K1, *ytf, K2 tog, rep from * to end.

K 6 rows.
Next row K2, (pick up and K 1, K4) 3 times, K7, (K4, pick up and K1) 3 times, K2 (41sts).
Commence lace patt.
1st row K1, *ytf, K2 tog, rep from * to end.
Rep 1st row 8 times more.
Bind off.

Finishing

Sew narrow lace around cuff and instep.
Run ribbon through eyelet for ties.

White lace bootees

Cast on 41sts. K 4 rows.
Commence lace patt.
1st row K1, *K1, ytf, K2 tog, rep from * to last st, K1.
2nd row P1, *P1, yrn, P2 tog, rep from * to last st, P1.
Rep 1st and 2nd rows 5 times more, then 1st row once.
K1 row.
Eyelet row
Next row K5, *ytf, K2 tog, K4, rep from * to end.
K1 row.
Rep 1st and 2nd patt rows once.

Divide for instep
1st row K16, *K1, ytf, K2 tog, rep from * twice, K1, turn.
Work 16 rows more in patt on center 11sts.
Next row P2 tog, P7, P2 tog. Break yarn.
With RS facing and 15 sts on needle, attach yarn at beg of instep, pick up and K 15sts along side of instep, K 9sts from center front, pick up and K 15sts along other side of instep, K 15sts from needle. K1 row across all sts (69sts). P1 row.
K1 row.
Rep last 3 rows twice more.
K2 rows.

Shape sole
As given for slipper socks.

Finishing

Sew sole and back seam and thread ribbon through eyelet row.

Christening robe in lace stitch

This lovely christening robe, designed in a delicate lace stitch separated by stockinette stitch and lace ladders, has the traditional fragile appearance of handmade lace. Trimmed or plain, it's so beautiful that you'll certainly keep it for years and years.

Size

Directions are for size birth to 6 months.
Length, 27in.
Sleeve seam, 5½in.

Gauge

9sts and 12 rows to 1in over stockinette stitch worked on No.1 needles.

Materials

Bear Brand or Fleisher or Botany Baby Zephyr
Nine 1oz skeins
One pair of No.1 needles
One pair of No.2 needles
¾yd narrow ribbon
17yd narrow lace, optional
Five small buttons

Note

A longer skirt may be made by working more patts before first decrease row. One ounce of yarn will work approximately 3¾in of lace patt. The additional trimming of lace may be omitted if a more simple garment is desired.

Skirt

Using No.2 needles, cast on 316sts.

K 4 rows.
Commence patt.
1st row *K2, ytf, K2 tog, K10, (ytf, sl 1, K2 tog, psso, ytf, K5) 6 times, ytf, sl 1, K2 tog, psso, ytf, K11, ytf, K2 tog, K1, rep from * 3 times more.
2nd row *K2, ytf, K2 tog, P71, K1, ytf, K2 tog, K1, rep from * 3 times more.
3rd row As 1st.
4th row As 2nd.
5th row *K2, ytf, K2 tog, K10, (K3, ytf, sl 1, K1, psso, K1, K2 tog, ytf) 6 times, K14, ytf, K2 tog, K1, rep from * 3 times more.
6th row As 2nd.
7th row *K2, ytf, K2 tog, K10, (ytf, sl 1, K2 tog, psso, ytf, K1) 12 times, ytf, sl 1, K2 tog, psso, ytf, K11, ytf, K2 tog, K1, rep from * 3 times more.
8th row As 2nd.
Rep 1st-8th rows 4 times more.
Work 1st dec row.
Next row *K2, ytf, K2 tog, K6, K2 tog, K2, (ytf, sl 1, K2 tog, psso, ytf, K5) 6 times, ytf, sl 1, K2 tog, psso, ytf, K2, K2 tog tbl, K7, ytf, K2 tog, K1, rep from * 3 times more.
Work 2nd-8th rows once, then 1st-8th rows 4 times more, noting that there is one st less on each st st panel (2sts less on WS rows between lace ladders).
Continue dec one st in this way on next and every 40th row until 3 dec rows have been worked (292sts).
Work 31 rows then dec on next row (284 sts).
Work 23 rows then dec on next row (276sts).
Work 23 rows then dec on

next row (268sts).
Work 14 rows ending with RS row.
Next row *K2, ytf, K2 tog, P3 tog, (P5, P3 tog) 7 times, K1, ytf, K2 tog, K1, rep from * to end.
Next row K2, ytf, K2 tog, K95, ytf, K2 tog, K3, ytf, K2 tog, K95, ytf, K2 tog, K1.
Next row K2, ytf, (K2 tog) twice, *ytf, K2 tog, rep from * 45 times more, K1, ytf, K2 tog, K3, ytf, (K2 tog) twice, *ytf, K2 tog, rep from * 45 times more, K1, ytf, K2 tog, K1.
Change to No.1 needles for yoke.
1st row Cast on 3sts, K5, ytf, K2 tog, K94, ytf, K2 tog, K3, ytf, K2 tog, K94, ytf, K2 tog, K1.
2nd row Cast on 3sts, K5, ytf, K2 tog, P93, K1, ytf, K2 tog, K3, ytf, K2 tog, P93, K1, ytf, K2 tog, K4.
3rd row (1st buttonhole) K5, ytf, K2 tog, K73, (ytf, K2 tog, K5) 3 times, ytf, K2 tog, K3, (ytf, K2 tog, K5) 3 times, ytf, K2 tog, K73, ytf, (K2 tog) twice, ytf, K2.
4th row K5, ytf, K2 tog, P72, (K1, ytf, K2 tog, P4) 3 times, K1, ytf, K2 tog, K3, ytf, K2 tog, (P4, K1, ytf, K2 tog) 3 times, P72, K1, ytf, K2 tog, K4.
5th row K5, ytf, K2 tog, K73, (ytf, K2 tog, K5) 3 times, ytf, K2 tog, K3, (ytf, K2 tog, K5) 3 times, ytf, K2 tog, K73, ytf, K2 tog, K4.

6th row As 4th.
Rep 5th and 6th rows 5 times more.

Divide for armholes

1st row Patt 48sts, bind off 10sts, patt to last 58sts, bind off 10sts, patt to last 4sts, K2 tog, ytf, K2.
Work on last group of sts for right back.
Work 1 row.
Dec one st at armhole edge of next 6 rows, then every RS row until 39sts rem.
Work 1 row.
Work 26 rows without shaping, working buttonhole on 1st and 15th rows.

Shape shoulder

1st row Bind off 7sts, patt to end.
2nd row Patt to end.
3rd row Bind off 6sts, patt to last 4sts, K2 tog, ytf, K2.
4th row Patt to end.
5th row Bind off 6sts, patt to end.
Bind off rem sts.
With WS of work facing, attach yarn to center 92sts and work to end. Complete front on these sts. Keeping patt correct, dec one st at each end of next 6 rows, then next 3 RS rows.
Work 13 rows without shaping.

Divide for neck

1st row Patt 29sts, bind off 16sts, patt 29 sts.
Work right shoulder on these sts.
**Dec at neck edge on next 7 rows, then every RS row until 19sts rem.
Work until armhole measures

Close-up of front panel stitch detail of the christening robe

same as right back to shoulder, ending at armhole edge.
Bind off 7sts at beg of next row, then bind off 6sts every other row twice. **
With WS of work facing, attach yarn to rem sts and work from ** to **.
With WS of work facing, attach yarn to last group of sts and complete as given for right back, omitting buttonholes.

Sleeves

Using No.1 needles, cast on 52 sts. K2 rows.
Continue in patt.
1st row K16, ytf, K2 tog, K5, ytf, K2 tog, K3, ytf, K2 tog, K5, ytf, K2 tog, K15.
2nd row P15, K1, ytf, K2 tog, P4, K1, ytf, K2 tog, K3, ytf, K2 tog, P4, K1, ytf, K2 tog, P15.
Keeping patt correct, inc one st at each end of next and every 6th row until there are 70sts. Continue without shaping until work measures 5½in, ending with a WS row.
Shape cap
Bind off 6sts at beg of next 2 rows.
Dec one st at each end of next and every RS row until 34sts rem.
Dec one st at each end of every row until 16sts rem.
Bind off rem sts.

Finishing

Press all pieces under a damp cloth with a warm iron. Sew seam of skirt to 3in below waistline.
Join shoulder seams.
Neckband Using No.1 needles, pick up and K 109sts evenly around neck edge. K3 rows. Bind off.
Sew sleeve seams. Sew in sleeves. Edge panels, wrists, neck and lower edge with lace if desired.
Sew on buttons to correspond with buttonholes.
Run ribbon through eyelet slotting and sew ends at sides of back opening and center front panel.

Shetland lace baby shawl

Because this shawl has few seams, the amount of finishing is minimal.

Size
About 60in square.

Gauge
About 4 sts and 8 rows to 1in over garter st worked on No.7 needles

---

Materials
Reynolds Angelina
9 skeins
One pair No.7 needles

Outer border

Using No.7 needles, cast on 8 sts.
1st row K2, (ytf, K2 tog) 3 times.
2nd and every other row K.
3rd row K2, ytf, K2 tog, ytf, K2, ytf, K2 tog.
5th row K2, ytf, K2 tog, ytf, K3, ytf, K2 tog.
7th row K2, ytf, K2 tog, ytf, K1, ytf, K2 tog, K1, ytf, K2 tog.
9th row K2, ytf, K2 tog, ytf, K3, (ytf, K2 tog) twice.
11th row K1, (K2 tog, ytf) twice, K3 tog, ytf, K2, ytf, K2 tog.
13th row K1, (K2 tog, ytf) twice, K2 tog, K2, ytf, K2 tog.
15th row K1, (K2 tog, ytf) twice, K2 tog, K1, ytf, K2 tog.
17th row K1, (K2 tog, ytf) 3 times, K2 tog.
18th row K.
Rep 1st—18th rows 21 times more. Bind off.

Main border

Pick up and K181 sts along straight edge of border.
1st row K.
2nd row K2, *K2 tog, ytf, K4, rep from * to last 5 sts, K2 tog, ytf, K3.
3rd and every other row K.
4th row K1, *K2 tog, ytf, K1, ytf, K2 tog, K1, rep from * to end.
6th row K2 tog, ytf, *K3, ytf, K3 tog, ytf, rep from * to last 5 sts, K3, ytf, K2 tog.
8th row K1, *ytf, K2 tog, ytf, K3 tog, ytf, K1, rep from * to end.
10th row K2, *ytf, K3 tog, ytf, K3, rep from * to last 5 sts, ytf, K3 tog, ytf, K2.
12th row K1, K2 tog, ytf, (K1, ytf, K2 tog, ytf, K3 tog, ytf) twice, K7, *(ytf, K2 tog, ytf, K3 tog, ytf, K1) 3 times, K6, rep from * to last 15 sts, (ytf, K2 tog, ytf, K3 tog, ytf, K1) twice, ytf, K2 tog, K1.
14th row K2 tog, ytf, (K3, ytf, K3 tog, ytf) twice, *K2, K2 tog, ytf, K1, ytf, K2 tog, K2, (ytf, K3 tog, ytf, K3) twice, ytf, K3 tog, ytf, rep from * to last 23 sts, K2, K2 tog, ytf, K1, ytf, K2 tog, K2, (ytf, K3 tog, ytf, K3) twice, ytf, K2 tog.
16th row K1, *(ytf, K2 tog, ytf, K3 tog, ytf, K1) twice, K2, K2 tog, ytf, K3, ytf, K2, tog, K3, rep from * to last 12 sts, (ytf, K2 tog, ytf, K3 tog, ytf, K1) twice.
18th row K2, *(ytf, K3 tog, ytf, K3) twice, (K2 tog, ytf) twice, K1, (ytf, K2 tog) twice, K3, rep from * to last 11 sts, ytf, K3 tog, ytf, K3, ytf, K3 tog, ytf, K2.
20th row K1, K2 tog, ytf, K1, *ytf, K2 tog, ytf, K3 tog, ytf, K4, (K2 tog, ytf) twice, K3, (ytf, K2 tog) twice, K4, rep from * to last 9 sts, ytf, K2 tog, ytf, K3 tog, ytf, K1, ytf, K2 tog, K1.
22nd row K2 tog, ytf, *K3, ytf, K3 tog, ytf, K4, (K2 tog, ytf) 3 times, K1, (ytf, K2 tog) 3 times, K1, rep from * to last 11 sts, K3, ytf, K3 tog, ytf, K3, ytf, K2 tog.
24th row K1, ytf, K2 tog, ytf, K3 tog, ytf, K5 (K2 tog, ytf) 3 times, *K3, (ytf, K2 tog) 3 times, K3, K2 tog, ytf, K4 (K2 tog, ytf) 3 times, rep from * to last 20 sts, K3, (ytf, K2 tog) 3 times, K5, ytf, K2 tog, ytf, K3 tog, ytf, K1.
26th row K2, ytf, K3 tog, ytf, K5, (K2 tog, ytf) 4 times, K1, (ytf, K2 tog) 4 times, *K7, (K2 tog, ytf) 4 times, K1, (ytf, K2 tog) 4 times, rep from * to last 10 sts, K5, ytf, K3 tog, ytf, K2.
28th row K1, K2 tog, ytf, K6, (K2 tog, ytf) 4 times, K3, (ytf, K2 tog) 4 times, *K1, K2 tog, ytf, K2, (K2 tog, ytf) 4 times, K3, (ytf, K2 tog) 4 times, rep from * to last 9 sts, K6, ytf, K2 tog, K1.
30th row K2 tog, ytf, K6, *(K2 tog, ytf) 5 times, K1, (ytf, K2 tog) 5 times, K3, rep from * to last 5 sts, K3, ytf, K2 tog.
32nd row K7, *(K2 tog, ytf) 5 times, K3, (ytf, K2 tog) 5 times, K1, rep from * to last 6 sts, K6.
34th row K1, K2 tog, K5, work as 30th row from * to last 5 sts, K2, K2 tog, K1. (179 sts.)
36th row K1, K2 tog, K5, *(K2 tog, ytf) 4 times, K3, (ytf, K2 tog) 4 times, K5, rep from * to last 3 sts, K2 tog, K1. (177 sts.)
38th row K1, K2 tog, K5, *(K2 tog, ytf) 4 times, K1, (ytf, K2 tog) 4 times, K1, K2 tog, ytf, K1, ytf, K2 tog, K1, rep from * to last 25 sts, (K2 tog, ytf) 4 times, K1, (ytf, K2 tog) 4 times, K5, K2 tog, K1. (175 sts.)
40th row K1, K2 tog, K5, *(K2 tog, ytf) 3 times, K3, (ytf, K2 tog) 3 times, K1, K2 tog, ytf, K3, ytf, K2 tog, K1, rep from * to last 23 sts, (K2 tog, ytf) 3 times, K3, (ytf, K2 tog) 3 times, K5, K2 tog, K1. (173 sts.)
42nd row K1, K2 tog, K5, *(K2 tog, ytf) 3 times, K1, (ytf, K2 tog) 3 times, K1, (K2 tog, ytf) twice, K1, (ytf, K2 tog) twice, K1, rep from * to last 21 sts, (K2 tog, ytf) 3 times, K1, (ytf, K2 tog) 3 times, K5, K2 tog, K1. (171 sts.)
44th row K1, K2 tog, K5, *(K2 tog, ytf) twice, K3, (ytf, K2 tog) twice, K1, rep from * to last 7 sts, K4, K2 tog, K1.
46th row K1, K2 tog, K5, *(K2 tog, ytf) twice, K1, (ytf, K2 tog) twice, K1, (K2 tog, ytf) 3 times, K1, (ytf, K2 tog) 3 times, K1, rep from * to last 17 sts, (K2 tog, ytf) twice, K1, (ytf, K2 tog) twice, K5, K2 tog, K1.
48th row K1, K2 tog, K5, *K2 tog, ytf, K3, ytf, K2 tog, K1, (K2 tog, ytf) 3 times, K3, (ytf, K2 tog) 3 times, K1, rep from * to last 15 sts, K2 tog, ytf, K3, ytf, K2 tog, K5, K2 tog, K1.
50th row K1, K2 tog, K5, *K2 tog, ytf, K1, ytf, K2 tog, K1, (K2 tog, ytf) 4 times, K1, (ytf, K2 tog) 4 times, K1, rep from * to last 13 sts, K2 tog, ytf, K1, ytf, K2 tog, K5, K2 tog, K1.
52nd row K1, K2 tog, K6, *ytf, K2 tog, K1, (K2 tog, ytf) 4 times, K3, (ytf, K2 tog) 4 times, K2, rep from * to last 34 sts, ytf, K2 tog, K1, (K2 tog, ytf) 4 times, K3, (ytf, K2 tog) 4 times, K1, K2 tog, ytf, K6, K2 tog, K1.
54th row K1, K2 tog, K7, *(K2 tog, ytf) 5 times, K1, (ytf, K2 tog) 5 times, K3, rep from * to last 7 sts, K4, K2 tog, K1. (159 sts.)
56th row K1, K2 tog, K5, *(K2 tog, ytf) 5 times, K3,

(ytf, K2 tog) 5 times, K1, rep from * to last 7 sts, K4, K2 tog, K1.

58th row K1, K2 tog, K5, *(K2 tog, ytf) 5 times, K1, (ytf, K2 tog) 5 times, K3, rep from * to last 5 sts, K2, K2 tog, K1.

60th row K1, K2 tog, K5, *(K2 tog, ytf) 4 times, K3, (ytf, K2 tog) 4 times, K2, ytf, K2 tog, K1, rep from * to last 27 sts, (K2 tog, ytf) 4 times, K3, (ytf, K2 tog) 4 times, K5, K2 tog, K1.

62nd row K1, K2 tog, K5, *(K2 tog, ytf) 4 times, K1, (ytf, K2 tog) 4 times, K2, ytf, K3 tog, ytf, K2, rep from * to last 25 sts, (K2 tog, ytf) 4 times, K1, (ytf, K2 tog) 4 times, K5, K2 tog, K1.

64th row K1, K2 tog, K5, *(K2 tog, ytf) 3 times, K3, (ytf, K2 tog) 3 times, K4, ytf, K2 tog, K3, rep from * to last 23 sts, (K2 tog, ytf) 3 times, K3, (ytf, K2 tog) 3 times, K5, K2 tog, K1.

66th row K1, K2 tog, K5, *(K2 tog, ytf) 3 times, K1, (ytf, K2 tog) 3 times, K11, rep from * to last 21 sts, (K2 tog, ytf) 3 times, K1, (ytf, K2 tog) 3 times, K5, K2 tog, K1. (147 sts.)

68th row K1, K2 tog, K5, *(K2 tog, ytf) twice, K3, (ytf, K2 tog) twice, K6, ytf, K2 tog, K5, rep from * to last 19 sts, (K2 tog, ytf) twice, K3, (ytf, K2 tog) twice, K5, K2 tog, K1.

70th row K1, K2 tog, K5, *(K2 tog, ytf) twice, K1, (ytf, K2 tog) twice, K5, K2 tog, ytf, K1, ytf, K2 tog, K5, rep from * to last 17 sts, (K2 tog, ytf) twice, K1, (ytf, K2 tog) twice, K5, K2 tog, K1.

72nd row K1, K2 tog, K5, *K2 tog, ytf, K3, ytf, K2 tog, K5, rep from * to last 3 sts, K2 tog, K1.

74th row K1, K2 tog, K5, *K2 tog, ytf, K1, ytf, K2 tog, K4, K2 tog, ytf, K1, ytf, K2 tog, ytf, K3 tog, ytf, K1, ytf, K2 tog, K4, rep from * to last 13 sts, K2 tog, ytf, K1, ytf, K2 tog, K5, K2 tog, K1.

76th row K1, K2 tog, K5,

*K2 tog, ytf, K5, K2 tog, ytf, K3, ytf, K3 tog, ytf, K3, ytf, K2 tog, K4, rep from * to last 11 sts, K2 tog, ytf, K6, K2 tog, K1.

78th row K1, K2 tog, K9, *K2 tog, ytf, (K1, ytf, K2 tog, ytf, K3 tog, ytf) twice, K1, ytf, K2 tog, K7, rep from * to last 5 sts, K2, K2 tog, K1.

80th row K1, K2 tog, K7, *K2 tog, ytf, (K3, ytf, K3 tog, ytf) twice, K3, ytf, K2 tog, K5, rep from * to last 5 sts, K2, K2 tog, K1.

82nd row K1, K2 tog, K4, *K2 tog, ytf, (K1, ytf, K2 tog, ytf, K3 tog, ytf) 3 times, K1, ytf, K2 tog, K1, rep from * to last 6 sts, K3, K2 tog, K1.

84th row K1, K2 tog, K2, K2 tog, *ytf, K3, ytf, K3 tog, rep from * to last 10 sts, ytf, K3, ytf, K2 tog, K2, K2 tog, K1. (129 sts.)

86th row K1, K2 tog, K2,

*ytf, K2 tog, ytf, K3 tog, ytf, K1, rep from * to last 4 sts, K1, K2 tog, K1.

88th row K1, K2 tog, K2, *ytf, K3 tog, ytf, K3, rep from * to last 8 sts, ytf, K3 tog, ytf, K2, K2 tog, K1.

90th row K5, *ytf, K2 tog, K4, rep from * to last 6sts, ytf, K2 tog, K4. (125 sts.)

91st row K.
Bind off loosely.
Work one more outer border and main border in the same way.
Make a third section in the same way, either binding off or leaving the sts on a holder to be woven to last row of center. Make a fourth section but do not bind off, continuing on these 125 sts for center.

Center

1st-8th rows K.

9th row K8, *ytf, K2 tog, K4, rep from * to last 3 sts,

K3.

10th and every other row K.

11th row K7, *ytf, K3 tog, ytf, K3, rep from * to last 4 sts, K4.

13th row As 9th.

15th row K.

17th row K8, ytf, K2 tog, K to last 9 sts, ytf, K2 tog, K7.

19th row K7, ytf, K3 tog, ytf, K to last 10 sts, ytf, K3 tog, ytf, K7.

21st row As 17th.

23rd row K.

Rep last 8 rows 27 times more, then rep 9th-14th rows once.
K8 rows more.
Bind off loosely or weave to last border section.

Finishing

Slip stitch border sections to center sides. Slip stitch corners together. Roll in a damp towel for 2 hours. Pin to measurement with rust-proof pins; allow to dry.

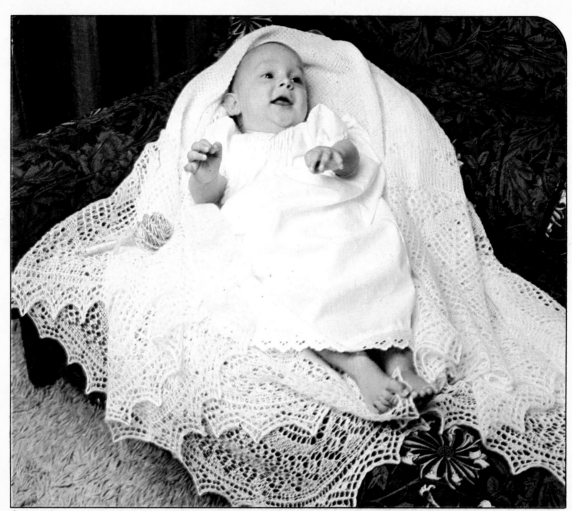
▲ *A perfect example of openwork stitches and fine yarn combining to make a soft and warm baby shawl*

Two~way baby sacque

Basic Wardrobe Knitting

Make an enchanting jacket for baby. This one has an unusual two-color band of pattern and lacy eyelets. You can either leave these open or thread with satin ribbon as an extra trimming, using the main color or the contrast.

Sizes
Directions are for 18in chest. The figures in brackets [] refer to the 20in size.
Sleeve seam, 5[5¾]in.
Center back length, 9[11]in.

Gauge
7 sts and 9 rows to 1in over stockinette stitch worked on No.3 needles.

Materials
Bernat Nylo Sports
2[3] 2oz balls of main color A
One ball of contrast B
One pair No.3 needles
One large stitch holder
Four small buttons
Narrow ribbon, if desired
Note K1y2rn is the abbreviation for insert needle as if to knit stitch, put yarn twice around needle, lift stitch over both loops in usual way.

Sleeves

Using No.3 needles and A, cast on 29[33] sts.
K 1 row.
Next row K1, *ytf, K2 tog, rep from * to end.
K 2 rows.
Next row K1[3], *inc, K2[1], rep from * to last 1[2] sts, inc[K2]. 39[47] sts.
Continue in 2-color pattern.
1st row With A, K3, *K1y2rn, K3, rep from * to end.
2nd row With B, K3, *keeping yarn at back of work, sl 1P dropping extra loop, K3, rep from * to end.
3rd row With B, K1, K1y2rn, K1, *ytf, sl 1P, ytb, K1, K1y2rn, K1, rep from * to end.
4th row With A, keeping yarn at back of work, K1, sl 1P, K1, *K2, sl 1P, K1, rep from * to end.
5th row With A, K1, ytf, sl 1P, ytb, *K1, K1y2rn, K1, ytf, sl 1P, ytb, rep from * to last st, K1.
Rep 2nd-5th rows once more, then 2nd-4th rows once.
Continue with A only.
Next row K1, ytf, sl 1P, ytb, K1, *K2, ytf, sl 1P, ytb, K1, rep from * to end.
K 2 rows.
Next row K1, ytf, K1, *ytf, K2 tog, rep from * to last st, ytf, K1. 41[49] sts.
K 1 row.
1st patt row P1, *K1, P1, rep from * to end.
2nd patt row K.
Rep last 2 rows until sleeve measures 5[5¾]in, ending with a 2nd patt row.

Shape cap
Keeping patt correct throughout, bind off 3[4] sts at beg of next 2 rows.
Dec one st at each end of next 4[5] RS rows. 27[31] sts.
Work 1 row.
Slip sts on holder until required.
Work the second sleeve in the same way as the first.

Skirt

Using No.3 needles and A, cast on 171[187] sts.
K 1 row.
Next row K6, *ytf, K2 tog, rep from * to last 5 sts, K5.
K 2 rows.
Next row K20, M1K, K to last 20 sts, M1K, K20. 173[189] sts.
Continue in 2-color pattern.
1st row With A, K8, *K1y2rn, K3, rep from * to last 5 sts, K5.
2nd row K5 A, join in B, K3, *sl 1P, K3, rep from * to last 5 sts, join in length of A to work garter st border, K5 A. On patt rows when B is used, twist A and B around each other when changing colors to avoid a gap.
3rd row K5 A, with B, K1, K1y2rn, K1, *ytf, sl 1P, ytb, K1, K1y2rn, K1, rep from * to last 5 sts, K5 A.
4th row With A, K6, sl 1P, K1, *K2, sl 1P, K1, rep from * to last 5 sts, K5.
5th row With A, K6, ytf, sl 1P, ytb, K1, *K1y2rn, K1, ytf, sl 1P, ytb, K1, rep from * to last 5 sts, K5.
Rep 2nd-5th rows once, then 2nd-4th rows once.
Next row With A, K6, ytf, sl 1P, ytb, *K3, ytf, sl 1P, ytb, rep from * to last 6 sts, K6.
Continue with A only.
K 2 rows.
Next row K5, ytf, K1, *ytf, K2 tog, rep from * to last 5 sts, ytf, K5. 175[191] sts. K 1 row.
Next row K5, P1, *K1, P1, rep from * to last 5 sts, K5.
Next row K.
Rep last 2 rows until work measures 5¾[6¾]in from cast-on edge.

Next row K2, ytf, K2 tog, K1, P1, *K1, P1, rep from * to last 5 sts, K5.
Next row K.

Next row K5 patt 39[42], bind off 6[8] sts, patt 74[80], bind off 6[8] sts, patt 38[41], K5.
Work on last set of sts for left

front.
Keeping garter st edge and patt correct, dec one st at armhole edge on next 4[5] RS rows.
Next row K6[8], *K2 tog, K2, rep from * to last 2 sts, K2 tog. 31[33] sts.
Slip sts on holder until required. With WS of work facing, attach yarn to center group of sts for back.
Keeping patt correct, dec one st at each end of next 4[5] RS rows.
Next row K2 tog [K0], *K3, K2 tog, rep from * to last 0[1] st, [K1]. 53[57] sts.
Slip rem sts on holder until required.
With WS of work facing, attach yarn to rem sts for right front.
Keeping patt and garter st edge correct, dec one st at armhole edge on next 4[5] RS rows.
Next row K2 tog, *K2, K2 tog, rep from * to last 6[8] sts, K6[8]. 31[33] sts.

Yoke

1st row With A, K across 31[33] sts from right front holder, K27[31] sts from 1st sleeve, 53[57] from back holder, 27[31] from 2nd sleeve and 31[33] sts from left front. 169[185] sts.
2nd row K5, ytf, K3 tog, ytf, *K2 tog, ytf, rep from * to last 5 sts, K5.
3rd row K2, ytf, K2 tog, K to end.
4th row K.
5th row K6[11], *K2 tog, K5, rep from * to last 9[13] sts, K3 tog [K2 tog], K6[11]. 145[161] sts.
6th row K.
7th row K5, *K3, K1y2rn, rep from * to last 8 sts, K8.
Work as given for 2-color patt at lower edge of coat, working from 2nd-5th rows once, then 2nd-4th rows once.
Next row K6[10], *ytf, sl 1P, ytb, K3, rep from * to last 7[11] sts, ytf, sl 1P, ytb, K6[10].
Next row K5[9], *K2 tog, K5, rep from * to last 7[12] sts, K2 tog, K5[10]. 125[140] sts.
K 1 row.
Next row K2, ytf, K2 tog, K to end.

114

▲ *Jacket in white and green*

Top right: detail of the jacket

Jacket in yellow and white ▶

Next row K5, K3 tog [K2 tog], *ytf, K2 tog, rep from * to last 5 sts, K5. 123[139] sts.
K 2 rows.

Next row K8[10], K2 tog, *K6[7], K2 tog, rep from * to last 9[10] sts, K9[10]. 109[125] sts.

Next row K8, *Kly2rn, K3, rep from * to last 5 sts, K5.
Work 2-color patt as before by rep 2nd-5th rows as for skirt, then 2nd-4th rows once.

Next row K6, *ytf, sl 1P, ytb, K3, rep from * to last 7sts, ytf, sl 1P, ytb, K6.

Next row K2, ytf, K2 tog, K1, *K1, K2 tog, rep from * to last 5[6] sts, K5[6]. 76[87] sts.
K 1 row.

Next row K7[5], *ytf, K2 tog, rep from * to last 5[6] sts, ytf, K5[6].
K 1 row. Bind off.

Finishing

Join sleeve and raglan seams. Sew on buttons to correspond with buttonholes. Leave eyelets as lace pattern or thread with narrow ribbon, sewing ends to wrong side.

Chevron stripes for a little girl

The cleverly striped chevron patterned skirt and neat stockinette stitch bodice make this delightful elfin dress ideal party wear for little girls up to four years old. The full skirt is shaped at the waist and the chevron pattern gives a scalloped edge to the hemline. And of course, color is vital!

Sizes
Directions are for 20in chest. The figures in brackets [] refer to the 22 and 24in sizes, respectively.
Length to shoulder, 13½[15: 16½]in.
Sleeve seam, 1½[2:2½]in.

Gauge
7 sts and 9 rows to 1in over stockinette stitch worked on No.3 needles.

Materials
Unger English Crepe
3[3:4] balls in main color A
2[2:2] balls in contrast B
2[2:2] balls in contrast C
1[1:1] ball in contrast D
One pair No.2 needles
One pair No.3 needles
Three small buttons

Front

Using No.3 needles and D, cast on 140[154:168] sts.
K 2 rows.
Commence patt.
1st row *K into front then into back of next st, K7[8:9], sl 1, K1, psso, K2 tog, K7[8:9], K into front then into back of next st, rep from * to end.
2nd row P.
116

Break off D.
These 2 rows form patt and are rep throughout skirt.
Continue in patt, working in stripes as follows:
14[16:18] rows C, 14[16:18] rows B, 14[16:18] rows A, 2[2:2] rows D, 8[10:12] rows C, 8[10:12] rows B and 2[2:2] rows A.
Continue with A only.
1st and 3rd sizes
Next row *K2 tog, rep from * to end. 70[84] sts.
2nd size
Next row K1, *K2 tog, rep from * to last st, K1. 78 sts.
Beg with a P row, work 3 rows st st.

Shape raglan armholes
Bind off 1[2:3] sts at beg of next 2 rows.
Next row K1, sl 1, K1, psso, K to last 3 sts, K2 tog, K1.
Next row K1, P to last st, K1.**
Rep last 2 rows until 48 sts rem, ending with a WS row.

Shape neck
Next row K1, sl 1, K1, psso, K14 sts, turn.
Next row P to last st, K1.
Next row K1, sl 1, K1, psso, K to last 3 sts, K2 tog, K1.
Next row P to last st, K1.
Rep last 2 rows until all sts are worked off.
With RS of work facing, sl center 14 sts onto a holder, attach A to rem sts and complete to match first side, reversing shaping.

Back

Work as given for front to **
Rep last 2 rows until 60 sts rem, ending with a WS row.

Divide for back opening
Next row K1, sl 1, K1, psso, K29 sts, turn.
Next row K4, P to last st, K1.
Next row K1, sl 1, K1, psso, K to end.
Next row K4, P to last st, K1.
Next row (make buttonhole) K1, sl 1, K1, psso, K to last 3 sts, ytf, K2 tog, K1.
Continue to shape raglan and work 4 sts in garter st at center edge until 17 sts rem, working 2nd buttonhole as before on 14th row from previous buttonhole. Slip 17 sts on holder for back neck.
With RS facing, attach yarn to rem sts, cast on 4 sts, K to last 3 sts, K2 tog, K1.
Complete to match first side, reversing shaping, keeping 4 sts in garter st at center edge and omitting buttonholes.

Sleeves

Using No.2 needles and A, cast on 42[48:52] sts.
Work 6 rows K1, P1 rib.
Change to No.3 needles.
Beg with a K row, continue in st st, inc one st at each end of 3rd and every following 4th row until there are 46[54:60] sts.
Continue without shaping until sleeve measures 1½[2:2½] in from beg, ending with a WS row.

Shape raglan cap
Bind off 1[2:3] sts at beg of next 2 rows.
Next row K1, sl 1, K1, psso, K to last 3 sts, K2 tog, K1.

Next row K1, P to last st, K1.
Rep last 2 rows until 6 sts rem.
Slip sts on holder.

Neckband

Join raglan seams.
Using No.2 needles and A, with RS facing, K across 17 sts on left back neck holder, K across 6 sts of left sleeve top, pick up and K16[18:20] sts down left front, K across 14 sts on holder at center front, pick up and K16[18:20] sts up right front, K across 6 sts of right sleeve top and K across 17 sts of right back neck. 92[96:100] sts.
1st row K4, *K1, P1, rep from * to last 4 sts, K4.
Rep last row twice more.
4th row (make buttonhole) K4, *K1, P1, rep from * to last 4 sts, K1, ytf, K2 tog, K1.
5th row As 1st.
6th row Bind off 4 sts, rib to last 4 sts, K4.
7th row Bind off 4 sts, rib to end.
Work 4 more rows in K1, P1 rib.
Bind off loosely in rib.

Finishing

Press each piece on wrong side under a damp cloth with a warm iron.
Join side and sleeve seams.
Stitch underflap neatly in position at bottom of back opening.
Fold neckband in half to WS and sl st.
Sew on buttons. Press seams.

▼*Pattern detail*   *Bright colors can look so pretty on little girls* ►

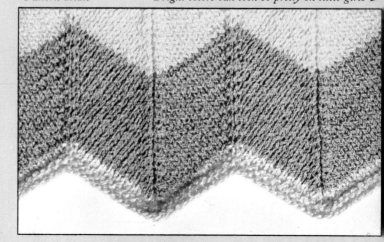

Drummer boy coat in fabric stitch

Basic Wardrobe Knitting

These delightful little coats with their fresh, simple lines are worked in a firm fabric stitch. The double-breasted front fastening is worked separately and can be adapted for either a boy or a girl. Contrast piping is made by working the invisible casting on method. Shoulder tabs and a back half-belt give a crisp, military air.

Sizes

Directions are for 20in chest. Length down center back, 16¼ [17¾:19¼]in.
Sleeve seam, 6½ [8½:10½]in. The figures in brackets [ ] refer to the 22 and 24in sizes respectively.

> **Basic gauge**
> 6sts and 7 rows to 1 inch measured over stockinette stitch worked on No.5 needles.
> **Gauge for this design**
> 7½sts and 13 rows on No.4 needles.

Materials

Reynolds Classique
5 [6:7] balls in main color A
2 balls in contrast B
One pair No.3 needles
One pair No.4 needles
Two stitch holders
Ten medium buttons
Two small buttons
Small quantity of Sports yarn in any color for casting on. This is removed afterwards.

Note

If the coat is being made for a girl, complete the left front first and mark the button positions on this side. The buttonholes are then worked on the right side. If making the coat for a boy, complete the right front first and work the buttonholes on the left front.

Back

Using No.3 needles and a length of odd wool, cast on 61 [67:73] sts. (This thread is removed later.)
** Next row With B, K1, *ytf, K1, rep from * to end. 121 [133:145] sts.
Next row K1, * ytf, sll, ytb, K1, rep from * to end.
Next row Ytf, sll, ytb, * K1, ytf, sll, ytb, rep from * to end.
Rep last 2 rows once more. Break B and remove thread used for casting on.**
Using A and No.4 needles, begin pattern:
1st row Sll, K to end.
2nd row Sll, K to end.
3rd row P1, * ytb, sll, ytf, P1, rep from * to end.
4th row K1, * ytf, sll, ytb, K1, rep from * to end.
These 4 rows form the pattern and are rep throughout.
Work 16 rows more.
1st dec row K29 [32:35], sll, K1, psso, K2 tog, K55 [61:67], sll, K1, psso, K2 tog, K29 [32:35].
Keeping pattern correct, work 15 rows more.
2nd dec row K28 [31:34], sll, K1, psso, K2 tog, K53 [59:65], sll, K1, psso, K2 tog, K28 [31:34].
Work 15 rows more.
Continue dec 4sts in this way on next and every 16th row until 89 [97:105] sts rem.
Work until 11 [12¼:13½]in,
ending with a WS row.

Shape armholes

Bind off 4 [5:6] sts at beg of next 2 rows.
Dec one st at each end of next 6 rows, then next 0 [1:2] RS rows.
Work 46[47:47] rows more.

Shape shoulders

Bind off at each armhole edge 5sts 0 [2:4] times and 4sts 10 [8:6] times.
Bind off rem sts.

Left front

Using No.3 needles and a length of odd wool, cast on 37 [41:45] sts.
Work from ** to ** as for back.
Next row With A, knit to last 22 [24:26] sts and leave these sts on holder for front panel.
Continue on No.4 needles with A in pattern as given for back, beginning with 2nd pattern row. Work 19 rows.
1st dec row K29 [32:35], sll, K1, psso, K2 tog, K18 [21:24].
Work 15 rows more.
2nd dec row K28 [31:34], sll, K1, psso, K2 tog, K17 [20:23].
Work 15 rows more.
Continue dec 2sts on next and every 16th row until 35 [39:43] sts rem.
Work until same length as back to armhole, ending at side edge.

Shape armhole

1st row Bind off 4 [5:6] sts, pattern to end.
Work one row.
Dec at armhole edge on next 6 rows, then next 0 [1:2] RS rows.
Work 29 rows more without shaping.

Shape neck

Dec one st at center front on next and every other row until 20 [21:22] sts rem.
Work until same length as back to shoulder, ending at the armhole edge.

Shape shoulder

Bind off 5sts at beg of every other row 0 [1:2] times and 4sts at beg of every other row 5 [4:3] times.

Right front

Cast on and work from ** to ** as for left front.
Next row With B and still using No.3 needles, K22 [24:26].
Slip these sts onto holder until required.
Continue in pattern with A and No.4 needles.
Work 20 rows.
1st dec row K18 [21:24], sll, K1, psso, K2 tog, K29 [32:35].
Work 15 rows more.
2nd dec row K17 [20:23], sll, K1, psso, K2 tog, K28 [31:34].
Work 15 rows more.
Continue as for left front, reversing all shapings.

Button strip

Slip 22 [24:26] sts from holder onto No.3 needles.
With B and RS work facing, K across sts from holder.
Continue in garter st (every row K) until strip is long enough to reach beg of neck shaping when slightly stretched.
Bind off.
Mark positions for four groups of buttons.
Work strip on other side in same way, working buttonholes when markers are reached as follows:
RS work facing, K3, bind off 3, K to last 6sts, bind off 3, K2.
Next row K3, cast on 3, K to last 3sts, cast on 3, K3.

Sleeves

Using No.3 needles and a length of odd wool, cast on 25 [27:29] sts.
Work as for back from ** to ** 49 [53:57] sts.
Continue on No.4 needles with A in 4 row pattern as for back.
Work 4 [4:12] rows.
Keeping pattern correct, inc one st at each end of next and every 8th [8th:12th] row until there are 69 [73:77] sts.
Work until sleeve measures 6½ [8½:10½]in or required length.

Shape cap

Bind off 4 [5:6] sts at beg of

next 2 rows.
Dec one st at each end of every
RS row until 33 sts rem.
Dec one st at each end of next
7 rows.
Bind off.

Neckband

Sew shoulder seams and sl st
button and buttonhole strips
to their respective sides.
Beginning 1 inch before seam of
front strip to front with A, and
using No.4 needles, K up 7 sts
from right front strip, K up 13
[14:15] sts up right front
neck to shoulder, K up 21
[23:25] sts from back, K up 13
[14:15] sts down left front
neck and K up 7 sts from left
front strip, finishing about 1
inch beyond front strip seam
to main section.
K one row.
Beginning with a 3rd pattern
row, work 6 rows in 4 row
pattern as for back. Break A.
Change to No.3 needles and B.
1st row K1, * ytf, sl1, ytb,
K1, rep from * to end.
2nd row Ytf, sl1, ytb,
* K1, ytf, sl1, ytb, rep
from * to end.
Rep 1st and 2nd rows once.
Break B, leaving a length of
yarn for working the invisible
binding off.
Bind off using a darning
needle as shown in Chapter 6.

Belt

With No.3 needles and B, cast
on 11 sts.
K 42 [48:54] rows. Bind off.

Shoulder tabs

With No.3 needles and B, cast
on 9 sts.
K 20 [22: 24] rows.

Shape point
1st row K1, sl1, K1, psso,
K to last 3 sts, K2 tog, K1,
K one row.
Rep last 2 rows once.
5th row K1, sl1, K2 tog,
psso, K1.
6th row Sl1, K2 tog, psso,
pull yarn through and
finish off.
Work another tab in the
same way.

▲ *Back view of the coats*

Finishing

Press very lightly under a damp
cloth with a warm iron.
Join side and sleeve seams.
Sew in sleeves.
Fold edge of neckband
sideways and sl st to bound-
off edge of front strips.
Sew belt to center back and
sew a button at either end.
Stitch cast-on edge of tabs
close to sleeve seam at shoulder.
Sew point in place toward
neckband and trim with a
small button.
Sew buttons to correspond
with buttonholes.
Press seams lightly.

Little drummer boy ►

▼ *Detail of invisible casting on*

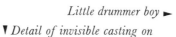

Pinafore with jacquard pockets

The jacquard pockets of this pretty pinafore are worked using the principles explained in Knitting Know-how Chapter 33.

Sizes
Directions are for 24in chest. The figures in brackets [ ] refer to the 26, 28 and 30in sizes, respectively.
Length down center back, 21 [22:24:26]in, adjustable.

Gauge
7 sts and 9 rows to 1in over stockinette stitch worked on No.4 needles.

Materials
Unger English Crepe 8[9:11:12]oz main color A
Small quantities of other, contrasting colors for pockets
One pair No.2 needles
One pair No.4 needles
Set of four No.2 double-pointed needles
Stitch holder

Back

Using No.4 needles and A, cast on 141[148:155:162] sts. Work 12 rows K1, P1 rib.
Beg with a K row continue in st st. Work 14 rows.
Next row K2 tog, K30 [32:34:36] sts, K2 tog tbl, K1, K2 tog, K67[70:73:76] sts, K2 tog tbl, K1, K2 tog, K to last 2 sts, K2 tog.
Beg with a P row, work 13 rows without shaping.
Next row K2 tog, K28[30: 32:34] sts, K2 tog tbl, K1, K2 tog, K65[68:71:74] sts, K2 tog tbl, K1, K2 tog, K to last 2 sts, K2 tog.

Beg with a P row, work 13 rows without shaping.
Continue dec 6 sts in this way on next and every 14th row 6 times more.
Continue without shaping until work measures 15[16: 17:18]in or desired length to underarm, ending with a WS row.

Shape armholes
Bind off 4 sts at beg of next 2 rows, then dec one st at each end of every row until 63[68:73:78] sts rem.
Continue without shaping until armholes measure 6[6:7:7]in from beg, ending with a WS row.

Shape shoulders
Bind off 5 sts at beg of next 4 rows and 4[5:6:7] sts at beg of next 2 rows.
Bind off rem sts.

Front

Work as given for back until work measures ½in less than back to underarm, ending with a WS row.

Shape neck
Next row K38[41:44:47] sts, turn.
Slip rem sts on holder.
Dec one st at neck edge on every row 9[10:11:12] times in all; *at the same time* when work measures same as back to underarm, shape armhole, ending with a WS row.

Shape armhole
Bind off 4 sts at beg of next row and dec one st at armhole edge on every row 11[12:13: 14] times in all.

Continue without shaping until armhole measures same as back to shoulder, ending at armhole edge.

Shape shoulder
Bind off at beg of next and every other row 5 sts twice and 4[5:6:7] sts once.
With RS of work facing, leave first 17[18:19:20] sts on holder for center neck, attach yarn to rem sts and complete to correspond to first side, reversing shaping.

Finishing

Press under a damp cloth with a warm iron. Join shoulder seams.
Armbands. Using No.2 needles and A, with RS facing, pick up and K113 [113:121:121] sts evenly around armhole. Work 8[8:10: 10] rows K1, P1 rib, dec one st at each end of every 4th row. Bind off in rib.
Join side seams.
Neckband. Using set of four No.2 needles and A, with RS facing, pick up and K176 [178:192:194] sts evenly around neck, including sts on holder. Work 8[8:10:10] rounds K1, P1 rib. Bind off in rib. Press seams.
Striped pockets. (Make 2) Using No.4 needles and A, cast on 30 sts.
Beg with a K row, work in st st and stripes of 1 row B, 1 row A and 1 row C. Work 34 rows. Break off B and C and continue with A only. K 1 row. Work 5 rows K1, P1 rib. Bind off in rib.
Christmas tree pocket. (Make 2) Using No.4 needles and A, cast on 30 sts. Beg with a K row, work in st st.
Work 34 rows as given on chart using colors as given. Using A only, work 6 rows K 1, P1 rib. Bind off in rib.
Boat and flower pocket. (Make 2) As for Christmas tree pocket, following chart.
Windmill pocket. (Make 2) Work as for Christmas tree pocket, following chart.
Turn in narrow hem around edge of pockets and stitch to pinafore. Press pockets.

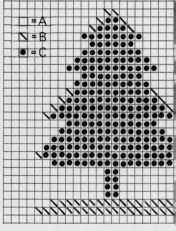

▲ *Christmas tree* ▼ *flower charts*

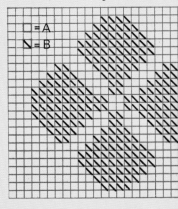

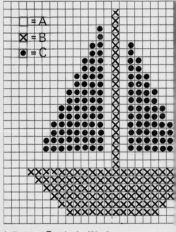

▲ *Boat* ▼ *windmill charts*

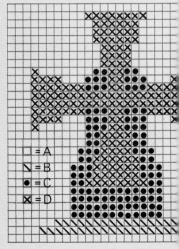

120

▲ *Christmas tree* ▼ *flower motifs*

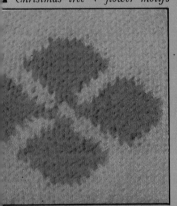

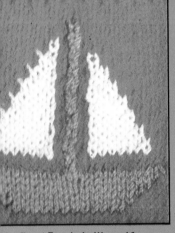

▲ *Boat* ▼ *windmill motifs*

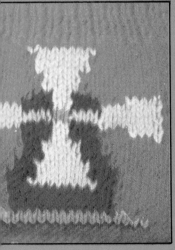

Fair Isle snowsuits

Make a snug snowsuit for a boy or a girl! Patterns for the matching mittens and cap will be in the next Basic Wardrobe chapter.

Sizes

Directions are for size 6.
The figures in brackets [] refer to sizes 8, 10 and 12.

Jacket
Sleeve seam, 10[11:12½:13½]in.
Length from edge to shoulder, 14½[16:18:19½]in.

Leggings
Front seam, 9[9:9½:9½]in.
Leg seam, 13½[16½:19½:22½]in.

> **Gauge**
> 5½sts and 7½ rows to 1in over stockinette stitch worked on No.5 needles.

Materials
(Make sure to buy all the yarn you'll need at one time.)
Reynolds Danskyarn 100% wool
Jacket. 5[6:7:7] balls in main color A
1 ball each in contrast colors B, C and D
14[16:18:20]in open-end zipper
Leggings. 5[6:7:7] balls in main color A
Elastic for waist and feet
Mittens. 2 balls in color A
Small amounts of B, C and D
Cap. 2 balls in color A
1 ball each in B, C and D
One pair No.5 needles
One pair No.3 needles
Stitch holder

Jacket back

Using No.3 needles and A, cast on 68[72:80:84] sts.
1st row K3, *P2, K2, rep from * to last st, K1.

2nd row K1, *P2, K2, rep from * to last 3sts, P2, K1.
Rep 1st and 2nd rows 6[7:6:8] times more, then 1st row once.
Next row Rib 12[7:13:9] sts, (inc in next st, rib 20[13:25:15] sts) 2[4:2:4] times, inc in next st, rib to end.
71[77:83:89] sts.
Change to No.5 needles.
Beg with a K row, continue in st st until 9½[10½:12:13]in, or desired length, from beg, ending with a P row.

Shape armholes
Bind off 3sts at beg of next 2 rows.
Dec one st at each end of next and every other row until 51 [55:59:63] sts rem.
Continue without shaping until work measures 14½[16:18:19½] in from beg, ending with a P row.

Shape shoulders
Bind off 5[5:6:6] sts at beg of next 4 rows, then 5[6:5:6] sts at beg of next 2 rows.
Slip rem 21[23:25:27] sts on holder.

Right front

Using No.3 needles and A, cast on 32[36:36:40] sts.
Work 15[18:15:19] rows rib as given for back.
Sizes 6, 10 and 12 only:
Next row (Rib 10[6:9] sts, inc in next st) 1[3:2] times, rib to end. 33[36:39:42] sts.
Change to No.5 needles.
Next row Bind off 12sts, K to end. 21[24:27:30] sts.
Beg with a P row, continue in st st until work measures same as back to underarm, ending at side edge.

Shape armhole
Bind off 3sts at beg of next row. Dec one st at armhole edge on next and every other row until 11[13:15:17] sts rem.
Continue without shaping until work measures same as back to shoulder, ending at armhole edge.

Shape shoulder
Sizes 6 and 8 only:
Bind off 5[6] sts at beg of next row. Work 1 row.
Bind off.

Sizes 10 and 12 only:
Bind off 5[5] sts at beg of next row and 5[6] sts at beg of following alt row. Work 1 row.
Bind off.

Left front

Using No.3 needles and A, cast on 32[36:36:40] sts.
Work 15[18:15:19] rows rib as given for back.
Sizes 6, 10 and 12 only:
Next row Rib 21[15:20] sts, (inc in next st, rib 10[6:9] sts) 1[3:2] times.
33[36:39:42] sts.
Change to No.5 needles and K to last 12sts, bind off 12sts.
Break off yarn and rejoin to rem sts. Complete as given for right front, reversing shapings.

Fair Isle bands

Using No.3 needles and A, with RS of right front facing, pick up and K 89[97:113:121] sts along front edge.
Next row P.
Change to No.5 needles.
Working rows 1-12 from chart, keeping odd rows in K and even rows in P and working the odd st as indicated at end of K rows and beg of P rows, work 3[3:1:1] rows from chart.

Shape neck
Bind off 8[8:11:11] sts at beg of next row. Dec one st at neck edge on every other row until 78[86:98:106] sts rem, ending with a WS row.
Work last 2 rows from chart.
Break off contrasts B, C and D.
Change to No.3 needles.
K 1 row.

Work 2 rows of P1, K1 rib.
Bind off tightly in rib.
Using No.3 needles and A, with RS of left front facing, pick up and K 89 [97:113:121] sts along front edge.
Next row P.
Change to No.5 needles and work rows 1-12 from chart, shaping neck as follows:
Work 4[4:2:2] rows from chart.
Bind off 8[8:11:11] sts at beg of next row. Dec one st at neck edge on next and every other row until 78[86:98:106] sts rem.
Work last 2 rows from chart.
Break off contrasts B, C and D.
Change to No.3 needles.
K 1 row.
Work 2 rows of K1, P1 rib.
Bind off tightly in rib.

Sleeves

Using No.3 needles and A, cast on 32[36:36:40] sts.
Work 15[17:15:19] rows rib as given for back.
Next row Work in rib, inc 4 [2:4:2] sts evenly across row.
36[38:40:42] sts.
Change to No.5 needles.
Beg with a K row, continue in st st, inc one st at each end of 3rd [3rd:5th:3rd] and every following 7th row until there are 52[56:60:64] sts.
Continue without shaping until work measures 10[11:12½:13½] in, or desired length, ending with a P row.

Shape cap
Bind off 3sts at beg of next 2 rows.
Dec one st at each end of next and every other row until 32 [34:36:38] sts rem.
Bind off 3sts at beg of next 6[6:8:8] rows.
Bind off rem sts.

Neck border

Sew shoulder seams.
Using No.3 needles and A, with RS facing, pick up and K 23[24:26:27] sts up right side of neck, K across sts on holder for back inc 5[5:7:7] sts evenly and pick up and K 23[24:26:27] sts down left side of neck.

2[76:84:88] sts.
Beg with a 2nd row, work
½[3½:4½:5½]in rib as given
for back.
Bind off in rib.

Leggings (right leg)

Using No.3 needles and A,
cast on 44[48:52:56] sts.
Work 10 rows rib as given for
jacket back, inc 4sts evenly
on last row.
48 [52:56:60] sts.
Change to No.5 needles.
1st row K.
2nd row P 11[12:13:14] sts,
1 1P, P 24[26:28:30] sts,
1 1P, P 11[12:13:14] sts.
Keeping sl st correct, work
2 rows more.
Next row Inc in first st,
K 22[24:26:28], M1K, K2,
M1K, K to last st, inc in last st.
Work 8[9:11:12] rows.
Next row Inc in first st,
work 24[26:28:30], M1K,
work 2, M1K, work to last st,
inc in last st.
Continue inc in this way on
every following 9th [10th:
12th:13th] row until there are
84[92:96:104] sts.
Continue without shaping
until work measures 12¾
[16:18¾:22]in from beg,
ending with a P row.
Inc one st at each end of next
and following 2[1:2:1] rows.
90[96:102:108] sts. Work 1
row.

Warm set for winter days ▶

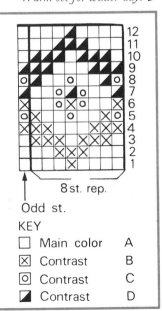

12
11
10
9
8
7
6
5
4
3
2
1

8 st. rep.

↑
Odd st.

KEY

☐	Main color	A
☒	Contrast	B
◉	Contrast	C
◪	Contrast	D

Fair Isle chart

Shape front and back edges
Bind off 2sts at beg of next
2 rows.
Dec one st at each end of 3rd
and every following 4th row
until 68[74:78:82] sts rem. **
Continue without shaping
until work measures 8[8:8½:
8½]in from bound-off sts,
ending with a K row.

Shape back
1st row P 48[48:60:60] sts.
Turn.
2nd and every other row K.
3rd row P 40[40:50:50] sts.
Turn.
5th row P 32[32:40:40] sts.
Turn.
Continue in this way until
P 8[8:10:10] and turn row

has been worked.
Next row K.
Next row P across all sts.
Change to No.3 needles.
Work 1 row of K1, P1 rib.
Bind off in rib.

Left leg

Work as for right leg to **.
Continue without shaping until
work measures 8[8:8½:8½]in
from bound-off sts, ending
with a P row.

Shape back
1st row K 48[48:60:60] sts.
Turn.
2nd and every other row P.
Complete as given for right
leg, reversing back shaping.

Finishing

Press each piece under a damp
cloth using a warm iron.

Jacket
Sew ends of front borders to
bound-off edge of ribbing. Sew
side and sleeve seams and
sew in sleeves. Fold neckband
in half to WS and sl st in place.
Sew in zipper. Press seams.

Leggings
Fold legs at sl st and press
creases. Join front, back and
leg seams. Make casing stitch
at waist, insert elastic and join
ends. Sew elastic at each side
of leg at ankles to go under
foot. Press seams.

Caps and mittens for snowsuits

A special for youngsters! Make these warm mittens and cozy cap to be worn as separates or match them with the snowsuits featured in the last Basic Wardrobe chapter. The hat can be worn as a simple pull-on or made to include snug earlaps which tie under the chin. Both the cap and the mittens are trimmed with Fair Isle using clear, vibrant colors.

Sizes

Cap. Width all around lower edge, 18[20]in.
Mittens. width all around above thumb, 6[7]in.
The figures in brackets [] refer to the larger size.

Gauge
5½sts and 7½ rows to 1in over stockinette stitch worked on No.5 needles

---

Materials

Reynolds Danskyarn 100% wool
Cap. 2 balls in main color A
1 ball each in contrast colors B, C and D
Mittens. 2 balls in main color A
Small amounts in contrast colors B, C and D
One pair No.5 needles
One pair No.3 needles

Cap

Using No.3 needles and A, cast on 128[144] sts.
Work 4 rows K1, P1 rib, inc one st at end of last row.
Change to No.5 needles.
Work rows 1-12 from chart.

124

Break off contrast yarns B, C and D.
Change to No.3 needles.
K 1 row, dec one st at beg of row. Work 3in of K1, P1 rib, ending with RS facing, to reverse work.
Next row P6[2], *P2 tog, P4, rep from * to last 8[4] sts, P2 tog, P6[2]. 108 [120] sts.
Change to No.5 needles.
Beg with a K row, work 1½ [2]in st st, ending with a P row.

Shape top

1st row (K7[8] sts, K2 tog) 12 times.
2nd and every other row P.
3rd row (K6[7] sts, K2 tog) 12 times.
5th row (K5[6] sts, K2 tog) 12 times.
7th row (K4[5] sts, K2 tog) 12 times.
9th row (K3[4] sts, K2 tog) 12 times.
11th row (K2[3] sts, K2 tog) 12 times.
13th row (K1[2] sts, K2 tog) 12 times.
14th row P.

Larger size only

15th row (K1, K2 tog) 12 times.

Both sizes

Next row (K2 tog) 12 times. 12sts.
Break yarn, thread through rem sts, draw up and fasten off securely.

Earlaps

Using No.3 needles and A, cast on 21sts.
1st row K2, *P1, K1, rep from * to last st, K1.

2nd row *K1, P1, rep from * to last st, K1.
Rep 1st and 2nd rows 8 times more.
Next row K1, K2 tog tbl, rib to last 3sts, K2 tog, K1.
Next row K1, P2 tog, rib to last 3sts, P2 tog tbl, K1.
Rep last 2 rows until 7sts rem.
Continue without shaping on these sts for 7in. Bind off.

Finishing

Press Fair Isle border under a damp cloth with a warm iron.
Join seam. Turn border to right side ½in above ribbing.
Using contrast yarns, make a large pompon (see Crochet Know-how page 196) and sew to center of crown.
Attach earlaps. Press seams.

Mittens

Right hand

Using No.3 needles and A, cast on 40[48] sts.
Work 4 rows K1, P1 rib, inc one st at end of last row.
Change to No.5 needles.
Work rows 1–12 from chart.
Break off contrast yarns.
Change to No.3 needles.
K 1 row, dec one st at beg of row.
Work 3in of K1, P1 rib, ending with RS facing, to reverse work.
Next row P4[3], *P2 tog, P3, rep from * to last 6[5] sts, P2 tog, P4[3]. 33[39] sts.
Change to No.5 needles.
Beg with a K row, work 2 [4] rows st st. **

Shape thumb

1st row K18[21], inc one st, K1, inc one st, K14[17]. Work 3 rows.
Next row K18[21], inc one st, K3, inc one st, K14[17]. Work 3 rows.
Continue inc in this way until there are 41[47] sts. Work 1 row.
Next row K27[30] sts. Turn.
Next row P9, cast on 2sts. Turn.
Work 10[12] rows on these 11 sts.

Shape top

1st row K2 tog tbl, K2, sl 1, K2 tog, psso, K2, K2 tog.
2nd row P.
3rd row K2 tog tbl, sl 1, K2 tog, psso, K2 tog.
Break yarn and thread through rem sts, draw up and fasten off.
With RS facing, pick up and K 2sts from 2 cast-on sts at base of thumb, K14[17].
Next row P across all 34[40] sts. Beg with a K row, continue in st st until work measures 4½[5]in from end of ribbing.

Shape top

1st row K2, (K2 tog, K10[13], K2 tog tbl, K2) twice.
2nd and every other row P.
3rd row K2, (K2 tog, K8 [11], K2 tog tbl, K2) twice.
5th row K2, (K2 tog, K6 [9], K2 tog tbl, K2) twice.
7th row K2, (K2 tog, K4[7], K2 tog tbl, K2) twice.
Break yarn and thread through rem sts, draw up and fasten off.

Left hand

Work as for right hand to **.

Shape thumb

Next row K14[17], inc one st, K1, inc one st, K18[21]. Work 3 rows.
Next row K14[17], inc one st, K3, inc one st, K18[21]. Work 3 rows.
Continue inc in this way until there are 41[47] sts. Work 1 row.
Next row K23[26] sts. Turn.
Next row Cast on 2sts, P9. Turn. Complete thumb as for right hand.
With RS facing, pick up and K 2sts from 2 cast-on sts at base of thumb, K18[21].
Next row P across all 34 [40] sts. Complete as for right hand.

Finishing

Press as directed for cap.
Join thumb and side seam.
Fold border to right side ½in above ribbing.
Press seams.

Fair Isle trimmed cap and mittens to team with snowsuits ►

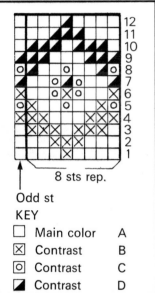

12
11
10
9
8
7
6
5
4
3
2
1

8 sts rep.

Odd st

KEY

☐	Main color	A
☒	Contrast	B
⊙	Contrast	C
◨	Contrast	D

Fair Isle chart ▲ and detail ▼

Striped sweater with raglan sleeves

Striped sweaters for a boy or a girl are child's play to knit in simple stockinette stitch, and the round neckline and the easy-fitting raglan sleeves make them ideal garments for indoor and outdoor play. Although stripes in blending or contrasting colors give a sporty look, the pattern can also be worked in a single color to make a simple classic sweater. The directions cover a wide size range.

Sizes

Directions are for 24in chest. The figures in brackets [] refer to the 26, 28, 30 and 32in chest sizes respectively. Side seam, 7½[9:10:11:12½]in. Sleeve seam, 9[10½:12¼:13½: 15]in.

Gauge
6sts and 8 rows to 1in over stockinette stitch worked on No.5 needles.

Materials
Dawn Wintuk Sports (2oz skeins)
2[3:3:3:3] skeins in main color A
2 skeins in contrast B
For a plain pullover, 4[5:5: 5:5] skeins in one color.
One pair No.3 needles
One pair No.5 needles
Stitch holder

Back

Using No.3 needles and A, cast on 80[86:92:98:104]sts. Work 14[16:18:18:18] rows K1, P1 rib.
Change to No.5 needles and
st st.
Beg with a K row, work in stripes as follows:
1st-6th rows Using A.
7th-10th rows Using B.
11th-12th rows Using A.
13th-14th rows Using B.
15th-16th rows Using A.
17th-18th rows Using B.
19th-20th rows Using A.
21st-24th rows Using B.
These 24 rows form the patt and are rep throughout. Work 24[34:40:48:60] more rows of patt, ending with a 24th [10th:16th:24th:12th] patt row.

Work raglan shaping
Bind off 1[1:2:2:3] sts at beg of next 2 rows.
3rd row K2, sl 1P, K1, psso, K to last 4sts, K2 tog, K2.
4th row P.
Keeping striped patt correct, rep last 2 rows until 30[32: 34:36:38]sts rem, ending with a P row.
Slip rem sts on holder.

Front

Work as for back until 42[44:46:48:50] sts rem on raglan shaping, ending with a P row.

Shape neck
1st row K2, K2 tog tbl, K10, turn. Work right shoulder on these sts.
** Keeping raglan shaping correct as before, dec one st at neck edge on next 6 rows. Continue raglan shaping until 3sts rem, ending with WS row.**
Next row K1, K2 tog.
Last row P2 tog. Draw yarn through and fasten off.

With RS facing, slip center 14[16:18:20:22] sts onto holder. Attach yarn to rem sts and work to end of row. Work from ** to ** as for right shoulder.
Next row K2 tog, K1.
Last row P2 tog. Draw yarn through and fasten off.

Sleeves

Using No.3 needles and A, cast on 38[40:42:44:46] sts. Work 14[18:18:20:20] rows K1, P1 rib, inc one st at each end of last row.
Change to No.5 needles and st st. Continue working in striped patt as for back, beg with 15th [15th:7th:7th:7th] patt row and inc one st at each end of 3rd and then every 6th [6th:8th:8th:8th] row until there are 56[60: 64:68:72] sts.
Work without shaping until next 24th [10th:16th:24th: 12th] patt row has been completed.

Shape raglan
Bind off 1[1:2:2:3] sts at beg of next 2 rows.
3rd row K2, sl 1P, K1, psso, K to last 4sts, K2 tog, K2.
4th row P.
Rep last 2 rows until 8sts rem, ending with a P row. Slip rem sts on holder.

Neckband

Using No.3 needles and A, with RS facing, K across 30[32:34:36:38] sts from back neck, K across 8sts from left sleeve cap, pick up and K 12sts down neck, K across 14[16:18:20:22] sts from center front, pick up and K 12sts up neck and K across 8sts from right sleeve cap. 84[88:92:96:100] sts.
Work 16[16:18:18:18] rows K1, P1 rib. Bind off in rib.

Finishing

DO NOT PRESS.
Sew raglan, side and sleeve seams. Fold neckband in half to WS and sl st.

Warm enough to wear outdoors ▶

Sweaters and caps in Aran

Warm and practical, this teenage twosome is suitable for both boys and girls. The simple design is ideal for a first attempt at Aran.

Sizes

Directions are for 30in chest. The figures in brackets [] refer to the 32, 34 and 36in sizes respectively.
Length to shoulder, 18[20¼:21:21¾]in.
Sleeve seam, 14½[15:15½:16]in.

Gauge
4½ sts and 7 rows to 1in over stockinette stitch worked on No.6 needles.

Materials

Reynolds Irish Fisherman
Sweater with round neck
12[13:13:14] balls
Sweater with turtleneck
13[13:14:15] balls
Cap
2[2:2:2] balls
One pair No.3 needles
One pair No.4 needles
One pair No.6 needles
One cable needle
One stitch holder

Sweater back

Using No.3 needles, cast on 81[89:93:101] sts.
1st row K1 tbl, *P1, K1 tbl, rep from * to end.
2nd row P1, *K1 tbl, P1, rep from * to end.
Rep these 2 rows until twisted rib measures 2[2:2½:2½]in, ending with a 1st row.
Next row Rib 7[11:11:15], K up 1, rib 9, P up 1, rib 7, 128

P up 1, rib 10, K up 1, rib 8[8:10:10], P up 1, rib 8 [8:10:10], K up 1, rib 9, P up 1, rib 7, P up 1, rib 9, K up 1, rib 7[11:11:15]. 90[98:102:110] sts.
Change to No.6 needles. Commence patt.
1st patt row K2, (P2, K2) 1[2:2:3] times, P2, sl next 2 sts onto cable needle and hold at back of work, K next st, K2 from cable needle, K1, sl next st onto cable needle and hold at front of work, K next 2 sts, K1 from cable needle—called C7—P2, Tw2F, P5, Tw2B, P2, C7, P2, (Tw2F, Tw2B) 4[4:5:5] times, P2, C7, P2, Tw2F, P5, Tw2B, P2, C7, P2, K2, (P2, K2) 1[2:2:3] times.
2nd patt row (K2, P2) 1[2:2:3] times, K4, P7, K2, P9, K2, P7, K2, P16[16:20:20], K2, P7, K2, P9, K2, P7, K4, (P2, K2) 1[2:2:3] times.
3rd patt row K2, (P2, K2) 1[2:2:3] times, P2, K7, P2, Tw2F, K5, Tw2B, P2, K7, P2, (Tw2B, Tw2F) 4[4:5:5] times, P2, K7, P2, Tw2F, K5, Tw2B, P2, K7, P2, K2, (P2, K2) 1[2:2:3] times.
4th patt row As 2nd patt row. These 4 rows form patt and are rep throughout the back and front.
Continue in patt until work measures 12[14:14½:15]in from beg or desired length to underarm, ending with a WS row.

Shape armholes
Bind off 5[6:6:7] sts at beg of next 2 rows.

Dec one st at each end of every RS row until 76[78:80:82] sts rem.
Continue without shaping until armholes measure 6[6¼:6½:6¾]in, ending with a WS row.

Shape shoulders
Bind off 5 sts at beg of next 6[4:4:2] rows; then 6 sts at beg of next 2[4:4:6] rows. Bind off rem sts.

Sweater front

Work as given for back until armholes measure 4¼[4½:4½:4¾]in, ending with a RS row.

Shape neck
1st row Patt 30[31:31:32] sts, bind off center 16[16:18:18] sts, patt 29[30:30:31] sts.
Complete left shoulder first.
** Dec one st at neck edge on next 7 rows, then one st on every RS row until 21 [22:22:23] sts rem.
Continue without shaping until armhole measures same as back to shoulder, ending at armhole edge.

Shape shoulder
At arm edge, bind off 5 sts every other row 3[2:2:1] times; then 6 sts every other row 1[2:2:3] times.**
With RS of work facing, attach yarn to rem shoulder sts and work right shoulder as for left shoulder from ** to **.

Sleeves

Using No.3 needles, cast on 43[43:47:47] sts.
Work 2[2:2½:2½]in twisted rib as given for back.
Change to No.6 needles and patt.
1st patt row K2[2:0:0], *(P2, K2) 1[[1:2:2] times, P2, C7, P2, Tw2F, P5, Tw2B, P2. C7, P2, (K2, P2) 1[1:2:2] times, K2[2:0:0].
2nd patt row K2[2:0:0], (P2, K2) 1[1:2:2] times, K2, P7, K2, P9, K2, P7, K2, (K2, P2) 1[1:2:2] times, K2[2:0:0].
3rd patt row K2[2:0:0], (P2, K2) 1[1:2:2] times, P2,

K7, P2, Tw2F, K5, Tw2B, P2, K7, P2, (K2, P2) 1[1:2:2] times, K2[2:0:0].
4th patt row As 2nd.
Continue in patt, inc one st at each end of next and every following 8th row, working extra sts into double seed st side panels as they are made, until there are 59[63:65:69] sts.
Continue without shaping until sleeve measures 14½[15:15½:16]in from beg or desired length to underarm, ending with a WS row.

Shape cap
Bind off 5[6:6:7] sts at beg of next 2 rows.
Dec one st at each end of next 6 rows, then each end of every RS row until 27 sts rem.
Bind off 3 sts at beg of next 4 rows. Bind off rem 15 sts.

Neckband or turtleneck collar

Join right shoulder seam.
Using No.3 needles, with RS facing, K up 20 [20:22:22] sts down left front neck, K up 16[16:18:18] sts from center front, K up 20[20:22:22] sts from right front neck and K up 34[34:36:36] sts from center back.
Work in twisted rib as given for back, working 2in for neckband and 6in for turtleneck collar.
Bind off in rib.

Finishing

Join left shoulder and neckband or collar. Turn neckband in half to WS and sl st.
Seam sleeves and sew into armholes. Join side seams. Press lightly under a damp cloth with a warm iron if desired, excluding ribbing.

Cap

Using No.4 needles, cast on 97 sts.
Work 5 rows twisted rib as given for sweater back.
6th row Rib 3, *K up 1, rib 2, K up 1, rib 7, K up 1,

rib 2, K up 1, rib 5, rep from * to last 14 sts, K up 1, rib 2, K up 1, rib 7, K up 1, rib 2, K up 1, rib 3.

Change to No.6 needles.

1st row *P3, Tw2B, P2, C7, P2, Tw2F, P2, rep from * to last st, P1.

2nd row *P5, K2, P7, K2, P4, rep from * to last st, P1.

3rd row *K3, Tw2B, P2, K7, P2, Tw2F, K2, rep from * to last st, K1.

4th row As 2nd.

Rep 1st, 2nd and 3rd rows once more.

8th row *P3, P up 1, P2, K2, P7, K2, P2, P up 1, P2, rep from * to last st, P1.

9th row *P4, Tw2B, P2, C7, P2, Tw2F, P3, rep from * to last st, P1.

Continue in patt, noting that there will now be 2 extra sts between the sts on ladder panels.

Work 10 rows in patt for the boy's cap and 14 rows in patt for the girl's.

Shape top

1st dec row *P2, P2 tog tbl, P2, K2, P7, K2, P2, P2 tog, P1, rep from * to last st, P1.

Work 5 rows without shaping, noting that there will be 2 sts less on each ladder panel.

2nd dec row *P1, P2 tog tbl, P2, K2, P7, K2, P2, P2 tog, rep from * to last st, P1.

Work 3 rows without shaping.

3rd dec row P2 tog, *P2, K2, P7, K2, P2, P3 tog, rep from * to last 17 sts, P2, K2, P7, K2, P2, P2 tog.

Work 3 rows without shaping.

4th dec row P2 tog, *P1, K2, P7, K2, P1, P3 tog, rep from * to last 15 sts, P1, K2, P7, K2, P1, P2 tog.

5th dec row K2 tog, *P2, K7, P2, sl 1, K2 tog, psso, rep from * to last 13 sts, P2, K7, P2, K2 tog.

Next row *P1, K2, P7, K2, rep from * to last st, P1.

6th dec row P2 tog, *P1, C7, P1, P3 tog, rep from * to last 11 sts, P1, K7, P1, P2 tog.

Next row *K2, P7, K1, rep from * to last st, K1.

7th dec row P2 tog, *K7, P3 tog, rep from * to last 9 sts, K7, P2 tog.

▲ *The Aran sweaters with round or turtleneck collar, paired with matching Aran knit caps*

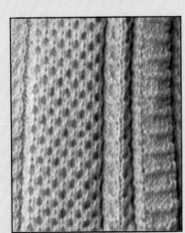

▲ *Close-up of the stitch detail*

Next row *K1, P7, rep from * to last st, K1.

Next row *P1, C7, rep from * to last st, P1.

8th dec row *K1, P1, P2 tog, P1, P2 tog tbl, P1, rep from * to last st, K1.

9th dec row *P1, K1, sl 1, K2 tog, psso, K1, rep from * to last st, P1.

10th dec row *K1, P3 tog, rep from * to last st, K1.

11th dec row *P1, sl 1, K2 tog, psso, rep from * to last st, P1.

Break off yarn, thread through rem sts and draw up. Fasten off.

Brim

Using No.4 needles, cast on 3 sts.

1st row K1, K1 putting yarn twice around needle—called K1y2rn—K1.

2nd row P1, sl 1 dropping extra yarn, P1.

3rd row K1, K up 1, K1y2rn, K up 1, K1.

4th row P2, sl 1 dropping extra yarn, P2.

5th row K1, K up 1, K1, K1y2rn, K1, K up 1, K1.

6th row P3, sl 1 dropping extra yarn, P3.

Continue inc 2 sts in this way on every K row until there are 19 sts.

Keeping center st correct, work 3 rows.

Next row K1, K up 1, K8, K1y2rn, K8, K up 1, K1.

Keeping center st correct, work 15 rows without shaping.

Keeping center st correct, dec one st at each end of next row. Work 3 rows.

Dec one st at each end of next and every K row until 3 sts rem. Bind off.

Finishing

Press pieces lightly under a damp cloth with a warm iron, excluding ribbing.

Seam cap from center top to edge.

Fold brim in half lengthwise along sl st fold line. Sew one long edge to center of cap.

Sl st other long edge beneath first.

Aran poncho and matching cap

A jaunty teenage Aran poncho and cap, designed to help you to practice Aran stitches without having to cope with complicated shaping at the same time. The poncho is made in two simple, separate strips and has a neatly fitting ribbed neckband.

Size
Poncho. Each piece measures 31in by 16½in, after blocking
Cap. To fit 20½ to 21½in circumference measured around the head

---
Gauge
9½ sts and 12 rows to 2in over stockinette stitch worked on No.7 needles.

Materials
Bear Brand, Botany or Fleisher Shamrock
8 2oz balls
One pair No.4 needles
One pair No.7 needles
One cable needle
One No.E crochet hook

Poncho

Using No.7 needles, cast on 145 sts.
P 1 row.
Commence patt.
1st row K2, *K1 tbl, P3, K1 tbl, P2, K1 tbl, P3, K1 tbl, P11, K1 tbl, P3, K1 tbl, P2, K1 tbl, P3, K1 tbl*, P7, sl next 2 sts onto cable needle and hold at front of work, K2, K2 from cable needle—called C4F—P7**, rep from * to ** once more, then from * to * once more, K2.

Basic Wardrobe Knitting

2nd row K2, *P1 tbl, K3, P1 tbl, K2, P1 tbl, K3, P1 tbl, K1, (K1, P1, K1 all into next st—called 3 in 1—P3 tog) twice, 3 in 1, K1, P1 tbl, K3, P1 tbl, K2, P1 tbl, K3, P1 tbl *, K7, P4, K7**, rep from * to ** once more, then from * to * once more, K2 (151 sts).
3rd row K2, *K1 tbl, P3, K1 tbl, P2, K1 tbl, P3, K1 tbl, P13, K1 tbl, P3, K1 tbl, P2, K1 tbl, P3, K1 tbl*, P6, sl next st onto cable needle and hold at back of work, K2, P1 from cable needle—called C3B—sl next 2 sts onto cable needle and hold at front of work, P1, K2 from cable needle—called C3F—P6**, rep from * to ** once more, then from * to * once more, K2.
4th row K2, *P1 tbl, K3, P1 tbl, K2, P1 tbl, K3, P1 tbl, K1, (P3 tog, 3 in 1) twice, P3 tog, K1, P1 tbl, K3, P1 tbl, K2, P1 tbl, K3, P1 tbl*, P6, P2, K2, P2, K6**, rep from * to ** once more, then from * to * once more, K2 (145 sts).
5th row K2, *K1 tbl, P3, K1 tbl, P2, K1 tbl, P3, K1 tbl, P11, K1 tbl, P3, K1 tbl, P2, K1 tbl, P3, K1 tbl*, P5, C3B, P2, C3F, P5**, rep from * to ** once more, then from * to * once more, K2.
6th row K2, *P1 tbl, K3, P1 tbl, K2, P1 tbl, K3, P1 tbl, K1, (3 in 1, P3 tog) twice, 3 in 1, K1, P1 tbl, K3, P1 tbl, K2, P1 tbl, K3, P1 tbl*, K5, P2, K4, P2, K5**, rep from * to ** once more, then from * to * once more, K2 (151 sts).

7th row K2, *K1 tbl, P3, sl next st onto cable needle and hold at front, P1, K1 tbl from cable needle—called C2F—sl next st onto cable needle and hold at back, K1 tbl, P1 from cable needle—called C2B—P3, K1 tbl, P13, K1 tbl, P3, C2F, C2B, P3, K1 tbl*, P4, C3B, P4, C3F, P4 **, rep from * to ** once more, then from * to * once more, K2.
8th row K2, *P1 tbl, K4, (P1 tbl) twice, K4, P1 tbl, K1, (P3 tog, 3 in 1) twice, P3 tog, K1, P1 tbl, K4, (P1 tbl) twice, K4, P1 tbl*, K4, P2, K6, P2, K4**, rep from * to ** once more, then from * to * once more, K2 (145 sts).
9th row K2, *K1 tbl, P4, sl next st onto cable needle and hold at front, K1 tbl, K1 tbl from cable needle—called C2F tbl—P4, K1 tbl, P11, K1 tbl, P4, C2F tbl, P4, K1 tbl*, P3, C3B, P6, C3F, P3 **, rep from * to ** once more, then from * to * once more, K2.
10th row K2, *P1 tbl, K4, (P1 tbl) twice, K4, P1 tbl, K1, (3 in 1, P3 tog) twice, 3 in 1, K1, P1 tbl, K4, (P1 tbl) twice, K4, P1 tbl*, K3, P2, K8, P2, K3**, rep from * to ** once more, then from * to * once more, K2 (151 sts).
11th row K2, *K1 tbl, P3, C2B, C2F, P3, K1 tbl, P13, K1 tbl, P3, C2B, C2F, P3, K1 tbl *, P2, C3B, P8, C3F, P2**, rep from * to ** once more, then from * to * once more, K2.
12th row K2, *P1 tbl, K3, P1 tbl, K2, P1 tbl, K3, P1 tbl, K1, (P3 tog, 3 in 1) twice, P3 tog, K1, P1 tbl, K3, P1 tbl*, K2, P2, K10, P2, K2**, rep from * to ** once more, then from * to * once more, K2 (145 sts).
These 12 rows form patt and are rep throughout.
Keeping 2 sts in garter st each end, rep patt rows 5 times more.

Shape shoulder
Next row Patt 78 sts, *K1 tbl, P2 tog, P1, K1 tbl, P2, K1 tbl, P1, P2 tog, K1 tbl*, P2 tog, P5, C4F, P5, P2 tog,

rep from * to * once more, patt next 11 sts, rep from * to * once more, K2 (137 sts).
Continue in patt for 23 more rows, noting that there will now be one st less at each side of last 3 chain cable and V panels.
Next row Bind off 78 sts, K to end (59 sts).
Change to No.4 needles.

Neck border
1st row *K1, P1, rep from * to last st, K1.
2nd row P1, sl 1, K1, psso, *K1, P1, rep from * to last 4 sts, K1, K2 tog, P1.
3rd row K1, P1, *P1, K1, rep from * to last 3 sts, P2, K1.
4th row P1, sl 1, K1, psso, *P1, K1, rep from * to last 4 sts, P1, K2 tog, P1.
Rep last 4 rows once more, then 1st and 2nd rows once more.
Bind off in rib.
Work another piece in same way.

Finishing

Press pieces under a damp cloth with a warm iron.
Join side edge of first piece to bound-off edge of 2nd piece, and side edge of 2nd piece to bound-off edge of first piece, including neck border edges.
Fringe. Cut a piece of stiff cardboard 1¾in wide and 5in long. Hold upright in left hand and knot yarn around near top. Using No.E crochet hook, put hook under loop and draw yarn through then under yarn and draw loop through again ,*wind yarn around cardboard from front to back, hook under loop at front then under yarn at back, draw through loop then draw through 2 loops on hook, rep from * for desired length, slipping loops off cardboard as it fills. When fringe fits all around poncho, break yarn but do not fasten off last st and leave a few yards of yarn for adjustment. Attach yarn at other end and work 1sc into each st of fringe, adjusting length if necessary. Top st around edges of poncho.

Cap

Using No.4 needles, cast on 91 sts.

Work 9 rows K1, P1 rib.

Next row P45 sts, P2 tog, P44 sts (90 sts).

Change to No.7 needles.

1st row (RS) P.

2nd row K1, *3 in 1, P3 tog, rep from * to last st, K1.

3rd row P.

4th row K1, *P3 tog, 3 in 1, rep from * to last st, K1.

5th row As 1st.

6th row As 2nd.

7th row *P3, K1 tbl, P2, K1 tbl, P3, rep from * to end.

8th row *K3, P1 tbl, K2, P1 tbl, K3, rep from * to end.
Rep 7th and 8th rows twice more.

13th row *P3, C2F, C2B, P3, rep from * to end.

14th row *K4, (P1 tbl) twice, K4, rep from * to end.

15th row *P4, C2F tbl, P4, rep from * to end.

16th row As 14th.

17th row *P3, C2B, C2F, P3, rep from * to end.

18th row As 8th.
Rep rows 7-18 once more.

Shape top

1st dec row P1, P2 tog, *K1 tbl, P2, K1 tbl, P2 tog, P2, P2 tog, rep from * to last 7 sts, K1 tbl, P2, K1 tbl, P2 tog, P1 (72 sts).

Work 3 rows rib tbl as now established, without shaping.

2nd dec row P2 tog, *rib 4, (P2 tog) twice, rep from * to last 6 sts, rib 4, P2 tog (54 sts).

Work 3 rows rib tbl.

3rd dec row P1, *K1 tbl, P2 tog, rep from * to last 2 sts, K1 tbl, P1 (37 sts).

Work 2 rows rib tbl.

4th dec row P1, *P2 tog, rep from * to end (19 sts).
Thread yarn through rem sts, draw up and fasten off.

Finishing

Press lightly under a damp cloth with a warm iron.
Join as shown. Make a tassel or pompon and sew to top.

◄ *Poncho featuring a simple Aran stitches pattern*

Frog-fastened coat and hat

This gently shaped knitted coat with matching pull-on hat will please any fashion-conscious teenage girl. The frog fastenings, which add a touch of distinction, can be made in either matching or contrasting yarn, or be purchased ready-made.

Sizes

Directions are for 34in bust. The figures in brackets [] refer to the 36 and 38in sizes respectively.

Length at center back, 35[36: 37]in, adjustable.

Sleeve seam,.17in, adjustable.

Hat. To fit average head.

N.B. One skein will add approximately 8in extra length to the coat if desired. If the hat is knitted separately allow one skein of yarn.

> **Gauge**
> 4½ sts and 6½ rows to 1in worked over st st on No.8 needles.

Materials

Columbia-Minerva Knitting Worsted 5[6:6] skeins
One pair No.6 needles
One pair No.8 needles
Four buttons
One No.E crochet hook

Coat back

Using No.6 needles, cast on 99[103:107] sts.

1st row *K1, P1, rep from * to last st, K1.

Rep 1st row 9 times more for seed st hem.

Change to No.8 needles.

Next row K15[17:19] sts, *K2 tog, K14, rep from * 4 times more, K to end. 94[98: 102] sts.

Beg with a P row, work 37[41:45] rows st st.

Any change in length should be made at this point.

Shape darts

1st dec row K20, sl 1, K1, psso, K to last 22 sts, K2 tog, K20.

Beg with a P row, work 7 rows st st.

Rep last 8 rows 7 times more. 78[82:86] sts.

Continue without shaping until work measures 26[26½: 27]in from beg, or desired length to underarm, ending with a P row.

Shape armholes

Bind off 5 sts at beg of next 2 rows.

Dec one st at each end of next and every other row 3 times. 60[64:68] sts.

Continue without shaping until armholes measure 7¼[7¾:8¼]in from beg, ending with a P row.

Shape shoulders

Bind off 6 sts at beg of next 2 rows; 6[7:7] sts at beg of next 2 rows; then 6[7:8] sts at beg of next 2 rows.

Bind off rem 24[24:26] sts.

Coat left front

Using No.6 needles, cast on 51[53:57] sts.

Work 10 rows seed st as given for back.

Change to No.8 needles.

Next row K15[18:21] sts, K2 tog, K14[25:14], K2 tog, K10[K0:K2 tog, K10], turn and slip rem 8 sts on holder for border. 41[44:47] sts.

Beg with a P row, work 37 [41:45] rows st st, or same number as for back.

Shape dart

1st dec row K20, sl 1, K1, psso, K to end.

Beg with a P row, work 7 rows st st.

Rep last 8 rows 7 times more. 33[36:39] sts.

Continue without shaping until work measures same as back to underarm, ending with a P row.

Shape armhole

Bind off 5 sts at beg of next row.

Work 1 row.

Dec one st at arm edge every other row 4 times. 24[27:30] sts.

Beg with a P row, work 20[22: 24] rows st st, ending at neck edge.

Shape neck

1st row Bind off 3[4:4] sts,

> ▼ *Detail showing frog fastening and the border stitch*

P to end.

2nd row K.

3rd row P2 tog, P to end.

Rep last 2 rows 2[2:4] times more. 18[20:21] sts.

Work 2[4:2] rows st st, ending at armhole edge.

Shape shoulder

At arm edge, bind off 6 sts once, 6[7:7] sts once and 6[7:8] sts once.

Coat right front

Using No.6 needles, cast on 51[53:57] sts.

Work 10 rows seed st as given for back.

Next row Seed st 8 and slip these sts on holder for border, change to No.8 needles, K10, K2 tog, K14, K2 tog[K0:K14, K2 tog], K to end. 41[44:47] sts.

Beg with a P row, work 37 [41:45] rows st st, or same number as for back.

Shape dart

1st dec row K until 22 sts rem, K2 tog, K to end.

Beg with a P row, work 7 rows st st.

Rep last 8 rows 7 times more. 33[36:39] sts.

Complete as given for left front, reversing all shapings.

Sleeves

Using No.6 needles, cast on 43[45:47] sts.

Work 10 rows seed st as given for back.

Change to No.8 needles.

Beg with a K row, continue in st st, inc one st at each end of 21st and every following 10th row until there are 55[57:59] sts.

Continue without shaping until work measures 17in from beg, or desired length to underarm. End with a P row.

Shape cap

Bind off 5 sts at beg of next 2 rows.

Dec one st at each end of next and every other row until 23 sts rem.

Bind off 3 sts at beg of next 4 rows.

Bind off rem 11 sts.

Finishing

Press each piece under a damp cloth using a warm iron. Join shoulder, side and sleeve seams. Press seams.

Left front border

Slip border sts from holder onto No.6 needles and with RS facing, attach yarn and work in seed st until border is long enough to fit to neck when slightly stretched. Replace 8 border sts on holder and join border to front.

Right front border

Work as given for left front border but attach yarn to back of work. Join border to front.

Neckband

Using No.6 needles and with RS facing, seed st across right front border sts, pick up and K16[18:20] sts to shoulder, pick up and K23 [23:25] sts across back neck, pick up and K16[18:20] sts down left front and seed st across left front border sts. 71[75:81] sts.
Work 9 rows seed st. Bind off in seed st.
Press borders lightly on WS. Sew in sleeves.

Frog fastenings

Using No.E hook make a tight chain of 14in. Skip first ch from hook and work 1ss into each ch to end. Pull out last st and leave end for sewing on. Fold into 3 loops at one end and sew to coat at neck, then sew remainder of cord in a long loop to edge of coat.
Work 4 frogs in this way down left front and 4 more to correspond on right front allowing long loop to protrude slightly beyond the edge of the border.
Sew on 4 buttons to left front at end of long loop to match loops on right front.

Hat

Crown

Using No.6 needles, cast on 83 sts, and work 30 rows seed st as given for coat back.

Shape top

1st dec row Seed st 7, P3 tog, (seed st 11, P3 tog) 5 times, seed st 3. 71 sts.
Seed st 3 rows.
2nd dec row Seed st 11, *P3 tog, seed st 9, rep from * to end. 61 sts. Seed st 3 rows.
3rd dec row Seed st 3, P3 tog, (seed st 9, P3 tog) 4 times, seed st 7. 51 sts.
Seed st 3 rows.
4th dec row Seed st 3, *P3 tog, seed st 3, rep from * to end. 35 sts.
Seed st 1 row.
5th dec row K1, P3 tog, * seed st 3, P3 tog, rep from * to last st, K1. 23 sts.
Seed st 1 row.
6th dec row *K1, P3 tog, rep from * to last 3 sts, K1, P2 tog. 12 sts.
Next row K1, *K2 tog, rep from * to last st, K1.
Break yarn and draw through all sts, fasten off securely and sew up back seam.

Brim

Using No.6 needles, cast on 13 sts and work in seed st for 25½in. Bind off in seed st.

Finishing

Join cast-on edge to bound-off edge. Place this seam to back seam of crown and pin evenly in position, stretching crown slightly to fit brim. Overcast to crown so that brim rolls up when finished.

Zipper~ fronted jacket

A zippered casual jacket designed to fit all sizes from teens to adults.

Sizes
Directions are for 32in bust or chest.
The figures in brackets [] refer to the 34, 36, 38, 40 and 42in sizes respectively.
Length from shoulder, 22[22:23½:23½:25:25]in, adjustable.
Sleeve seam, 17[17½:17½: 18:18:18]in, adjustable.

Gauge
12 sts and 15 rows to 2in over patt worked on No.5 needles.

Materials
Unger Tosca
6[6:7:7:8:8] balls
One pair No.4 knitting needles
One pair No.5 knitting needles
One 20[20:22:22:24:24]in open-ended zipper

Back

Using No.4 needles, cast on 99 [105:111:117:123:129] sts.
1st row Sl 1, *K1, P1, rep from * to last 2 sts, K2.
2nd row Sl 1, *P1, K1, rep from * to end.
Rep these 2 rows 5 times more.
Change to No.5 needles.
Commence patt.
1st row Sl 1, K0[1:0:1:0:1], *P2, K2, rep from * to last 2[3:2:3:2:3] sts, P1[2:1:2:1:2], K1.
2nd row Sl 1, P0[1:0:1:0:1], *K2, P2, rep from * to last 2[3:2:3:2:3] sts, K2[3:2:3:2:3].
134

These 2 rows form patt and are rep throughout.
Continue in patt until work measures 14½[14½:15:15: 15½:15½]in from beg, or desired length to underarm, ending with a WS row.

Shape raglan sleeves
Bind off 4 sts at beg of next 2 rows.
Keeping patt correct, dec one st at each end of every row until 61[55:69:63:77:71] sts rem, then every other row until 27[27:29:29:31:31] sts rem.
Bind off.

Right front

Using No.4 needles, cast on 49[51:55:57:61:63] sts.
Work 12 rows rib as given for back, inc one st at beg of last row for the 34 and 42in sizes

▼ *Stitch detail showing zipper*

only. 49[52:55:57:61:64] sts.
Change to No.5 needles.
Commence patt.
32 and 40in sizes only
1st row Sl 1, *K2, P2, rep from * to last 4 sts, K2, P1, K1.
2nd row As 1st.
34 and 42in sizes only
1st row Sl 1, *P2, K2, rep from * to last 3 sts, P2, K1.
2nd row Sl 1, P1, *K2, P2, rep from * to last 2 sts, K2.
36 and 38in sizes only
Work 2 rows patt as given for 1st size back.
All sizes
Continue in patt until work measures same as back to raglan shaping, ending with a RS row.

Shape raglan sleeves
Bind off 4 sts at beg of next row.
Keeping patt correct, dec one st at raglan edge on every row until 30[27:34:30:38:35] sts rem, then on every other row until work measures 19[19:21:21:23:23]in from beg, ending with a WS row.

Shape neck
Next row At neck edge bind off 5[5:6:5:7:7] sts, patt to last 2 sts, K2 tog.
Continue dec at raglan edge as before, *at the same time* dec one st at neck edge on next 6 rows.
Continue shaping raglan edge only until 2 sts rem. Bind off.

Left front

Using No.4 needles, cast on 49[51:55:57:61:63] sts.
Work 12 rows rib as given for back, inc one st at end of last row for the 34 and 42in sizes only. 49[52:55:57:61:64] sts.
Change to No.5 needles.
Commence patt.
32 and 40in sizes only
1st row Sl 1, P1, *K2, P2, rep from * to last 3 sts, K3.
2nd row As 1st.
34 and 42in size only
1st row Sl 1, *P2, K2, rep from * to last 3 sts, P2, K1.
2nd row Sl 1, K1, *P2, K2, rep from * to last 2 sts, K2.
36 and 38in sizes only
Work 2 patt rows as given for 1st size back.

All sizes
Keeping patt correct and reversing all shaping, complete to correspond to right front.

Sleeves

Using No.4 needles, cast on 43[45:47:49:51:53] sts.
Work 13 rows in rib as given for back.
Next row Rib 4[1:2:3:4:1], *inc in next st, rib 4[5:5:5:5:6], rep from * to last 4[2:3:4:5:3] sts, inc in next st, rib to end.
51[53:55:57:59:61] sts.
Change to No.5 needles and patt as given for back, inc one st at each end of 3rd and every following 7th row until there are 83[85:87:89:91:93] sts, working extra sts into patt.
Continue without shaping until sleeve measures 17[17½:17½:18:18:18]in from beg, or desired length to underarm. End with a WS row.

Shape raglan sleeves
Bind off 4 sts at beg of next 2 rows.
Keeping patt correct, dec one st at each end of every row until 53[51:65:63:77:75] sts rem, then every other row until 15 sts rem. Bind off.

Neckband

Join raglan seams.
Using No.4 needles, with RS work facing pick up and K 17[17:18:18:19:19] sts from right front neck edge, 15 sts from sleeve, 27[27:29: 29:31:31] sts from back neck, 15 sts from sleeve and 17[17: 18:18:19:19] sts from left front neck edge.
91[91:95:95:99:99] sts.
Beg with the 2nd row, work 2in rib as given for 1st size back. Bind off loosely in rib.

Finishing

Press lightly with a cool iron under a dry cloth on the WS. Join side and sleeve seams. Sew in sleeves. Fold neckband in half and sl st to WS. Sew in zipper. Press seams.

His and hers zippered jacket ▶

Raglan cardigans

These useful matching cardigans can be made in a wide range of sizes to fit both you and your daughter. The pattern panels are optional and the design may be worked entirely in reversed stockinette stitch. Both cardigans button to the neck for extra warmth and comfort.

Sizes
Directions are for 28in bust or chest.
The figures in brackets [] refer to the 30, 32, 34, 36 and 38in sizes respectively.
Length down center back, 19½[20½:22:23:23½:24]in.
Sleeve seam, 13[14:16:17: 18:18]in.

Gauge
6sts and 8 rows to 1in over stockinette stitch worked on No.5 needles.

Materials
Dawn Wintuk Sport 4[4:5:6:7:7] 2oz skeins
One pair No.3 needles
One pair No.5 needles
Cable needle
Seven buttons

Note
To work the cardigan entirely in reversed stockinette stitch, follow directions exactly as given, omitting the panel patt on fronts and sleeves.

Back

Using No.3 needles, cast on 86[92:98:104:110:116] sts.
Work 1[1:1½:1½:1½:1½]in
136

K1, P1 rib.
Change to No.5 needles.
Beg with a P row continue in reversed stockinette stitch until work measures 12[12½:13½: 14:14:14]in from beg, ending with a K row.

Shape armholes
Bind off 2sts at beg of next 2 rows.
Dec one st at each end of next and every other row until 24[26:28:30:32:34] sts rem.
Work 1 row.
Bind off.

Left front

Using No.3 needles, cast on 43[46:49:52:55:58] sts.
Work 1[1:1½:1½:1½:1½]in K1, P1 rib.
Change to No.5 needles.
Commence patt:
1st row P25[27:29:32:34:36] sts, K1, P1, K1, P10, K1, P1, K1, P to end.
2nd row K2[3:4:4:5:6] sts, ytf, sl 1, ytb, K1, ytf, sl 1, ytb, K10, ytf, sl 1, ytb, K1, ytf, sl 1, ytb, K to end.
3rd row P25[27:29:32:34:36] sts, K1, P1, sl next st on cable needle and hold at front of work, P next st then K st on cable needle—called C2L—P8, sl next st on cable needle and hold at back of work, K next st then P st on cable needle—called C2R— P1, K1, P to end.
4th row K2[3:4:4:5:6] sts, ytf, sl 1, ytb, K2, ytf, sl 1, ytb, K8, ytf, sl 1, ytb, K2, ytf, sl 1, ytb, K to end.
5th row P25[27:29:32:34:36]

sts, K1, P2, C2L, P6, C2R, P2, K1, P to end.
6th row K2[3:4:4:5:6] sts, sl 1 as before, K3, sl 1, K6, sl 1, K3, sl 1, K to end.
7th row P25[27:29:32:34:36] sts, K1, P3, C2L, P4, C2R, P3, K1, P to end.
8th row K2[3:4:4:5:6] sts, sl 1, (K4, sl 1) 3 times, K to end.
9th row P25[27:29:32:34:36] sts, K1, P4, C2L, P2, C2R, P4, K1, P to end.
10th row K2[3:4:4:5:6] sts, sl 1, K5, sl 1, K2, sl 1, K5, sl 1, K to end.
11th row P25[27:29:32:34:36] sts, K1, P5, C2L, C2R, P5, K1, P to end.
12th row K2[3:4:4:5:6] sts, sl 1, K6, sl 2, K6, sl 1, K to end.
13th row P25[27:29:32:34:36] sts, K1, P6, sl next st onto cable needle and hold at front of work, K next st then K st on cable needle, P6, K1, P to end.
14th row K2[3:4:4:5:6] sts, sl 1, K14, sl 1, K to end.
15th row P25[27:29:32: 34:36] sts, K1, P6, make a bobble on next 2sts by knitting then purling then knitting into each st.
Turn.
Beg with a P row work 4 rows st st on these 6sts.
Now with left-hand needle pass 2nd st over first st, 3rd st over first st, then sl first st back onto left-hand needle.
Sl 5th st over 4th st and 6th st over 4th st. Replace first st on right-hand needle, P6, K1, P to end.
16th row K2[3:4:4:5:6] sts sl 1, K14, sl 1, K to end.
These 16 rows form panel patt and are rep throughout.
Continue in patt until work measures same as back to underarm, ending with a WS row.

Shape armhole
Bind off 2sts at beg of next row, patt to end.
Work 1 row.
Dec one st at beg of next and every other row until work measures 17[17½:19:19½:20: 20½]in from beg, ending at center front edge.

Shape neck
Bind off 6sts at beg of next row and dec one st at neck edge on the next 5[6:7:8:9: 10] rows; *at the same time* continue to dec at armhole edge as before until 2sts rem. K2 tog. Fasten off.

Right front

Work as given for left front, reversing all shaping and noting that first patt row will read as follows:
1st row P2[3:4:4:5:6] sts, K1, P1, K1, P10, K1, P1, K1, P to end.

Sleeves

Using No.3 needles, cast on 42[44:46:48:50:52] sts.
Work 2[2:2½:2½:2½:2½]in K1, P1 rib.
Change to No.5 needles.
Commence patt:
1st row P13[14:15:16:17: 18] sts, K1, P1, K1, P10, K1, P1, K1, P to end.
2nd row K13[14:15:16:17: 18] sts, sl 1, K1, sl 1, K10, sl 1, K1, sl 1, K to end.
These 2 rows form patt.
Continue in patt as given for left front, keeping center 16 sts in patt and inc one st at each end of 5th and every following 6th row until there are 66[70:74:80:84:88] sts.
Continue without shaping until sleeve measures 13 [14:16:17:18:18]in from beg, ending with a WS row.

Shape cap
Bind off 2sts at beg of next 2 rows.
Dec one st at each end of next and every other row until 4[4:4:6:6:6] sts rem. Work 1 row.
Bind off.

Borders

Using No.3 needles, cast on 10sts.
Work in K1, P1 rib.
Work ¾[1¼:1¼:½:1¼:½]in.
Next row (buttonhole row) Rib 3, bind off 3sts, rib to end.
Next row Rib 3, cast on 3 sts, rib to end.
Make 5 more buttonholes in

this way at intervals of
2¾[2¾:3:3¼:3¼:3½]in,
measured from the center
of the previous buttonhole.
Continue until border
measures 17[17½:19:19½:20:
20½] in from beg.
Bind off in rib.

Work other border in same
way, omitting buttonholes.

Finishing

Press lightly.
Join raglan, side and sleeve
seams using backstitch and

overcasting welts and cuffs.
Attach borders to center
front edges from RS (P side).

Neckband

Using No.3 needles, with RS
facing, pick up and K85

[93:97:107:115:119] sts
evenly around neck.
Work 7[7:8:8:8:8] rows
K1, P1 rib making
buttonhole as before on 4th
and 5th rows.
Bind off in rib.
Sew on buttons.

The classic camel turtleneck

Even for the relative beginner, this classic ribbed turtleneck knits up easily and, of course, would make an ideal gift for either a boy or a girl. Work it in the traditional camel or white, as illustrated, or choose any other color to suit your taste. If you've forgotten some of the abbreviations used here, look back to Knitting Know-how Chapter 1.

Sizes

Directions are for 32in bust or chest.
Length down center back, 23½ [23¾:24:24¼]in.
Sleeve seam 17½in.
The figures in brackets [] refer to the 34, 36 and 38in sizes respectively.

Gauge
for this design
6sts and 8 rows to 1in on No.5 needles.

Materials

Bear Brand or Fleisher or Botany Twin-Pak Win-Knit
5 [6:6:7] balls
One pair No.3 needles
One pair No.5 needles
2 stitch holders

Note

For a truly professional finished look, use the invisible binding off method for completing the collar. Directions for this are given in Knitting Know-how Chapter 6.

Back

Using No.3 needles cast on 96 [102:108:114] sts.
1st row K2, P4 [P1:P4:K3, P4], * K4, P4, rep from * to last 2 [5:0:3] sts, K2 [K4, P1: 0:K3].
2nd row P2, K4 [K1:K4: P3, K4], * P4, K4, rep from * to last 2 [5:0:3] sts, P2 [P4, K1:0:P3].
These 2 rows form the rib and are rep throughout back.
Work 22 rows more.
Change to No.5 needles and continue in rib.
Work until 98 rows from beg, or desired length to armholes.

Shape armholes
Bind off 1 [2:3:4] sts at beg of next 2 rows.
Dec one st at each end of next and every other row until 82 [82:86:86] sts rem.
Work 41 [39:41:39] rows without shaping.

Shape shoulders
1st row K2, sl1, K1, psso, rib to last 4sts, K2 tog, K2.
2nd row P2, P2 tog, rib to last 4sts, P2 tog tbl, P2.
Rep last 2 rows 8 [8:9:9] times, then first row once.
Leave rem 44sts on holder.

Front

Using No.3 needles cast on 110 [116:122:128] sts.
1st row K1 [K4:P3, K4: K2], * P4, K4, rep from * to last 5 [0:3:6:] sts, P4, K1 [0:P3:P4, K2].
2nd row P1 [P4:K3, P4: P2], *K4, P4, rep from * to last 5 [0:3:6] sts, K4, P1 [0:K3: K4, P2].

Work 22 rows more in rib.
Change to No.5 needles and continue in rib.
Work until 98 rows from beg, or until same desired length as back.

Shape armholes
Bind off 4 [5:6:7] sts at beg of next 2 rows.
Dec one st at each end of next 6 [8:8:10] rows.
Work 44 [44:46:46] rows without shaping.

Shape shoulders
Bind off 19 [19:21:21] sts at beg of next 2 rows.
Leave rem 52 sts on holder for neck.

Sleeves

Using No.3 needles cast on 54 [56:58:60] sts.
1st row P1 [2:3:4], K4, *P4, K4, rep from * to last 1 [2:3:4] sts, P1 [2:3:4].
2nd row K1 [2:3:4], P4, *K4, P4, rep from * to last 1 [2:3:4] sts, K1 [2:3:4].
Continue in rib for 22 rows more.
Change to No.5 needles and continue in rib, working extra sts into rib pattern as they are added. Work 2 rows.
Inc 1 st at each end of next and every 8th row until there are 80 [84:88:92] sts.
Work until sleeve measures 17½in or desired length, ending with a WS row.

Shape cap
1st row K2, sl1, K1, psso, rib to last 4sts, K2 tog, K2.
2nd row P2, P2 tog, rib to last 4sts, P2 tog tbl, P2.
Rep last 2 rows twice.
7th row as 1st.
8th row P3, rib to last 3sts, P3.
Rep 7th and 8th rows until 32 sts rem.
Repeat 1st and 2nd rows 3 times.
Bind off.

Collar

Sew left shoulder seam.
Using No.5 needles rib across sts from back and front holders (96 sts). Work 43 rows in K4, P4 rib. Bind off.

Finishing

Sew collar and right shoulder seam.
Sew side and sleeve seams.
Sew in sleeves.
Press lightly using a damp cloth with a cool iron.

These pullovers have been specially designed to look good on a boy or a girl, since the elasticity of the rib allows for contours! The continental shaping which has been used is of particular interest and is actually simpler to do, with better results, than the standard American type of shaping. It gives a close-fitting look, letting the clear lines of the rib reach over the shoulder from the front to the sloping back seam. The shoulder seam itself is set behind the shoulder.

Sweaters for boys or girls ►
▼ Stitch detail of rib

Tailored vest

Soft, random-dyed yarn makes this vest ideal for either town or country wear. The neat edging uses a special "invisible" method of casting on. (See Knitting Know-how Chapter 3 for directions telling how to use this method on any garment.)

Sizes

Directions are for 32in bust. The figures in brackets [] refer to the 34 and 36in sizes respectively.
Length down center back, 21½ [22:22½]in.

Gauge

6sts and 8 rows to 1in over stockinette stitch worked on No.4 needles.

Materials

Reynolds Firefly
4[5:6] balls
One pair No.4 needles
One pair No.5 needles
One No.4 circular needle
Five pearl buttons

Back

Using No.4 needles and any length of contrasting yarn, cast on 49[51:55] sts by the one needle method. (This thread is removed later.)
Next row With main yarn, K1, *ytf, K1, rep from * to end. 97[101:109] sts.
Next row K1, *ytf, sl 1, ytb, K1, rep from * to end.
Next row Ytf, sl 1, *ytb, K1, ytf, sl 1, rep from * to end.
Rep last 2 rows once.
Next row K1, *P1, K1, rep

from * to end.
Next row P1, *K1, P1, rep from * to end.
Rep last 2 rows 3 times more.
Change to No.5 needles. Beg with a K row, continue in st st, dec one st at each end of the 7th and then every other row until 81[85:93] sts rem, ending with a P row.
Continue in st st, inc one st at each end of the 7th and then every 10th row until there are 93[99:105] sts, ending with a P row.
Continue without shaping until work measures 13in from beg, ending with a P row.

Shape armholes

Bind off 5[6:7] sts at beg of next 2 rows.
Dec one st at each end of next and every other row until 69[73:77] sts rem.
Continue without shaping until armholes measure 7½ [7¾:8]in from beg, ending with a P row.

Shape shoulders

Bind off 8sts at beg of next 2 rows and 8[9:10] sts at beg of following 2 rows.
Bind off rem 37[39:41] sts.

Left front

Using No.5 needles and main yarn, cast on 29 [31:33] sts.
Work in st st throughout.
K 1 row.
Cast on 3sts at beg of next P row and then at beg of following 2 P rows.
Dec one st at beg of next and every other row 8 times in all; *at the same time* inc one st at

front edge on every row 10[10:12] times in all, ending with a P row.
Keeping front edge even, continue in st st, inc one st at armhole edge on the 7th and then on every following 10th row until there are 46 [49:52] sts.
Continue without shaping until work measures same as back to underarm, less ribbing, ending at armhole edge.

Shape armhole and front edge

Bind off 5[6:7] sts at beg of next row.
Work 1 row.
Dec one st at armhole edge on next and every other row 7 times in all; *at the same time* dec one st at front edge on next and then on every following 3rd row until 16 [17:18] sts rem.
Continue without shaping until armhole measures same as back to shoulder, ending at armhole edge.

Shape shoulder

Bind off 8sts at beg of next row, work 1 row, then bind off 8[9:10] sts at same edge once again.

Right front

Cast on as for left front.
Beg with a P row, continue in st st and complete as given for left front, reversing all shaping.

Front border

Join shoulder seams.
Mark position for 5 buttons on left front, placing the first 1in above last bottom curve shaping and placing the 5th 4 rows below first front edge shaping.
Using No.4 needles and the same casting on method as given for the back, cast on 217[221:225] sts.
Change to No.4 circular needle and main yarn, turning at the end of each row and working back and forth as if using straight needles.
Continue as given for back

on 433[441:449] sts, working 8 rows in K1, P1 rib when "invisible" edge has been completed and making buttonholes as markers are reached on 4th and 5th ribbing rows, as follows:
Next row Rib 74[78:82] sts, *bind off 3sts, rib 10, rep from * 4 times more, rib to end.
Next row Rib to end, casting on 3sts above those bound off in previous row. Bind off in rib.

Armbands

Using No.4 needles and the same casting on method as given for back, cast on 63 [67:71] sts. Complete as given for front border, omitting buttonholes and working 4 rows K1, P1 rib. Bind off in rib.

Finishing

Press each piece under a damp cloth with a cool iron, omitting ribbing on back hem and borders. Remove casting-on thread. With RS facing, beg at right front side seam and pin bound-off edge of front border around right front edge, around neck and down left front, making sure buttonholes come on right front. Sew on border. Sew on armhole borders in same way. Join side seams, including ribbing. Press seams very lightly. Sew on buttons.

Soft, subtly shaded vests with neat "invisible" cast-on edge ▶
▼ Details of "invisible" edging

140

Fabric-stitch sleeveless pullover

A knitted pullover like this is a garment dear to the heart of the fashion-conscious American woman because of its great versatility. Wear it with a tailored blouse and pleated skirt, or team it with pants, a heavy sweater and a handsome belt. The interesting fabric stitch of this design gives a firm texture without being too bulky, and the deep armholes make it ideal for wearing over set-in or raglan sleeved sweaters. We made it in Unger Roxanne, which is warm but light and comes in beautiful colors.

Sizes
Directions are for 34in bust. The figures in brackets [] refer to the 36, 38 and 40in sizes respectively.
Length down center back, 26 [26½:27:27½]in.

Gauge
6sts and 8 rows to 1in over st st worked on No.6 needles.

Materials
Unger Roxanne
5 [6:7:7] balls
One pair No.6 needles
One pair No.4 needles
Set of No.4 double-pointed needles

Back

Using No.6 needles, cast on 110 [118:126:134] sts.
1st row K2, *P2, K2, rep from * to end.
2nd row P2, *K2, P2, rep

from * to end.
3rd row As 1st.
4th row As 2nd.
5th row Place the right-hand needle behind the next st, K the following st, then K the first st and sl both sts off left-hand needle tog— called cross 2—*P2, cross 2, rep from * to end.
6th row As 1st.
7th row As 2nd.
8th row As 1st.
9th row As 2nd.
10th row As 1st.
11th row P2, *cross 2, P2, rep from * to end.
12th row As 2nd.
These 12 rows form patt and are rep throughout.
Keeping patt correct, dec one st at each end of next and every following 10th row 6 times in all, then inc one st at each end of every following 12th row 4 times. Continue without shaping until work measures 16[16: 16½:16½]in from beg, ending with a WS row.

Shape armholes
Dec one st at each end of next and every following 4th row 17 [18:19:20] times in all.
Continue without shaping until armholes measure 10 [10½:10½:11]in from beg, ending with a WS row.

Shape neck and shoulders
Next row Bind off 5sts, patt 8[10:12:14] sts, bind off 44 [46:48:50] sts, patt to end.
Complete left shoulder first. Bind off 5sts at armhole edge every other row twice, then 4 [6:8:10] sts once.
With WS of work facing, attach

yarn to rem sts and work to correspond to first side.

Front

Work as given for back until front measures same to underarm.

Shape armholes
Next row Dec one st at each end of this row.
Work 3 rows without shaping.
Rep last 4 rows once more.

Shape neck
Next row Dec one st, patt 34 [37:40:43] sts, bind off 30 [32:34:36] sts, patt to last 2sts, dec one st.
Complete right shoulder first. Dec one st at neck edge on next 7 rows and *at the same time* dec one st at armhole edge on every 4th row 14 [15: 16:17] times more.
Continue without shaping until armhole measures same as back to shoulder, ending at armhole edge.

Shape shoulder
Bind off 5sts at armhole edge every other row twice, then 4 [6:8:10] sts once.
With WS of work facing, attach yarn to rem sts and work to correspond to first side.

Finishing

Press lightly.
Join shoulder seams.
Armbands Using No.4 needles and with RS of work facing, pick up and K118 [126:126:134] sts evenly around armhole.
Work in K2, P2 rib.
Work 1 row.
Work 5 more rows, dec one st at each end of every row.
Bind off in rib.
Join side seams.
Neckband Using No.4 double-pointed needles and with RS of work facing, pick up and K196 [204:208:216] sts evenly around neck.
Work in rounds of K2, P2 rib. Work 11 rounds.
Next round *K2, P2 tog, rep from * to end.
Bind off in rib.

Knitted knight's tunic

The knights of old wore a tunic for extra warmth without bulk, and for a decorative colorful effect. Whether you wear them over casual clothes or with a dressier outfit, tunics are still the ideal garment to wear for an extra layer of warmth with maximum freedom of movement. This one opens down the front.

Sizes
Directions are for 34in bust. The figures in brackets [ ] refer to the 36, 38, 40in sizes respectively.
Length at center back, 31[32:33:34]in.

Gauge
6 sts and 8 rows to 1in over st st worked on No.8 needles.

Materials
Spinnerin Wintuk Sport 5[6:6:6] skeins
One pair No.5 needles
4 frog closings or clasps

Back

Using No.5 needles, cast on 90[96:102:108] sts.
Beg with a K row work in st st.
Work 1 row.
Inc one st at each end of every row until there are 100[106:112:118] sts.
Commence patt.
1st–6th rows K.
7th row K.
8th row P.
Rep last 2 rows twice more. These 12 rows form patt and are rep throughout.
144

Continue in patt until work measures 24[25:25½:26½]in from beg, ending with a WS row.

Shape armholes
Bind off 6 sts at beg of next 2 rows.
Dec one st at each end of every row until 80[84:88:92] sts rem.
Continue without shaping until armholes measure 7[7:7½:7½]in ending with a WS row.

Shape shoulders
Bind off 9 sts at beg of next 4 rows.
Bind off 8[9:10:11] sts at beg of next 2 rows.

▼ *The tunic with a distinctive metal clasp fastening*

Bind off rem sts.

Left front

Using No.5 needles, cast on 40[43:46:49] sts.
Beg with a K row work in st st.
Work 1 row.
Inc one st at each end of every row until there are 50[53:56:59] sts.
Continue in patt as for back until work measures same as back to armhole, ending with a WS row.

Shape armhole
Bind off 6 sts at beg of next row.
Dec one st at armhole edge on every row 4[5:6:7] times.
Continue without shaping until armhole measures 5in from beg, ending at center front edge.

Shape neck
Bind off 7 sts at beg of next row.
Dec one st at neck edge on every row 7[8:9:10] times.
Continue without shaping until armhole measures same as back to shoulder, ending at armhole edge.

Shape Shoulder
Bind off 9 sts every other row twice.
Bind off rem 8[9:10:11] sts.

Right front

Work as for left front, ending with a RS row before armhole shaping.

Finishing

Press lightly.
Join shoulder seams using back st.

Armbands
Pick up and K95[95:101:101] sts evenly around armhole with RS facing. Beg with a P row work 5 rows st st, inc one st at each end of every row. Bind off loosely.
Join side seams using back st and leaving 9in free at bottom of seams to form side vents.

Vents
Pick up and K54 sts evenly along one side of vent, with RS facing. Beg with a P row work 5 rows st st, dec one st at lower edge of vent and inc one st at other end of row. Bind off loosely.
Work 3 other vent edges.

Front facings
Pick up and K173[179:182:188] sts along edge of right front, with RS facing. Beg with a P row work 5 rows st st, dec one st at lower edge of every row. Bind off loosely.
Work left front in same way.
Fold all st st edges to WS of tunic and slip st in place, joining mitered corners.

Collar
Pick up and K70[74:84:88] sts evenly around neck, with RS facing and beg 3 sts in from center front edges. Beg with a K row work 5 rows garter st, 4 rows st st, 6 rows garter st and 12 rows st st. Bind off loosely.
Fold collar in half to WS and slip st in place, sewing down side edges.
Sew on closings.

Tunic with link fastening ▶

Sleeveless summer top

Make this pretty top to wear with suits, skirts and all kinds of pants.

Sizes
Directions are for 32in bust. The figures in brackets [] refer to the 34, 36 and 38in sizes respectively.
Length to back neck, 16¾[17:17¼:17½]in.

> ### Gauge
> 7½ sts and 9 rows to 1in over stockinette stitch worked on No.2 needles.

Materials
Bernat Pompadour
6[6:7:7] 1oz balls
One pair No.1 needles
One pair No.2 needles
One pair No.3 needles
One No.B crochet hook

Back

Using No.1 needles, cast on 125[131:137:143] sts.
Beg with a K row, work 4 rows st st.
1st patt row Using No.3 needles, K.
2nd patt row (wrong side) Using No.3 needles, K1, *K3 tog, before slipping sts off left-hand needle K into first st again, then K 2nd and 3rd sts tog, slip all 3sts off left-hand needle—called K3 into 3—rep from * to last st, K1.
3rd patt row As 1st patt row.
4th patt row As 2nd patt row.
5th-14th patt rows Using No.2 needles and beg with a K row, work in st st.
Rep 1st-14th rows 6 times
146

more, then 1st-10th rows once.

Shape armholes
1st row Using No.2 needles, bind off 6[6:6:9] sts, K to end.
2nd row Using No.2 needles, bind off 6[6:6:9] sts, P to end.
3rd row Using No.2 needles, bind off 3 sts, K to end.
4th row Using No.2 needles, bind off 3 sts, P to end.
5th row Using No.3 needles, bind off 3 sts, K to end.
6th row Using No.3 needles, bind off 3 sts (1 st on right-hand needle), *K3 into 3, rep from * to last st, K1. 101[107:113:113] sts.
Rep 1st and 2nd patt rows throughout remainder of back. Work without shaping until armholes measure 5¾[6:6¼:6½] in, ending with 2nd patt row.

Shape neck
1st row Keeping patt correct, work 34[37:37:37] sts, bind off center 33[33:39:39] sts, patt to end.
Complete this shoulder first.
Work 1 row.
**Bind off 3 sts at neck edge every other row 3 times.

Shape shoulder
Bind off 7 sts at arm edge; then 9 sts on next arm edge row; then 9[12:12:12] sts on arm edge row. **
With WS of work facing, attach yarn to rem sts for other shoulder and work 2 rows.
Complete as for first shoulder from ** to **.

Front

Work as given for back.

Finishing

DO NOT PRESS.
Join shoulder and side seams using a backstitch seam.
Turn first 5 st st rows at lower edge to WS and slip st in place.
Neck edging Using No.B crochet hook, with RS of work facing, work picot edging evenly around neck edge, *1sc, 1sc into next st, ch3, 1sc into same place as last sc, rep from * to end. Work edging around armholes in same way.
Alternative knitted picot edging
Neck edge Join left shoulder seam.
Using No.2 needles, with RS of work facing, pick up and K13 sts down right side of back neck, pick up and K33 [33:39:39] sts from center back bound-off edge, pick up and K13 sts up left side of back and 13 sts down left side of front, pick up and K33[33:39:39] sts from center front bound-off edge and pick up and K13 sts up right side of front. 118[118:130: 130] sts. Work picot edge.
K into front and back of first st, turn, K2, turn, bind off 6 sts, slip st on right-hand needle back on left-hand needle and rep from * until all sts have been worked off.
Armhole edging Join right shoulder seam.
Using No.2 needles, with RS of work facing, pick up and K92[96:100:104] sts and work as for neck edging.

*Pretty, yet quick and easy to knit ►
▼ Detail of the bodice stitch*

Diamond patterned pullover

This charming classic pullover is superbly simple and made using a soft light yarn for feminine flattery.

Sizes

Directions are for 34in bust. The figures in brackets [ ] refer to the 36 and 38in sizes respectively.
Length from lower edge to shoulder, 24[24½:25]in.
Sleeve seam, 17[17½:18]in.

Gauge
7 sts and 9 rows to 1in over stockinette stitch worked on No.3 needles.

Materials

Bernat Pompadour 9[10:10] 1oz skeins
One pair No.1 needles
One pair No.3 needles
One set of No.1 double-pointed needles
Stitch holder

Front

Using No.1 needles, cast on 125[131:137] sts.
Work in K1, P1 rib for 1in.
Change to No.3 needles.
Commence wide rib panels.
Next row K8[11:14], P1, *K17, P1, rep from * to last 8[11:14] sts, K to end.
Next row P8[11:14], K1, *P17, K1, rep from * to last 8[11:14] sts, P to end.
Rep last 2 rows 3 times more.
Commence diamond patt.
1st row K8[11:14], P1, *K8, ytf, K2 tog tbl, K7, P1, rep from * to last 8 [11:14] sts, K to end.

Detail of the diamond pattern

2nd and every other row P8[11:14], K1, *P17, K1, rep from * to last 8[11:14] sts, P to end.
3rd row K8[11:14], P1, *K6, K2 tog, ytf, K1, ytf, K2 tog tbl, K6, P1, rep from * to last 8[11:14] sts, K to end.
5th row K8[11:14], P1, *K5, K2 tog, ytf, K3, ytf, K2 tog tbl, K5, P1, rep from * to last 8[11:14] sts, K to end.
7th row K8[11:14], P1, *K4, K2 tog, ytf, K5, ytf, K2 tog tbl, K4, P1, rep from * to last 8[11:14] sts, K to end.
9th row K8[11:14], P1, *K3, K2 tog, ytf, K7, ytf, K2 tog tbl, K3, P1, rep from * to last 8[11:14] sts, K to end.
11th row K8[11:14], P1, *K2, K2 tog, ytf, K9, ytf, K2 tog tbl, K2, P1, rep from * to last 8[11:14] sts, K to end
13th row K8[11:14], P1, *K1, K2 tog, ytf, K11, ytf, K2 tog tbl, K1, P1, rep from * to last 8[11:14] sts, K to end.
15th row K8[11:14], P1, *K3, ytf, K2 tog tbl, K7, K2 tog, ytf, K3, P1, rep from * to last 8[11:14] sts, K to end.
17th row K8[11:14], P1, *K4, ytf, K2 tog tbl, K5, K2 tog, ytf, K4, P1, rep from * to last 8[11:14] sts,

K to end.
19th row K8[11:14], P1, *K5, ytf, K2 tog tbl, K3, K2 tog, ytf, K5, P1, rep from * to last 8[11:14] sts, K to end.
21st row K8[11:14], P1, *K6, ytf, K2 tog tbl, K1, K2 tog, ytf, K6, P1, rep from * to last 8[11:14] sts, K to end.
23rd row K8[11:14], P1, *K7, ytf, sl 1, K2 tog, psso, ytf, K7, P1, rep from * to last 8[11:14] sts, K to end.
25th row K8[11:14], P1, *K8, ytf, K2 tog tbl, K7, P1, rep from * to last 8[11:14] sts, K to end.
27th row K8[11:14], P1, *K17, P1, rep from * to last 8[11:14] sts, K to end.
28th row As 2nd.
Rep 27th and 28th rows 10 times more.
These 48 rows form patt.
Rep 1st-48th rows once more, then 1st-20th rows once.

Shape armholes
Keeping patt correct, bind off 3 sts at beg of next 2 rows.
Next row K1, K3 tog, patt to last 4 sts, K3 tog tbl, K1.
Work 3 rows patt without dec.
Rep last 4 rows 13[14:14] times more.

Shape neck
Next row K1, K3 tog, patt 14[14:16] sts, bind off 27 [29:31] sts, patt to last 4 sts, K3 tog tbl, K1.
Complete right shoulder first.
Dec one st at neck edge on next 6 rows; *at the same time*, continue to dec on raglan edge every 4th row 4[4:5] times more. K last 2 sts tog. Fasten off.
With WS of work facing, attach yarn to rem sts and complete to match first shoulder.

Back

Using No.1 needles, cast on 125[131:137] sts.
Work in K1, P1 rib for 1in.
Change to No.3 needles.
Beg with a K row, work in st st until back measures same as front to armholes, ending with a P row.

Shape armholes
Bind off 3 sts at beg of next 2 rows.
Next row K1, K3 tog, K to last 4 sts, K3 tog tbl, K1.
Work 3 rows without dec.
Rep last 4 rows 19[20:21] times more.
Slip rem sts on holder.

Right sleeve

Using No.1 needles, cast on 58[60:62] sts.
Work in K1, P1 rib for 2in.
Change to No.3 needles.
Beg with a K row, work in st st, inc one st at each end of 7th and every following 6th row until there are 96[100: 104] sts.
Work without shaping until sleeve measures 17[17½:18]in from beg, ending with a P row.

Shape cap
Bind off 3 sts at beg of next 2 rows.
Next row K1, K3 tog, K to last 4 sts, K3 tog tbl, K1.
Work 3 rows without dec.
Rep last 4 rows 18[19:20] times more.**
Next row Bind off 6 sts, K to last 4 sts, K3 tog tbl, K1
Work 1 row. Bind off rem sts.

Left sleeve

Work as given for right sleeve to **.
Next row K1, K3 tog, K to end.
Next row Bind off 6 sts, P to end.
Work 1 row. Bind off rem sts.

Finishing

Press very lightly.
Join raglan edges of sleeves to raglan edges of back and front
Neckband Using set of No.1 double-pointed needles, with RS facing, pick up and K124 [128:138] sts evenly around neck, including sts from holder.
Work in rounds of K1, P1 rib for 2in.
Bind off loosely in rib.
Join side and sleeve seams.
Fold neckband in half to WS and sl st down.

Aran style sweater

Here is the pattern for an elegant, well-styled pullover with wide rib turtleneck and edging, which you will find a joy to knit and wear. Although this attractive sweater has an Aran look, there are no traveling stitches requiring the use of a cable needle. The zigzag lines are achieved by increasing and decreasing at either side of each pattern.

Size

Directions are for 38in bust. Length at center back, 22in. Sleeve seam, about 17½in.

Gauge
6 sts and 8 rows to 1in over st st on No.4 needles.

Materials

Dawn Wintuk Sports
7 2oz skeins
One pair No.2 needles
One pair No.4 needles

Back

Using No.2 needles, cast on 122 sts.
1st row P2, *K2, P2, rep from * to end.
2nd row K2, *P2, K2, rep from * to end.
Rep first and 2nd rows until work measures 2½in.
Change to No.4 needles and patt.
1st row K1, *P1, K2, P18, K2, P1, rep from * to last st, K1.
2nd row K1, *K1, P2, K18,

P2, K1, rep from * to last st, K1.
3rd row K1, lift thread before next st and make one st by knitting into it—called K up 1—, *P1, K2, P8, P2 tog, P8, K2, P1, K up 1, rep from * to last st, K1. 123 sts.
4th row K1, *K2, P2, K17, P2, K1, rep from * to last 2 sts, K2.
5th row K1, *P2, K up 1, K2, P2 tog, P13, P2 tog, K2, K up 1, P1, rep from * to last 2 sts, P1, K1.
6th row K1, *K3, P2, K15, P2, K2, rep from * to last 2 sts, K2.
7th row K1, *P3, K up 1, K2, P2 tog, P5, K into front and back and front and back of next st—called M4—, P5, P2 tog, K2, K up 1, P2, rep from * to last 2 sts, P1, K1.
8th row K1, *K4, P2, K6, P4, K6, P2, K3, rep from * to last 2 sts, K2.
9th row K1, *P4, K up 1,

▼ *Close-up detail of pattern*

K2, P2 tog, P4, K4, P4, P2 tog, K2, K up 1, P3, rep from * to last 2 sts, P1, K1.
10th row K1, *K5, P2, K5, P4, K5, P2, K4, rep from * to last 2 sts, K2.
11th row K1, *P5, K up 1, K2, P2 tog, P3, sl 2, K2 tog, p2sso, P3, P2 tog, K2, K up 1, P4, rep from * to last 2 sts, P1, K1.
12th row K1, *K6, P2, K9, P2, K5, rep from * to last 2 sts, K2.
13th row K1, P1, *P5, K up 1, K2, P2 tog, P5, P2 tog, K2, K up 1, P5, M4, rep from * ending last rep P6, K1.
14th row K2, *K6, P2, K7, P2, K6, P4, rep from * ending last rep K8.
15th row K1, P1, *P6, K up 1, K2, P2 tog, P3, P2 tog, K2, K up 1, P6, K4, rep from * ending last rep P7, K1.
16th row K2, *K7, P2, K5, P2, K7, P4, rep from * ending last rep K9.
17th row K1, P1, *P7, K up 1, K2, P2 tog, P1, P2 tog, K2, K up 1, P7, sl 2, K2 tog, p2sso, rep from * ending last rep P8, K1.
18th row K1, *K9, P2, K3, P2, K8, rep from * to last 2 sts, K2.
19th row K1, *P9, K up 1, K2, P3 tog, K2, K up 1, P8, rep from * to last 2 sts, P1, K1.
20th row K1, *K10, P2, K1, P2, K9, rep from * to last 2 sts, K2.
21st row K1, *P4, M4, P5, K2, P1, K2, P5, M4, P3, rep from * to last 2 sts, P1, K1.
22nd row K1, *K4, P4, K5, P2, K1, P2, K5, P4, K3, rep from * to last 2 sts, K2.
23rd row K1, *P4, K4, P5, K2, P1, K2, P5, K4, P3, rep from * to last 2 sts, P1, K1.
24th row K1, *K4, P4, K5, P2, K1, P2, K5, P4, K3, rep from * to last 2 sts, K2.
25th row K1, *P4, sl 2, K2 tog, p2sso, P3, P2 tog, K2, K up 1, P1, K up 1, K2, P2 tog, P3, sl 2, K2 tog, p2sso, P3, rep from * to last 2 sts, P1, K1.
26th row K1, *K9, P2, K3, P2, K8, rep from * to last 2 sts, K2.

27th row K1, *P7, P2 tog, K2, K up 1, P3, K up 1, K2, P2 tog, P6, rep from * to last 2 sts, P1, K1.
28th row K1, *K8, P2, K5, P2, K7, rep from * to last 2 sts, K2.
29th row K1, P1, *P5, P2 tog, K2, K up 1, P5, K up 1, K2, P2 tog, P5, M4, rep from * ending last rep P6, K1.
30th row K2, *K6, P2, K7, P2, K6, P4, rep from * ending last rep K8.
31st row K1, P1, *P4, P2 tog, K2, K up 1, P7, K up 1, K2, P2 tog, P4, K4, rep from * ending last rep P5, K1.
32nd row K2, *K5, P2, K9, P2, K5, P4, rep from * ending last rep K7.
33rd row K1, P1, *P3, P2 tog, K2, K up 1, P9, K up 1, K2, P2 tog, P3, sl 2, K2 tog, p2sso, rep from * ending last rep P4, K1.
34th row K1, *K5, P2, K11. P2, K4, rep from * to last 2 sts, K2.
35th row K1, *P3, P2 tog, K2, K up 1, P5, M4, P5, K up 1, K2, P2 tog, P2, rep from * to last 2 sts, P1, K1.
36th row K1, *K4, P2, K6, P4, K6, P2, K3, rep from * to last 2 sts, K2.
37th row K1, *P2, P2 tog, K2, K up 1, P6, K4, P6, K up 1, K2, P2 tog, P1, rep from * to last 2 sts, P1, K1.
38th row K1, *K3, P2, K7, P4, K7, P2, K2, rep from * to last 2 sts, K2.
39th row K1, *P1, P2 tog, K2, K up 1, P7, sl 2, K2 tog, p2sso, P7, K up 1, K2, P2 tog, rep from * to last 2 sts, P1, K1.
40th row K1, *K2, P2, K17, P2, K1, rep from * to last 2 sts, K2.
41st row K1, P2 tog, *K2, K up 1, P17, K up 1, K2, P3 tog, rep from * ending last rep P2 tog, K1.
42nd row K1, *K1, P2, K19, P2, rep from * to last 2 sts, K2.
43rd row K1, *P1, K2, P5, M4, P7, M4, P5, K2, rep from * to last 2 sts, P1, K1.
44th row K1, * K1, P2, K5, P4, K7, P4, K5, P2, rep from * to last 2 sts, K2.

45th row K1, *P1, K2, P5, K4, P7, K4, P5, K2, rep from * to last 2 sts, P1, K1.

46th row K1, *K1, P2, K5, P4, K7, P4, K5, P2, rep from * to last 2 sts, K2.

47th row K1, *P1, K up 1, K2, P2 tog, P3, sl 2, K2 tog, p2sso, P7, sl 2, K2 tog, p2sso, P3, P2 tog, K2, K up 1, rep from * to last 2 sts, P1, K1.

48th row As 4th.
The patt is formed by rep rows 5—48 throughout.
Work without shaping until work measures about 15½in, ending with a WS row.

Shape armholes
Bind off 3 sts at beg of next 2 rows.
Bind off 2 sts at beg of next 2 rows.
Dec one st at each end of next and every other row 7 times in all.
Work without shaping until armholes measure about 6½in, ending with a 42nd patt row.

Shape shoulders
Bind off 6 sts at beg of next 8 rows; then 5 sts at beg of next 2 rows. Slip rem sts onto holder.

Front

Work as for back until armholes measure about 4½in, ending with a 26th patt row.

Shape neck
1st row Patt 41. Turn.
Complete first shoulder on these sts.
**Bind off at neck edge every other row 3 sts once, 2 sts once and one st 7 times.
Work until armhole measures same as back to shoulder, ending at armhole edge.

Shape shoulder
Bind off 6 sts every other row 4 times; and 5 sts once.**
With right side of work facing, slip center 17 sts onto holder.
Attach yarn to rem sts and patt to end of row. Work 1 row.
Work second shoulder in same

▲ *Aran style sweater showing overall zigzag pattern*

manner from ** to **.

Sleeves

Using No.2 needles, cast on 50 sts.
Work in rib as on back until work measures 2½in.
Change to No.4 needles and patt as on back.
Continue working in patt as established inc one st at each end of 9th and every following 8th row until there are 75 sts.
Work until sleeve measures about 17½in ending with a WS row.

Shape cap
Bind off 3 sts at beg of next 2 rows.
Bind off 2 sts at beg of next 10 rows.
Dec one st at beg of next 28 rows.
Bind off 2 sts at beg of next 6 rows.
Bind off rem sts.

Collar

Press lightly.
Join left shoulder seam.
Using No.2 needles and with right side facing, pick up and

K120 sts evenly around neck edge.
1st row P1, K2, *P2, K2, rep from * to last st, P1.
2nd row K1, P2, *K2, P2, rep from * to last st, K1.
Rep first and 2nd rows until collar measures 5½in or desired depth. Bind off.

Finishing

Press lightly.
Join right shoulder seam and collar.
Join side and sleeve seams.
Sew in sleeves.

Short or long coat and pants

This smart mix and match outfit can be made with either a long or a short coat. The raised basket stitch has a rich tweed effect.

Size

Directions are for 32in bust and 34in hips.
The figures in brackets [ ] refer to the 34, 36 and 38in bust sizes, and 36, 38, and 40in hip sizes respectively.
Long coat. Length to shoulder 43[43½:44:44½]in, adjustable.
Short coat. Length to shoulder, 31[31½:32:32½]in, adjustable.
Sleeve seam, 17½in adjustable.
Pants. Inside leg, 28[28½: 29:29½]in, adjustable.

Gauge
6 sts and 8 rows to 1in over plain basket st and 9 sts and 11 rows to 1in over raised basket st worked on No.5 needles.

Materials

Reynolds Classique
Long coat. 19[19:20:20] balls
Short coat. 15[16:16:17] balls
Pants. 9[10:10:10] balls
One pair No.3 needles
One pair No.5 needles
Long coat. 10 buttons
Short coat. 8 buttons
One snap fastener
Waist length elastic
One No.E crochet hook

Coat back

Using No.3 needles, cast on 177[182:187:192] sts for long coat or 157[162:167:172] sts for short coat.
Beg with a K row, work 1½in st st ending with a K row.
Next row P2, *P twice into next st, P4, rep from * to end. 212[218:224:230] sts for long coat, 188[194:200:206] sts for short coat.
Change to No.5 needles.
Commence raised basket st patt.
1st row K1, *with yarn at back of work sl 3P, ytf, P3, rep from * to last st, K1.
2nd row K1, *K3, ytf, sl 3P, ytb, rep from * to last st, K1.
3rd row As 1st.
4th row As 2nd.
5th row K1, *M1K, K3 tog, M1K, K3, rep from * to last st, K1.
6th row P.
7th row K1, *P3, ytb, sl 3P, ytf, rep from * to last st, K1 skipping ytf before knitting last st.
8th row K1, *ytf, sl 3P, ytb, K3, rep from * to last st, K1.
9th row As 7th.
10th row As 8th.
11th row K1, *K3, M1K, K3 tog, M1K, rep from * to last st, K1.
12th row P.
These 12 rows form patt and are rep throughout.
Rep 12 patt rows once more.**
Continue in patt, dec one st at each end of next and every following 12th row until 152[158:164:170] sts rem. 30 dec long coat, 18 dec short coat.
Continue without shaping until work measures 36½in from hemline for long coat or 24½in from hemline for short coat, or desired length to

underarm allowing for 1½in hem and ending with a WS row.

Shape armholes

Bind off 9 sts at beg of next 2 rows.
Dec one st at each end of next and following 5[8:8:11] alt rows. 122[122:128:128] sts.
Continue without shaping until armholes measure 6½[7:7½:8]in, ending with a WS row.

Shape shoulders

Bind off 9 sts at beg of next 6 rows; then 10 sts at beg of next 2 rows. Bind off rem 48[48:54:54] sts.

Coat left front

Using No.3 needles, cast on 92[97:102:107] sts for long coat or 82[87:92:97] sts for short coat and work as given for back to **. 110[116:122:128] sts for long coat and 98[104:110:116] sts for short coat.
Continue in patt, dec one st at beg of next and every following 12th row until 80[86:92:98] sts rem.
Continue without shaping until work measures same as back to underarm, ending with a WS row.

Shape armhole

Bind off 9[9:15:15] sts at beg of next row. Work 1 row.
Dec one st at beg of next and following 5[8:8:11] alt rows. 65[68:68:71] sts.
Continue without shaping until armhole measures 4½[5:5½:6]in from beg, ending with a RS row.

Shape neck

Bind off at neck edge, 12[15:15:18] sts once; then 3 sts every other row twice.
Dec one st at neck edge on every other row until 38 sts rem.
Continue without shaping until armhole measures same as back to shoulder, ending with a WS row.

Shape shoulder

At arm edge, bind off 9 sts

every other row 3 times.
Work 1 row.
Bind off rem 11 sts.
Mark position for buttons on left front, first to come ½in below neck edge, last to come 6in above hemline for long coat or 4in above hemline for short coat, with 8 more evenly spaced between for long coat or 6 more for short coat.

Coat right front

Work as given for left front, but reverse all shaping and, as markers are reached, make buttonholes as follows:
Next row (RS) Patt 4 sts, bind off 3 sts, patt to end.
Next row Patt to end, casting on 3 sts above those bound off.

Sleeves

Using No.3 needles, cast on 57[57:62:62] sts.
Beg with a K row, work 1in in st st, ending with a K row.
Next row P2, *P twice into next st, P4, rep from * to end. 68[68:74:74] sts.
Change to No.5 needles.
Continue in patt as given for back, inc one st at each end of 7th and every following 8th row until there are 92[92:98:98] sts, then at each end of every 6th row until there are 116[116:122:122] sts.
Continue without shaping until sleeve measures 17½in from hemline, or desired length to underarm allowing 1in for hem and ending with a WS row.

Shape cap

Bind off 9[9:12:12] sts at beg of next 2 rows.
Dec one st at each end of next and following 11[14:14:17] alt rows. 74[68:68:62] sts.
Bind off 2 sts at beg of next 12 rows, 3 sts at beg of next 6[4:4:2] rows and 4 sts at beg of next 4 rows. Bind off rem 16 sts.

Finishing

Press pieces under a damp cloth with a warm iron.
Join shoulder seams.

Front and neck edge

Using No.E hook and RS facing, work 1 row sc up right front, around neck and down left front, turn and work second row sc. Fasten off. Join side and sleeve seams. Sew in sleeves. Turn hems to WS and slip stitch in place. Press seams. Sew on buttons.

Pants left leg

Using No.3 needles, cast on 137[142:147:152] sts. Beg with a K row, work 1½in st st, ending with a K row.
Next row P2, *P twice into next st, P4, rep from * to end. 164[170:176:182] sts. Change to No.5 needles and work 72 rows in raised basket st patt as given for coat.
Next row K1, *P1, P2 tog, K1, K2 tog, rep from * to last st, K1. 110[114:118:122] sts.
Next row K1, *P2, K2, rep from * to last st, K1.
Continue in plain basket st patt.
1st row K1, *P2, K2, rep from * to last st, K1.
2nd row K1, *K2, P2, rep from * to last st, K1.
3rd and 4th rows As 2nd.
5th and 6th rows As 1st.
These 6 rows form patt.
Continue in patt, dec one st at each end of 5th and every following 8th row until 90[96: 102:108] sts rem.
Continue without shaping until work measures 19[19½: 20:20½]in from beg, or adjust leg length here allowing 1½in for hem and ending with a WS row.
Inc one st at each end of next and every following 8th row until there are 102[108:114: 120] sts, then each end of every 6th row until there are 114[120:126:132] sts, ending with an inc row.
Inc one st at each end of next 5 rows, ending with a WS row. 124[130:136:142] sts.
Dec one st at each end of next and following 6 alt rows, then each end of every 4th row until 76[82:88:94] sts rem. Work 1[3:5:7] rows after last dec, ending with a WS row.**

Shape back
Next row Patt 41[45:49:53] sts, turn and patt to end.
Next row Patt 37[41:45:49] sts, turn and patt to end.
Continue to work 4 sts less on every other row until row reads patt 17, turn and patt to end.
Change to No.3 needles.
Beg with a K row continue in st st for 1in, ending with a P row.
Bind off.

Pants right leg

Work as given for left leg to **. Work 1 more row.

Shape back
Work as given for left leg until row reads patt 17, turn and patt to end.
Change to No.3 needles.
Beg with a P row, continue in st st for 1in, ending with a P row. Bind off.

Finishing

Press as given for coat. Join back and front seams. Join leg seams. Turn hems at lower edge and waist to WS and slip stitch in place. Press seams. Thread elastic through hem at waist and secure.

▲ *The pants suit* ▼ *Stitch detail*

Pants suit with two-tone jacket

Basic Wardrobe Knitting

Sizes

Directions are to fit 32in bust and 34in hips.
The figures in brackets [] refer to the 34, 36 and 38in bust sizes, and the 36, 38 and 40in hip sizes respectively.
Jacket. Length at center back, 27[27½:28:28½]in. Sleeve seam, 21[21:21½:21½]in.
Pants. Inside leg seam, 29[30:30½:31½]in.

Gauge

7 sts and 8 rows to 1in over st st worked on No.4 needles.
8 sts and 8 rows to 1in over patt worked on No.4 needles.

Materials

Spinnerin Mona
Jacket. 4[5:5:6] balls in dark color A
7[8:9:10] balls in light color B
7 buttons
Pants. 11[12:13:13] balls in dark color A
One pair No.2 needles
One pair No.4 needles
Waist length of elastic

Pants left leg

**Using No.2 needles and A, cast on 160[166:174:180] sts and work 7 rows st st beg with a K row.
Next row K to form ridge for hemline.
Change to No.4 needles and continue in st st beg with a K row, until work measures 10[11:11½:12½]in from hemline, ending with a P row.

Shape leg

Next row K39[40:42:44], K2 tog tbl, K78[82:86:88], K2 tog, K39[40:42:44]. 158 [164:172:178] sts.
Work without shaping until leg measures 14[15:15½:16½] in from hemline, ending with a P row.
Next row K39[40:42:44], K2 tog tbl, K76[80:84:86], K2 tog, K39[40:42:44]. 156 [162:170:176] sts.
Work without shaping until leg measures 18[19:19½:20½]in from hemline, ending with a P row.
Next row K38[39:41:43], K2 tog tbl, K76[80:84:86], K2 tog, K38[39:41:43]. 154 [160:168:174] sts.
Work without shaping until leg measures 22[23:23½:24½]in from hemline, ending with a P row.
Next row K38[39:41:43], K2 tog tbl, K74[78:82:84], K2 tog, K38[39:41:43]. 152 [158:166:172] sts.
Work without shaping until leg measures 26[27:27½:28½]in from hemline, ending with a P row.
Next row K37[38:40:42], K2 tog tbl, K74[78:82:84], K2 tog, K37[38:40:42]. 150 [156:164:170] sts.
Work without shaping until leg measures 29[30:30½:31½] in from hemline, ending with a P row.
Mark center of last row with colored thread.

Shape front and back seams

Bind off 4 sts at beg of next 2 rows, then dec 1 st at each end of next 3 rows. 136[142: 150:156] sts. Work 1 row.
Dec 1 st at each end of next

and every other row until 128 [134:142:148] st rem.
Work 7[9:9:11] rows without shaping.
Next row K2 tog, K60[63: 67:70], K2 tog tbl, K2 tog, K to last 2 sts, K2 tog. 124[130:138:144] sts.
Work 7 rows.
Next row K2 tog, K58[61: 65:68], K2 tog tbl, K2 tog, K to last 2 sts, K2 tog, 120[126:134:140] sts.
Work 5 rows.
Next row K2 tog, K56[59: 63:66], K2 tog tbl, K2 tog, K to last 2 sts, K2 tog. 116[122:130:136] sts.
Work 5 rows.
Continue dec in this way on next and every following 6th row until 88[94:102:108] sts rem.
Continue without shaping until work measures 9[9½:9½: 10]in from colored marker ending with a P row.**

Shape back

***1st row** K44[47:51:54], turn.
2nd and every other row P.
3rd row K33[35:38:40], turn.
5th row K22[23:25:26], turn.
7th row K11[11:12:12], turn.
9th row K across all sts picking up loop at point where work was turned and knitting it tog with next st to avoid hole.
Change to No.2 needles and work in K1, P1 rib for 1in.
Bind off in rib.

Right leg

Work as for left leg from ** to **.
Next row K.
Work as for left leg from *** to end, reading P for K and K for P.

Finishing

With WS facing, block each piece by pinning out around edges and omitting ribbing, press lightly using a cool iron and a dry cloth.
Using a flat seam for ribbing and a fine backstitch seam for remainder, join front, back and leg seams.
Fold hems at hemline to

wrong side and slip stitch hem in place. Work casing stitching inside waistband and thread with elastic. Press seams.

Jacket back

NB When working in stripe patt carry yarn not in use loosely along side of work.
Using No.2 needles and A, cast on 129[137:145:153] sts. Work 5 rows garter st.
Change to No.4 needles, attach B and work in patt as follows:
1st row (RS) Using B, *K1, ytf, K2, sl 1, K2 tog, psso, K2, ytf, rep from * to last st, K1.
2nd row Using B, P.
Rep last 2 rows twice more.
7th row Using A, as 1st.
8th row Using A, as 2nd.
These 8 rows form patt.**
Continue in patt until back measures 10in, ending with RS row.
Change to No.4 needles and continue in patt until back measures 20in, ending with RS facing.

Shape armholes

Keeping patt correct, bind off 3 sts at beg of next 2 rows, then dec 1 st at each end of every row until 109[117:125: 133] sts. rem.
Work 1 row.
Dec 1 st at each end of every other row until 97[101:105:109] sts rem.
Work without shaping until back measures 27[27½:28:28½] in, ending with a WS row.

Shape shoulders

Bind off 9[9:9:10] sts at beg of next 4 rows, then 8[9:10:9] sts at beg of following 2 rows. Bind off rem 45[47:49:51] sts.

Left front

Using No.2 needles and A, cast on 65[69:73:77] sts. K 5 rows.
Change to No.4 needles, attach B and patt as follows:
1st and 3rd sizes only.
Work as for back from ** to **.
2nd and 4th sizes only.
1st row (RS) Using B, *K1,

154

ytf, K2, sl 1, K2 tog, psso,
K2, ytf, rep from * to last
5 sts, K1, ytf, K2, K2 tog tbl.
2nd row Using B, P.
Rep last 2 rows twice more.
7th row Using A, as 1st.
8th row Using A, as 2nd.
These 8 rows form the patt.
***All sizes** Continue in
patt until front measures
10in, ending with RS facing.
Change to No.4 needles and
continue in patt until front
measures 20in, ending with
same patt row as back,
ending with WS row.

**Shape armhole and front
edge**
Next row Keeping patt
correct, bind off 3 sts, patt to
last 2[3:2:3] sts, K2[3:2:3]
tog. 61[64:69:72] sts.
Next row P.
Dec 1 st at armhole edge on
every row *at the same time* dec
1 st at neck edge on next and
every other row until 50[54:58:
62] sts rem.
Work 1 row.
Dec 1 st at each end of next
and every other row until 38
sts rem.
Keeping armhole edge
straight, continue dec 1 st at
neck edge on every other row as
before until 26[27:28:29] sts
rem.
Work without shaping until
front measures same as back
to shoulder, ending with RS
facing.

Shape shoulder
At armhole edge, bind off
9[9:9:10] sts every other row
twice. Work 1 row.
Bind off rem 8[9:10:9] sts.

Right front

Using No.2 needles and A,
cast on 65[69:73:77] sts. K 5
rows.

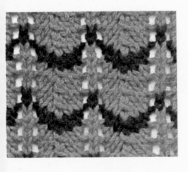

Change to No.4 needles, attach
B and work in patt as
follows:
1st and 3rd sizes only.
Work as for back from ** to
**
2nd and 4th sizes only.
1st row (RS) Using B, K2
tog, K2, ytf, *K1, ytf, K2,
sl 1, K2 tog, psso, K2, ytf,
rep from * to last st, K1.
2nd row Using B, P.
Rep last 2 rows twice more.
7th row Using B, as 1st.
8th row Using B, as 2nd.
These 8 rows form patt.
Work as for left front from
*** to end, reversing shaping.

Sleeves

Using No.2 needles and A,
cast on 50[52:54:56] sts and
work in K1, P1 rib for 3½in.
Next row (Rib 1, pick up and
K yarn before next st—called
M1—) 2[5:2:5] times, *inc in
next st, M1, rep from * to last
2[5:2:5] sts, (rib 1, M1) 1[4:1:
4] times, rib 1. 145[145:157:

157] sts.
Change to No.4 needles,
attach B and patt as follows:
1st row (RS) Using B, *K1,
ytf, K4, sl 1, K2 tog, psso,
K4, ytf, rep from * to last
st, K1.
2nd row Using B, P.
Rep last 2 rows twice more.
7th row Using A, as 1st.
8th row Using A, as 2nd.
These 8 rows form patt.
Continue in patt until sleeve
measures 12½in, ending with a
WS row.

Shape sleeve sides
Next row *K1, ytf, K3,
sl 2, K3 tog, p2sso, K3, ytf,
rep from * to last st, K1. 121
[121:131:131] sts.
Next row P.
Next row *K1, ytf, K3,
sl 1, K2 tog, psso, K3, ytf,
rep from * to last st, K1.
Keeping patt correct, rep last
2 rows until sleeve seam
measures 16½in, ending with
WS facing.
Next row *K1, ytf, K2,

sl 2, K3 tog, p2sso, K2, ytf,
rep from * to last st, K1.
97[97:105:105] sts.
Next row P.
Next row *K1, ytf, K2,
sl 1, K2 tog, psso, K2, ytf,
rep from * to last st, K1.
Keeping patt correct, rep
last 2 rows until sleeve seam
measures about 21[21:21½:
21½]in, ending with same patt
row as back before armhole
shaping.

Shape cap
Bind off 3 sts at beg of next
2 rows.
Dec 1 st at each end of
every other row until 73
[65:73:65] sts rem.
Work 1 row.
Dec 1 st at each end of every
row until 29 sts rem.
Bind off.

Finishing

Omitting garter st, block and
press as for pants. Join
shoulder, side and sleeve
seams.
Sew in sleeves.

Left front border
Using No.2 needles and A,
cast on 11 sts.
1st row (RS) K2, (P1, K1)
4 times, K1.
2nd row (K1, P1) 5 times,
K1.
Rep last 2 rows until border
fits up left front and around to
center of back when slightly
stretched.
Bind off in rib.

Right front border
Work as for left border
working 7 buttonholes,
first to come ½in above lower
edge, 7th at start of neck
shaping and remainder
evenly spaced between.
First mark positions of
buttons on left front, then
work buttonholes as markers
are reached.
Buttonhole row. (RS)
Rib 4, bind off 3, rib to end.
On next row cast on 3 sts
above those bound off.
Join borders at center back
and stitch in position.
Press seams.
Sew on buttons.

155

Smart outfits for larger sizes

Five smart outfits from one pattern, specially designed for larger sizes—from forty inch to forty-eight inch bust. Almost an entire wardrobe, this wonderful pattern will make a sleeveless dress and jacket, a blouse and skirt, a short-sleeved dress, a long-sleeved dress and a sleeveless jacket.

Sizes
Directions are for 40in bust. The figures in brackets [] refer to the 42, 44, 46 and 48in bust sizes respectively.
Dress. 42[44:46:48:50]in hips. Length to shoulder, 43[44:45: 46:47]in, or as desired.
Jacket. Length to shoulder, 25[26:27:28:29]in. Sleeve seam, 17in, or as required.

> **Gauge**
> **Dress.** 7 sts and 9 rows to 1in over st st worked on No.3 needles.
> **Jacket.** 6½ sts and 9 rows to 1in over st st worked on No.3 needles.

Materials
Dress. Unger's English Crepe
19[21:23:25:27] balls
One pair No.3 needles
12in zipper
Jacket. Reynolds Classique
10[10:11:12:12] balls
One pair No.3 needles
11 buttons

Dress back

Cast on 175[183:191:199:207] sts.

1st row K1, *P1, K1, rep from * to end.
Rep 1st row until work measures 3in ending with a WS row.
Continue in st st beg with a K row.
Work 4in (for longer or shorter dress work more or fewer rows at this point).
1st dec row K40[42:44:46: 48], sl 1, K1, psso, K until 42[44:46:48:50] sts rem, K2 tog, K to end.
Work 7 rows st st beg with a P row.
Rep last 8 rows 19 times more. 135[143:151:159:167] sts.
Work 39[41:43:45:47] rows without shaping.

Shape for bust
1st row K40[42:44:46:48], K up 1 tbl, K until 40[42:44: 46:48] sts rem, K up 1 tbl, K to end.
Work 7 rows st st beg with a P row.
Rep last 8 rows 5 times more. 147[155:163:171:179] sts.
Continue on these sts until work measures 35[35½:36: 36½:37]in, or desired length ending with a P row.

Shape armholes
Bind off 12[13:14:14:14] sts at beg of next 2 rows.
Dec one st at beg of every row until 99[105:111:117:123] sts rem.
Work without shaping until armholes measure 8[8½:9:9½: 10]in, ending with a K row.

Shape neck
1st row P33[35:37:39:41], bind off 33[35:37:39:41], P to end.

Work on these sts for right shoulder.

Shape shoulder
1st row Bind off 7[7:8:9:9] sts, K to last 2 sts, K2 tog.
2nd row P2 tog, P to end.
Rep last 2 rows once more.
5th row Bind off 7[8:8:8:9] sts. K to last 2 sts, K2 tog.
6th row P.
Bind off rem 7[8:8:8:9] sts.
With RS facing, attach yarn to rem sts and K to end.

Shape second shoulder
Work to correspond to first shoulder.

Dress front

Work as given for back until armhole shaping is completed and armholes measure 5½[6:6½:7:7½]in, ending with a K row.

Shape neck
1st row P38[40:42:44:46] sts, bind off 23[25:27:29:31] sts, P to end.
Work on last set of sts only for left shoulder, dec one st at neck edge on next and every other row until 28[30:32: 34:36] sts rem. Work 1 row. (When working second side work 2 rows instead of 1.)

Shape shoulder
Bind off 7[7:8:9:9] sts every other row twice; then bind off 7[8:8:8:9] sts every other row twice.
With RS of work facing, attach yarn to rem sts and work second side to correspond.

Finishing

Press pieces lightly on wrong side using a damp cloth and a warm iron. Join left shoulder seam.

Neckband
With RS facing, pick up and K121[125:129:133:137] sts around neck edge.
Work in seed st for 11[11:11: 12:12] rows. Bind off in seed st.
Join right shoulder seam. Press shoulder seams.

Armbands
With RS facing, pick up and K133[141:149:157:163] sts around armhole. Work in seed st for 11[11:11:12:12] rows. Bind off in seed st.
Join right side seam and left side leaving 12in open for zipper about 3in below armhole. Sew in zipper. Press seams on wrong side.

Jacket back

Cast on 127[133:139:145:151] sts.
1st row K1, *P1, K1, rep from * to end.
Rep first row 11 times more for seed st border.
Continue in st st beg with a K row.
Work until 16½[17:17½:18: 18½]in from cast-on edge, ending with a P row.

Shape armholes
Bind off 8 sts at beg of next 2 rows.
Dec one st at beg of every row until 95[101:107:113:119] sts rem.
Work without shaping until armholes measure 8½[9:9½:10: 10½]in, ending with a P row.

Shape shoulders
Bind off 8[8:9:9:10] sts at beg of next 4 rows.
Bind off 7[8:8:9:9] sts at beg of next 4 rows.
Bind off rem 35[37:39:41:43] sts.

Jacket left front

Cast on 81[85:89:93:97] sts.
Work in seed st as for back for 12 rows.
Next row K to last 9 sts, seed st 9.
Next row Seed st 9, P to end.
Rep last 2 rows until work measures same length as back to armhole, ending at side edge.

Shape armhole and border
1st row Bind off 8 sts, K to last 9 sts, seed st 9.
2nd row Seed st 9, P to end.
3rd row Sl 1, K1, psso, K to last 11 sts, K2 tog, lift thread before next st and K into back of it—called K up 1

tbl—, seed st to end.

4th row Seed st 10, P to end.

5th row Sl 1, K1, psso, K to last 10 sts, seed st 10.

6th row As 4th.

7th row Sl 1, K1, psso, K to last 12 sts, K2 tog, K up 1 tbl, seed st to end.

8th row Seed st 11, P to end. Continue in this way for 10 more rows working the K2 tog, K up 1 tbl on 11th and 15th rows and dec at armhole edge on K rows. 65[69:73:77:81] sts.

Work bust shaping

1st row K24[26:28:30:32], K2 tog, K24[26:28:30:32], K2 tog, K up 1 tbl, seed st to end.

2nd row Seed st 14, P to end.

3rd row K to last 14 sts, seed st to end.

4th row As 2nd.

5th row K to last 16 sts, K2 tog, K up 1 tbl, seed st to end.

6th row Seed st 15, P to end.

7th row K to last 15 sts, seed st to end.

8th row As 6th.

9th row K23[25:27:29:31], K2 tog, K to last 17 sts, K2 tog, K up 1 tbl, seed st to end.

10th row Seed st 16, P to end. Continue to work bust dec every 8th row from last dec *at same time* working the K2 tog, K up 1 tbl before the seed st border every 4th row as before until there are 23 seed sts, ending at center front edge.

Shape lapel

1st row Bind off 14[15:16:17:18] sts, work to end.

2nd row K to seed st border, seed st to end.

NB The seed st border sts are now kept straight but work the K2 tog (omitting the K up 1 tbl) every 4th row as before, also working the bust dec every 8th row as before *at the same time* dec one st at neck edge every WS row until 7[8:8:8:9] bust dec have been worked and 33[32:34:36:38] sts rem. End at armhole edge.

Dress with contrasting jacket ▶

▲ *Sleeveless and slimming for larger sizes*

▲ *Adaptation for a sleeveless blouse and skirt*

For 42, 44, 46 and 48in sizes only Continue on these sts until armhole measures same as back to shoulder, ending at armhole edge.

Shape shoulder
1st row Bind off 8[8:9:9:10] sts, K to end.
2nd row For 40in size only Dec one st.
For all sizes P to end.
Rep last 2 rows once more.
5th row Bind off 7[8:8:9:9] sts, K to end.
6th row As 2nd.
Bind off rem sts.

Jacket right front

Cast on 81[85:89:93:97] sts.
Work 12 rows seed st as for back.
Next row Seed st 9, K to end.
Next row P to last 9 sts, seed st to end.
Rep last 2 rows 11[13:15:17: 158

19] times more.
1st buttonhole row Seed st 3, bind off 3 sts, seed st 3, K to end.
2nd buttonhole row P to last 6 sts, seed st 3, cast on 3 sts, seed st 3.
Continue in patt making 4 more buttonholes with 24 rows between each of the buttonholes.
Next row Seed st 9, K to end.

Shape armholes
1st row Bind off 8 sts, P to last 9 sts, seed st to end.
2nd row Seed st 9, K up 1 tbl, sl 1, K1, psso, K to end.
3rd row P2 tog, P to last 10 sts, seed st 10.
4th row Seed st 10, K to end.
5th row As 3rd.
6th row Seed st 10, K up 1 tbl, sl 1, K1, psso, K to end.
Continue as established until 61[65:69:73:77] sts rem, ending at front edge.

Work bust shaping
1st row Seed st 14, K up 1 tbl, sl 1, K1, psso, K24[26:28: 30:32], sl 1, K1, psso, K to end.
Continue working to correspond with left front, working bust dec every 8th row and inc number of seed st border for lapel every 4th row until 23[23:23:24:24] sts are in seed st, then shape lapel and continue to correspond to other side.

Sleeves

Cast on 65[67:69:71:73] sts. Work in seed st for 12 rows as for back.
Continue in st st beg with a K row. Work 4in.
Inc one st at each end of next and every 10th[10th:8th: 8th:8th] row until there are 85[89:93:97:101] sts.
Work without shaping until sleeve measures 17in or

desired length ending with a P row.

Shape cap
Bind off 8 sts at beg of next 2 rows.
Dec one st at beg of every row until 39 sts rem.
Dec one st at each end of every row until 27 sts rem.
Bind off.

Collar

Cast on 21[25:29:33:37] sts. Work one row seed st as given for back.
Continue in seed st casting on 6 sts at beg of next 10 rows 81[85:89:93:97] sts.
Work 26[28:30:32:34] rows in seed st. Bind off loosely.

Cuffs

Cast on 75[77:79:81:83] sts. Work in seed st as for back for 6 rows.

▲ *Adaptation to make a short-sleeved dress*

▲ *Adaptation to make a long-sleeved dress and sleeveless jacket*

7th row Seed st 5, K to last 5 sts, seed st to end.

8th row Seed st 5, P to last 5 sts, seed st to end.

Rep last 2 rows once more.

11th row Seed st 5, bind off 3, K to last 5 sts, seed st to end.

12th row Seed st 5, P to last 5 sts, cast on 3 sts, seed st 5.

Rep 7th and 8th rows 8 times more, then rep 11th and 12th rows once.

Work 7th and 8th rows twice more.

Work 6 rows seed st. Bind off in seed st.

2nd cuff

Work as for first cuff to end of 10th row.

11th row Seed st 5, K to last 8 sts, bind off 3 sts, seed st 5.

12th row Seed st 5, cast on 3 sts, P to last 5 sts, seed st 5.

Rep 7th and 8th rows 8 times more, then rep 11th and 12th rows once.

Rep 7th and 8th rows twice more.

Work 6 rows seed st. Bind off in seed st.

Pockets

Cast on 39 sts.

Work 10 rows seed st as given for back.

11th row Seed st 7, K to last 7 sts, seed st to end.

12th row Seed st 7, P to last 7 sts, seed st to end.

Rep last 2 rows 16 times more.

Work 4 rows seed st.

49th row Seed st 18, bind off 3 sts, seed st to end.

50th row Seed st 18, cast on 3 sts, seed st to end.

Work 4 rows in seed st. Bind off in seed st.

Finishing

Press pieces on wrong side under a damp cloth with a warm iron.

Join shoulder seams, side seams and sleeve seams. Press seams.

Sew in sleeves. Sew collar to neck edge placing center of cast-on sts to center back of neck with ends in center of lapels. Sew one cuff to each sleeve with buttonhole on outer edge. Sew pocket to each front above border. Sew on buttons to correspond to buttonholes.

Mixing and matching the patterns

By using the basic patterns it is possible to adapt the garments for a simple change of style.

Dress with long sleeves

Work the dress as given, omitting armbands.

Using No.3 needles and Unger's English Crepe, work sleeves as given for the jacket, omitting cuffs.

Dress with short sleeves

Using No.3 needles and Unger's English Crepe, cast on 77[81:85:89:93] sts. Work 12 rows seed st.

Continue in st st beg with a K row, inc one st at each end of next and every 8th row until there are 85[89:93:97:101] sts.

Work without shaping until sleeve measures 5in or desired length.

Complete as given for jacket sleeve.

Sleeveless jacket

Work back, fronts and collar as given for jacket, omitting sleeves, buttonholes and pockets.

Work the armbands by first joining shoulder seams.

Using No.3 needles and with RS facing, pick up and K123 [127:131:135] sts around armhole edges. Work 6 rows seed st. Bind off. Seam sides.

Beaded angora evening top

Soft angora yarn, a simple lace pattern and the sparkle of beads add up to an elegant evening top.

Size
Directions are for 32in bust. The figures in brackets [ ] refer to the 34, 36 and 38in sizes respectively.
Length to shoulder, 20¼ [20½:20¾:21]in.

Gauge
6 sts and 8 rows to 1in over patt worked on No.5 needles.

Materials
Spinnerin Frostlon Petite 9[10:11:12] balls
One pair No.3 needles
One pair No.5 needles
One pair No.2 needles
750 beads to fit yarn
NB. Thread 350 beads onto each of 3 balls of yarn

Back

Using No.3 needles, cast on 103[109:115:121] sts.
Beg with a K row, work 5 rows st st.
Picot hemline (WS) K1, *ytf, K2 tog, rep from * to end.
Change to No.5 needles and beaded yarn.
1st row K2, *ytf, sl 1, push bead up to stitch so that it sits in front of slipped stitch, ytb—called B1 —, K1, rep from * to last st, K1.
2nd row P.
3rd row K1, *B1, K1, rep from * to end.
4th row P.

160

Rep 1st to 4th rows once. Break off bead yarn and continue in patt.
1st patt row K1, *ytf, K2 tog tbl, K1, K2 tog, ytf, K1, rep from * to end.
2nd patt row P.
3rd patt row K1, *ytf, K1, sl 1, K2 tog, psso, K1, ytf, K1, rep from * to end.
4th patt row P.
5th patt row K1, *K2 tog, ytf, K1, ytf, K2 tog tbl, K1, rep from * to end.
6th patt row P.
7th patt row K2 tog, *(K1, ytf) twice, K1, sl 1, K2 tog, psso, rep from * to last 5 sts, (K1, ytf) twice, K1, K2 tog tbl.
8th patt row P.
These 8 rows form the patt and are rep throughout.
Work 8 rows more.
Change to No.3 needles.

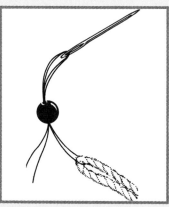

▲ *Threading bead onto the yarn*

Work 16 rows.
Change to No.2 needles.
Work 8 rows.
Change to No.3 needles.
Work 16 rows.
Change to No.5 needles.
Continue in patt until work measures 13¾in ending with

8th patt row.

Shape armholes
Bind off 6[7:8:9] sts at beg of next 2 rows.
Bind off 2 sts at beg of next 4 rows.
Dec one st at each end of next and every other row until 73[75:77:79] sts rem.
Bead rem of back by adding beads on every 1st and 5th patt rows between K2 tog tbl and K2 tog by slipping the stitch between and placing a bead in front of ss.
Continue until armholes measure 6½[6¾:7:7¼] in, ending with a WS row.

Shape neck
1st row Patt 22[23:24:25], bind off 29 sts, patt to end. Complete left shoulder on these sts.
2nd row P.
3rd row Bind off 3 sts, patt to end.
4th row Bind off 5[6:7:8] sts, P to end.
5th row Bind off 3 sts, patt to end.
6th row Bind off 5 sts, P to end.
7th row Bind off 2 sts, patt to end.
8th row Bind off rem 4 sts.
With WS of work facing, attach yarn to rem sts.
1st row Bind off 3 sts, P to end.
2nd row Bind off 5[6:7:8] sts, patt to end.
3rd row Bind off 3 sts, P to end.
4th row Bind off 5 sts, patt to end.
5th row Bind off 2 sts, P to end.
6th row Bind off rem 4 sts.

Front

Work as given for back until armholes measure 2¾[3:3¼:3½]in, ending with a WS row.

Shape neck
1st row Patt 26[27:28:29], bind off 21 sts, patt to end. Complete right front on these sts.
2nd row P.
3rd row Bind off 3 sts, patt

to end.
4th row P.
5th row Bind off 3 sts, patt to end.
6th row P.
7th row Bind off 2 sts, patt to end.
8th row P.
Dec one st at beg of next and every other row until 14[15:16:17] sts rem.
Work until armhole measures same as back to shoulder, ending at armhole edge.

Shape shoulder
At arm edge, bind off every other row, 5[6:7:8] sts once; 5 sts once; then 4 sts once. With WS facing, attach yarn to rem sts and work left front to correspond.

Neckband

Join left shoulder seam. Using No.3 needles, with RS of work facing and beaded yarn, pick up and K49 sts across back, pick up and K30 sts down left front neck, 21 sts from center front and 30 sts up right front. **P 1 row.
2nd row K1, *B1, K1, rep from * to last st, K1.
3rd row P.
4th row K2, *B1, K1, rep from * to end.
Picot row K1, *ytf, K2 tog, rep from * to last st, K1.
Change to No.2 needles. Beg with a K row, work 4 rows st st. Bind off loosely.**

Armbands

Join right shoulder seam and neckband.
Using No.3 needles and beaded yarn, pick up and K86[90:92:96] sts evenly around armhole.
Work as for neckband from ** to **.
Work another band in the same manner.

Finishing

Press lightly under a dry cloth if required.
Join side seams.
Fold hemlines to wrong side along picot rows and slip stitch in place.

Lacy dress in circular knitting

Knitted circularly so that there are no side seams, the skirt of this scoop-necked dress, in a pretty lacy stitch, hangs particularly well. The sleeves are raglan-shaped, and are finished with a ribbed cuff to match the neckline edge.

Sizes
Directions are for 34in bust. The figures in brackets [ ] refer to the 36, 38 and 40in sizes respectively.
Length from shoulder to lower edge, 45[46¾:48½:50¼]in, adjustable.
Sleeve seam, 12½[12½:13½:13½] in.

Gauge
7½ sts and 9½ rows to 1in over stockinette stitch worked on No.4 needles.

Materials
Unger English Crepe 20[22:24:27] 1oz balls
One No.3 circular needle 29in long
One No.2 circular needle 14in long
One large stitch holder

Dress

Begin at lower edge of skirt. Using 29in No.3 circular needle cast on 396[432:468:504]sts. Work back and forth.
1st row *K1, P1, rep from * to end.
2nd row *P1, K1, rep from * to end.
Rep these 2 rows 5 times more.
162

Basic Wardrobe Knitting

Join work into a circle and continue in rounds. Place marker thread at beginning of round.
1st round *K4, ytf, K4, sl 1, K2 tog, psso, K4, ytf, K3, rep from * to end of round.
2nd and every other round K.
3rd round *K5, ytf, K3, sl 1, K2 tog, psso, K3, ytf, K4, rep from * to end of round.
5th round *K6, ytf, K2, sl 1, K2 tog, psso, K2, ytf, K5, rep from * to end of round.
7th round *K7, ytf, K1, sl 1, K2 tog, psso, K1, ytf, K6, rep from * to end of round.
9th round *K4, (ytf, sl 1, K2 tog, psso, ytf, K1) 3 times, K2, rep from * to end of round.
10th round K.
These 10 rounds form patt. Rep 1st—10th rounds 7[8:9:10] times more. If the length is to be altered, work more or fewer patterns at this point, allowing 1in for each patt. Work the 1st patt round once.
1st dec round *K2 tog, K16, rep from * to end of round. 374[408:442:476] sts.
Next round *K4, ytf, K3, sl 1, K2 tog, psso, K3, ytf, K4, rep from * to end of round.
Continue in patt as established, noting that 1 less st is worked at the beg of each patt rep. Work until 5 more patts have been completed, then work 1st patt round skipping last K st of round.
2nd dec round *K2 tog, K15, rep from * to end of round.

352[384:416:448] sts.
Next round *K4, ytf, K3, sl 1, K2 tog, psso, K3, ytf, K3, rep from * to end of round. Continue in patt as established, working 1 st less at beg and end of each patt rep until 3 more patts have been completed. Work 1st patt round once.
3rd dec round *K2 tog, K14, rep from * to end. 330[360:390:420] sts.
Next round *K3, ytf, K3, sl 1, K2 tog, psso, K3, ytf, K3, rep from * to end of round. Continue in patt as established, working 2 sts less at beg and 1 st less at end of each patt rep until 3 complete patts have been worked. Work 1st patt round once, skipping last K st.
4th dec round *K2 tog, K13, rep from * to end. 308[336:364:392] sts.
Next round *K3, ytf, K3, sl 1, K2 tog, psso, K3, ytf, K2, rep from * to end of round. Continue in patt as established, working 2 sts less at each end of every patt rep until 3 more patts have been completed. Work 1st patt round once.
5th dec round *K2 tog, K12, rep from * to end. 286[312:338:364] sts.
Next round *K2, ytf, K3, sl 1, K2 tog, psso, K3, ytf, K2, rep from * to end.
Continue in patt as established, working 3 sts less at beg and 2 sts less at end of each patt rep until 3 more patts have been completed. Work 1st patt round once, skipping last K st and ending with ytf.
6th dec round *K2 tog, K11, rep from * to end of round. 264[288:312:336] sts.
Next round *K2, ytf, K3, sl 1, K2 tog, psso, K3, ytf, K1, rep from * to end of round. Continue in patt as established, working 3 sts less at each end of every patt rep until work measures 30[31:32:33]in, or desired length to waist.
Change to different patt which is used throughout bodice and sleeves.
1st round *K1, ytf, K4,

sl 1, K2 tog, psso, K4, ytf, rep from * to end of round.
2nd and every other round K.
3rd round K2, *ytf, K3, sl 1, K2 tog, psso, K3, ytf, K3, rep from * to end of round ending with K1 instead of K3.
5th round K2 tog, *ytf, K1, ytf, K2, sl 1, K2 tog, psso, K2, ytf, K1, ytf, sl 1, K2 tog, psso, rep from * to last 10 sts, ytf, K1, ytf, K2, sl 1, K2 tog, psso, K2, ytf, K2 tog, ytf.
7th round *Ytf, sl 1, K1, psso, K2, ytf, K1, sl 1, K2 tog, psso, K1, ytf, K3, rep from * to end of round.
9th round K1, *ytf, sl 1, K2 tog, psso, ytf, K1, rep from * to end of round, skipping last K st.
10th round K.
These 10 rounds form the bodice patt.
Rep 1st—10th rounds once more.
Inc round Inc for the sides as follows: *inc in first st, work in patt until 11[12:13:14] patts have been worked, inc in last st*, rep from * to * thus increasing 2 sts at each side.
Marker threads placed at each inc will make counting easier. Work 9 rounds patt, knitting the extra inc sts.
Rep last 10 rounds 3 times more. 8 sts have now been increased at each side. Mark beg of round in center of 8 st panel 4 sts in.
Work without shaping until work measures 39[40¼:41½:42¾]in, ending after a K round.

Shape front raglan armholes

1st row Bind off 4 sts, work in patt until 11[12:13:14] patts have been worked, K4, turn and work back and forth on these sts only.
2nd row Bind off 4 sts, P to end.
3rd row K2, sl 1, K1, psso, work to last 4 sts, K2 tog, K2.
4th row P.
Rep last 2 rows 3[5:7:9] times more.

hape front neck

st row K2, sl 1, K1, psso, att 40[43:46:49] sts, turn and vork on these sts only.

nd row P.

rd row K2, sl 1, K1, psso, att to last 2 sts, K2 tog.

th row P.

Rep last 2 rows 3[4:5:6] times nore.

*Continue to dec at armhole dge on next and every RS ow; *at the same time* dec one st t neck edge on every 4th ow until 21[16:23:18] sts em. Continue to dec at armhole edge as before, but keep neck edge straight until sts rem, P3. Bind off.

With RS facing, sl first 36 38:40:42] sts on stitch holder, ttach yarn to rem sts.

1st row Patt to last 4 sts, K2 og, K2.

2nd row P.

3rd row Dec one st, patt to ast 4 sts, K2 tog, K2.

4th row Rep 2 rows 3[4:5:6] times more.

Complete as for first side, vorking from ** to end.

Shape back raglan armholes

With RS facing, attach yarn o rem sts, bind off 4 sts at beg of next 2 rows.

3rd row K2, sl 1, K1, psso, att to last 4 sts, K2 tog, K2.

4th row P.

Rep last 2 rows 6[8:10:12] imes more.

Shape back neck

1st row K2, sl 1, K1, psso, patt 34[37:40:43], turn and vork on these sts only.

2nd row P.

3rd row K2, sl 1, K1, psso, patt to last 2 sts, K2 tog.

4th row P.

Rep last 2 rows 0[1:2:4] times more. Complete from ** of first side of front neck to end.

With RS of work facing, sl first 42[44:46:48] sts onto a st holder, attach yarn to rem sts and work to correspond to other side.

Sleeves

Using 14in No.2 circular needle, cast on 74[74:86:86] sts. Work back and forth

throughout sleeve.

Work 16 rows K1, P1 rib.

Change to 29in No.3 circular needle. Work in patt as given for bodice adding 1 K st at each end to allow for seaming.

1st row K1, *K1, ytf, K4, sl 1, K2 tog, psso, K4, ytf, rep from * to last st, K1.

2nd row P.

Continue in patt as established until 10th row has been completed, then inc one st at each end of next and every 6th row until there are 98 [102:106:110] sts, working the inc sts into patt as they are made.

Work without further shaping until sleeve measures 12½[12½: 13½:13½]in, ending with a P row.

Shape cap

Bind off 4 sts at beg of next 2 rows.

3rd row K2, sl 1, K1, psso, patt to last 4 sts, K2 tog, K2.

4th row P.

Rep last 2 rows until 18 sts rem. Slip sts on st holder for neck ribbing.

Finishing

Press each piece lightly on WS under damp cloth using warm iron. Join sleeve seams. Sew sleeve into armhole.

Slip the 42[44:46:48] sts from back st holder onto 29in No.3 circular needle, slip sts from one sleeve cap onto needle, slip 36[38:40:42] sts from front and sts from second sleeve cap all onto same needle. Attach yarn to end of 18 sts of right sleeve and pick up and K34 sts to st holder, rib 42[44:46: 48] sts from holder, then pick up and K34 sts to left sleeve, rib 18 sts sleeve and pick up and K66 sts to stitch holder, rib 36[38:40:42] sts from holder, pick up and K66 sts to right sleeve and rib 18 sts from sleeve. 314[318:322: 326] sts. Join sts.

Work in rounds of K1, P1 rib for 12 rounds. Bind off in rib.

Above left: a charming dress knitted in a fine lace pattern
Below left: a close-up detail of the lace pattern

Basic Wardrobe Knitting

Bridal coat in lace stitch

This superb design represents all that is best in hand knitting. Shown here as an exquisite bridal coat, the same pattern would make an evening coat if it were knitted in a bright colored yarn. Alternatively, by carrying the button loop fastening down to the hem, the coat would make an elegant coat-dress for evening occasions. The hood is optional and can be omitted, leaving a mandarin collar. The pearl trim is optional.

Size
Directions are for 34-36in bust with 36-38in hips. Length from center back, 58in. Sleeve seam, 18in.

Gauge
7 sts and 9 rows to 1in over stockinette stitch worked on No.3 needles.

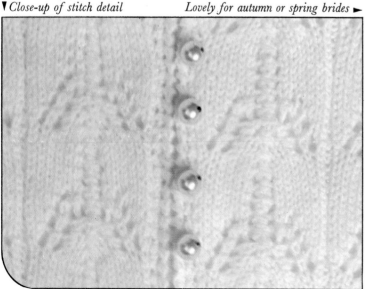
▼ *Close-up of stitch detail*

Lovely for autumn or spring brides ▶

Gauge for this pattern
7½ sts and 9 rows to 1in over patt worked on No.3 needles.

Materials
Bernat Meadowspun (1oz skeins)
Coat. 19 skeins
Hood. 2 skeins
One pair No.3 needles
One No.D crochet hook
70 pearls (optional)

Back

Using No.3 needles, cast on 250 sts.
1st row K1, P8, *K6, ytf, sl 1, K2 tog, psso, ytf, K6, P16, rep from * ending P8, K1 instead of P16.
2nd and every other row K9, *P15, K16, rep from * ending K9 instead of K16.
3rd row As 1st.

5th row As 1st.
7th row As 1st.
9th row K1, P8, *K1, ytf, K1, ytf, sl 1, K1, psso, K2, sl 1, K2 tog, psso, K2, K2 tog, ytf, K1, ytf, K1, P16, rep from * ending P8, K1, instead of P16.
11th row K1, P8, *K2, ytf, K1, ytf, sl 1, K1, psso, K1, sl 1, K2 tog, psso, K1, K2 tog, ytf, K1, ytf, K2, P16, rep from * ending P8, K1, instead of P16.
13th row K1, P8, *K3, ytf, K1, ytf, sl 1, K1, psso, sl 1, K2 tog, psso, K2 tog, ytf, K1, ytf, K3, P16, rep from * ending P8, K1, instead of P16.
15th row K1, P8, *K4, ytf, sl 1, K1, psso, ytf, sl 1, K2 tog, psso, ytf, K2 tog, ytf, K4, P16, rep from * ending P8, K1, instead of P16.
16th row As 2nd.
These 16 rows form the patt and are rep throughout.
Continue in patt until work measures 8in from beg, ending with a RS row.
1st dec row K7, K2 tog, *P15, sl 1, K1, psso, K12, K2 tog, rep from * ending sl 1, K1, psso, K7.
Continue in patt with 1 st less in the P panels at each side and 2 sts less in the rem P panels, until work measures 14in from beg, ending with a RS row.
2nd dec row K6, K2 tog, *P15, sl 1, K1, psso, K10, K2 tog, rep from * ending sl 1, K1, psso, K6.
Continue in patt until work measures 20in from beg, ending with a RS row.
3rd dec row K5, K2 tog, *P15, sl 1, K1, psso, K8, K2 tog, rep from * ending sl 1, K1, psso, K5.
Continue in patt until work measures 26in from beg, ending with a RS row.
4th dec row K4, K2 tog, *P15, sl 1, K1, psso, K6, K2 tog, rep from * ending sl 1, K1, psso, K4.
Continue in patt until work measures 32in from beg, ending with a RS row.
5th dec row K3, K2 tog,

*P15, sl 1, K1, psso, K4, K2 tog, rep from * ending sl 1, K1, psso, K3.
Continue in patt until work measures 38in from beg, ending with a RS row.
6th dec row K2, K2 tog, *P15, sl 1, K1, psso, K2, K2 tog, rep from * ending sl 1, K1, psso, K2.
Continue in patt until work measures 44in from beg, ending with a RS row.
7th dec row K1, K2 tog, *P15, sl 1, K1, psso, K2 tog, rep from * ending sl 1, K1, psso, K1 (138 sts).
Continue in patt with 2 sts in each P panel.
Work 34 rows.

Shape armholes
Bind off 8 sts at beg of next 2 rows; then 2 sts at beg of next 4 rows.
Dec one st at beg of every row until 104 sts rem.
Continue without shaping until armholes measure 6¾in from beg, ending with a WS row.

Shape shoulders
Bind off 6 sts at beg of next 4 rows; then 5 sts at beg of next 2 rows.

Shape back neck
Next row Bind off 5 sts, patt 14 sts, bind off 32 sts, patt to end.
Complete this side first.
1st row Bind off 5 sts, patt to last 2 sts, dec one st.
2nd row Dec one st, patt to end.
3rd row Bind off 6 sts, patt to last 2 sts, dec one st.
Work 1 row.
Bind off 5 rem sts.
Attach yarn to rem sts at neck edge.
1st row Dec one st, patt to end.
2nd row Bind off 6 sts, patt to last 2 sts, dec one st.
3rd row Dec one st, patt to end.
Bind off 5 rem sts.

Left front

Using No.3 needles, cast on 119 sts.
1st row K1, P8, *K6, ytf,

sl 1, K2 tog, psso, ytf, K6, P16, rep from * ending P1, K1, instead of P16.

2nd and every other row K2, *P15, K16, rep from * ending K9 instead of K16. Continue in patt as set until work measures 8in from beg, ending with a RS row.

1st dec row K2, *P15, sl 1, K1, psso, K12, K2 tog, rep from * ending sl 1, K1, psso, K7. Continue in patt until work measures 14in from beg, ending with a RS row.

2nd dec row K2, * P15, sl 1, K1, psso, K10, K2 tog, rep from * ending sl 1, K1, psso, K6. Continue in patt until work measures 20in from beg, ending with a RS row.

3rd dec row K2, *P15, sl 1, K1, psso, K8, K2 tog, rep from * ending sl 1, K1, psso, K5. Continue in patt until work measures 26in from beg, ending with a RS row.

4th dec row K2, *P15, sl 1, K1, psso, K6, K2 tog, rep from * ending sl 1, K1, psso, K4. Continue in patt until work measures 32in from beg, ending with a RS row.

5th dec row K2, *P15, sl 1, K1, psso, K4, K2 tog, rep from * ending sl 1, K1, psso, K3. Continue in patt until work measures 38in from beg, ending with a RS row.

6th dec row K2, *P15, sl 1, K1, psso, K2, K2 tog, rep from * ending sl 1, K1, psso, K2. Continue in patt until work measures 44in from beg, ending with a RS row.

7th dec row K2, *P15, sl 1, K1, psso, K2, K2 tog, rep from * ending sl 1, K1, psso, K1 (70 sts). Continue in patt with 2 sts in each P panel. Work 34 rows.

Shape armhole
At arm edge, bind off 8 sts once, then 2 sts every other row twice.

Dec one st at armhole edge on every other row until 53 sts rem.

Continue without shaping until armhole measures 5½in from beg, ending at center front edge.

166

Shape neck
Next row Bind off 11 sts, patt to end.

Keeping armhole edge straight, dec one st at neck edge on every row 4 times, then one st on every other row twice, ending at armhole edge.

Shape shoulder
1st row Bind off 6 sts, patt to end.
2nd row Dec one st, patt to end.
3rd row Bind off 5 sts, patt to end.
4th row As 2nd.
5th row As 1st.
6th row As 2nd.
Keeping neck edge straight, bind off at neck edge 5 sts every other row twice; then 6 sts once.

Right front

Using No.3 needles, cast on 119 sts.

1st row K1, P1, *K6, ytf, sl 1, K2 tog, psso, ytf, K6, P16, rep from * ending P8, K1, instead of P16.

2nd and every other row K9, *P15, K16, rep from * ending K2 instead of K16. Continue in patt as set until work measures 8in from beg, ending with a RS row.

1st dec row K7, K2 tog, *P15, sl 1, K1, psso, K12, K2 tog, rep from * ending K2. Complete to correspond to left front, reversing shaping, and work 1 more row before commencing armhole shaping.

Sleeves

Using No.3 needles, cast on 56 sts.

1st row K3, *P2, K4, rep from * ending K3 instead of K4.
2nd row P3, *K2, P4, rep from * ending P3, instead of P4.
These 2 rows form the patt. Continue in patt inc one st at each end of 19th and every following 10th row until there are 74 sts.
Continue without shaping until sleeve measures 12½in from beg, ending with a RS row.

Next row K2, *P1, (inc one st by picking up loop between needles and P tbl, P2) 4 times, inc one st as before, P1, K2, rep from * to end (104 sts).
Next row P2, *K6, ytf, sl 1, K2 tog, psso, ytf, K6, P2, rep from * to end.
Continue in patt as given for top of back.
Work 49 more rows.

Shape cap
Bind off 8 sts at beg of next 2 rows, then dec one st at beg of every row until 44 sts rem.
Bind off 2 sts at beg of next 4 rows; then 3 sts at beg of next 2 rows.
Bind off rem 30 sts.

Hood

Front panel
Using No.3 needles, cast on 206 sts.
1st row P2, *K6, ytf, sl 1, K2 tog, psso, ytf, K6, P2, rep from * to end.
Continue in patt as for top of back until work measures 7in from beg.
Bind off.

Back panel
Using No.3 needles, cast on 70 sts.
Work 9in patt as given for front panel.
Bind off.

Finishing

Press each piece under a damp cloth with a warm iron.
Join shoulder seams.
Sew sleeves into armholes, easing fullness on each side of shoulder seam.
Join side and sleeve seams.
Join bound-off and side edges of back hood panel to bound-off edge of front hood panel.
Press all seams.
Hood border. Thread 12 pearls onto a ball of yarn.
Join in yarn and work a row of sc along face edge of hood, working one sc into each st.
End with ch1 but do not turn work.
Work a row of sc back along row just worked—called crab

st—bringing a pearl to back of work at the point of each lace panel and working the st in the usual way. Cut yarn and fasten off.
Baste hood to neck edge of coat, beg 1¼in from center front edges of coat and easing in the fullness evenly.
Collar. Attach yarn to right side of neck at center front edge. Work a row of firm sc right around neck edge, working through edges of both hood and coat. Turn with ch1 Work 10 more rows of sc, turning with ch1 at end of every row except last row.
End last row with ch1 but do not turn work.
Work a row of crab st as given for hood border.
Cut yarn and fasten off.
Front edges. Attach yarn to left center front edge at top of collar and work a row of sc down left center front edge, along cast-on edges of left front, back and right front and up right center front edge to top of collar, working into every other row along center front edges and into each st along cast-on edges.
Cut yarn but do not turn.
Thread 35 pearls onto ball of yarn.
Attach yarn at neck and work a row of crab st down right center front edge, working the first 12 pearls into the first and then every 5th st and the remainder into every 9th st. Continue to work in crab st along lower edges of right front, back and left front.
Cut yarn and thread rem 23 pearls onto ball of yarn.
Attach yarn and continue in crab st, working pearls up left front edge to match the lower 23 pearls on right front.
Continue up left front edge, working button loops to match 12 rem pearls on right front by working ch2 and skipping one st.
Cut yarn and fasten off.
Press borders lightly.
If desired, omit pearl trimming and sew on 12 small buttons, making button loops as given.

Slipper socks knitted in rounds

Either of these patterns provides an original and useful way of practicing knitting and shaping in rounds. With instructions given for two different styles in two different sizes, these slipper socks are warm, comfortable and colorful. Make them for yourself or, better yet, as novelty gifts for many different occasions.

Sizes

Striped slipper socks. To fit size 6½ or 7½ slipper soles. Length from top to base of heel, 22in.

Bobble-trimmed slipper socks. To fit size 4½ or 5½ slipper soles. Length from top to base of heel, excluding cuff, 15in.

Gauge
5½ sts and 7½ rows to 1in over st st worked on No.5 needles; 6 sts and 8 rows to 1in over st st worked on No.3 needles.

Materials
Reynolds Danskyarn
Striped slipper socks. Two balls each of green, blue and yellow; three of red
Slipper soles size 6½ or 7½
Bobble-trimmed slipper socks. Five balls
Slipper soles size 4½ or 5½
One set of 4 No.3 double-pointed needles
Spool of shirring elastic

Striped slipper sock

Using set of 4 No.3 needles and blue, cast on 77 sts, 28 on

168

▲ *Detail of striped version*

first needle, 21 on second needle and 28 on third needle.
1st round *P1, K5, P1, rep from * to end of round.
Rep this round 7 times more.
Next round Using green, K to end.
Using green, rep 1st round 7 times more.
Next round Using red, K to end.
Using red, rep 1st round 15 times more.
Next round Using yellow, K to end.
Using yellow, rep 1st round 7 times more.
These 40 rounds form striped patt, noting that 1st round with new color is always K to end.
Continue in patt until work measures 5½in from beg.
Next round *P1, K2, K2 tog, K1, P1, rep from * to end. 66 sts.
Continue in striped sequence, working rib as established until work measures 13½in from beg.

Shape leg
Next round Work 1, sl 1, K1, psso, work to last 3 sts, K2 tog, work 1.
Work 4 rounds without shaping.
Rep last 5 rounds 5 times more. 54 sts.
Continue in patt until work measures 20½in from beg.

Divide for heel
Work across 13 sts, sl last 13 sts of round onto other end of same needle, making 26 sts for heel, divide rem sts onto 2 needles and leave for instep.
Keeping stripes as established, work heel in rows.
1st row Sl 1, P to end.
2nd row Sl 1, K to end.
Rep these 2 rows 6 times more. Bind off.
Sl all instep sts onto 1 needle.
With RS facing and keeping stripes as established, pick up and K10 from side of heel, rib across instep sts, pick up and K10 from other side of heel. 48 sts.
Work in rows for remainder of sock.

Shape instep
1st row P7, P2 tog tbl, P1, rib 28 sts, P1, P2 tog, P to end.
2nd row K9, rib 28 sts, K9.
3rd row P6, P2 tog tbl, P1, rib 28 sts, P1, P2 tog, P to end.
4th row K8, rib 28 sts, K8.
Continue to dec in this way on every other row until 34 sts rem, ending with a RS row.
Next row P2 tog tbl, P1, rib 28 sts, P1, P2 tog.
Next row K2, rib 28 sts, K2.
Next row P2, rib 28 sts, P2.
Keeping stripes as established, rep last 2 rows until work measures 7in from where sts were picked up at heel, ending with a WS row.

Shape toe
1st row K1, sl 1, K1, psso, rib to last 3 sts, K2 tog, K1.
2nd row P2. rib to last 2 sts, P2.
Rep last 2 rows until 14 sts rem, ending with a WS row. Bind off.

Finishing
Press lightly under a damp cloth with a warm iron. Sew sock to slipper sole, using zigzag stitch.
Thread 4 rows shirring elastic inside top edge of each leg, on WS of work, using a darning needle and running stitches.

Bobble-trimmed slipper sock

▲ *Detail of bobble version*

Using set of 4 No.3 needles, cast on 64 sts, 22 on first needle, 20 on second needle and 22 on third needle.
1st round *P1, K3, rep from * to end of round.
2nd round As 1st.
3rd round *P1, K1, make bobble by K1, P1, K1, P1, K1 all into next st, turn and K5, turn and P5, turn and K5, turn and P5 tog—called MB—K1, rep from * to end of round.
4th to 8th rounds As 1st.
Rep last 6 rounds 3 times more, then 3rd round once, then 1st round twice.
Next round P to end to mark foldline of cuff.
Work 1½in K1, P1 rib.
Turn work inside out to reverse pattern.
Work in rib as given for 1st round until work measures 3½in from foldline.
Next round (P1, K3) 4 times, (P1, K1, MB, K1) twice, (P1, K3) 4 times, (P1, K1, MB, K1) twice,

(P1, K3) 4 times.
Last round sets position of bobble panels and these are worked on every 6th round as given for cuff.

Shape leg
Next round P1, sl 1, K1, psso, patt to last 2 sts, K2 tog.
Work 4 rounds without shaping.
Rep last 5 rounds 5 times more. 52 sts.
Continue in patt until work measures 13in from foldline.

Divide for heel
Sl last 11 sts onto spare needle, work across first 12 sts of round onto same needle, making 23 sts for heel, divide rem sts onto 2 needles and leave for instep.
Keeping rib correct, work across heel sts on rows for 2in. Bind off.
With RS facing, pick up and K12 along side of heel, patt across 29 sts for instep and pick up and K12 along other side of heel. 53 sts.
Keeping patt as established, work instep in rows.
1st row P12 sts, patt 29, P12.
2nd row K2, sl 1, K1, psso, K8, patt 29, K8, K2 tog, K2.
3rd row P11 sts, patt 29, P11.
4th row K2, sl 1, K1, psso, K7, patt 29, K7, K2 tog, K2.
Continue in this way, dec 2 sts on every other row until 35 sts rem, ending with a WS row.
Next row K1, sl 1, K1, psso, patt 29, K2 tog, K1.
Next row P2 sts, patt 29, P2.
Next row Sl 1, K1, psso, patt 29, K2 tog. 31 sts.
Continue in patt without shaping until work measures 4½in from where sts were picked up at heel.
Work in rib and bobble patt as given for cuff, i.e. bobble on every rib, shape toe by dec one st at each end of next and every following 3rd row until 15 sts rem. Bind off.

Finishing

As given for striped slipper sock. Turn cuff to RS at foldline.

The two slipper sock versions ▶

Jacquard pattern housecoats

Basic Wardrobe Knitting

These lounge robes, worked in a jacquard pattern, are trimmed with knitted loops.

Sizes

Directions are for 32in bust. The figures in brackets [] refer to the 34, 36 and 38in sizes respectively.

Long version. Length from top of shoulder, 48[49:50:51]in, excluding loop edging.

Short version. Length from top of shoulder, 32[33:34:35]in, excluding loop edging. Sleeve seam, 12[13:13:13½]in, excluding loop edging.

Materials

Bucilla Paradise

Long version. 24[25:27:28] skeins of main color A 12[13:14:15] skeins of contrast B

Short version. 15[17:19:21] skeins of main color A 7[9:10:12] skeins of contrast B One pair No.3 needles One pair No.6 needles 15 buttons for long version and 11 buttons for short version

Long version

Left front

Using No.3 needles and A, cast on 73[73:79:79] sts. Work 5 rows garter st.
**Change to No.6 needles. Commence loop patt.
1st row (RS) P.

170

2nd row K1, *K next st winding yarn 4 times over needle and around 1st, 2nd and 3rd fingers of left hand, then over needle again, draw 5 loops through, then place loops back on left-hand needle and K tog with st tbl—called ML—K1, rep from * to end.
3rd row P.
4th row K.
These 4 rows form loop patt. Rep them twice more, then 1st and 2nd rows once. **
Attach B. Commence patt.
1st row K1A [K1A: K0: K0], *K3B, 1A, rep from * to last 0[0:3:3] sts, K0[K0:K3B: K3B].
2nd row P1A[P1A:P0:P0], *P1A, 1B, 2A, rep from * to last 0[0:3:3] sts, P0[P0:P1A, 1B, 1A:P1A, 1B, 1A].
These 2 rows form patt and are rep throughout.
Continue in patt until work

▼ *Detail of two-color effect*

measures 8in from top of loop edging, ending with a WS row.
Dec one st at beg of next and every following 6th row until 47[50:53:56] sts rem.
Continue without shaping until work measures 40[41: 41½:42]in from top of loop edging, ending with a WS row. ***

Shape front edge

Dec one st at end of next and every other row until 43[46: 49:52] sts rem, ending with a WS row.

Shape armhole and front edge

Next row Bind off 4sts, patt to last 2sts, K2 tog.
Next row Patt to end.
Dec one st at armhole edge on every row; *at the same time* dec one st at front edge on every following 4th row until 28[31:34:35] sts rem.
Continue dec one st at front edge on every following 4th row as before; *at the same time* dec one st at armhole edge on next and every other row until 24[25:27:29] sts rem.
Keeping armhole edge straight, continue dec one st at front edge on every following 3rd row until 18[19:20:21] sts rem.
Continue without shaping until armhole measures 7[7: 7½:8]in from beg, ending with a WS row.

Shape shoulder

Bind off 6[7:6:7] sts at arm edge every other row once, then 6[6:7:7] sts every other row twice.

Right front

Work as given for left front, reversing all shaping.

Back

Using No.3 needles and A, cast on 145[145:155:155] sts. Work 5 rows garter st.
Work as given for left front from ** to **.
Attach B and work in patt as given for left front until back measures 8in from top of

loop edging, ending with a WS row.
Dec one st at each end of next and every following 6th row until 95[101:107:113] sts rem.
Continue without shaping until back measures same as front to underarm, ending with a WS row. ****

Shape armholes

Bind off 4 sts at beg of next 2 rows.
Dec one st at each end of every row until 71[77:83:85] sts rem, then one st at each end of every other row until 65[69:73:77] sts rem.
Continue without shaping until back measures same as front to shoulder, ending with a WS row.

Shape shoulders

Bind off 6[7:6:7] sts at beg of next 2 rows; 6[6:7:7] sts at beg of next 4 rows.
Bind off rem 29[31:33:35] sts.

Sleeves

Using No.3 needles and A, cast on 93[93:95:95] sts.
Work 5 rows garter st.
Change to No.6 needles and work 6 rows in loop patt as given for left front.
Attach B and continue in patt as given for left front, dec one st at each end of 5th and every following 4th row until 71[73:75:77] sts rem.
Continue without shaping until sleeve measures 12[13:13: 13½]in from top of loop edging, ending with a WS row.

Shape cap

Bind off 4 sts at beg of next 2 rows.
Dec one st at each end of next and every other row until 33 [37:33:31] sts rem, then one st at each end of every row until 23 sts rem. Bind off.

Finishing

Press pieces lightly on WS under a dry cloth with a cool iron, omitting garter st and loop edges. Join shoulder, side and sleeve seams. Sew in sleeves.

Left front edge. Using No.3 needles and A, cast on 10 sts. Work in garter st until edge fits from hem to beg of neck shaping when slightly stretched. Sew in position. Commence loop patt.
***** **1st, 2nd and 3rd rows** K.
4th row (K1, ML) 4 times, K2.
5th and 6th rows K. *****
Rep these 6 rows until edge fits along left front neck to center back neck. Bind off.
Right front edge. Using No.3 needles and A, cast on 10 sts.
Work in loop patt as given for left front edge from ***** to *****, noting that 4th row will read: K2, (ML K1) 4 times.
Mark positions for 15 buttons on left front edge, first to come 14[14½:15:15½]in from lower edge and 15th to come 1in below beg of neck shaping, with 13 evenly spaced between.
Continue in loop patt until edge fits up right front, along right front neck to center back neck, making buttonholes when markers are reached as follows:
Buttonhole row (RS facing) K6, bind off 2 sts, K to end. Next row K to end, casting on 2 sts above those bound off. Bind off.
Using flat st join center back seam of front edges. Sew edges in position. Press seams. Sew on buttons.

Short version

Left front

Using No.3 needles and A, cast on 61[61:67:67] sts. Work 5 rows garter st. Work as given for left front of long version from ** to **. Attach B and work in patt as given for left front of long version until work measures 8in from top of loop edge, ending with a WS row.
Dec one st at beg of next and every following 6th row until 47[50:53:56] sts rem.
Continue without shaping until front measures 24[25:25½:26]in from top of loop

▲ *The fanciful loop edging on both versions (short on left, long on right) is made in contrasting color*

edging, ending with a WS row.
Complete as given for left front of long version from ***.

Right front

Work as given for left front, reversing all shaping.

Back

Using No.3 needles and A, cast on 121[121:131:131] sts. Work 5 rows garter st.

Work as given for left front from ** to **.
Attach B and work in patt until back measures 8in from top of loop edging, ending with a WS row.
Dec one st at each end of next and every following 6th row until 95[101:107:113] sts rem.
Continue without shaping until back measures same as front to underarm, ending with a WS row.
Complete as given for back of long version from ****.

Sleeves

Work as given for long version.

Finishing

As given for long version.
Left front edge. Work as given for long version.
Right front edge. Work as given for long version, making 11 buttonholes, the first to come 4[4:4½:4½]in from lower edge and the 11th 1in below beg of neck shaping.

Lacy bed jacket

Easy to knit, easy to wear!

Size

Directions are for 34in bust. The figures in brackets [ ] refer to the 36, 38 and 40in sizes respectively.
Length at center back, 17½ [17¾:18:18¼]in.

Gauge

8 sts and 10 rows to 1in over st st worked on No.2 circular needle. 8 sts and 10 rows to 1in over patt worked on No.5 needles.

Materials

Reynolds Angelina 5[6:6:7] balls
One No.1 circular needle 24in
One No.2 circular needle 24in
One pair No.5 needles
7 small buttons
1yd 1in wide ribbon
3yds narrow ribbon
4yds narrow lace

Cape sleeves

Using No.2 circular needle, cast on 199[215:231:247] sts. Work back and forth in rows.
K 2 rows.
3rd row (ribbon slotting row) K1, *y2on, K2 tog, rep from * to end.
4th and 5th rows K.
Change to No.5 needles and patt.
1st row (WS) K1, P to last st, K1.
2nd row K2, *insert needle into next 3 sts as if to P3 tog but work P1, K1, P1, K next st, rep from * to last st, K1.

172

These 2 rows form patt.
Rep 1st and 2nd rows until work measures 6in from cast-on edge ending with a 2nd row.
Next row K3 tog, *P2 tog, rep from * to last 2 sts, K2 tog. Change to No.2 circular needle and work in rows.
K 2 rows.
Next row (ribbon slotting row) K1, *y2on, K2 tog, rep from * to end.
K 2 rows.
Change to No.5 needles.
Rep 1st and 2nd rows for patt until work measures 10in from cast-on edge, ending with a 2nd row.
Last row K1, *P2 tog, rep from * to last 2 sts, K2 tog.
Slip sts onto holder.
Work second cape sleeve

▲ *Detail of lace and ribbon insert*

in the same manner.

Main section

Using No.1 circular needle,

cast on 280[296:312:328] sts. Work in rows of K1, P1 rib for 2¼in.
Change to No.2 circular needle, and work in rows of st st, beg with a K row.
Continue in st st until work measures 12¼in from cast-on edge, ending with a P row.

Divide for armholes
1st row K61[64:67:70], bind off 16[18:20:22], K126[132: 138:144], bind off 16[18:20: 22], K61[64:67:70].
Complete left front on last group of sts.
Next row P to last 2 sts, K2.
Next row K2, sl 1, K1, psso, K to end.
Next row P to last 2 sts, K2.
Rep last 2 rows 4[5:6:7] times more.

Shape neck
1st row K2, sl 1, K1, psso, K34, K2 tog, turn, slip rem 16[18:20:22] sts onto holder.
**2nd row P to last 2 sts, K2.
3rd row K2, sl 1, K1, psso, K to last 2 sts, K2 tog.
4th row P to last 2 sts, K2.
Rep last 2 rows until 4 sts rem.
Last row K4 tog. Fasten off.**
With WS facing, attach yarn to center group of sts for back.
1st row K2, P to last 2 sts, K2.
2nd row K2, sl 1, K1, psso, K to last 4 sts, K2 tog, K2.
3rd row K2, P to last 2 sts, K2.
Rep 2nd and 3rd rows 4[5:6:7] times more.

Shape back
1st row K2, sl 1, K1, psso, K34, K2 tog, turn.
Complete right back on these sts, working from ** to ** as for left front.
With RS of back facing, slip next 36[40:44:48] sts onto holder and attach yarn to next st.
***1st row K2 tog, K to last 4 sts, K2 tog, K2.
2nd row K2, P to end.
Rep 1st and 2nd rows until 4 sts rem.
Last row K4 tog. Fasten off.***

With WS facing, attach yarn to rem sts for right front.
1st row K2, P to end.
2nd row K to last 4 sts, K2 tog, K2.
Rep last 2 rows 4[5:6:7] times more.

Shape neck
1st row K2, P28, turn.
Complete as for left back from *** to ***.

Yoke

Using No.2 circular needle, K16[18:20:22] sts from front, pick up and K30 sts up side of raglan, K50[54:58:62] sts from top of first cape sleeve, pick up and K29 sts down side of raglan, K46 [50:54:58] sts from center back, pick up and K29 sts from side of raglan, K50[54: 58:62] sts from second cape sleeve, pick up and K30 sts down side of raglan and K16 [18:20:22] sts from front. 286[302:318:334] sts.
Continue in st st beg with a P row.
Work 5 rows.
1st dec row K7, *K2 tog tbl, K16[18:20:22], K2 tog, K16, rep from * to last 27 [29:31:33] sts, K2 tog tbl, K16[18:20:22], K2 tog, K7.
Work 3 rows.
2nd dec row K7, *K2 tog tbl, K14[16:18:20], K2 tog, K16, rep from * to last 25 [27:29:31] sts, K2 tog tbl, K14[16:18:20], K2 tog, K7.
Work 3 rows.
3rd dec row K7, *K2 tog tbl, K12[14:16:18], K2 tog, K16, rep from * to last 23[25: 27:29] sts, K2 tog tbl, K12 [14:16:18], K2 tog, K7.
Work 3 rows.
4th dec row K7, *K2 tog tbl, K10[12:14:16], K2 tog, K16, rep from * to last 21 [23:25:27] sts, K2 tog tbl, K10[12:14:16], K2 tog, K7.
Work 1 row.
5th dec row K7, *K2 tog tbl, K8[10:12:14], K2 tog, K16, rep from * to last 19[21:23:25] sts, K2 tog tbl, K8[10:12:14], K2 tog, K7.

Work 1 row.
6th dec row K7, *K2 tog tbl, K6[8:10:12], K2 tog, K16, rep from * to last 17 [19:21:23] sts, K2 tog tbl, K6[8:10:12], K2 tog, K7.
Work 1 row.

7th dec row K7, *K2 tog tbl, K4[6:8:10], K2 tog, K16, rep from * to last 15[17:19: 21] sts, K2 tog tbl, K4[6:8: 10], K2 tog, K7.
Work 1 row.

8th dec row K7, *K2 tog tbl, K2[4:6:8], K2 tog, K16, rep from * to last 13[15:17: 19] sts, K2 tog tbl, K2[4:6:8], K2 tog, K7.
Work 3 rows.

9th dec row K7, *K2 tog tbl, K0[2:4:6], K2 tog, K16, rep from * to last 11[13:15: 17] sts, K2 tog tbl, K0[2:4:6], K2 tog, K7.
Work 3 rows.

Next row K1, *K2 tog, K1, rep from * to end.
Work 5 rows.
Change to No.1 circular needle, and work in rows of K1, P1 rib for 1in.
Bind off.

Front edgings

Button strip
Using No.1 circular needle, with RS of left front facing, pick up and K190[192:196: 198] sts from beg of st st to neck edge. Work 6 rows K1, P1 rib. Bind off in rib. Mark position for 7 buttons on strip.

Buttonhole strip
Work as for button strip, working buttonholes as markers are reached on 3rd row by binding off 3 sts and on 4th row casting on 3 sts above those bound off on previous row.

Finishing

Press lightly.
Fold hem in half to wrong side and slip stitch in place. Thread with 1in wide ribbon. Thread narrow ribbon through sleeve slottings and sew ends. Sew lace below ribbon slottings and around yoke.

Matching Fair Isle sweaters

Sizes

Ladies'. Directions are for 36in bust.
The figures in brackets [] refer to the Ladies' 38 and 40in sizes respectively.
Length at center back, 21[22: 23]in, adjustable.
Sleeve seam, 18[19:20]in, adjustable.
Men's. Directions are for 38in chest.
The figures in brackets [] refer to the Men's 40 and 42in sizes respectively.
Length at center back, 23½ [24½:25½]in, adjustable.
Sleeve seam, 17½[17½:18]in, adjustable.

Gauge

6 sts and 8 rows to 1in over st st worked on No.4 needles.
6½ sts and 8½ rows to 1in over st st worked on No.3 needles.

Materials

Reynolds Cashmere Lamb
Ladies'. 7[8:9] balls main color A, coral
1 ball each of 5 colors B, C, D, E and F: white, gray, dark brown, beige and medium brown
One pair No.3 needles
One pair No.4 needles
One circular needle No.4
4 small buttons
One large stitch holder
One No.D crochet hook
Men's. 8[9:9] balls main color A, natural
2 balls 1st contrast B, white
1 ball each of 4 colors C, D, E and F: gold, medium brown, dark brown and camel

174

One pair No.4 needles
One pair No.3 needles
One set of 4 No.4 double point needles

Circular yoked sweater

Front

Using No.3 needles and A, cast on 113[117:121] sts.
Work 4in K1, P1 rib.
Change to No.4 needles
Work in st st, beg with a K row and inc one st at each end of 7th and every following 8th row until there are 121 [127:133] sts.
Continue without shaping until work measures 14[14½: 15]in or length required, ending with a P row.

Shape armholes

Bind off 6 sts at beg of next 2 rows.
Dec one st at each end of next and every other row until 103 sts rem. P 1 row.

Shape for yoke

1st row K2 tog, K33, K2 tog, slip rem 66 sts onto holder. Continue on 35 sts for left side.
Dec one st at each end of every K row until 3 sts rem.
Last row K2 tog, K1. Bind off.
With RS facing, slip first 29 sts onto holder for yoke and attach yarn to rem 37 sts. Finish to match other side.

Back

Using No.3 needles, cast on 112[116:120] sts and work as for front, noting that there is one st less. When shaping for yoke, slip only 28 sts instead of 29 sts onto holder.

Sleeves

Using No.3 needles, cast on 60[62:64] sts.
Work 4in K1, P1 rib.
Change to No.4 needles.
Continue in st st beg with a K row, inc one st at each end of 5th and every following 6th row until there are 84[90:96] sts.
Work until sleeve measures 18[19:20]in or desired length (allowing 2in for turn-back cuff), ending with a P row.

Shape cap

Bind off 6[6:8] sts at beg of next 2 rows.
Dec one st at each end of every K row until 36 sts rem.
Slip sts onto holder for yoke.

Yoke

Sew up raglan seams.
With RS facing, slip first 14 sts of back onto holder.
Beg from center back with A and first double-pointed needle, pick up and K rem 14 sts of back, pick up and K31[34:37] sts from raglan side, K36 sts from sleeve holder, using 2nd needle, pick up and K31[34:37] sts from next raglan side, K29 sts from front holder, pick up and K31[34:37] sts from next raglan side, using 3rd needle K36 sts from 2nd sleeve, pick up and K31[34:37] sts from last raglan side and 14 sts from center back. 253[265: 277] sts.
Using A, P 1 row. Attach F.
Next row *K3A, 1F, rep from *, ending 1A.
Next row *P1F, 1A, rep from * ending 1F.
Next row K1A, *1F, 3A, rep from * to end of row. Break off F.
Using A, P 1 row. Break off A.
Using B, K 1 row. P 1 row.
Continue working from chart.
1st size Skip first 6 sts of chart 1. Work rem 19 sts of chart 1, K40 sts of both charts 2 and 1 five times, then the 15 sts of chart 2 once, ending round with first 19 sts of chart 1.
Continue with rem 24 rows of charts, beg K rows from 7th st and P rows from 19th st at front edge of garment. Dec on chart on 9th and every other

Star and tapered star motifs for yoke. Tapered stars alternate with stars

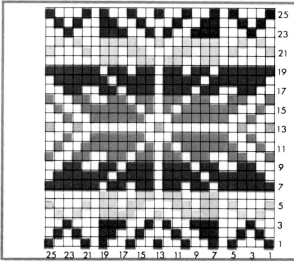

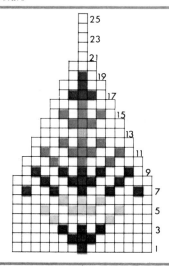

ow is worked by K2 tog tbl.
After completing 25 chart
rows using B, P 1 row.
Next row *K1, K2 tog, rep
from * to end of row. Break
off B.
Using A, P 1 row.
Next row *K3A, 1F, rep
from * to end.
Next row *P1F, 1A, rep
from * to end.
Next row K1A, *1F, 3A, rep
from * to end. Break off F.
Using A, P 1 row.
Next row *K2, K2 tog, rep
from * to end of row. P 1 row.
Change to No.3 needles.
Work 1in K1, P1 rib. Bind off
loosely in rib.*
2nd size Work from chart. K
from 1st row of chart 1
followed by 1st row of chart 2
across 11 sts, ending with 25
sts from chart 1, noting that
dec on 9th and every other
row is made by K2 tog tbl.
Complete from * to * as for
1st size.
3rd size Work as for 2nd
size, working every row with
5 sts in B before and after sts
from charts.
All sizes Sew up back
opening leaving 4½in open.
Crochet 1 row sc around both
opening edges. Work 2nd row
sc on RS making 4 loops for
buttonholes.

Banded sweater

Back

Using No.3 needles, cast on
115[121:127] sts. Work 1½in
K1, P1 rib.
Change to No.4 needles.
Work in st st beg with a K
row until work measures
11[11½:11½]in, ending with a
P row.
Continue in st st, working 39
rows from chart. If desired,
continue in st st until work
measures 15½[16:16]in or
desired length, ending with a
P row.
Shape armholes
Bind off 6 sts at beg of next
2 rows.
Next row K1, K2 tog, K
to last 3 sts, sl 1, K1, psso, K1.
Next row P.**
Rep last 2 rows until 37[39:
41] sts rem, ending with a P

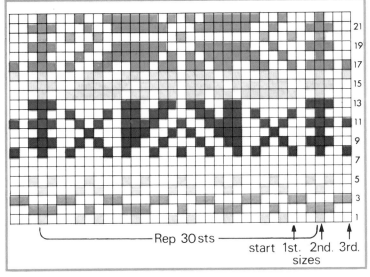

▼ *Bottom half of banded sweater motif. Work rows 19 to 1 for top half.*
The whole of the star motif is worked over 39 rows

— Rep 30 sts —

start 1st. 2nd. 3rd.
sizes

row. Slip sts onto holder.

Front

Work as given for back until
57[59:61]sts rem, ending with
a P row.

Shape neck
1st row K1, K2 tog, K17,
turn and slip rem sts onto
holder.
2nd row P to end.

3rd row K1, K2 tog, K to
last 3 sts, sl 1, K1, psso, K1.
Rep 2nd and 3rd rows 6 times
more, then 2nd row once.
Next row K1, K3 tog, K1.
Next row P3.
Next row K1, K2 tog.
Next row P2 tog and fasten
off.
With RS facing, slip first 17
[19:21] sts onto holder.
Attach yarn to rem sts, K to
last 3 sts, sl 1, K1, psso, K1.

Complete to correspond to
other side.

Sleeves

Using No.3 needles, cast on
47[49:51] sts and work 3in
K1, P1 rib.
Change to No.4 needles.
Continue in st st beg with a
K row, inc one st at each end
of 5th and every following 6th
row until there are 85[89:93]
sts. Work until sleeve measures
19[19:19½]in or required
length, ending with a P row.
Place a marker thread at each
end of last row. Work 8 rows
more.

Shape cap
Rep from ** to ** as for
back until 47 sts rem, ending
with a P row.
Next row K1, (K2 tog, K18,
sl 1, K1, psso, K1) twice.
Continue to dec in center of
every 6th row 4 times more;
at same time dec at each end of
every K row until 9 sts rem,
ending with a P row. Slip
sts onto holder.

Neckband

Join raglan seams, sewing last
8 rows of sleeve cap above
marker threads to bound-off
sts at armhole.
Using No.3 needles and with
RS facing, K across sts of
right sleeve, back neck and
left sleeve, knitting 2 tog
across each raglan seam, pick
up and K14 sts down front
neck, K front sts and pick up
and K14 sts up other side of
neck. 98[102:106] sts.
Work 2½in in K1, P1 rib. Bind
off loosely in rib.

Finishing

Yoked sweater
Press with a damp cloth and
warm iron, omitting ribbing.
Sew up side and sleeve seams.
Sew on buttons to correspond
to loops.
Banded sweater
Press with a warm iron over
a damp cloth. Join side and
sleeve seams. Fold neckband
in half to wrong side and slip
stitch in place.

Man's fabric-stitch vest

This comfortable knit vest will be a handsome addition to any man's wardrobe. What's more, it's fun to make!

Sizes
Directions are for 38in chest. The figures in brackets [ ] refer to the 40, 42 and 44in sizes respectively.
Length down center back, 20½ [21½:22:23]in.

Gauge
6sts and 8 rows to 1in over stockinette stitch worked on No.5 needles.

Materials
Dawn Wintuk Sports 4[5:5:5] 2oz skeins
One pair No.3 needles
One pair No.5 needles
Five buttons
Stitch holder

Back

Using No.5 needles, cast on 119[125:131:137] sts.
1st row K1, *P1, K1, rep from * to end.
2nd row P1, *K1, P1, rep from * to end.
Continue in K1, P1 rib until work measures 11[11½:12: 12½]in from beg.

Shape armholes
Bind off 6sts at beg of next 2 rows.
Dec one st at each end of every row until 81[85:89:93] sts rem.
Continue without shaping until armholes measure 5½[6:6:6½]in from beg.
Inc one st at each end of next

and every following 10th row until there are 87[91:95:99] sts.
Continue without shaping until armholes measure 9½[10:10:10½]in from beg.

Shape shoulders and neck
Next row Bind off 7sts, rib 28[29:30:31], bind off 17 [19:21:23] sts, rib to end.
Complete left shoulder first. Bind off 7sts at armhole edge at the beg of next row, then 7sts every other row twice and 5[6:7:8] sts once; *at the same time* bind off 3sts at neck edge every other row 3 times.
With WS facing, attach yarn to rem sts and work to correspond to first side.

Left front

Using No.5 needles, cast on 3sts.
Commence patt and shaping:
1st row P1, K1, P1.
2nd row Inc in first st (center edge), K to last st, inc in last st (side edge).
3rd row K twice into first st, P1, K1, P1, K twice into last st.
4th row K twice into first st, K to last st, K twice into last st.
Keeping patt correct, inc one st at each end of every row 3[5:7:9] times more.
Continue to inc one st at center edge on every row 12 times more; *at the same time* cast on 9sts at side edge 4 times. 63[67:71:75] sts.
Dec one st at side edge on every 8th row 4 times, then inc one st at this edge on every 6th row 6 times;

at the same time, when inc at center front edge are completed, work even for ¼[½:¾:1]in, ending at center front edge and working a buttonhole on next 2 rows as follows:
Next row Patt 2sts, bind off 2sts, patt to end.
Next row Patt to last 2sts, cast on 2sts, patt 2sts.
Work 4 more buttonholes in this way at intervals of 2½ [2½:2½:2¾]in measured from center of previous buttonhole.
Work until side edge measures 10½[11:11½:12]in from beg, ending at side edge.

Shape armhole and front
Next row Bind off 6sts, patt to last 2sts, work 2 tog.
Dec one st at neck edge on every following 3rd row 21[22:23:24] times more; *at the same time* dec one st at armhole edge on every row 14[16:18:20] times.
Continue until armhole measures 5½[6:6:6½]in from beg, ending at armhole edge.
Inc one st at beg of next and every following 10th row 3 times in all. Continue until armhole measures same as back to shoulder, ending at armhole edge.

Shape shoulder
Bind off at beg of next and every other row 7sts 3 times and 5[6:7:8] sts once.

Right front

Work as given for left front, reversing all shaping and omitting buttonholes.

Finishing

Press lightly.
Join shoulder seams using backstitch.
Armbands Using No.3 needles, RS facing, pick up and K 102[108:108:114] sts evenly around armhole. K 2 rows. Bind off.
Right front edge Using No.3 needles, beg at side edge and pick up and K 43 [45:47:49] sts to center point. K 2 rows, inc one st at center point on each row. Bind off. Using No.3 needles, beg at center point and pick up and K 25[27:29:31] along shaped edge, 65[68:71:74] along center front straight edge, 64[67:67:70] along shaped edge of neck and 19[20:21:22] sts to center back neck. K 2 rows, inc one st at center point on each row. Bind off.
Left front edge Using No.3 needles, beg at center back neck and pick up and K 19[20:21:22]sts, 64[67:67:70] along shaped edge of neck, 65 [68:71:74] along center front straight edge and 25 [27:29:31] along shaped edge to center point. K 2 rows, inc one st at center point on each row. Bind off. Using No.3 needles, beg at center point and pick up and K 43[45:47:49] sts to side edge. K 2 rows, inc one st at center point on each row. Bind off.
Join side and armband seams. Join right and left front edges at center point.
Buttonhole stitch around buttonholes and sew on buttons

▼ *The vest front is in rice stitch, giving a fabric effect*

Aran cardigan

One charm of authentic Aran designs is that they suit both men and women.

Sizes

Directions are for 36in bust or chest.
The figures in brackets [] refer to the 38, 40, 42 and 44in sizes respectively.
Length down center back, 24[24½:25:25½:26]in, adjustable.
Sleeve seam, 17[17½:18:18½: 19]in, adjustable.

Gauge
5 sts and 7 rows to 1in over double seed stitch worked on No.6 needles.

Materials

Fleisher's Shamrock 10[11:12:12:13] 2oz balls
One pair No.3 needles
One pair No.6 needles
One cable needle
Two stitch holders
Five buttons

Back

Using No.3 needles, cast on 94[98:102:106:110] sts.
1st row *K1 tbl, P1, rep from * to end.
Rep 1st row 7 times more.
Next row K to end, inc 16 sts evenly across row. 110[114:118:122:126] sts.
Change to No.6 needles.
1st row (wrong side) (K1, P1) 3[4:5:6:7] times, *K2, P6, K7, P4, K6, P6, K2*, P32 sts, rep from * to * once, (K1, P1) 3[4:5:6:7] times.
2nd row (K1, P1) 3[4:5:6:7]

times, *P2, sl next 2 sts onto cable needle and hold at back of work, K2, K2 from cable needle—called C4B—K2, P6, K2, sl next 2 sts onto cable needle and hold at front of work, P1, K2 from cable needle—called K2F—P6, C4B, K2, P2*, (C4B, sl next 2 sts onto cable needle and hold at front of work, K2, K2 from cable needle—called C4F) 4 times, rep from * to * once, (K1, P1) 3[4:5:6:7] times.
3rd row (P1, K1) 3[4:5:6:7] times, *K2, P6, K6, P2, K1, P2, K6, P6, K2*, P32 sts, rep from * to * once, (P1, K1) 3[4:5:6:7] times.
4th row (P1, K1) 3[4:5:6:7] times, *P2, K6, P5, sl next st onto cable needle and hold at back of work, K2, P1 from cable needle—called P1B—K1, K2F, P5, K6, P2*, K32 sts, rep from * to * once, (P1, K1) 3[4:5:6:7] times.
5th row (K1, P1) 3[4:5:6:7] times, *K2, P6, K5, P2, K1, P1, K1, P2, K5, P6, K2*, P32 sts, rep from * to * once, (K1, P1) 3[4:5:6:7] times.
6th row (K1, P1) 3[4:5:6:7] times, *P2, K2, C4F, P4, P1B, K1, P1, K1, K2F, P4, K2, C4F, P2*, (C4F, C4B) 4 times, rep from * to * once, (K1, P1) 3[4:5:6:7] times.
7th row (P1, K1) 3[4:5:6:7] times, *K2, P6, K4, P2, (K1, P1) twice, K1, P2, K4, P6, K2*, P32 sts, rep from * to * once, (P1, K1) 3[4:5:6:7] times.
8th row (P1, K1) 3[4:5:6:7] times, *P2, K6, P3, P1B, (K1, P1) twice, K1, K2F, P3, K6, P2*, K32 sts, rep from

* to * once, (P1, K1) 3[4:5:6:7] times.
9th row (K1, P1) 3[4:5:6:7] times, *K2, P6, K3, P2, (K1, P1) 3 times, K1, P2, K3, P6, K2*, P32 sts, rep from * to * once, (K1, P1) 3[4:5:6:7] times.
10th row (K1, P1) 3[4:5:6:7] times, *P2, C4B, K2, P2, P1B, (K1, P1) 3 times, K1, K2F, P2, C4B, K2, P2*, (C4B, C4F) 4 times, rep from * to * once, (K1, P1) 3[4:5:6:7] times.
11th row (P1, K1) 3[4:5:6:7] times, *K2, P6, K2, P2, (K1, P1) 4 times, K1, P2, K2, P6, K2*, P32 sts, rep from * to * once, (P1, K1) 3[4:5:6:7] times.
12th row (P1, K1) 3[4:5:6:7] times, *P2, K6, P1, P1B, (K1, P1) 4 times, K1, K2F, P1, K6, P2*, K32 sts, rep from * to * once, (P1, K1) 3[4:5:6:7] times.
13th row (K1, P1) 3[4:5:6:7] times, *K2, P6, K1, P2, (K1, P1) 5 times, K1, P2, K1, P6, K2*, P32 sts, rep from * to * once, (K1, P1) 3[4:5:6:7] times.
14th row (K1, P1) 3[4:5:6:7] times, *P2, K2, C4F, P1, K2F, (P1, K1) 4 times, P1, P1B, P1, K2, C4F, P2*, (C4F, C4B) 4 times, rep from * to * once, (K1, P1) 3[4:5:6:7] times.
15th row (P1, K1) 3[4:5:6:7] times, *K2, P6, K2, P2, (K1, P1) 4 times, K1, P2, K2, P6, K2*, P32 sts, rep from * to * once, (P1, K1) 3[4:5:6:7] times.
16th row (P1, K1) 3[4:5:6:7] times, *P2, K6, P2, K2F, (P1, K1) 3 times, P1, P1B, P2, K6, P2*, K32 sts, rep from * to * once, (P1, K1) 3[4:5:6:7] times.
17th row As 9th.
18th row (K1, P1) 3[4:5:6:7] times, *P2, C4B, K2, P3, K2F, (P1, K1) twice, P1, P1B, P3, C4B, K2, P2*, (C4B, C4F) 4 times, rep from * to * once, (K1, P1) 3[4:5:6:7] times.
19th row As 7th.
20th row (P1, K1) 3[4:5:6:7] times, *P2, K6, P4, K2F, P1, K1, P1, P1B, P4, K6, P2*, K32 sts, rep from * to * once,

(P1, K1) 3[4:5:6:7] times.
21st row As 5th.
22nd row (K1, P1) 3[4:5:6:7] times, *P2, K2, C4F, P5, K2F, P1, P1B, P5, K2, C4F, P2*, (C4F, C4B) 4 times, rep from * to * once, (K1, P1) 3[4:5:6:7] times.
23rd row As 3rd.
24th row (P1, K1) 3[4:5:6:7] times, *P2, K6, P6, sl next 3 sts onto cable needle and hold at front of work, K2, K2 P1 from cable needle, P6, K6, P2*, K32 sts, rep from * to * once, (P1, K1) 3[4:5:6:7] times.
These 24 rows form patt and are rep throughout back.
Continue in patt until work measures 15[15½:16:16½:17] in or required length to underarm, ending with a WS row.

Shape armholes

Bind off 8 sts at beg of next 2 rows.
1st raglan row K1, sl 1, K1, psso, patt to last 3 sts, K2 tog, K1.
2nd raglan row K1, P1, patt to last 2 sts, P1, K1.
Rep these 2 rows until 32 [34:36:38:40] sts rem.
Bind off.

Left front

Using No.3 needles, cast on 29 sts.
Work 24 rows K1, P1 rib for pocket lining.
Slip sts onto holder.
Using No.3 needles, cast on 48[50:52:54:56] sts.
Work 8 rows twisted rib as given for back.
Next row K to end, inc 8 sts evenly across row. 56[58:60:62:64] sts.
Change to No.6 needles.
Commence patt.
1st row (wrong side) K1, P16, K2, P6, K7, P4, K6, P6, K2, (K1, P1) 3[4:5:6:7] times.
2nd row (K1, P1) 3[4:5:6:7] times, P2, C4B, K2, P6, K2, K2F, P6, C4B, K2, P2, (C4B, C4F) twice, K1.
Continue in patt as given until 24 rows have been worked, K front edge st on every row.

Next row K1, P16, K2, sl next 29 sts onto stitch holder, work in patt across 29 pocket lining sts, K2, (K1, P1) 3[4:5:6:7] times.
Continue until work measures same as back to armhole, ending at armhole edge.

Shape armhole and neck
Next row Bind off 8 sts, patt to last 2 sts, dec one. Work 1 row.

▲ *Stitch details of Aran patterns*

Next row K1, Sl 1, K1, psso, patt to end.
Next row Dec one, patt to last 3 sts, P1, K1.
Continue in this way, dec one st at armhole edge on every other row and one st at neck edge on every 3rd row 16[17:18:19:20] times in all until all sts are worked off.
Pull yarn through last st Fasten off.

Right front

Work as given for left front, reading patt row in reverse and reversing all shapings.

Sleeves

Using No.3 needles, cast on 46[48:50:52:54] sts.
Work 3in twisted rib as given for back.
Next row K to end, inc 14 sts evenly across row. 60[62:64:66:68] sts.
Change to No.6 needles.
1st row K1[K2:P1, K2:K1, P1, K2:P1, K1, P1, K2], P6, K2, P16, K2, P6, K2, P16, K2, P6, K1[K2:K2, P1: K2, P1, K1:K2, P1, K1, K2, P1, K1,

P1].
2nd row P1[P2:K1, P2: P1, K1, P2:K1, P1, K1, P2], C4B, K2, P2, (C4B, C4F) twice, P2, C4B, K2, P2, (C4B, C4F) twice, P2, C4B, K2, P1[P2:P2, K1:P2, K1, P1:P2, K1, P1, K1].
Continue in patt as given, working 2 honeycomb panels and 3 plaited cables and inc one st at each end of next and every 6th row until there are 80[84:88:92:96] sts. Work inc in double seed st.
Continue without shaping until sleeve measures 17 [17½:18:18½:19]in or desired length, ending with a WS row.

Shape cap
Bind off 8 sts at beg of next 2 rows.
Work 1st and 2nd raglan rows as given for back until 2[4:6:8:10]sts rem.
Bind off.

Buttonhole band

Using No.3 needles, cast on 10 sts. Work in twisted rib as given for back.
Work 3 rows.
Next row Rib 4 sts, bind off 2 sts, rib 4 sts.
Next row Rib 4 sts, cast on 2 sts, rib 4 sts.
Continue in rib working 4 more buttonholes in this way at 3[3¼:3½:3¾:4]in intervals, until band measures 56[58: 60:62:64]in when slightly stretched.
Bind off.

Finishing

Using No.3 needles and with RS pocket top facing, work 7 rows twisted rib as given for back. Bind off. Complete other pocket top in same way. Sew in sleeves. Join side and sleeve seams. Sew around pocket linings and sides of pocket tops. Sew on buttonhole band, with buttonholes on left front for a man's garment and right front for a woman's. Sew on buttons to correspond to buttonholes. Press lightly under a damp cloth with a warm iron.

Seamless pullover in fisherman's knitting

Your first project in fisherman's knitting, a seamless sweater for an outdoor man. The firmness of the fabric, which results from the traditional stitch, makes this an ideal garment to wear in cold or windy weather.

Size

Directions are for 38in chest. The figures in brackets [] refer to the 40, 42 and 44in sizes respectively.
Length at Center back, 23[23: 23½:23½]in.
Sleeve seam, 18in, adjustable.

Gauge
7 sts and 9 rows to 1in over st st worked on No.3 circular needle.

Materials

Spinnerin Wintuk Sport 7[7:8:8]skeins
One No.2 14in or 24in circular needle
One No.3 14in or 24in circular needle
One set of 4 No.2 double-pointed needles
One set of 4 No.3 double-pointed needles

NB This pullover is entirely seamless and requires no finishing after knitting.
Yarn should be joined at mock seams by leaving ends to darn into work on completion.

Pullover

Using No.2 circular needle, cast on 264[276:288:300] sts.
1st row *P1, K2, P1, rep from * to end. Join into a
180

---

circle and place marker thread before first st to mark beginning of round.
Next round *P1, K2, P1, rep from * to end of round. Rep last round until work measures 3in.
Change to No.3 circular needle.
Next round *P into front and back of next st to make one st, K130[136:142:148], P1, rep from * once.
Continue in st st with mock seam sts.
1st round *K1, P1, K130 [136:142:148], P1, rep from * once more.
2nd round *P2, K130[136: 142:148], P1, rep from * once more.
Rep 1st and 2nd rounds until work measures 12in from cast-on edge ending with a 1st round.
Begin yoke pattern and underarm gusset.
1st round *K into front and back and front of first st, P132[138:144:150], rep from * once more.
2nd round *K3, P132[138: 144:150], rep from * once more.
3rd round *K3, P1, K130 [136:142:148], P1, rep from * once more.
Rep 3rd round once more.
Rep 2nd round twice more.
7th round *Inc once in each of next 2 sts, K1, P1, K130 [136:142:148], P1, rep from * once more.
8th round *K5, P1, K130 [136:142:148], P1, rep from * once more.
9th round *K5, P132[138: 144:150], rep from * once more.
Rep 9th round once more.
Rep 8th round once more.

12th round *K5, P1, (K2, P2) 32[34:35:37] times, K2 [0:2:0], P1, rep from * once more.
13th round *Inc, K2, inc, K1, P1, K130[136:142:148], P1, rep from * once more.
14th round *K7, P1, (P2, K2) 32[34:35:37] times, P2 [0:2:0], P1, rep from * once more.
15th round *K7, P1, K130 [136:142:148], P1, rep from * once more.
Continue in this way, working center 130[136:142:148] sts in 4 row patt, keeping seam sts correct and inc one st at each side of each gusset on every 6th row until 14 rows more have been worked. There should now be 11 sts between seam sts on gusset.
Break yarn at end of last round.

Divide for armholes

Slip gusset sts and seam sts (13 sts at each side) onto holder or thread until needed. Work front on center 130[136:142:148] sts working in rows.
**1st row P.
2nd row K.
3rd row K.
4th row P.
Rep 1st—4th rows once more then 1st and 2nd rows once.

Work center patt panel

1st patt row K.
2nd patt row P.
3rd patt row K2[5:8:11], *K10, P1, K10, rep from * to last 2[5:8:11] sts, K to end.
4th patt row K1, P1[4:7:10], * P9, K3, P9, rep from * to last 2[5:8:11] sts, P to last st, K1.
5th patt row K2[5:8:11], *K8, (P1, K1) twice, P1, K8, rep from * to last 2[5:8:11] sts, K to end.
6th patt row K1, P1[4:7:10], * P7, (K1, P2) 3 times, P5, rep from * to last 2[5:8:11] sts, P to last st, K1.
7th patt row K2[5:8:11], *K6, P1, K2, P3, K2, P1, K6, rep from * to last 2[5:8:11] sts, K to end.
8th patt row K1, P1[4:7:10], * P5, K1, P2, (K1, P1) 3 times, P1, K1, P5, rep from *

---

to last 2[5:8:11] sts, P to last st, K1.
9th patt row K2[5:8:11], *K4, (P1, K2) twice, P1, (K2, P1) twice, K4, rep from * to last 2[5:8:11] sts, K to end.
10th patt row K1, P1[4:7: 10], *P3, (K1, P2) twice, K3, (P2, K1) twice, P3, rep from * to last 2[5:8:11] sts, P to last st, K1.
11th patt row K2[5:8:11], *K5, P1, K2, (P1, K1) 3 times, K1, P1, K5, rep from * to last 2[5:8:11] sts, K to end.
12th patt row K1, P1[4:7: 10], *P4, (K1, P2) twice, (K1, P2) 3 times, P2, rep from * to last 2[5:8:11] sts, P to last st, K1.
13th patt row K2[5:8:11], *K6, P1, K2, P3, K2, P1, K6, rep from * to last 2[5:8:11] sts, K to end.
14th patt row K1, P1[4:7: 10], *P5, K1, P2, (K1, P1) 3 times, P1, K1, P5, rep from * to last 2[5:8:11] sts, P to last st, K1.
15th patt row K2[5:8:11], *K7, (P1, K2) 3 times, K5, rep from * to last 2[5:8:11] sts, K to end.
16th patt row K1, P1[4:7: 10], *P6, K1, P2, K3, P2, K1, P6, rep from * to last 2[5:8: 11] sts, P to last st, K1.
17th patt row K2[5:8:11], *K8, (P1, K1) 3 times, K7, rep from * to last 2[5:8:11] sts, K to end.
18th patt row K1, P1[4:7: 10], *P7, (K1, P2) 3 times, P5, rep from * to last 2[5:8: 11] sts, P to last st, K1.
19th patt row K2[5:8:11], *K9, P3, K9, rep from * to last 2[5:8:11] sts, K to end.
20th patt row K1, P1[4:7: 10], *P8, (K1, P1) 3 times, P7, rep from * to last 2[5:8: 11] sts, P to last st, K1.
21st patt row K2[5:8:11], *K10, P1, K10, rep from * to last 2[5:8:11] sts, K to end.
22nd patt row K1, P1[4:7: 10], *P9, K3, P9, rep from * to last 2[5:8:11] sts, P to last st, K1.
23rd patt row As 21st.
24th patt row K1, P1[4:7: 10], *P10, K1, P10, rep from * to last 2[5:8:11] sts, P to last st, K1.

▲ *A modern interpretation of the traditional fisherman's pullover*

25th patt row K.
26th patt row P.
P 1 row. K 2 rows. P 1 row.
Rep last 4 rows once more.
P 1 row. K 2 rows.
Next row P2[0:2:0], *K2,
P2, rep from * to end.
K 1 row.

Next row K2[0:2:0], *P2,
K2, rep from * to end.
Rep last 4 rows until 14 rows
more have been worked.
P 1 row. K 1 row.

For 42 and 44in sizes only
K 1 row. P 2 rows. K 1 row.**

For all sizes divide for shoulders

1st row K48[50:52:54], then
complete this shoulder on
these sts.
***2nd row** P2 tog, P to end.
3rd row P to last 2 sts, P2
tog.
4th row K2 tog, K to end.
5th row K to last 2 sts, K2
tog.
6th row P2 tog, P to end.
7th row P to last 2 sts, P2
tog.
8th row K2 tog, K to end.
9th row K to last 2 sts, K2
tog.
P 2 rows. K 1 row.
Slip sts onto holder.***
With RS facing, slip center
34[36:38:40] sts onto holder
and leave for neckband.
Attach yarn to rem sts and K
to end. Complete other
shoulder to correspond,
working from *** to ***,
reversing shaping.

Back
With RS facing, attach yarn
to rem 130[136:142:148] sts
and work from ** to ** as
for front.

Work shoulders
K 1 row. P 2 rows. K 1 row.
Rep last 4 rows twice more.
Bind off right shoulder as
follows:
Hold back and front together
with WS touching.
Bind off both shoulders
together on RS by *K first
st from back and front tog,
K next 2 sts tog, lift first st
over 2nd, rep from * until all
shoulder stitches are bound off.
Slip center 50[52:54:56] sts
onto holder for neckband and
bind off 2nd shoulder in same
way.

Neckband
Using No.3 circular needle,
K sts from back holder, pick up
and K 14 sts down right side of
neck, K across sts from front
holder and pick up and K 14
sts up left side of neck.
1st round *P1, K2, P1, rep
from * to end.
Rep 1st round for 1in.
If preferred, neckband may be
made longer and folded in

half to WS and slip stitched in
place.

Sleeves
Using set of 4 No.3 dp needles,
with RS facing, work gusset
sts on first needle, P1, K11,
P1, pick up and K110[110:
118:118] sts evenly around
armhole, dividing the stitches
on 3 needles. Work in rounds.
1st round P1, K11, P1, K2,
*P2, K2, rep from * to end.
2nd round P1, K2 tog tbl,
K7, K2 tog, P1, K to end.
3rd round P1, K9, P3, *K2,
P2, rep from * to end.
4th round P1, K9, P1, K to
end.
Rep last 4 rounds until 12
more rounds have been
worked, dec one st each side of
gussets every 6th round.
Next round P1, K5, P to end.
Rep last round once more.
Next round P1, K5, P1, K to
end.
Next round P1, K2 tog tbl,
K1, K2 tog, P1, K to end.
Next 2 rounds P1, K3, P to
end.
Next 2 rounds P1, K3, P1,
K to end.
Next round P1, K3, P to end.
Next round P1, K3 tog,
P to end.
Next round P3, K to end.
Next round P1, K1, P1, K
to end.
Next round P3, K2 tog tbl,
K to last 2 sts, K2 tog.
Next round P1, K1, P1, K
to end.
Next round P3, K to end.
Next round P1, K1, P1, K
to end.
Rep last 4 rounds until
57[61:61:65] sts rem.
Work until sleeve measures
15in or 3in less than desired
length, dec one st at beg of
last round.
Change to No.2 dp needles.
1st round *P1, K2, P1, rep
from * to end.
Rep 1st round until cuff
measures 3in.
Bind off in rib.

Blocking
Press lightly on wrong side
under a damp cloth using a
warm iron. Darn in ends
including joining first row ends
to complete lower edge circle.

181

Chapter 1

Crochet Know-how

Introduction to crochet

Crochet is a most important look in the world of fashion today. It works up very quickly so it is of particular interest to the woman whose time is very limited and who would like to add crochet designs to her wardrobe or her home. Once the three basic steps have been mastered, there are dozens of patterns for one to work with, like the traditional American Granny squares pictured on the opposite page (see Chapter 4 on how to make these squares). One useful feature about these squares is that they can be carried around in a handbag, worked separately and then joined together to make anything from a bedspread to a shawl or a vest.

Although crochet is simple, it provides marvelously crisp textures and color effects, which makes it ideal for heavy or unusual garments. Fringed shawls, ponchos, tote bags, and even belts made in crochet are so very easy to do and, in turn, do so much to liven up your wardrobe.

If you knit, you will probably notice that anything that you crochet tends to use more yarn than a design that is knitted. However, because the crochet rows are deeper than the knitted rows, you will be able to finish the work in a much shorter time, whether it's a man's tie, an elegant evening dress or a cosy afghan.

Equipped for action

Crochet hooks are made of steel, plastic and aluminum. Steel hooks range in size from number 00, the smallest, to number 12, the largest. Plastic and aluminum hooks range in size from B, the smallest, to P (jumbo), the largest. Below is a list of sizes for American and English plastic and aluminum hooks. (Alternative U.S. sizes for steel hooks are in parentheses.) Where it is necessary to use a smaller than size 1 steel crochet hook, it will be stated clearly in the garment directions.

U.S.		English	
B (1)		2.00	
C (2)		2.50	
D (3)		3.00	
E (4)		3.50	
F (5)		4.00	
G (6)		4.50	
H (8)		5.00	
I (9)		5.50	
J (10)		6.00	
K (10½)		6.50	
P or jumbo			

The following tools will also be helpful:
☐ Metal or wooden ruler ☐ Scissors
☐ Rustless pins ☐ Large blunt sewing needles
☐ Iron and ironing board with pad ☐ Pressing cloths
☐ Cloth or plastic bag to keep work clean

Take care with yarn

All types of yarns are suitable for crochet—whether thick or thin, natural or man-made fibers—not only the fine cottons or linens used for the more traditional types of fine crochet.

If you are not absolutely certain that you can achieve the same gauge, then it is wisest to buy the brand of yarn specified in the directions. A different brand may make it difficult for you to obtain the correct measurements. But as in knitting, if you can obtain the number of stitches and rows given in the directions, then you can use any other yarn that gives the same number of stitches and rows to the inch. (See Yarn Chart, pages 10-11.) Always buy sufficient quantity to complete the garment so that all the yarn comes from the same dye lot. Another dye lot may vary very slightly and cause unwanted stripes. When working with balls of crochet cotton, always use the end from the center of the ball as it flows more smoothly when being worked.

The importance of gauge

Gauge is one of the most important factors towards successful work. If you do not get the number of stitches and rows to one inch that are stated in the directions your garment cannot have the correct measurements when completed.

Beginners should practice trying to obtain the correct gauge, but if it proves very difficult to obtain while trying to hold hook and yarn comfortably, then different hook sizes should be tried.

Before beginning a garment, work a four inch square. If you find you have fewer stitches to the inch than given, then use a smaller hook; if on measuring you find you have too many stitches to the inch, then you must use a larger hook.

Common abbreviations

(Complicated abbreviations will be explained as they occur.)

alt	=alternate	**rem**	=remaining
beg	=beginning	**rep**	=repeat
ch	=chain(s)	**rnd**	=round
cl	=cluster	**sc**	=single crochet
dc	=double crochet	**RS**	=right side
dec	=decrease	**sdc**	=short double
gr	=group		crochet
hdc	=half double	**sp**	=space
	crochet	**ss**	=slip stitch
in	=inch	**st(s)**	=stitches
inc	=increase	**WS**	=wrong side
patt	=pattern	**yoh**	=yarn over hook
		yrh	=yarn around hook

N.B. It should be noted that yoh is the first movement in crochet and forms an important part of every stitch.

An asterisk * means to repeat directions following the * as many extra times as specified.

Repeat instructions in parentheses as many times as specified. For example: (5ch, dc into next dc) 5 times, means to make all that is in brackets 5 times. Multiple means the number of stitches necessary to complete one pattern. If the pattern is 4 sts, the number of chains should be evenly divisible by 4. If the pattern reads "multiple of 4 sts, plus 1" then an extra chain stitch is required in addition to the multiple of 4.

How to begin

The beginning of crochet is to make a slip loop in the yarn and place it on the hook.

1. To make a slip loop: Wrap yarn around first and second fingers of left hand. Insert hook under front loop and draw the back loop through to form a new loop, slipping it off fingers and transferring it to the hook. Pull the loop tight.

2. Holding yarn and hook: Before making a chain, which is the next step, it is necessary to know how to hold the hook and the yarn correctly.

The hook is held in your right hand in the same way as you hold a pen or pencil. This means you hold it between thumb and first finger, letting the hook rest against the second finger, which controls it in moving through the stitches. The left hand is used to hold the work as it is made, and to control the yarn from the ball. Control the yarn by passing it over the first and second fingers of the left hand, then under the third finger and around the little finger—letting the yarn flow loosely.

3. Chain stitch: Hold the stitch you have made between thumb and first finger of left hand.

Pass hook from left to right under the yarn over your left hand fingers, and over the hook. This is called 'yarn over hook' (yoh) and is a most important part of all stitches. Draw yarn through loop on hook. This makes 1 chain stitch (ch).

4. Repeat this step until you have as many chain stitches as you need, being careful to move your left-hand thumb and finger up the chain to hold the stitch you have just made. Practice making chains until you can hold hook and yarn comfortably.

5. To fasten off: Cut yarn about six inches from work. Thread loose end through the one remaining loop on the hook and pull it tightly.

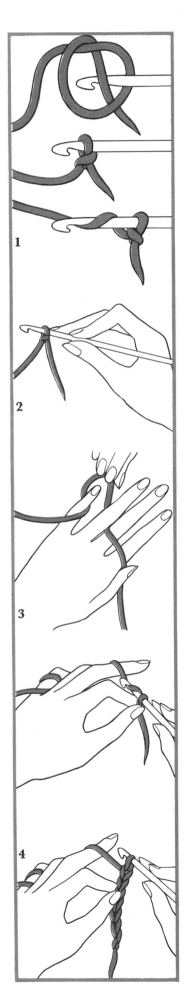

Chapter 2

Singles and doubles

To begin crocheting, make a chain and then work back along that chain with your chosen stitch. The top edge of this row forms a new chain base for the next row. Remember to pick up the top two loops of the chain formed by the previous row, unless otherwise instructed. This creates an even surface.

Chain stitch (ch)

Make a loop on hook, * wrap yarn over hook and draw yarn through the preceding loop; repeat from * for the desired length. Each loop is counted as one chain stitch.

Single crochet (sc)

Make a chain the required length, plus two turning chain stitches.
1st row. Skip the first two chains. * Insert hook in next chain, yarn over hook, draw through loop (2 loops on hook), yarn over hook, and draw through both loops (1 loop on hook). This makes one single crochet. Repeat from * to end of chain. Turn.
2nd row. Ch2, skip first single crochet.* Insert hook through next single crochet (picking up both loops), yarn over hook, draw loop through (2 loops on hook), yarn over hook, draw loop through both loops on hook (1 loop on hook), repeat from * in every single crochet stitch, working last single crochet into turning chain on previous row. Turn.
Repeat 2nd row until the work measures the required length. End off.
Occasionally check the number of stitches at the end of each row, to make sure you have worked the full number of stitches that you had at the end of the second row.

Double stitch (dc)

Make the required length of chain plus 3 turning chains.
1st row. Skip first 3 chains, * yarn over hook, insert hook into next chain, yarn over hook, draw through one loop (3 loops on hook), yarn over hook, and draw through 2 loops (2 loops on hook), yarn over hook, and draw through remaining 2 loops on hook (1 loop on hook). This makes one double crochet. Repeat from * to end of chain, turn.
2nd row. Ch2, skip the first double * 1 double in next double, repeat from * to end of row, working last double into second chain of turning chain, turn.
Repeat 2nd row until the work measures the required length. Remember to check the number of stitches you have worked at the end of each row to maintain the shape of your work.
Always draw up the first stitch to its full height. Proper loop formation gives the finished stitch its full and soft appearance. If the top of the stitch is finished off too loosely a ragged effect will be produced.

Turning chains

When working rows (as opposed to rounds), it is necessary to add extra chain stitches at the beginning of each row as a 'fake' stitch to bring you up to the level of stitching for this row. These extra stitches are called turning chains and count as the first stitch of the row to be worked (unless otherwise stated). To compensate for this extra stitch, you must skip the first stitch of the row and work the first actual pattern stitch into the second stitch of the previous row. At the end of each row the last stitch is then worked into the turning chain of the previous row.
These turning chains give a neat, firm edge to your work. The following table is a guide to the number of chains to be worked to give the right depth of the stitch being replaced.
N.B. Some patterns give directions for working the turning chains at the end of the row before turning to start the next row. You may do this if you prefer, but in this book, the turning chain is given at the beginning of each row.

Single crochet	— 2 turning chain
Short double	— 2 turning chain
Double crochet	— 3 turning chain
Treble stitch	— 4 turning chain
Double treble stitch	— 5 turning chain

N.B. 'Chain stitches' usually referred to as 'chain'.

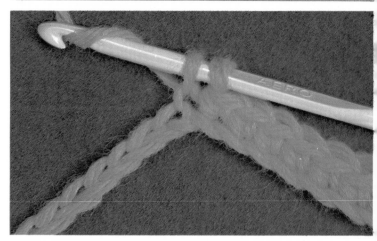

▲ *Beginning single crochet along the first chain*

▼ *Double crochet gives a deeper row*

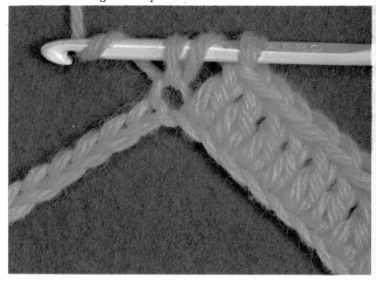

Variations of the double stitch

1. Short double (sdc) or half double (hdc)

Make the required length of chain, plus 2 turning chain.
1st row. Skip first 2ch, * yoh, insert hook into next ch, yoh, draw through one stitch (3 loops on hook), yoh, draw through all loops on hook (1 loop on hook), (this makes 1 sdc), repeat from * to end of ch. Turn.
2nd row. Ch2, * 1 sdc into next sdc, rep from * to last sdc, 1 sdc into 2nd of 2 turning ch. Turn. Rep 2nd row for length required.

2. Treble stitch (tr)

To begin, first work the required length of chain, plus 4 turning chain.
1st row. Skip first 4ch, * yarn twice over hook—called y2oh—insert hook into next ch, yoh, draw loop through ch, yoh, draw loop through first 2 loops on hook, yoh, draw loop through next two loops on hook, yoh, draw loop through last 2 loops on hook, (this makes 1 tr), rep from * to end of ch. Turn.
2nd row. Work 4ch. Work 1 tr into next tr, rep from * to end of row, working last tr into 4th ch of turning ch. Turn. Rep 2nd row for length required.

3. Double treble (dtr)

Work these stitches in the same way as treble, passing the yarn over hook three times, instead of twice. Then work the loops off in the same way, two at a time, until one loop remains on hook.

4. Double around double

This stitch is frequently used in designs where a deeply ridged effect is required. Make the ridge by working around the double in the previous row, instead of working into the chain at the top of the stitches. Shown here is a sample of double already worked, with the hook in position to work the next stitch around the double in the previous row. The ridge is made by the top chain on the previous row being left free on the reverse side of the work.

5. Double between double

To crochet with the stitches alternating more definitely, work into the space between the doubles in the previous row. The illustration shows ordinary double with the hook in position to work the next double into the space in the previous row.
The last two stitches show how you can change the appearance of a familiar stitch by varying the way you insert the hook.

Slip stitch (ss)

This stitch is used chiefly for joining or in intricate patterns, and it is the shortest in height of all the crochet stitches.
Make the required length of chain.
1st row. Skip first ch, * pass hook through top loop of next ch, yoh, draw yarn through both stitches on hook, rep from * to end of ch. Turn. This makes 1 slip stitch (ss).
2nd row. Ch 1, * 1 ss into next ss, rep from * working last ss into turning ch of previous row.
Repeat second row for length required. Fasten off.

▲ *Short double (sdc) or half double (hdc) stitch*

▲ *Treble stitch (tr)*

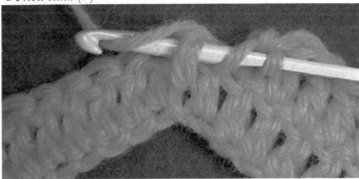

▲ *Double around double stitch*

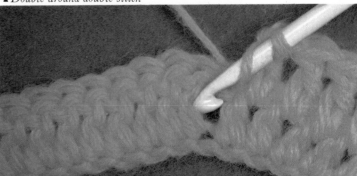

▲ *Double between double stitch*

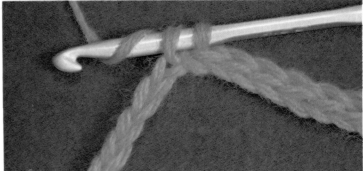

▲ *Slip stitch*

Chapter 3

Increasing and decreasing

Knowing how to increase and decrease stitches is an important step in crochet, but one that becomes very simple with just a little practice. Once you master the methods, you can tackle almost any crochet item. Try the pillow cover shown and prove it!

Increasing

1. The simplest way to increase is to work two stitches into one. This can be done at each end of a row, or at one end only.

2. The second method is to add as many chains as the number of stitches to be increased, plus the turning chain at the end of the row. This way, an increase at the left side of the work is made at the end of a right side row, and an increase at the right side of the work is made at the end of a wrong side row. When the work is turned, the new chain is worked the same as a starting chain.

3. Mark the place where the increase is to be made with a length of colored thread. If the increase is to be made to the right, work two stitches into the stitch before the marker.

4. If the increase is to be made to the left, work these stitches into the stitch after the marker.

If the increases are to be repeated in following rows, they are moved one stitch to the right, or one stitch to the left, depending on which side the increase is required.

5. To make a double increase, follow the same instructions, but work three stitches instead of two into the foundation stitch.

Decorative increasing

Make a more decorative increase the following way. Mark the place where the increase is to be made on the wrong side of the work. Then, working on the wrong side, make one chain before the marker if you want the increase to be to the left, or after the marker if you want it to be to the right. On the next row (right side) work the increase stitch into the chain made on the previous row.

1. Increasing by working two stitches into one. This is the simplest method, and can be worked at either end of a row

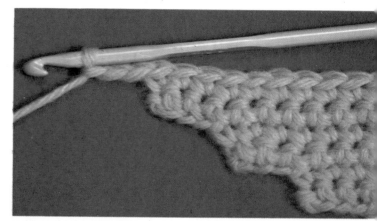

2. Increasing with a chain

3. Increasing to the right. This is made by marking the position for increasing, and working two stitches into one to the right of the marker

4. Increasing to the left. This is made by marking the position for increasing, and working two stitches into one to the left of the marker

5. Double increasing. This is the same method as for single increasing, but three stitches instead of two are worked into one

186

Decreasing

To decrease one stitch at the side edge, skip the first stitch at the beginning of the row and insert the hook into the second stitch. Work to within the last two stitches in the usual way, skip the next stitch and insert the hook into the last stitch.

To decrease several stitches, work the row and turn, leaving the stitches to be decreased at the end of a row, unworked.

5. There is a way to avoid ugly steps in your work where several stitches have to be decreased at once. For example, if three are to be decreased, work along the row to the last three stitches, skip the next two and work one slip stitch into the last stitch: turn with one chain, skip the slip stitch, work a single crochet into the next stitch, and then continue along the row in the normal way.

Decreasing a stitch in the middle of a row

7. Work two single or double crochet, but keep the last loop of each stitch on the hook. Then draw a loop through all the loops that are remaining on the hook.

Marking position for decreases

When making decreases in the middle of a row, make sure you mark the spot with a length of contrasting colored yarn. Then work the decrease in the two stitches before the marker if it is a right decrease, or in the two stitches after it if it is a left decrease. For example, to decrease on single crochet, insert the hook into the first of these two stitches, yoh, and draw one loop through, keeping it on the hook. Insert the hook into the second stitch, yoh and draw another loop through so that there are three loops on the hook. Then, yoh, draw loop through all loops.

When decreasing or increasing on garments, use the method that gives the neatest edges, as it will be easier to sew together.

6. *Decreasing at the end of a row. This can be worked on either side, producing the slanting edge shown*

7. *Decreasing a stitch in the middle of a row. It is very important to use a marker to keep the decreasing even*

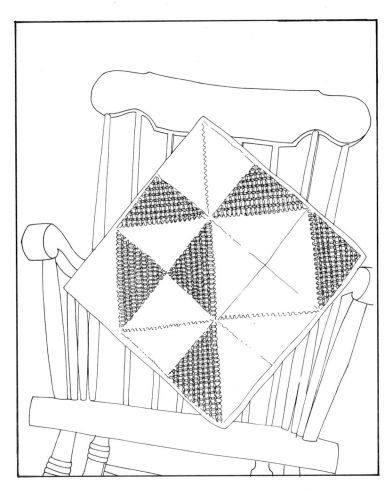

These unusual pillow covers have been made from crocheted squares, each made up of two colors and then joined together. This method could be used for anything which is made with squares—a vest, handbag, or an afghan would all look attractive in carefully chosen colors.

Pillows made with colored squares

The pillow is made with squares crocheted in two colors and then sewn together to form a cover. Each measures $5\frac{1}{2}$ inches square. You can use odd scraps of yarn, but do make sure you choose yarns of similar thickness.

To make a square

Work 3 ch.

1st row. Work 2 dc into 3rd ch from hook. Turn. Continue in rows of dc working 3 ch at beg of each row to turn, and inc 2 dc at each end of every row. Work until about $7\frac{1}{2}$ inches wide.

Join contrast yarn with ss and continue, dec 2 dc at each end of every row by leaving last loop of each 3 dc to be decreased on hook, then drawing yarn through all loops. This decreases 2 dc. Work until 3 dc rem.

Last row. Work 3 dc, leaving last loop of each on hook, then draw loop through all loops on hook.

Work 8 more squares in same manner; sew tog on wrong side.

To make the border

Work 2 rows of sc around edges, working 2 extra sc in each corner st.

Work another side in the same way.

You can, if you like, instead of working two sides, work just one and back it with any strong fabric in a contrasting or blending color. Vary the arrangement of the squares and colors too, to make your own design.

Chapter 4

Crochet in rounds

Crochet in rounds produces beautiful results from the simplest American Granny squares to the finest Irish crochet.

To make a circle

Make the central circle from a short chain, looped round to form a circle and joined by 1 ss into the first ch. Into this first circle work twice the number of stitches of the original chain, and complete the round by joining to the first stitch with a ss. Shape is made in the next rounds by the position of the increased stitches.

> **N.B.** Before making anything in crochet of any size, you must know how to join yarn securely. Join new yarn with a slip stitch, work the chain to form the first stitch and work over both the ends for a few stitches.

▼ *Joining chains to form a circle*   ▼ *The disc when almost complete*

Crocheting into spaces (sp)

When following a pattern it is often necessary to work into a space made in the previous row, instead of working into or around the stitch. The illustration shows the third round of an American Granny square and illustrates how to change to a different colored yarn with a slip stitch while working into a chain space.

The traditional American Granny square

Afghan squares are fun and easy to do

An afghan is the name given to a knitted or crocheted blanket or coverlet. These are often made in strips or sections for easy handling, then put together when all the sections are complete. The beautiful afghan shown on the opposite page is made of small squares crocheted in a traditional, much-used design called the American Granny design.

It is common to use odd lengths of wool or left-over scraps of any color for making afghans, but if you have to buy wool, the afghan can take on added sophistication by having a planned color scheme. Choose one color for the background or main color, and two or more colors to tone or contrast. Arrange the finished squares at random as in the illustration, or in lines, or in squares of color for a neat, symmetrical design.

How to make a Granny square

Use 2 different shades of yarn.

With first color, ch4 and join with a ss to form a circle.

1st round. Ch3, 2dc into circle, ch 1, * 3dc into circle, ch 1 ; rep from * twice. Join into 3rd ch with ss. Break off yarn.

2nd round. Join 2nd color into last sp with a ss, ch2, 2dc into same sp, ch 1, 3dc into same sp, ch 1, * 3dc, ch 1, 3dc, ch 1 into next sp, rep from * twice. Join into 3rd ch with ss. Break off yarn.

3rd round. With first color, join into last sp with ss. Continue working groups of 3dc, with ch 1 between, along sides; and 2 groups of 3dc, with ch 1 between, into each corner.

Work 3 more rounds in same manner, alternating colors.

When squares are ready to be joined, sew them together on one side, or crochet together using single crochet.

Finish ends by darning into same color yarn so that it is invisible. Either side of the crochet can be treated as the right side.

◄ *Working into a space*

The color scheme for this richly blended afghan was taken from the colors seen in a harbor in Malta, where these pictures were taken ►

189

Chapter 5

Crochet a vest in squares

You have already seen how to work squares using just two colors in Crochet Know-how Chapter 4. The vest design featured here is based on the use of four colors arranged in different combinations in squares of four rounds each. You will need to work sixty-two of these, plus two half-squares for the front shaping. You can make every square different by varying the number of colors and their sequence in each square. (If you do this, you might chart your plan before you begin.) Or you can simply make each square using the same combination.

For the vest shown, you will need a total of 16 ounces of fingering yarn and a No.D crochet hook. If you intend to use one main color as the last round of every square, you will need more of this color in proportion to the three contrasting colors.

The measurements are for a 34-36in bust size, with an underarm length of 17½in. This size is based on a 3½in square, joined together in rows of ten. To vary the bust size, use a different size of hook to work a smaller or larger square. For example, to make a 30-32 in size use a hook which will work a 3in square, ten of which when joined together will give you the size you want. Add extra rows of squares to alter the length of the vest to a sweeping midi worn over flowing evening trousers. Take away one or two rows and you have a snug bolero.

190

Size

To fit a 34-36in bust.
Length to center back, 24½in.

> **Gauge**
> Each square measures 3½ x 3½in worked on No.D crochet hook.

Materials

Fingering yarn
4oz each of 4 colors
One No.D crochet hook

To make a square

Ch4. Join with a ss to first ch to form circle.
1st round Ch3, 2dc into circle, ch2, *3dc into circle, ch2, rep from * twice. Join with a ss to 3rd of first 3ch.
2nd round Ch2, work 3dc, ch2, 3dc into first ch2 space to form corner, *ch 1, work 3dc, ch2, 3dc into next ch2 space to form corner, rep from * twice. Join with a ss to 1st of first 2ch.
3rd round Ch3, 2dc into first ch space, ch 1, *work 3dc, ch2, 3dc into corner ch2 space, ch 1, 3dc into next ch 1 space, ch 1, rep from * twice, work 3dc, ch2, 3dc into last corner space, ch 1. Join with a ss to 3rd of first 3ch.
4th round Ch2, 3dc into next ch 1 space, ch 1, * work 3dc, ch2, 3dc into corner ch2 space, ch 1, 3dc into ch 1 space, ch 1, 3dc into ch 1 space, ch 1, rep from * twice, work 3dc, ch2, 3dc into last corner ch2 space, ch 1, 2dc into next ch space. Join with a ss to 1st of first 2ch. Fasten off.

Make 61 more squares in this way, varying the theme by using only one color or combinations of two, three or four colors.

To make a half square

Ch32.
1st row Into 3rd ch from hook work 1 dc, 1 dc into next ch, ch 1, skip 1 ch, work 1 dc into each of next 3ch, ch 1, skip 1 ch, work 1 dc into each of next 3ch, ch 1, skip 1 ch, work 1 dc into each of next 3ch leaving last loop of each dc on hook, skip 1 ch, work 1 dc into each of next 3ch leaving last loop of each dc on hook, yoh and draw through all 7 loops on hook, ch 1, skip 1 ch, work 1 dc into each of next 3ch, ch 1, skip 1 ch, work 1 dc into each of next 3ch, ch 1, skip 1 ch, work 1 dc into each of last 3ch. Turn.
2nd row Ch3, into first ch loop work 3dc, ch 1, skip 3dc, 3dc into next ch loop, ch 1, skip 3dc, work 3dc into next ch loop leaving last loop of each dc on hook, skip corner cluster, work 3dc into next ch loop leaving last loop of each

dc on hook, yoh and draw through all 7 loops on hook, ch 1, skip 3dc, work 3dc into next ch loop, ch 1, skip 3dc, work 3dc into next ch loop, 1 dc in turning ch. Turn.
3rd row Ch3, into first ch loop work 3dc, ch 1, skip 3dc, 3dc into next ch loop leaving last loop of each dc on hook, skip corner cluster, work 3dc into next ch loop leaving last loop of each dc on hook, yoh and draw through all 7 loops on hook, ch 1, skip 3dc, 3dc into next ch loop, 1 dc into turning ch. Turn.
4th row Ch3, work 3dc into first ch loop leaving last loop of each dc on hook, skip corner cluster, work 3dc into next ch loop leaving last loop of each dc on hook, yoh and draw through all 7 loops on hook, 1 dc into turning ch. Fasten off.
Make one more half-square in the same way varying the colors according to your theme.

Finishing

Darn in all ends. Press each square under a damp cloth with a warm iron. Sew or crochet 10 squares together to form 1 row and join 5 rows in same way (50 squares). To 4 center squares of last row join 2 rows of 4 squares for center back (58 squares). Skip first and last square at end of last row and join 2 rows of 1 square to 2nd and 9th squares, leaving 3rd and 8th squares on last row to form underarm. Join half motif to first and 10th squares of last row to form neck shaping. Join 2nd square to first of 4 center back squares and 9th square to 4th of 4 center back squares to form shoulders. Press.
With RS facing beg at underarm square of lower edge and work 1 round sc up front, around neck, down front and around lower edge. Join with ss to first st. Work around armholes in same way. Press. If you prefer, work a picot edge (see Crochet Know-how page 200).

Chapter 6

Ideas for motifs

Motifs have endless uses, not only for pillows and covers but also for fashion ideas. A change of colors, yarn or shape of motif can completely alter the finished look.

Colors and yarns

Try out several color ideas until you find something you particularly like. It could be a collection of gay chunky wools worked with a large hook so that the motifs grow quickly and are then joined (see Crochet Know-how, Chapter 4) to form a long scarf. Or trim the lower edges and sleeves of an evening blouse with a row of motifs worked in a fine metallic yarn. Just remember that if you are using only one color you do not need to break the yarn, but simply continue with the next round, omitting the slip stitch used to join in a new color.

Directions are given for the same color combinations as those shown in the illustrations. Try using your own choice of colors and see the difference if you work in only one or two. Or work with the darkest color in the center and graduate out to the pale one.

Square motif

With center color, ch10. Join into a circle with a ss.

1st round. Using same color, ch3 to form the first st, work 23dc into circle. Join with ss into 3rd of first 3ch. Break yarn, leaving an end to darn in later.

2nd round. Using 1st contrast, join to top of last st of preceding round with a ss, ch3 to form first st, ch5, 1dc into same st as first st, ch7, *skip 5dc of preceding round, work 1dc, ch5, 1dc all into next dc, ch7, rep from * twice. Join with ss into 3rd of first 3ch.

3rd round. Ch3 to form firm st, work 4dc, ch5, 5dc all into first ch5 space of preceding round, ch3, *skip ch7 space, 5dc, ch5, 5dc all into next ch5 space, ch3, rep from * twice. Join with ss into 3rd of first 3ch. Break yarn, leaving end for darning.

4th round. Using second contrast, join as before, ch3 to form first st, 1dc into each of next 4dc of preceding round, work 3dc, ch5, 3dc all into next ch5 space, work 1dc into each of next 5dc, ch7, *1dc into each of next 5dc, work 3dc, ch5, 3dc all into next ch5 space, 1dc into each of next 5dc, ch7, rep from * twice. Join with ss into 3rd of first 3ch. Break yarn, leaving end for darning.

5th round. Join in third contrast as before, ch3 to form first st, 1dc into each of next 7dc of preceding round, 9dc into next ch5 space, 1dc into each of next 8dc, ch3, 1sc into 4th (center) ch of ch7, ch3, *1dc into each of next 8dc, 9dc into next ch5 space, 1dc into each of next 8dc, ch3, 1sc into 4th ch of ch7, ch3, rep from * twice. Join with ss into 3rd of first 3ch. Break yarn, leaving end for darning.

6th round. Join in fourth contrast as before, ch1, work 1sc into each dc or sc of preceding round, working 3sc into each ch3 space. Join with ss to first ch. Break yarn and darn in end. Be careful when doing this to darn into the same color, so that the ends are invisible and the pattern not spoiled. If you have used wool or cotton, pin out the motif to form a good, regular shape and press under a damp cloth with a warm iron. Do not press too heavily or the stitches will be flattened. Do not press man-made fibers. Sew the motifs together at points where they touch each other.

Star motif with 8 points

Using center color, ch7. Join into a circle with a ss.

1st round. Ch2 to form first st, work 23sc into circle. Join with ss to 2nd of first 2ch. Break yarn, leaving end for darning.

2nd round. Join contrast yarn with ss to top of last st worked, ch4, 1dc into same st as first st, ch1, *skip 2sc of preceding round, 1dc, ch2, 1dc all into next sc, ch1, rep from * 6 times. Join with ss into 2nd of first 4ch.

3rd round. With same color, ch2, 1dc, ch2, 2dc all into first ch space of preceding round, 1sc into next ch1 space, *2dc, ch2, 2dc all into next ch2 space, 1sc into next ch1 space, rep from * 6 times. Join with ss into 2nd of first 2ch. Break yarn.

4th round. Join in first color as before, ch2, 2dc, ch1, 3dc all into first ch2 space of preceding round, 1sc on each side of sc of preceding round, *3dc, ch1, 3dc all into next ch2 space, 1sc on each side of next sc, rep from * 6 times. Join with ss into 2nd of first 2ch. Break yarn, leaving end for darning.

5th round. Join in contrast as before, ch2, 1sc into each of next 3dc, 1sc, ch3, 1sc all into first ch1 space, 1sc into each of next 4sts, *1sc into each of next 4sts, 1sc, ch3, 1sc all into next ch1 space, 1sc into each of next 4sts, rep from * 6 times. Join with ss into 2nd of first 2ch. Break yarn and darn in all ends. Complete as for square motif if pressing is required.

◄ *Star motif*

Square motif

Wagon wheels

To make the large round

Ch4. Join into circle with ss.

1st round. Ch3, * (yoh, insert hook into the circle and draw a loop through) twice, yoh and draw through all loops, ch1, rep from * 7 more times. Join with ss into 3rd ch. Cut yarn and fasten off.

2nd round. Join new color into last ch sp with a ss, ch2, (1dc, ch2) into same sp,* (2dc, ch2) into next ch sp, rep from * 6 times (8 dc groups). Join with a ss into 2nd ch. Cut yarn and fasten off.

3rd round. Join new color into last ch sp with a ss, ch2, (1dc, ch1, 2dc, ch1) into same sp,* (2dc, ch1, 2dc, ch1) into next ch sp, rep from * to end (16 dc groups). Join as before. Cut yarn and fasten off.

4th round. Join new color into last sp with ss, ch2, (2dc, ch1) into same sp,* (3dc, ch1) into next ch sp, rep from * to end (16 dc groups). Cut yarn and fasten off.

5th round. Change color and rep 4th round once more.

To make the small round

Make a ch and work 1st round as above but do not break yarn.

2nd round. Ch2, (1dc, ch2) into next sp,* (2dc, ch2) into each sp to end. Join with ss. Cut yarn and fasten off.

Chapter 7

Crochet Know-how

Decorative trimmings

Small crochet trims are easy to handle, quickly worked, perfect for using up all those left-over odds and ends, and are a marvelous way of adding finish and individuality to clothes and accessories. Take a baby's bonnet, trim it with bunches of cord and pastel rosettes like a miniature bouquet of flowers, and fasten mittens and bootees with ties trimmed to match. Add a bold military touch to a jacket with a richly scrolled frog fastening and crocheted buttons. Dangle groups of crochet spirals from the ends of a slender cord belt. Make them in glittering yarn to fringe an evening bag, or let the whole idea go to your head with narrow cords or flower rosettes to twist into an elaborate party hair style.

Cords and rosettes trim a baby's outfit

Cords, rosettes and spirals

You can make a pretty bag for a little girl out of colorful felt wit a crocheted cord handle and a bunch of rosettes in one corner t give a decorative touch. Trim your key ring by adding a fe spirals made in brightly colored yarn.

To make a cord
Ch7, joining to form a circle with a ss. Ch2 and work 1 dc int each ch. Do not join with a ss but continue working around wit 1 dc into each previous dc until desired length is reached. Finis off. You can trim the cord with rosettes and spirals.

To make a rosette
Ch16.
1st row. Into 4th ch from hook work 4dc, * 5dc into next ch, re from * to end. Finish off.
You will see the rosette forms a small curl or rose shape. The en can be secured by a few small stitches sewn through the cente The longer the chain, and the thicker the yarn and hook which yo use, the larger the rosette will be.

To make a spiral
Ch20.
1st row. Work 2dc into 4th ch, * 3dc in next ch, rep * to end c ch. Cut yarn and finish off the spiral.

Bag and key with crochet trims

Buttons

Small buttons like the ones shown are not just decorative—they're practical too! They often make a smart alternative to ordinary buttons on knitted or crocheted garments.

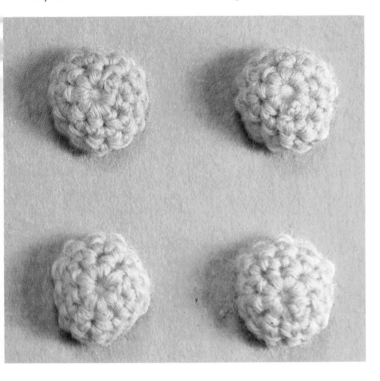

To make a button

Ch4, joining to form a circle with a ss.

1st round. Ch 1, work 7sc into circle. Do not join with a slip stitch. Continue in sc working * 2sc into next sc, 1 sc into each of next 2sc, rep from * 8 times. Work 1 sc into each of next 12sc. Dec by working as follows: * insert hook into next sc, yoh, draw through loop (2 loops on hook), insert hook into next sc, yoh, draw through loop (3 loops on hook), yoh, draw through all loops on hook, 1 sc into next sc, rep from * 5 times until opening is almost closed, stuffing with cotton batting as you work. Finish off and close any opening which is left.

You can vary the size of the button by increasing more or fewer stitches at the beginning. The number of stitches you work before decreasing will alter its depth.

▼ *Begin the button with a flat circle*   ▼ *Continue working over the filling*

Buttonholes

Horizontal buttonholes

Work until the position for the buttonhole is reached. When this is worked along with the main part of a cardigan, for example, always finish at the center front edge before working the buttonhole row. On the next row, work a few stitches to where the buttonhole is required, work two or more chain stitches for the size of the button, skip the corresponding number of stitches in the row below (picture **1**), then pattern to end of row. On the following row, work in pattern over the chain stitches made in the previous row to complete buttonhole (picture **2**).

Vertical buttonholes

Work until the position for the buttonhole is reached. On the next row, work a few stitches to where the buttonhole is required, turn and work back and forth for the required number of rows over these stitches deep enough for the size of button being used, ending at inner edge (picture **3**). Work in slip stitch down inner edge of rows to the last complete row worked, work across the remaining stitches for the same number of rows, then continue across all stitches (picture **4**).

1. *Horizontal buttonholing by chains*   **2.** *Horizontal buttonhole completed*

3. *Vertical buttonholing by rows*   **4.** *Vertical buttonhole completed*

Pompons and tufts

Pompons and tufted fringe are trims which can add an interesting touch to wardrobe and household items alike. Give new life to pillows, scatter rugs or bedspreads by adding a cluster of jewel-bright pompons. Use a large pompon at the end of the cord on a window shade or drapes. A huge pompon will do wonders for a plain wool cap—and you can add a matching one to your scarf! Tufted fringe, too, has a wide variety of uses. As you may have found, though, instructions all too often just say, "finish with a pompon" or "add fringe," but give you no details on how to go about it. This chapter tells you how to do both.

Small pompons

To make small pompons, wind lengths of yarn around two or more fingers. When you think you have wound enough for the size pompon you want, slip the strands off your fingers carefully and tie tightly around the center. With sharp scissors, snip both looped ends of yarn and arrange them to form a ball. It may be necessary to trim the ends so that the finished shape is neat and round.

Make cord belts with pompons or knot cord ends and spread out as tassels

Large pompons

For large pompons, you will need to use a cardboard frame. Decide on the diameter of the pompon you want and draw two circles of this diameter on the cardboard. From the center of each circle cut out a smaller circle: the larger this inner circle, the more wool you will need to complete the pompon and the heavier it will be when finished. If you don't have a compass, a cup or small bowl will be large enough to draw the outer circle and a coin or egg-cup is often a good size for the inner circle.

Place the two circles together and with one or more strands begin to wind the yarn around the frame as evenly as possible. When the center hole is almost filled, thread the yarn into a darning needle and continue until the hole is completely filled. To make a fat and well-shaped pompon, you must continue to work until the center circle is tightly filled.

When you have done this, take a pair of sharp scissors and begin to cut the strands of yarn at the outside edge, working in line with the edge of the cardboard and placing the scissors between the cardboard circles. Once you have cut all the strands, you are ready to begin the final stage.

Gently, with the tips of the scissors, begin to open the cardboard rings until they are far enough apart for you to tie a strong strand of yarn tightly around all the threads where they pass through the center of the rings. If you plan to sew the pompon onto a garment, you may like to leave the ends of the tying yarn hanging so that you can use them for sewing on. Once the center is tied, continue to remove both rings of cardboard.

When you have finished this step, fluff the pompon into a complete ball and trim the uneven ends.

For a multi-colored pompon, work all the colors together. If you want a striped effect, work around the ring in one color and then in another. Or, work in sections of one color at a time if you want to make a patchwork pompon.

Tufted fringing

From the illustration, you can see how to give a baby's poncho a soft, frothy edge by adding a tufted fringe.

The number and size of the tufts on each strand, as well as the distance between the tufts, can be altered according to your own taste. You can make a short, thick fringe by working only a few chain stitches between each tuft, or a deeper, more delicate fringe by spacing the tufts much farther apart—all you need to do is simply work more chain stitches between the tufts.

Begin by preparing the tufts. Decide on the size you want and cut a piece of cardboard this width and several inches long. Then wind the yarn around the full length of the cardboard and cut along the edges. If each tuft on the strand is to be a different width, then you will need one piece of cardboard for each width. The illustrations on the opposite page show a strand of wool made with three different sized tufts.

Now prepare the strands. Begin the first strand by making 9 chain stitches with a crochet hook. Open out the last chain stitch and place the desired number of threads in the loop. When the tuft is in place, pull the open stitch tight to grip all the threads in the center of the tuft. Continue by making 9 chain stitches before inserting the next tuft.

Complete the number of tufts you want in this way and join the strand, when completed, to the edge of the work with a slip stitch. Cut the yarn and fasten off the ends. Join other strands at even intervals along the edge to be trimmed. Finally, when the fringe is completed, you can anchor each tuft even more securely by working several small stitches through the center of tuft and chain with a fine, matching sewing thread or yarn.

▲ *Winding the yarn onto the frame*

▲ *Cutting yarn between circles*   ▼ *The finished pompon*

▲ *Working the chain between tufts*   ▲ *Joining a tuft to the chain*

▼ *Baby's poncho with tufted fringe and pompon tie*

Braids, borders and edgings

One of the great things about crochet is the many different types of trimming you can make with it. Braids and borders can look very attractive if you use a combination of colors, and they can be worked in a wide range of materials from fine cotton to colored string to make pillow and curtain edges, hat bands, belts and hairbands. Crochet edgings in a single color are also pretty and need not be limited to trimmings for household linen or crochet garments. They look just as attractive as borders for knitted garments. Try trimming a plain sweater with a crochet edging in a contrasting color, as shown in the illustration on the opposite page, to make a simple neckline look more interesting.

Braids and borders

Braid in two colors

With blue, crochet a chain the desired length, working it to a number of stitches divisible by 10, plus 1.

1st row. With blue, work 1hdc into 3rd ch from hook, 1hdc into each ch to end. Break yarn. Turn and work other side of ch. Join blue with ss to first st of commencing ch, ch2, 1hdc into each st to end. Break yarn and fasten off. Complete remaining rows on one side before turning and working the other side to correspond.

2nd row. Join cream with ss to first st, ch2, 1sc into each of next 2hdc, *skip 2hdc, insert hook into space between 2 rows of hdc along commencing ch immediately below 2nd skipped st, yoh and draw through a long loop to reach row being worked, 1sc into first hdc skipped, yoh and draw through both loops on hook, 1sc into each of next 3hdc, rep from * to end. Break yarn and fasten off. Do not turn work.

3rd row. Join cream with ss to 2nd of first 2ch, ch2, *ch2, yoh, insert hook into same st as last st, yoh and draw through 2 loops, yoh and insert hook into same st, yoh and draw through all 3 loops on hook, skip 3sc, 1sc into next st, rep from * to end. Break yarn and fasten off. Turn work.

Complete as for first side, working 2nd row with long st sloping in

opposite direction, thus—join cream with ss to 2nd of first 2ch, ch2, 1sc into each of next 2hdc, *insert hook into same space as first long st on other side, yoh and draw a long loop through, 1sc into next hdc, yoh and draw through 3 loops on hook, 1sc into each of next 3hdc, rep from * to end. Break yarn and fasten off. Do not turn work. Complete as for first side. Darn in all ends.

Border 1 in three colors

Crochet a chain the desired length with blue. Turn

1st row. With blue, 1sc into 2nd ch from hook, 1sc into next ch, *ch3, skip 2ch, 1sc into each of next 2ch, rep from * to end. Turn. Break off blue and fasten off.

2nd row. With cream, join with ss into first sc, ch1, 1sc into next sc, *into ch3 space work 1sc, 3dc, 1sc, 1sc into each of next 2sc, rep from * to end. Turn. Break off cream and fasten off.

3rd row. With light green, join with ss to first sc, 1sc into first sc, ch2, join with ss into side of last sc to form picot, 1sc into next sc, *ch2, 1sc into 2nd of 3dc, ch2, 1sc into next sc, 1 picot as before, 1sc into next sc, rep from * to end. Break off green and darn in all ends.

Border 2 in three colors

Crochet a chain the desired length with blue. Turn.

1st row. With blue, 1sc into 2nd ch from hook, *1sc into next ch, rep from * to end. Break off blue and fasten off. Turn.

2nd row. With cream, join with ss into first sc, 1sc into same sc, *ch7, skip 3sc, into 4th sc work 1sc, ch1, turn and work 4sc into ch7 space, ch1, turn, work 1sc into each of 4sc just worked, 1sc into last sc worked before ch7, rep from * to end. Break off cream and fasten off. Turn.

3rd row. With light green, join with ss into first sc, *1sc into each of first 3sc, into 4th sc work 3sc, 3sc into part of ch7 space not covered by sc, skip 1sc, rep from * to end. Break off light green and darn in all ends.

Edgings

The simplest of all edgings is formed by working two or more rows of single crochet along the garment edge.

The first row of crochet must be worked evenly onto the knitted edge for a neat and attractive crochet design. If the stitches of this first row are worked unevenly, the finished appearance will be completely spoiled.

Here we give you four more edges which can be worked just as quickly and easily. Use them as borders on the front of a plain cardigan or around the cuffs and neck of a basic sweater to give a couture finish to your favorite pattern.

Crab stitch edging

This is the simplest of all the variations of single crochet and can be worked backward and forward along an edge in rows, or continuously around a circular opening such as a cuff.

1st row. Work along edge using single crochet. If working a circular edge, join with a slip stitch to the first stitch.

2nd row. If the work is circular, work back along the round already made, working one single crochet in each single crochet and working from left to right instead of the normal right to left. If you are working in rows, then do not turn the work; simply make one single crochet in each single crochet already made. Fasten off.

▲ *Crab stitch edging*
▼ *Reversed crab stitch edging*

Reversed crab stitch edging

1st row. Work along edge using single crochet. Turn.

2nd row. Ch2, skip first single crochet, *1sc into next sc, rep from * to end. Do not turn.

3rd row. Into each sc of previous row work 1sc, working from left to right. Fasten off.

▼ *Twisted stitch edging*

Twisted stitch edging

1st row. Work along edge using single crochet. Turn.

2nd row. *Insert hook into first sc, yoh and draw a loop through loosely, turn the hook on itself in order to twist the stitches, yoh and draw through all loops, rep from * to end. Fasten off.

▼ *Cluster stitch edging*

Cluster stitch edging

1st row. Work along edge using single crochet. Break yarn.

The 2nd row is worked in the same direction as the 1st.

2nd row. Join yarn with ss to first sc, ch2, *1sc into next st, (yoh, insert hook into ch to right of sc just worked and draw through one loose st) 3 times into same stitch, yoh and draw through all loops, ch1, skip 1sc, rep from * to end. Fasten off.

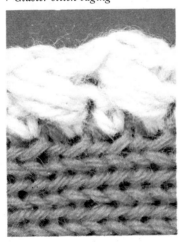

Sweater showing crochet neck edging

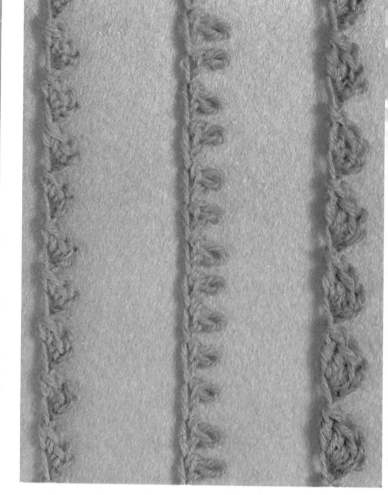

More ideas
for edgings

Picot edgings

Picot edgings can be made in thick yarns to give a chunky edge or in cotton for a delicate cobweb effect.

Small picot edging

* Ch3, work 2sc into the first of these 3ch. Without turning the work rep from * until the strip is the required length. Finish off.

Lace picot

Ch2, * into the first of these 2ch insert the hook, yoh, and draw through one loop. There are now 2 loops on hook. Into the loop nearest the hook point ch2. Slip both loops off hook and insert hook back into only the loop farther to the left of work. Without turning the work, rep from * until the edging is the desired length. Finish off.

Ring picot

* Ch5, work 1 dc into the first of these 5ch. Without turning the work, rep from * until the edging is the desired length. Finish off.

Left to right: small picot edging, lace picot, leaf picot

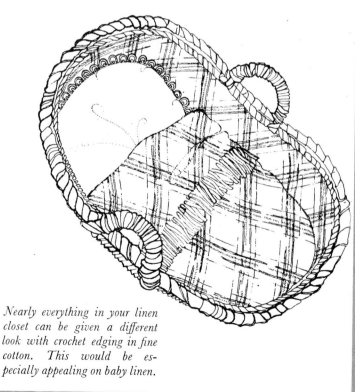

Nearly everything in your linen closet can be given a different look with crochet edging in fine cotton. This would be especially appealing on baby linen.

Ribbon-threaded edgings

These edgings are pretty in a variety of yarns, but, whichever yarn you choose, don't use too small a crochet hook, since the work must be open enough to allow the ribbon to slide through easily.

Clover edging

Work a number of chains divisible by 8, plus 1, for the desired length.

1st row. 1sc into 2nd ch from hook, *1sc into next ch, rep from * to end. Turn.

2nd row. Ch2, skip first sc, *ch3, skip 3sc and into next sc work 1sc, ch5 to form picot, (1tr into same sc, 1 picot of ch5) twice and 1sc all into same sc forming clover group, ch3, skip 3sc, 1sc into next sc, rep from * to end. Finish off.

Thread ribbon between sc of first row.

Scalloped edging

Work a number of chains divisible by 4, plus 2, for the desired length.

1st row. 1sc into 4th ch from hook, *ch1, skip 1ch, 1sc into next ch, rep from * to end. Turn.

2nd row. Ch2, *ch6, skip 1ch and 1sc and 1ch of previous row, 1sc into next sc, rep from * to end. Turn.

3rd row. Ch2, *3sc into next ch6 loop, ch3, 1ss into side of last sc worked to form picot, 3sc into same ch6 loop, 1sc into sc between loops, rep from * to end. Finish off. Thread ribbon in first row.

▲ *Clover edging*   ▼ *Scalloped edging*

Threaded trimmings give a charming edge to a little dress or a shawl

Mitered corners and "V"-necks

Crochet Know-how

Crochet tunic with "V"-neck

Although most crochet patterns give detailed directions, it is helpful to know how shaping is worked, particularly when adapting a favorite design to crochet. Previous chapters tell you how to choose the right stitch for a garment and all about gauge. This chapter gives directions for working a pointed and a rounded mitered corner, sleeve underarm shaping and "V"-necklines.

The tunic illustrated here shows the effective use of "V"-neck shaping, which is defined by an edging in a single contrasting color. The contrasting color theme can be continued at the hem and around the armholes. A "V"-neck tunic is a smart and useful addition to any wardrobe as it can be worn with a variety of separates to liven up the most ordinary outfit. Team it with a skirt and turtleneck sweater or with an open-necked shirt and pants as illustrated.

Pointed mitered corner

To make a separate band having a pointed mitered corner, first measure the length of band required and make the necessary number of chains. Mark the stitch which is to be the innermost point of the corner with colored thread. The band is worked from the inside to the outside edge.

1st row (right side). Work 1sc into 2nd ch from hook, then work 1sc into each ch to the last ch before the marked corner ch, ch2 and continue working 1sc into each ch to end. Turn.

2nd row. Ch2, work 1sc into each sc and 1sc into each of the 2ch at corner. Turn.

Continue in this way, working 2ch at corner on every RS row working 1 more sc on each RS row before making the 2ch and working 1sc into each of these 2ch on WS rows until the band is the required depth. Fasten off.

Any number of chains may precede and follow the corner stitches, depending on the angle of the corner, but always work one more stitch before corner chain on each RS row.

Rounded mitered corner

Prepare the band as for pointed mitered corner.

1st row (right side). Work 1sc into 2nd ch from hook, then 1sc into each ch to marked corner st, work 3sc into corner st and 1sc into each ch to end. Turn.

2nd row. Ch2, work 1sc into each sc to end. Turn. Repeat these 2 rows until band is the required depth, working 3sc into center stitch of the 3 corner stitches on each RS row.

Sleeve underarm shaping

To give a good underarm fit, the same number of stitches should be decreased on the back and front of a garment and at the commencement of the sleeve cap shaping. Work until the back and front side seams and the sleeve seam are the required length.

1st row. Ss over first 5 sts, work 1sc into each sc to last 5 sts. Turn.

2nd row. Ch2, skip 1sc, work 1sc into each sc to last 2sc, skip 1sc, work 1sc into last sc. Turn.

Repeat the 2nd row for a depth of 1½in. Fasten off.

"V"-neckline

The depth of the "V"-neck is entirely a matter of choice, but keep in mind that the deeper the "V," the more gradual the shaping, and that a high "V" must decrease more rapidly in order to complete the shaping before reaching the shoulder level. On a 34in bust size an average depth for a "V"-neck is approximately 10in from the shoulder, which means that the shaping must be commenced at least 3in before the armhole shaping. Mark the position of the center stitch and work each side separately.

1st row (right side). Ch2, work 1sc into each sc, skip 1sc before marked center st, work 1sc into center st. Turn.

2nd row. Ch2, work in sc to end. Rep 2nd row twice more.

5th row. Ch2, work 1sc into each sc, skip last sc but one at

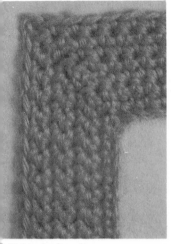

▲ *Pointed mitered corner*

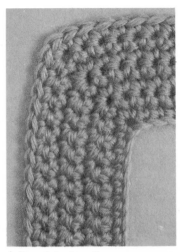

▲ *Rounded mitered corner*

▲ *Sleeve underarm shaping*

▼ *"V"-neck shaping*

neck edge, work 1sc into last sc. Turn.
Repeat rows 2-5 until required number of stitches have been decreased at neck edge, then continue without shaping, if necessary, to a depth of 10in.
With RS of work facing, attach yarn to center st.
1st row. Ch2, skip 1sc, work 1sc into each sc to end. Turn. Work 3 rows without shaping.

Repeat these 4 rows to match first side.
An alternative method of shaping may be worked as follows:
1st row (right side). Ch2, work 1sc into each sc to last 2 sts before center st, insert hook into next sc, yoh and draw loop through, insert hook in last sc, yoh and draw loop through (3 loops on hook),

yoh and draw through all loops in hook (1 dec made), work 1sc into center st. Turn.
Work 3 rows without shaping.
5th row. Ch2, work 1sc into each sc to last 3sc, 1 dec in next 2sc, 1sc in last sc. Turn.
Repeat rows 2-5 until required number of stitches have been decreased at neck edge, then continue without shaping, if necessary, to a depth of 10in.

With RS of work facing, attach yarn to center st.
1st row. Ch2, insert hook in next st, yoh, draw loop through, insert hook in next st, yoh and draw loop through, yoh and draw through 3 loops on hook, work 1sc into each sc to end. Turn. Work 3 rows without shaping.
Repeat these 4 rows to match first side.

Chapter 10

Tubular crochet

The technique of tubular crochet is the same as knitting in rounds, and has the advantage of doing away with bulky seams. Almost any crochet stitch can be adapted to this method but remember that the right side of the work is always facing you. It is particularly useful for working seamless skirts, handbags, hats or layette garments.

▲ *Tubular Russian stitch*　　　▼ *Tubular twisted stitch*

▲ *Joining foundation chain into a ring*　　▼ *Tubular rib stitch*

▼ *Tubular rose stitch*

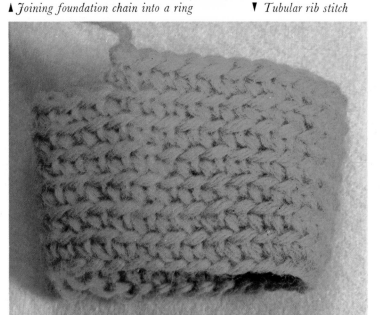

Tubular crochet

Commence with the number of chains which are required to give the total circumference of the article being made. Join into a ring with a slip stitch into the first foundation chain. Continue working in rounds with the chosen stitch for the necessary depth. With the stitches illustrated here it is not necessary to join the end of each round with a slip stitch, but it is advisable to mark the beginning of the first round with a colored thread so that you know where to finish.

Tubular rib stitch

Work each round in single crochet on a foundation chain joined into a ring, but insert the hook into the back loop only of each single crochet.

Tubular Russian stitch

Work each round in single crochet on a foundation chain joined into a ring.

Tubular twisted stitch

Work a foundation chain joined into a ring. Insert hook in center of foundation chain with the hook pointing downward, pass the hook over the yarn on the left index finger and, to make 3rd loop on hook, yoh by working from left to right, pull yarn through chain, pass the yarn over the hook from left to right (instead of the normal way from right to left), pull yarn through 3 loops on hook. This completes one stitch. On following rounds insert hook through both loops of stitch of previous round.

Tubular rose stitch

Work each round in half doubles on a foundation chain joined into a ring.

Handbag: *Join required number of ch into circle. Work patt for depth needed. Seam bottom edge and gather top edge onto frame.*
Bolster: *Make ch as for handbag. Work in patt for length of bolster. Make 2 wagon wheel motifs. Pad bolster and stitch 1 motif to each end.*
Napkin ring: *Make ch as for bag. Work in patt for required depth.*

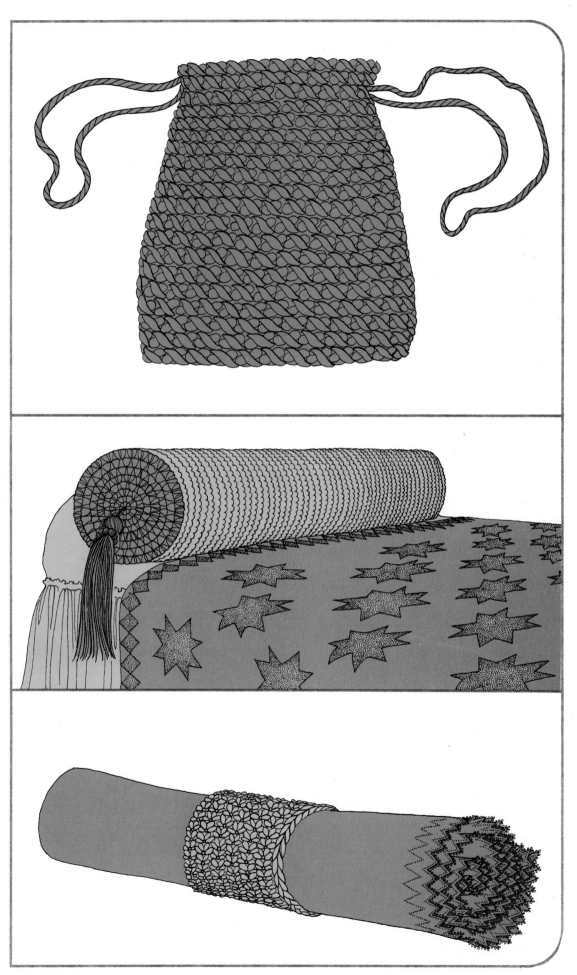

205

Chapter 11

Introduction to fabric stitches

These very firm, fabric-like stitches can be used for garments which receive a lot of wear—suits, jackets, skirts, coats and dresses, for instance. When you are working these stitches, choose a plain, untextured kind of yarn rather than anything fancy, or the fabric effect will tend to become lost. You will find that the close, compact nature of the stitches uses yarn very quickly, so allow a little extra when you are working out a garment pattern.

When you have completed all the stitch swatches, they could be stitched together to make a colorful pillow cover. If you make each square 4 inches by 4 inches and allow 9 squares for the front and the back of the pillow, you will arrive at a pillow measuring 12 inches square. Three of each pattern in different, vividly contrasting colors would make a completely original and individual furnishing accessory.

Double single crochet

Make a chain of the desired length.
1st row. Insert hook into 3rd ch from hook, draw yarn through, yoh, draw through 1 loop, yoh, draw through 2 loops on hook to form 1 double single crochet, work 1 double single crochet into each ch to end. Turn.
This row forms the pattern and is repeated throughout by inserting the hook into each st of the previous row and beginning each row with 2ch as the turning ch.

Up and down stitch

Make a number of chains divisible by 2, plus 1.
1st row. Into 3rd ch from hook work 1sc, *1dc into next ch, 1sc into next ch, rep from * to end. Turn.
2nd row. Ch2, *1sc into dc, 1dc into sc, rep from * to last st, 1sc into last st. Turn.
The 2nd row forms the pattern and is repeated throughout.

Double up and down stitch

Make a number of chains divisible by 4, plus 1.
1st row. Into 3rd ch from hook work 1sc, 1dc into each of next 2ch, *1sc into each of next 2ch, 1dc into each of next 2ch, rep from * to end. Turn.
2nd row. Ch2, 1sc into 2nd dc, *1dc into each of next 2sc, 1sc into each of next 2dc, rep from * to last 2sts, 1dc into each of last 2sc. Turn.
The 2nd row forms the pattern and is repeated throughout.
206

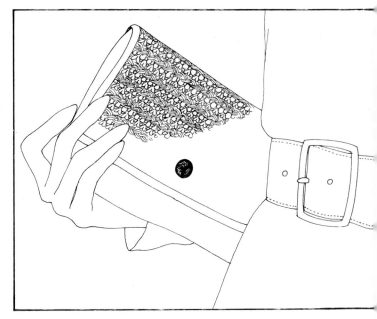

Fabric-look clutch bag in double single crochet

Raised basket weave stitch

Make a number of chains divisible by 4, plus 3.
1st row. Into 2nd ch from hook work 1sc, 1sc into each ch to end Turn.
2nd row. Ch2, 1sc into each sc to end. Turn.
3rd row. Ch2, work 1sc into each of next 2sc working into the back loop only of the row below, *work 1sc into next sc inserting the hook into the corresponding st on the row below the previous row and drawing up a long loop, work 1sc into each of next 3sc working into back loop only of the row below, rep from * to end Turn.
4th row. As 2nd.
5th row. Ch2, *work 1sc into next sc inserting the hook in the corresponding st on the row below the previous row and drawing up a long loop, work 1sc into each of next 3sc working into back loop only of the row below, rep from * to last 2sts, work 1sc into next sc inserting hook and drawing up a loop as before, 1sc into back loop only of last sc. Turn.
Rows 2-5 form the pattern and are repeated throughout.

Leaf stitch

Make a number of chains divisible by 2, plus 1.
1st row. Into 3rd ch from hook work 2sc, skip 1ch, *2sc into next ch, skip 1ch, rep from * to last st, 2sc into last st. Turn.
2nd row. Ch2, *skip 1sc, work 2sc into 2nd sc of group, rep from * to end. Turn.
The 2nd row forms the pattern and is repeated throughout.

Little leaf stitch

Make a number of chains divisible by 2, plus 1.
1st row. Into 3rd ch from hook work 1sc, ch1, 1sc into same st skip 1ch, *1sc, ch1, 1sc into next st, skip 1ch, rep from * to last st, 1sc, ch1, 1sc into last st. Turn.
2nd row. Ch2, *into ch between 2sc of previous row work 1sc, ch1 1sc, rep from * to end. Turn.
The 2nd row forms the pattern and is repeated throughout.

Up and down stitch ▲
Double up and down stitch ▼

Raised basket weave stitch ▲
Leaf stitch ▼

Double single crochet ▼

Little leaf stitch ▼

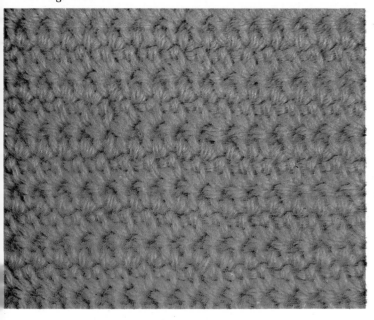

More firm fabric stitches

There are many variations of the closely-worked crochet stitches which give a fabric effect. The ones shown here produce a slightly bulkier fabric than those on the previous page as the stitches are grouped together in chunky clusters. To make the attractive peasant skirt illustrated, simply work two strips of crochet, one for the skirt back and one for the front, using any of the fabric stitches in this chapter. Work in a single bright color or, for a striking effect, in horizontal stripes of contrasting colors. Join the two strips along the side edges, gather the waist on a cord and tie in front. Work a fringe around the hem.

Cluster stitch
Make a number of chains divisible by 3.
1st row. Into 3rd ch from hook work 2dc, skip 2ch, *1sc and 2dc into next ch, skip 2ch, rep from * to last st, 1sc in last st. Turn.
2nd row. Ch2, 2dc into first sc, *1sc and 2dc into each sc of previous row, rep from * ending with 1sc in turning ch. Turn.
The 2nd row forms pattern and is repeated throughout.

Claw stitch
Make a number of chains divisible by 2.
1st row. Into 4th ch from hook work 1dc, *skip 1ch, 2dc into next ch, rep from * to end.
2nd row. Ch3 to form 1st st, 1dc into st between 1st and 2nd dc of previous row, * work 2dc between next 2dc of previous row, rep from * to end. Turn.
The 2nd row forms pattern and is repeated throughout.

Elongated basket stitch
Make a number of chains divisible by 3, plus 1.
1st row. Into 2nd ch from hook work 1sc, 1sc into each ch to end. Turn.
2nd row. Ch2, 1sc into each sc to end. Turn.
3rd row. Ch3, 1dc into each of next 2sc, *(inserting hook in the space between one st and the next on first sc row, work 1dc drawing up a long loop) 3 times, 1dc into each of next 3sc, rep from * to end. Turn.
4th row. As 2nd.
5th row. Ch3, (inserting hook between one st and the next on row below previous row, work 1dc drawing up a long loop) twice, *1dc into each of next 3sc, (inserting hook between one st and the next on row below previous row, work 1dc drawing up a long loop) 3 times, rep from * to end. Turn.
Rows 2-5 form pattern and are repeated throughout.

Paving stone stitch
Make a number of chains divisible by 2.
1st row. Into 3rd ch from hook work 1dc, ch2, 1sc into next ch, *skip 2ch, 2dc into next ch, ch2, 1sc into next ch, rep from * to end. Turn.
2nd row. Ch2, *work 2dc, ch2 and 1sc into 2ch loop of previous row, rep from * to end, 1sc in turning ch. Turn.
The 2nd row forms pattern and is repeated throughout.

Straw stitch
Make a number of chains divisible by 10, plus 6.
1st row. Into 3rd ch from hook work 1sc, 1sc into each of next 3ch, *1dc into each of next 5ch, 1sc into each of next 5ch, rep from * to end. Turn.
2nd row. Ch3, 1dc into each of next 4sc, *1sc into each of next 5dc, 1dc into each of next 5sc, rep from * to end. Turn.
3rd row. Ch2, 1sc into each of next 4dc, *1dc into each of next 5sc, 1sc into each of next 5dc, rep from * to end. Turn.
Rows 2 and 3 form pattern and are repeated throughout.

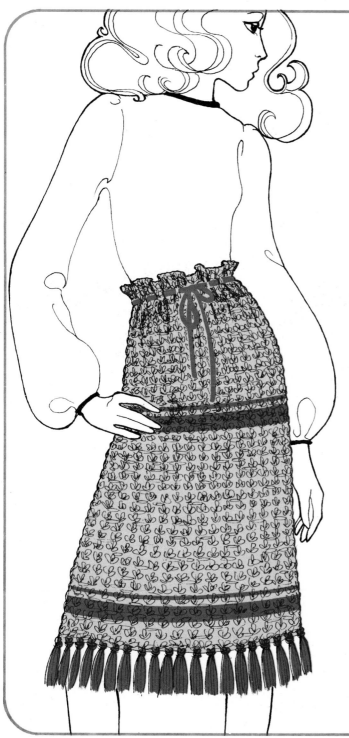

▲ *Cluster stitch, a particularly close fabric stitch*

▲ *Claw stitch, a fairly firm fabric stitch suitable for lightweight jackets*

◄ *Elongated basket stitch*   ▲ *Paving stone stitch*   ▼ *Straw stitch*

Chapter 12

Introduction to jacquard effects

Jacquard effects can be obtained by using two or more colors. Working in several colors gives a close fabric, so use a hook one size larger than normal for the thickness of yarn.

Jacquard patterns give working directions in two ways, either by each row or by means of a chart. Where the former method is used, the background or main color will be given as main color A, the second color to be used will be given as contrast color B, and so on. If a chart is used, the main color is represented by a white, open square and the contrast color by a black dot. Subsequent colors would then be represented by different symbols, such as an X or O, and these would be shown in the directions. In the jacquard patterns illustrated, both methods are given so that you may become familiar with them.

Where the yarn has to be carried over 3 or more stitches in a pattern, it may be advisable in the following row to work over the yarn when working the central stitch or stitches of a block. To do this on the right side of the work, insert the hook through the stitch to be worked and under the loop of yarn on the wrong side, then work the stitch in the usual way. When working on the wrong side, insert the hook under the loop of yarn and then into the stitch to be worked and complete the stitch in the usual way. In the following pattern directions, this will be referred to as "working over main or contrast yarn." This prevents over-long loops at the back of the work and makes it easier to keep an even gauge.

Using contrast yarn in jacquard

When a contrast color has to be worked in during the work, the last 2 loops of the last stitch in the main color are drawn through with the yarn of the contrast color, always keeping the yarn on the wrong side of the work (see illustration).

Reverting to main color in jacquard

When reverting to the main color after working a group of stitches in a contrast color, the last 2 loops of the last stitch in the contrast color are drawn through with the yarn of the main color, always keeping the yarn on the wrong side of the work (see illustration).

Two-color square jacquard pattern

The pattern consists of multiples of 7 stitches, plus 6 and a turning chain. Ch22 using A.

1st row. Using A, work 1dc into 4th ch from hook, 1dc into each ch to end. Turn. 20dc.

2nd row (right side). Join in contrast color B, ch2 in A and work 3rd ch in B, skip first dc, *using B work 1dc into each of next 4dc ending 4th dc by drawing A through last 2 loops on hook, using A work 1dc into each of next 3dc ending 3rd dc by drawing B through last 2 loops on hook, rep from * to last 5 sts, using B work 1dc into each of next 4dc ending 4th dc by drawing A through last 2 loops, 1dc into turning ch with A. Turn.

210

Top: working with the contrast yarn in jacquard crochet
Bottom: reverting to the main color yarn

3rd row (wrong side). Keeping yarn not in use on wrong side ch2 in A, work 3rd ch in B, skip first dc, using B work 1dc into next dc, 1dc into each of next 2dc working over main color loop of row below, 1dc into next dc drawing A through last 2 loops, * using A work 1dc into next dc, 1dc into next dc working over contrast color loop of row below, 1dc into next dc drawing B through last 2 loops, using B work 1dc into next dc, 1dc into each of next 2dc working over main color loop, 1dc into next dc drawing A through last 2 loops, rep from * to last dc, 1dc into turning ch with A. Turn.

4th row. Using A ch3, skip first dc, 1dc into each dc to end, working over yarn loops on 2 central dc of each block in B and 1 central dc of each block of A, ending with 1dc into turning ch. Turn. These 4 rows form pattern and are repeated throughout. They can also be worked from the chart.

Two-color diamond jacquard pattern

This pattern consists of multiples of 6 stitches, plus 1 and a turning chain. Ch21 using A.

1st row. Using A, work 1dc into 4th ch from hook, 1dc into each ch to end. Turn. 19dc.

2nd row (right side). Using A, ch3, join in B, skip first dc, using

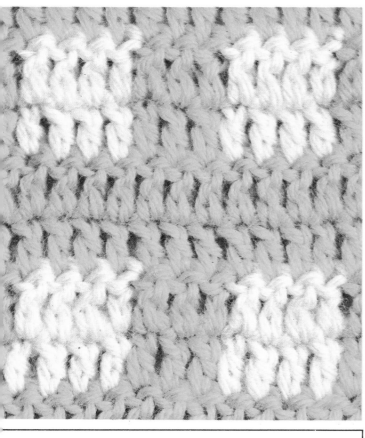

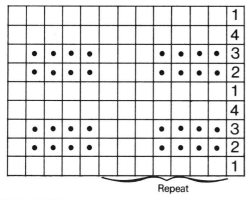

Top: two-color square jacquard pattern
Bottom: chart for the two-color square jacquard pattern

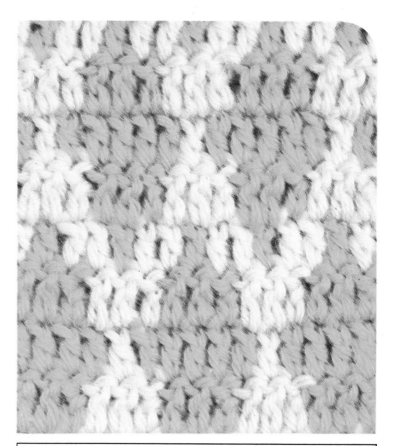

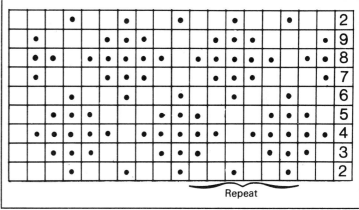

Top: two-color diamond jacquard pattern
Bottom: chart for the two-color diamond jacquard pattern

A work 1dc into next 2dc drawing B through last 2 loops of last dc, *using B work 1dc into next dc drawing A through last 2 loops, using A work 1dc into next 2dc drawing B through last 2 loops of last dc, rep from * to last 4dc, using B work 1dc into next dc drawing A through last 2 loops, using A work 1dc into last 3dc working last dc into turning ch. Turn.

3rd row (wrong side). Keeping yarn not in use on wrong side, ch3 in A, skip first dc, 1dc into next dc drawing B through last 2 loops, *using B work 1dc into each of next 3dc working over yarn loop on central dc and drawing A through last 2 loops of last dc, using A work 1dc into each of next 3dc working over yarn loop on central dc and drawing B through last 2 loops of last dc, rep from * to last 5dc, using B work 1dc into each of next 3dc working over yarn loop on central dc and drawing A through last 2 loops of last dc, using A work 1dc into last 2dc working last dc into turning ch. Turn.

Continue changing yarns in this way and working over loops on row below, keeping yarn not in use on wrong side of work.

4th row. Ch2 in A, work 3rd ch in B, skip first dc, *using B work 1dc into next 5dc, using A work 1dc into next dc, rep from * to end working last dc into turning ch. Turn.

5th row. As 3rd.

6th row. As 2nd.

7th row. Ch2 in A, work 3rd ch in B, skip first dc, using B work 1dc into next dc, *using A work 1dc into next 3dc using B work 1dc into next 3dc, rep from * to last 5dc, using A work 1dc into next 3dc, using B work 1dc into next dc, using A work 1dc into turning ch. Turn.

8th row. Ch2 in A, work 3rd ch in B, skip first dc, using B work 1dc into next 2dc, * using A work 1dc into next dc, using B work 1dc into next 5dc, rep from * to last 4dc, using A work 1dc into next dc, using B work 1dc into next 2dc, using A work 1dc into turning ch. Turn.

9th row. As 7th.

Rows 2-9 form pattern and are repeated throughout. They can also be worked from the chart.

More jacquard patterns from charts

Whether working jacquard patterns in two colors or more, the method is the same as that given on page 210. Since jacquard patterns produce a thick fabric, it is better to limit the colors used to three when working garments.

Base your designs for jacquard crochet on geometric shapes or simple designs—cross-stitch embroidery patterns can be used as a guide for motifs. Don't attempt anything too complicated because the depth of crochet stitches will not allow very fine detail.

Copy the design you have chosen onto squared graph paper calculating one stitch for each square. Leave the stitches to be worked in the main color as an empty square and mark the stitches to be worked in a contrasting color as a black dot in a square. If you wish to use a third color in the design, mark these stitches as a crossed square. Work the design in single or double crochet, remembering that single crochet will give a closer overall pattern, whereas double stitches are fairly long and will distort a rounded shape.

When changing from one color to another, be sure to draw through the last loops of the last stitch with the yarn of the next color. Always keep the yarns not in use at the back of the work. Also, when working over a group of stitches, remember to work over the loop of yarn on the row below to avoid overlong loops at the back of the work.

The white cottage motif shows how a simple design can be converted into a chart and worked in crochet. Designs such as this could be worked for pockets or as motifs for pillows.

You can use up remnants of yarn while practicing the three jacquard patterns on these pages, trying out color variations of the patterns. If test squares of crochet are worked to the same size, they can be joined together to make a colorful afghan.

▼ *Two-color triangle jacquard pattern*

▲ *Three-color geometric jacquard pattern showing one repeat*
▼ *Chart for three-color geometric jacquard pattern*

▼ *Chart for two-color triangle jacquard pattern*

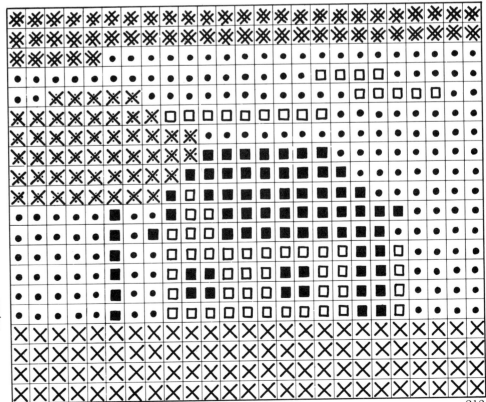

▲ *Two-color checked jacquard pattern*
▼ *Chart for two-color checked pattern*

▲ *A simple picture worked in crochet from a chart. Using six colors, the motif produces a thick fabric suitable for a mat or potholder. Chart for cottage motif* ▼

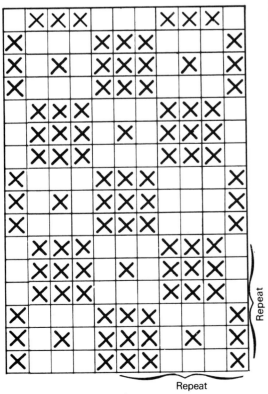

213

Chapter 13

Crochet plaid patterns

These patterns are interesting to work using remnants of different colored yarns, and the results can be truly original. Worked in heavy yarn, they make extremely attractive rugs for either the house or the car. However, if the rug is to be used on an uncarpeted floor, it is advisable to back the work with a non-slip textured fabric such as fine foam rubber. Cotton yarn makes an effective washable bath mat.

The plaid pattern is prepared in two separate stages. The mesh background is made first and then vertical rows of chains are worked onto it to form the pattern. The colors can be as varied as you like, both on the background and the vertical chains, and a very authentic-looking plaid can be produced in this way. If you want to make your own original pattern, remember to keep the colors used for the background rows, as well as those used for the chains, in a correct, pre-planned sequence. Otherwise, your results will look completely haphazard.

Preparing the mesh background
Make an even number of chains.
1st row. Work 1dc into 5th ch from hook, *ch1, skip 1ch, 1dc into next ch, rep from * to end. Turn.
2nd row. Ch4, skip first dc and first space, *1dc into next dc, ch1, skip 1 space, rep from * ending with 1dc into 3rd ch of turning ch. Turn. The 2nd row forms the pattern and is repeated for the required length, changing colors as desired.

Working vertical chains to form plaid pattern
Contrast yarn is used double throughout. Make a slip loop in contrast yarn. Holding the mesh background with right side facing you, begin at bottom right-hand corner of work and insert hook through slip loop. Keep working threads at back of work and insert hook from the front into the first space of the mesh background and work toward the top of the background, thus:
Draw yarn through space and through the stitch on hook.
Continue working from * to * until the top of the work is reached, then work last chain stitch over top of mesh background and through loop on hook.
Make vertical chains in this way into all spaces across mesh background, changing colors as required. Particular care must be taken with the tension of the chains to avoid any loosening or tightening of the mesh background.

Crochet plaid pattern
This pattern requires multiples of 12ch, plus 8, to give a pattern repeat of 6 spaces, plus 4 spaces, and an additional 3 turning ch.
Make sample as follows:
Using main color, ch35 (12×2+8+3=35).
1st row. Work 1dc into 5th ch from hook, *ch1, skip 1ch, 1dc into next ch, rep from * to end. Turn. 16 spaces.

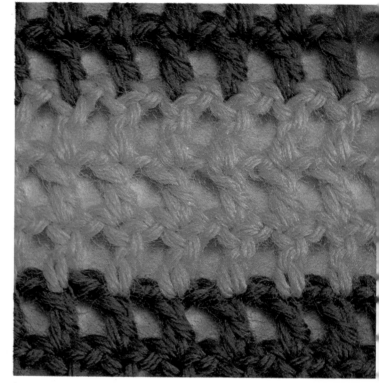

▲ *The mesh background formed from evenly spaced doubles*
▼ *Working vertical chains to form the plaid pattern*

214

▲ *A colorful lassie in her plaid pattern dress*

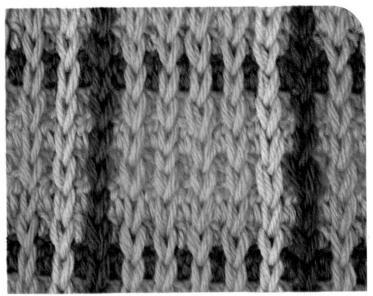

▲ *The right side of the three-color crochet plaid pattern*
▼ *The wrong side of the three-color crochet plaid pattern*

▼ *An example of a crochet plaid pattern in two colors*

2nd row. Ch4, *skip 1 space, 1dc into next dc, ch1, rep from * ending with 1dc into 3rd ch of turning ch. Turn.
Repeat 2nd row twice more.
Join in 2nd color and repeat 2nd row.
Join in 3rd color and repeat 2nd row.
Join in main color and repeat 2nd row 4 times.
Join in 2nd color and repeat 2nd row.
Join in 3rd color and repeat 2nd row.
Join in main color and repeat 2nd row 4 times. Fasten off. Using main color double, make a slip loop. Insert hook into loop and then into first space at bottom right-hand corner of mesh background. Hold yarn at back of work and draw yarn through space and through loop on hook. Work toward the top of the background in this way in each space. Fasten off.
Repeat in next 3 spaces.
Using 2 strands of 2nd color, work into 5th space in same way.
Using 2 strands of 3rd color, work into 6th space in same way.
Repeat with main color in next 4 spaces, 2nd color in next space, 3rd color in next space and main color in last 4 spaces.
Fasten off.

Chapter 14

Lacy-look stitches

This chapter shows how groups of stitches can be worked to form intricate and lacy-looking patterns. All the stitches on these pages are open stitches with the exception of lattice stitch, which forms an attractive diamond pattern on a close fabric background.

Any leftover remnants of yarn can be used to practice these stitches, using a medium size hook.

Fan stitch

Make a number of chains divisible by 8, plus 1.

1st row. Into 2nd ch from hook work 1sc, work 1sc into each ch to end. Turn.

2nd row. Ch2, 1sc into each sc to end. Turn.

3rd row. Ch5, skip 3sc, *(1dc, ch3, 1dc) into next sc, ch2, skip 3sc, 1dc into next sc, ch2, skip 3sc, rep from * ending with 1dc into last st. Turn.

4th row. Ch2, *2sc into next space, ch1, 5sc into next space between dc, ch1, 2sc into next space, ch1, rep from * ending with 2sc into last space, skip last ch and work 1sc into turning ch. Turn.

5th row. Ch2, 1sc into first sc, ch1, work petals thus: *yoh, insert hook into first sc of 5sc of previous row, yoh, pull through loop, yoh, put hook into same sc, yoh, pull through loop, yoh, put hook into same sc, yoh, pull through loop, yoh, pull through all 7 loops on hook, rep from * into each of next 4sc, ch1, skip 1ch and 2sc, work 1sc into next ch1 space, ch1, skip 2sc and 1ch, rep from * ending with 1sc and skipping last ch. Turn.

6th row. Ch5, *1sc into space between 2nd and 3rd petals of next petal group, ch2, 1sc into space between 3rd and 4th petals, ch2, (1dc, ch2, 1dc) all into next sc between petal groups, ch2, rep from * skipping 2ch and 1dc from last rep. Turn.

7th row. Ch2, 3sc into first space, work 2sc into every space to end, 1sc into 2nd ch of turning ch. Turn.

Rows 2-7 form pattern and are repeated throughout.

Lattice stitch

Make a number of chains divisible by 4, plus 3.

1st row. Into 2nd ch from hook work 1sc, work 1sc into each ch to end. Turn.

2nd row. Ch2, 1sc into each sc to end. Turn.

3rd row. As 2nd.

4th row. Ch2, 1sc into each of next 2sc, insert hook from front to back of work in first st of first row, yoh, draw up long loop, yoh and pull through first loop on hook, skip 4sts on first row, insert hook from front to back in next space, *yoh, draw up long loop, yoh and pull through first loop on hook, yoh and draw through all 3 loops on hook, skip 1sc behind this st, work 1sc into each of next 3sc, insert hook into same space as last loop worked, yoh, draw up loop, yoh and draw through first loop on hook, skip 4sts on first row, insert hook from front to back in next space, rep from *, ending with 3sc. Turn.

Rep 2nd row 3 times more.

8th row. Ch2, 1sc into next sc, insert hook into st formed where loops join in 4th row, yoh, draw up loop, yoh and draw through first loop on hook, yoh and draw through both loops, skip sc behind this st, work 1sc into each of next 3sc, *insert hook from front to back in same place as first loop, yoh, draw up loop, yoh and draw through first loop on hook, insert hook in st joining next 2 loops on 4th row, yoh, draw up loop, yoh and draw through first loop on hook, yoh, draw through all 3 loops on hook, skip 1sc behind this st, work 1sc into each of next 3sc, rep from * to end, with last loop pulling yarn through first loop on hook, insert hook in last sc on 4th row, yoh, draw through loop, yoh, draw through all 3 loops on hook, skip 1sc behind this st, work 1sc into each of next 3sc. Turn. Rep 2nd row 3 times more.

12th row. Ch2, 1sc into next 2sc, insert hook from front to back into st formed on 8th row, yoh, draw up loop, yoh, pull through first loop on hook, *insert hook into next joining loops in 8th row, yoh, draw up loop, yoh, draw through first loop on hook, yoh, draw through all 3 loops on hook, skip 1sc behind this st, work 1sc into each of next 3sc, insert hook in same place, yoh, draw up loop, yoh and draw through first loop on hook, rep from * ending with 3sc. Turn.

Rows 5-12 form pattern and are repeated throughout.

Triangle stitch

Make a number of chains divisible by 3, plus 2.

1st row. Into 2nd ch from hook work 1sc, 1sc into each ch to end. Turn.

2nd row. Ch4, *skip 2sc, work 1dc into next sc, insert hook into 2nd skipped sc behind dc just worked, work 1dc, ch1, rep from * ending with 1dc. Turn.

3rd row. Ch2, skip first dc, work 1sc into each st to end, ending with 1sc into 3rd ch of turning ch. Turn.

Rows 2 and 3 form pattern and are repeated throughout.

Crazy stitch

Make a number of chains divisible by 6, plus 2.

1st row. Into 2nd ch from hook work 1sc, *ch2, skip 2ch, work 3dc into next ch, ch2, skip 2ch, 1sc into next ch, rep from * ending with 1dc into last ch. Turn.

2nd row. *Ch2, 1sc into space before 3dc group of previous row, ch2, 3dc into 3rd dc of previous row, rep from * ending with 1dc into space between last sc and turning ch. Turn.

The 2nd row forms pattern and is repeated throughout.

Chainmail stitch

Make a number of chains divisible by 2, plus 1.

1st row. Into 2nd ch from hook work 1sc, 1sc into each ch to end. Turn.

2nd row. Ch3, skip first sc, *insert hook in next st, yoh, draw yarn through, yoh, draw through first loop on hook, yoh, draw through first loop on hook, yoh, draw through 2 loops on hook, ch1, skip 1sc, rep from *, ending with 1dc into last st. Turn.

3rd row. Ch2, work 2sc into each space of previous row to end. Turn.

Rows 2 and 3 form pattern and are repeated throughout.

Using these stitches for a stole

Any of these attractive, intricate stitches can be used to make an elegant stole.

Begin and end with two rows of doubles and allow for five extra doubles at each end of the rows to give a border effect. When completed, trim the short edges with a row of scallops by working four chains, skipping one double, then working one single crochet into the next double. If you wish, add a fringe to the next scalloped row.

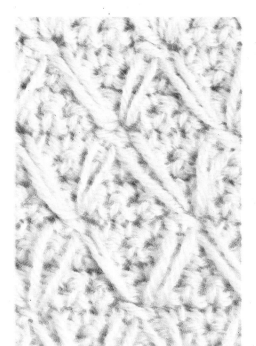

Fan stitch ▲

Chainmail stitch ▼

Lattice stitch ▲

Triangle stitch ▲

▼ *A pretty edging for a stole crocheted in triangle stitch*

Crazy stitch ▼

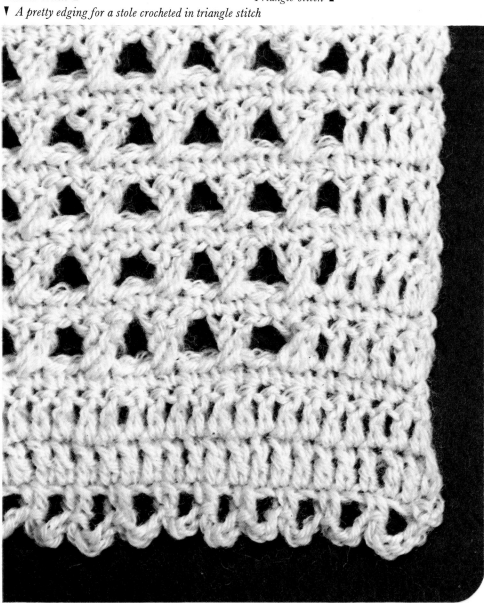

Crochet
Know-how

Arch stitches

These simple crochet stitches, based on a series of chains to form arches, comprise a very popular group of patterns. Because these stitches are so open and lacy, they have a great variety of uses—from warm stoles and ponchos to gossamer baby shawls and fashion garments.

A pretty way to try out arch stitches would be to make long lacy sleeves to fit into a sleeveless dress. Choose the shape of sleeve you want and either buy or make a paper pattern. As you work the sleeve, increase and decrease to obtain the shape, keeping to the pattern outline as closely as possible. You will find a straight, long sleeve or bell-shaped sleeve easiest to work. The illustration shows the use of festoon stitch on a bell-shaped sleeve.

Simple arch stitch

Make a loose chain divisible by multiples of 4, plus 2.
1st row. Into 2nd ch from hook work 1sc, *ch5, skip 3ch, 1sc into next ch, rep from * to end working 1sc into last ch. Turn.
2nd row. *Ch5, 1sc into first ch loop, rep from * to end. Turn. The 2nd row forms pattern and is repeated throughout.

Fancy arch stitch

Make a loose chain divisible by multiples of 4, plus 2, noting that the 1st row of chain loops should consist of an odd number of loops to keep the pattern symmetrical.
1st row. Into 2nd ch from hook work 1sc, *ch5, skip 3ch, 1sc into next ch, rep from * to end working 1sc into last ch. Turn.

▼ *Simple arch stitch*

▲ *Fancy arch stitch which has an asymmetrical effect*

▲ *Festoon stitch consisting of doubles and single crochet forming arches*

2nd row. *Ch3, 3dc into central ch of loop, ch3, 1sc into central ch of next loop, rep from * ending with 1sc into sc of previous row. Turn.
3rd row. Ch5, *1sc into center dc of 3dc group, ch3, 3dc into next sc of previous row, ch3, rep from * ending with ch2, 1dc into top of turning ch. Turn.
4th row. *Ch3, 3dc into next sc, ch3, 1sc into center dc of next dc group, rep from * ending with 1sc into turning ch. Turn.
Rows 3 and 4 form pattern and are repeated throughout.

Festoon stitch on arches

Make a loose chain divisible by multiples of 4, plus 2.
1st row. Into 2nd ch from hook work 1sc, 1sc into each ch to end. Turn.
2nd row. Ch3, skip first sc, *1dc into next sc, ch3, 1dc into same sc, skip 3sc, rep from * to last 2sc, skip 1sc, 1dc into last sc. Turn.
3rd row. Ch1, 1sc into first dc, *5sc into ch3 loop, rep from * ending

Arch stitch with picots results in a firmer look

Arch stitch with clusters, ideal for stoles and ponchos

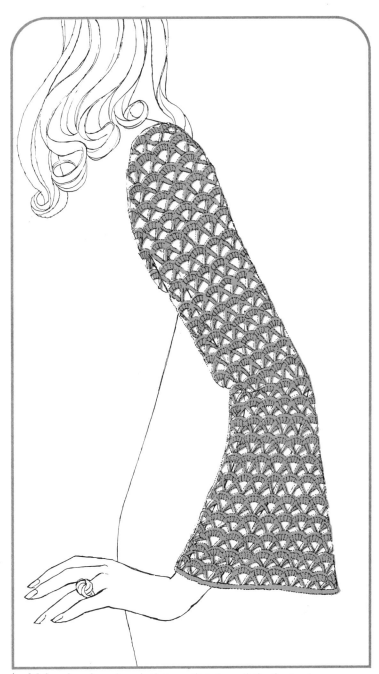

Make a long lacy sleeve in festoon stitch for a distinctive touch

with 1sc into top of turning ch. Turn.
4th row. Ch3, *1dc into center sc of 5sc group, ch3, 1dc into same sc, rep from * ending with 1dc into last sc. Turn.
Rows 3 and 4 form pattern and are repeated throughout.

Arch stitch with picots
Make a loose chain divisible by multiples of 4, plus 2.
1st row. Into 2nd ch from hook work 1sc, *ch5, skip 3ch, 1sc into next ch, rep from * ending with 1sc into last ch. Turn.
2nd row. Ch3, *1sc into ch5 loop, ch3, ss into first ch to form picot, 1sc into same ch loop, ch4, rep from * ending with 1dc into last sc of previous row. Turn.
3rd row. Ch7, *1sc, 1 picot, 1sc all into ch4 loop, ch4, rep from * ending with 1dc into top of turning ch. Turn.
4th row. Ch3, *1sc, 1 picot, 1sc all into ch4 loop, ch4, rep from * ending with 1sc, 1 picot, 1sc into ch7 loop, 1dc into 4th ch of turning ch. Turn.
Rows 3 and 4 form pattern and are repeated throughout.

Arch stitch with clusters
Work a loose chain divisible by multiples of 4, plus 2.
1st row. Into 2nd ch from hook work 1sc, 1sc into each ch to end. Turn.
2nd row. Ch1, 1sc into next sc, *ch4, skip 3sc, 1sc into next sc, rep from * ending with 1sc into last sc. Turn.
3rd row. Ch1, 1sc into next sc, into first loop work 1sc, into same loop, (yoh, draw yarn very loosely through ch loop) 3 times, yoh and draw through all loops on hook, yoh and draw through single loop on hook—called 1 cluster—1sc into same loop, ch4, *1sc, 1 cluster, 1sc all into next ch loop, ch4, rep from * ending with 1sc into last sc. Turn.
4th row. Ch5, *into next ch4 loop work 1sc, 1 cluster, 1sc, ch4, rep from * ending with 1sc into each of last sc. Turn.
5th row. Ch1, 1sc into next sc, *into next ch4 loop work 1sc, 1 cluster, 1sc, ch4, rep from * ending by skipping 4ch of last rep, then 1sc into 2nd of first 5ch. Turn.
Rows 4 and 5 form pattern and are repeated throughout.

Chapter 15

Introduction to filet crochet

Filet lace is one of the most interesting forms of crochet and its uses are numerous. Worked in fine cotton, it makes beautiful and long-wearing net curtains. In thicker yarn, filet crochet can be used to make anything from a pretty bedspread to a fashionable sweater. This chapter describes how to work a mesh ground—a group of spaces joined by doubles—and includes a chart for filet crochet.

Mesh ground

This consists of a group of spaces joined by doubles made by working *ch2, 1dc, rep from * for required length, ending with 1dc. The next and following rows are worked in the same way, working the doubles into the doubles of the previous row.

Beginning with a block

To begin the first row with a block of doubles make 3 extra chains to stand as the first double and make next double in the 4th chain from hook. Complete first block of 4 doubles by working 1 double in each of the next 2 chains.

Beginning with a space

To begin the first row with a space, make 5 extra chains of which the first 3 chains stand as the first double. Then work 1 double in the 8th chain from hook.

Beginning with a block of doubles

If the row begins with a block over a block of doubles, without increases or decreases, turn work, chain 3 to stand as first double, skip first double and work 1 double into next 3 doubles, or required number of doubles to complete block.

▲ *Mesh ground of doubles and spaces*
▼ *Sample beginning with a block of doubles*

▲ *Beginning with a block of doubles*
▼ *Sample of alternating doubles and spaces*

▲ *Beginning with a space*
▼ *Making mesh ground beginning with a space*

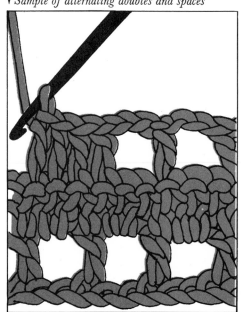

Beginning with alternating doubles and spaces

If the row begins with a block of doubles over a space, chain 3 to stand as first double, *work 2 doubles into space of previous row, 1 double into next double, rep from * to end. If the row begins with a space over a block of doubles, chain 5, skip 3 doubles and work 1 double into last double of block. Vary blocks of doubles and spaces as pattern requires.

Mesh ground of doubles and spaces

If the row begins with a space over a space, without increases or decreases, turn work, chain 5 and work 1 double into 2nd double of previous row.

Sample of filet crochet

Working methods of filet crochet are very often given by means of a chart, but unlike knitting, each square on the chart does not necessarily represent just one stitch. A chart and row by row directions are given for this sample so that you may become familiar with this method. In this case, each open square on the chart represents a chain 2 space plus a connecting double, and each cross represents a block of 2 doubles plus a connecting double. Begin at the bottom right-hand corner of the chart for the 1st row, turn work and read from left to right for the 2nd row, and so on. Ch50.

1st row. Work 1dc into 8th ch from hook (standing as first dc and first ch2 space), *ch2, skip 2ch, 1dc into next ch, rep from * to end. Turn. (15 spaces.)

2nd row. Ch5 (standing as first dc and first ch2 space), skip ch2 space, 1dc into next dc, 2dc into next ch2 space, 1dc into next dc, 2dc into next ch2 space, 1dc into next dc, (2 blocks), ch2, skip ch2 space, 1dc into next dc, (1 space), (2dc into ch2 space, 1dc into dc) twice, (ch2, skip ch2 space, 1dc into dc) 3 times, (2dc into ch2 space, 1dc into dc) twice, ch2, skip ch2 space, (2dc into ch2 space, 1dc into dc) twice, ch2, skip 2ch, 1dc into top of 3rd turning ch. Turn.

3rd row. Ch5, skip 1dc and 2ch, 1dc into next dc, 2 blocks over next 2 blocks working 1dc into each dc, 1 space over 1 space, ch2, skip 2dc, 1dc into dc, (1 space over 1 block), 1dc into each of next 3dc, 2dc into ch2 space, 1dc into 1dc, (1 block over 1 space), 1 space over 1 space, 2dc into ch2 space, 1dc into 1 dc, 1dc into each of next 3dc, (1 block over 1 space, 1 block over 1 block), 1 space over 1 block, 1 space over 1 space, 2 blocks over 2 blocks, ch2, skip 2ch, 1dc into 3rd of turning ch. Turn.

Continue working in this way from the chart, noting that 14 rows form one complete pattern repeat.

	X	X		X	X				X	X		X	X	14

▲ *Chart for filet crochet pattern*
◄ *Part of the filet crochet pattern worked from directions and chart*
▼ *The filet crochet pattern makes a pretty dressing table runner*

221

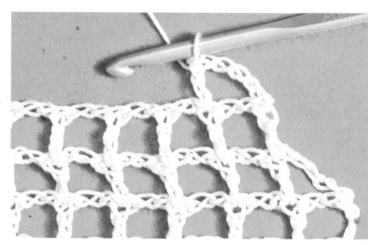

Shaping corners in filet

Shaping and making corners in filet crochet is not difficult but the continuity of the pattern must be kept accurate. Here are some useful hints for increasing and decreasing on spaces and blocks and a pretty filet crochet edging to sample.

Decreasing a space at the end of a row
At the end of the row where shaping is required, do not work last space but turn work, ch5 and work 1dc into 2nd dc of row below (Figure 1).

Decreasing a space at the beginning of a row
Work last space of previous row, turn. On next row, ch1, work 1ss into each of the next 2 ch sts, 1ss into next dc, ch5, skip 2ch, 1dc into next dc, *ch2, skip 2ch, 1dc into next dc, rep from * to end (Figure 2).

Increasing a space at the beginning of a row
Complete the row before shaping is required; turn work. On next row, ch7 (2 for base, 3 for side and 2 for top of space), work 1dc into last dc of previous row, *ch2, skip 2ch, 1dc into next dc, rep from * to end (Figure 3).

Decreasing a block at the end of a row
Work in pattern to the last 4dc, work 1dc, turn.
Next row. Ch3 if next row commences with a block, 3dc and then continue in pattern. Begin with ch5 if next row commences with a space, skip 2ch or 2dc, depending on whether you are working over a space or a block, 1dc into next dc, continue in pattern.

Increasing a block at the beginning of a row
Complete to the end of the row before shaping is required, turn work and ch5. Work 1dc into 4th ch from hook and 1dc into 5th ch from hook, then continue working in pattern to end.

Filet crochet edging
Work this edging from the chart, noting that each open square represents a space and each dot a block of doubles. Ch24 and start 1st row: Work 1dc into 4th ch from hook, 1dc into each of next 2ch, (ch2, skip 2ch, 1dc into next ch) 5 times, 1dc into each of rem 3ch. Turn. Begin chart from * for 2nd row, reading from right to left, then left to right for each row. Note the 8 row pattern repeat from * to *. Continue this repeat for required length, finishing with 8th row, then shape corner by mitering edge as follows:
1st row. Ss across first block, ch5, 3 blocks, 1 sp, 1 block, turn.
2nd row. Ch3, 1 block, 1 sp, 2 blocks, 1 sp, turn.
3rd row. Ss across 2ch and 1dc, ch5, 1 block, 1 sp, 1 block, turn.
4th row. Ch3, 1 block, 2 sps, turn.
5th row. Ss across 2ch and 1dc, ch5, 1 block, turn.
6th row. Ch3, 1 block, turn.

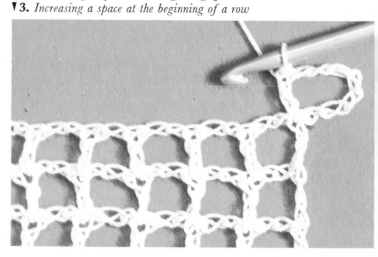

▲1. *Decreasing a space at the end of a row*

▲2. *Decreasing a space at the beginning of a row*
▼3. *Increasing a space at the beginning of a row*

7th row. As 6th.
8th row. (to turn corner) Ss across top of last row, ch3, 2dc into side of 7th row block, ss into 3rd of 5ch, ch2, ss into corner of next 5ch, ch3, 2dc into sp, ss into 3rd of 5ch, turn, ss across block, 1 sp, 1 block, turn.
9th row. Ch3, 1 block, 2 sp, 2dc into next sp, ss into 3rd of 5ch, ch3, 2dc into next sp, ss into 3rd of 5ch, turn.
10th row. Ss across 9th row block, (1 sp, 1 block) twice, turn.
11th row. Ch3, 1 block, 1 sp, 2 blocks, 1 sp, ch2, ss into 3rd of 5ch, ch3, 2dc into next sp, join with ss to corner of block, turn.
12th row. Ss across 11th row block, 1 sp, 3 blocks, 1 sp, 1 block, turn.
Continue from chart from ** to ** for required length.

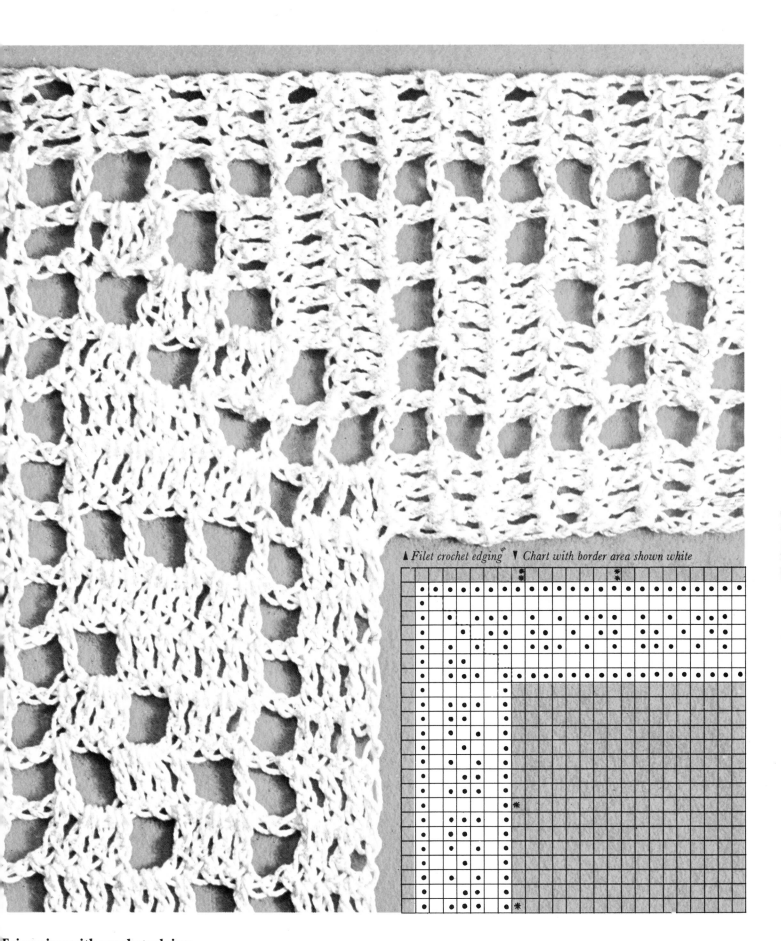

▲ *Filet crochet edging* ▼ *Chart with border area shown white*

Trimming with crochet edging

Filet crochet can be used for both edgings and for insertions on household linens. For edgings, make a narrow hem on the cloth first, machine stitching it or hemming by hand. The crochet edging is attached with either backstitch or slip stitch, working along the edge of the crochet. For inserting crochet, use a decorative stitch, but make sure that the stitch does not conflict with the pattern of the crochet.

Chapter 16

Traditional Irish crochet lace

Traditional Irish crochet lace is renowned throughout the world and, as with Aran and Shetland knitting, is synonymous with all that is beautiful in handicrafts.

This chapter deals with the preparation of three mesh backgrounds and gives directions for working various decorative motifs.

Shown here is a delightful snood that is sure to start your fingers itching.

Irish crochet can be used to make a wide range of garments, from the finest and most intricate of wedding gowns and baby robes, to simpler things such as shawls, scarves and stoles. Irish crochet makes pretty edgings too, worked in fine crochet cotton. Illustrated here are three delicate mesh backgrounds onto which the traditional motifs, such as shamrock, roses and leaves, can be sewn. The variations which can be achieved must be seen to be believed, and if you ever have the opportunity to see an exhibition of this breathtakingly beautiful craft a visit is well worthwhile—if only for the countless ideas you will gather.

The illustration below shows an elegant example of Irish crochet worked in the finest cotton. The rose motif is set off against a background of diamond picot mesh, forming a traditional design.

▼ *A beautiful example of Irish crochet*

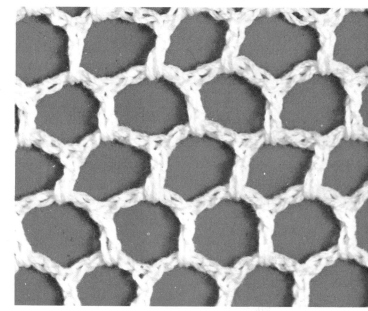

▲ *Honeycomb pattern mesh*

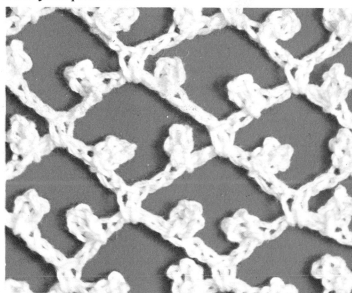

▲ *Diamond picot pattern mesh*
▼ *Shamrock pattern mesh*

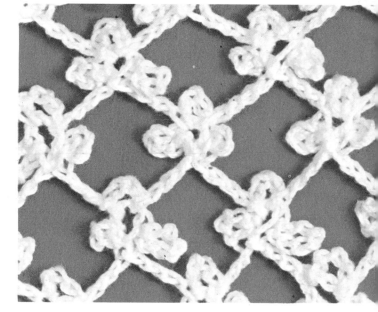

Mesh backgrounds

The patterns for the mesh backgrounds given here form the basis of many beautiful pieces of Irish crochet.

Honeycomb pattern mesh
Make a chain divisible by 4, plus 11.
1st row. Into 10th ch from hook work 1dc, *ch4, skip 3ch, 1dc into next ch, rep from * to end. Turn.
2nd row. Ch8, 1dc into first ch4 loop of previous row, *ch4, 1dc into next ch4 loop, rep from * to end. Turn.
The 2nd row forms pattern and is repeated throughout.

Diamond picot pattern mesh
Make a chain divisible by 7, plus 2.
1st row. Into 2nd ch from hook work 1sc, *ch2, ch5 and ss into first of these 5ch to form picot, ch3, 1 picot, ch2, skip 6ch, 1sc into next ch, rep from * to end. Turn.
2nd row. Ch2, 1 picot, ch3, 1 picot, ch2, 1sc into ch3 loop between picots of previous row, *ch2, 1 picot, ch3, 1 picot, ch2, 1sc into next ch3 loop, rep from * to end. Turn.
The 2nd row forms pattern and is repeated throughout.

Shamrock pattern mesh
Make a loose chain divisible by 5.
1st row. *Ss into 5th ch from hook to form picot, ch7, ss into 5th ch from hook to form 2nd picot, close the shamrock by working 1ss into bottom of first picot, skip 4ch, 1sc into next ch, ch8, rep from * ending with 1sc into last ch. Turn.
2nd row. Ch11, work 1ss into ch2 space between picots of previous row, ch4, 1ss into same ch2 space, *ch8, 1ss into 5th ch from hook, ch7, 1ss into 5th ch from hook, 1ss into bottom of first picot, ch3, 1ss into ch2 space of next 2 picot group, ch4, 1ss into same ch2 space, rep from * to end. Turn.
The 2nd row forms pattern and is repeated throughout, ending with 1sc into 3rd ch of 11 turning chain.

Snood

Materials
1 ball Coats & Clark's O.N.T. Speed Cro-Sheen
One No.B crochet hook
Length round hat elastic

To work
Using No.B crochet hook, ch39.
Work as given for honeycomb patt mesh, inc one sp at beg of each row by working 1 extra dc and ch4 into first sp until there are 14 sp. Work 6 rows without shaping. then dec one sp at beg of each row until 8 sp rem. Do not break off yarn.

Finishing
Using No.B crochet hook, work edging along sides and ends, *2sc into next sp, 1sc into next sp, rep from * along all 4 sides. Join with ss to first sc. Work 2 more rounds sc. Fasten off. Thread elastic through edging and secure on WS. Trim with motifs.

Glamorous snood in honeycomb mesh. *The motifs are on page 228 ►*

225

Collector's Piece

These delicate lace cuffs are an example of the exquisite results once achieved in Irish crochet. Worked at the end of the 19th century with the finest cotton and crochet hook, they show a variety of motifs including roses, trefoils and grapes on a mesh background. Crochet work of such delicacy first appeared in Ireland towards the middle of the 19th century in the work school of the Ursuline nuns in County Cork, and gradually spread to the northern counties. Country people, both men and women, flocked to learn the new skill, as they desperately needed a money-making cottage craft. Irish crochet became very popular as a fashion accessory just before the First World War, both at home and abroad. The smartest women were to be seen with crochet lace trims on their dresses, jackets, hats and parasols. Under the pressure of modern living, few people have the time, skill or patience required to produce quite such delicate works of art, but with a little perseverance beautiful examples of the craft can still be achieved.

Irish crochet motifs

Here are four pretty motifs which are used on the mesh backgrounds given on page 225. The rose motif was used on the Medici snood.

To give greater depth to Irish crochet lace, particularly when working in a very fine cotton, an almost three-dimensional effect is achieved by working over a separate thread of yarn. To begin work, estimate the length of separate thread you will require to complete a motif, then work a row of single crochet over this thread for the required number of stitches.

On the 2nd row, work one single crochet into each single crochet, still working over the thread, and by pulling the thread tightly the rows of single crochet can be made to lie in a curve.

To work a ring, first coil the separate thread into a loop once or twice, depending on the thickness required, then work a round of single crochet over this thread, joining with a slip stitch to complete ring. Where rings are required at varying intervals, continue working in single crochet over the separate thread until the next position is reached, then coil the thread in the same way and work another ring of single crochet.

Irish crochet rose motif

Ch8 and close into a circle with a ss.

1st round. Ch1, into circle work 15sc, ending with ss into first ch.

2nd round. *Work 1sc and 1hdc into 1st sc, work 3dc into

next sc, work 1hdc and 1sc into next sc, rep from * ending with a ss into 1st sc.

3rd round. Work 1sc into same place as ss, *ch10, 1sc between 2sc of previous round, rep from * ending with a ss into 1st sc.

4th round. Work 15sc into each ch loop, ending with a ss into 1st sc. Fasten off.

Irish crochet leaf and stem motif

Begin with 12sc worked along a separate thread and leaving an end long enough to form the stem later. Turn.

1st row. Ch1, work 10sc over thread and with hook inserted between one sc and the next of previous row. Turn.

2nd row. Ch1, work 5sc over thread and on sc sts of previous row, then work 9sc on thread only. Turn.

3rd row. Ch1, work 12sc over thread and on sc sts of previous row. Turn.

4th row. Ch1, work 6sc over thread and on sc sts of previous row, then work 9sc on thread only. Turn.

5th row. Ch1, work 15sc over thread and on sc of previous row. Turn.

6th row. Ch1, work 6sc over thread and on sc of previous row, then work 6sc on thread only. Turn.

7th row. Ch1, work 12sc over thread and on sc of previous row, then work 1dc into the first free st of 2nd row of 2nd petal and 1sc into 2nd free st. Turn.

8th row. Ch1, work 5sc over thread and on sc of previous row, then work 5sc on thread only. Turn.

9th row. Ch1, work 10sc over thread and on sc of previous row, 1dc into the first free st of 2nd row of 1st petal and 1sc into 2nd free st, work 4sc on thread only and attach this tail to the base of the leaves with a ss. Fasten off.

For the stem, return to the ends of yarn left at the beginning and work in sc over thread only. Fasten off.

Irish crochet branch and leaves motif

For each leaf, begin with 14sc worked over a thread. Turn. On the return row ch1, then, working over the thread and into the front loop only of the sc of the previous row, work 13sc and 6sc into last sc.

Continue working along other side of these sc, again working over thread and picking up facing loops of the sts, work 11sc. Turn.

On the return row ch1, working over thread and picking up both loops of all sts work 15sc, 5sc into sc at tip of leaf and 12sc along other half of leaf. Turn.

Working back in the same way, ch1, 14sc, 5sc into tip of leaf and 14sc on other half of leaf. Fasten off.

Make a second leaf in the same way.

For the branch, ch13 and join to the base of one leaf with a ss. Work back along this ch with a row of sc or dc. Attach second leaf to completed branch as illustrated.

Irish crochet three petal flower motif

Over a triple loop of separate thread work 24sc and join into a circle with a ss.

1st round. *Work 21sc over thread only, skip 7sc of circle, 1ss into next sc of circle, rep from * twice more.

2nd round. Fill inside of each petal formed by working 1dc, ch1, into every other sc of circle. Join with ss to petal edge. Fasten off. For the stem, ch13 and join to the space between two petals with a ss. Work back along this ch with a row of sc or dc. Fasten off all ends.

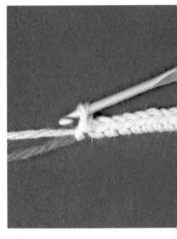

▲ *Work single crochet over thread*
▼ *Working 2nd row over thread*

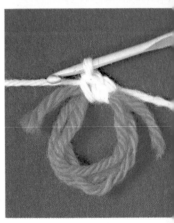

▲ *Working ring over loop of thread*
▼ *Work along thread for next ring*

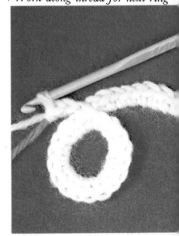

▲ *Irish crochet rose motif*　　　▲ *Leaf and stem motif*

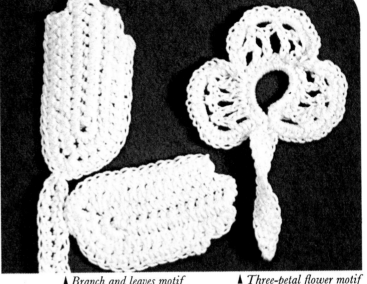

▲ *Branch and leaves motif*　　　▲ *Three-petal flower motif*

Irish rose cameo

Size
Oval motif measures 1¾in by 1¼in when worked on No.12 steel crochet hook

Materials
Spool of sewing thread or machine twist No.50
One No.12 steel crochet hook
Oval frame
Silk and cardboard for backing

Note
This motif is lovely when worked in a larger version. For example, to make a motif measuring 5in in diameter, use Coats & Clark's O.N.T. Speed Cro-Sheen and a No.B hook

Center rose motif
Ch8. Join into a ring with ss into first ch.
1st round Ch1, work 12sc into ring. Join with ss.
2nd round *Ch5, skip 1sc; 1sc into next sc, rep from * all around. Join with ss (6 loops).
3rd round Into each loop work 1sc, 1hdc, 5dc, 1hdc, 1sc. Join with ss (6 petals).

Background
4th round *Ch7, ss into same sc as worked on 2nd round from back, rep from * to end. Join with ss (6 loops).
5th round Into each loop work 1sc, 1hdc, 7dc, 1hdc, 1sc. Join with ss.
6th round *Ch1, ch5 and join with ss to first ch to form

picot, ch2, 1 picot, ch1, join to 2nd dc of next petal with 1sc, ch1, 1 picot, ch2, 1 picot, ch1, join to 5th dc of same petal with 1sc, rep from * to end.
7th round Continue with loops of ch and picot, joining each with 1sc into center of ch2 loop of previous round.
8th round Continue with loops of ch9, joining each with 1sc into center of ch2 loop of previous round, end round with 4ch joined to center of first ch9 loop.
9th round 5sc into same loop, 10sc into each following loop 11 times, 5sc into rem half loop. Join with ss.
10th round Ch1, *1sc into each of next 4sc picking up back loop only, ch5, skip 1sc, rep from * to end. Join with ss. Fasten off, leaving 12in end of thread for sewing motif to backing.

Finishing oval motif
Wet crochet to shrink it. While still damp, pin out to shape on padded surface with pin in every ch5 loop of last round. Leave until dry before removing pins. Cut silk and cardboard to fit frame, allowing ⅜in to cover edge of cardboard. Run basting thread ⅛in from edge of material, cover cardboard and secure at back. Attach motif to backing working sts through backing.

Cameo with fine Irish rose motif ▶

Chapter 17

Crochet Know-how

Introduction to Tunisian crochet

If you are interested in knitting, but haven't attempted crochet yet, you may enjoy learning the art of Tunisian crochet, a technique which combines the methods of both knitting and crochet to produce a soft, yet firm fabric. Tunisian crochet differs from both knitting and crochet in one distinctive feature—it is always worked on the right side, and is never turned. Once you have mastered the basic techniques, you will find Tunisian crochet very rewarding.

Tunisian crochet

Tunisian crochet is the complete combination of crochet and knitting and draws on the techniques of both crafts to achieve the finished fabric. Because of the way in which it is worked, Tunisian crochet produces strong, thick fabrics which are ideal for sportswear, coats, suits and heavier garments, although lighter fabrics can also be achieved. Depending on the stitch used, the finished appearance can resemble crochet or it can look surprisingly like knitting.

Using an afghan hook
The fabric is not produced with an ordinary, short crochet hook but with a special afghan crochet hook which looks exactly like a knitting needle, but with a hook at one end instead of a point. These are available in one length but, just as with crochet hooks, in a large range of sizes.

As with both knitting and crochet, the size of hook required depends on your own particular gauge, the thickness of the yarn being used and the firmness required for the final look. Experimenting with yarns and hook sizes will soon give you a very clear idea of how to achieve the desired results.

Working Tunisian crochet
Tunisian crochet takes from crochet the basic principle of beginning with a chain as explained in Crochet Know-how Chapter 1. But instead of completing one stitch and then passing on to the next, it becomes like knitting and one loop from each stitch is lifted onto the hook as you work along the length of starting chain, from the right toward the left.

Although one row has now been worked, it requires a second row to complete the pattern. This is worked from left to right without turning the work around and reduces the number of loops until only one remains, when you should again have reached the right-hand edge of the work.

Once you have practiced a little, you will find the work grows quickly and is not in any way complicated.

Classic Tunisian stitch

Begin with a chain consisting of an even number of stitches.

Foundation row. Insert hook into 2nd ch from hook, put yarn around hook—called yrh—and draw one loop through ch, *insert hook into next ch, yrh and draw through one loop, rep from * to end. The number of loops on the hook should now be the same as the number of chains worked at the beginning.

2nd row. Do not turn work, yrh and draw loop through first loop on hook, *yrh and draw through 2 loops on hook, rep from * until one loop remains. This is working from left- to right-hand edge.

3rd row. Ch1, *insert hook from right to left through first upright thread of previous row, yrh and draw through one loop, rep from * into every upright thread working along the row to the left. Once again, the number of loops on the hook should be the same as the number of chains worked at the beginning.

4th row. As 2nd.

The 3rd and 4th rows are repeated for the desired length. Always finish with a 2nd row and for a neat finish work 1 row single crochet into the last row of upright threads.

Because of the way in which Tunisian crochet is worked, it has a tendency to twist sideways. This can be corrected when the finished work is pressed, but can be lessened by not working too tightly as you go along. It will be tighter if the "yrh" is not pulled adequately through the stitch so that only a tiny loop is formed and also if the yarn is held too tightly or if too fine a hook is used. When starting to work toward the right, never pull the first stitch so tightly that you flatten or pull down the height of the row.

Double Tunisian stitch

Worked over an even number of chains.
Foundation row. Yrh, insert hook into 3rd ch from hook, yrh and draw through ch, yrh and draw through 2 loops, *yrh, insert hook into next ch, yrh and draw through 2 loops, rep from * to end.
2nd row. As 2nd row of classic Tunisian stitch.
3rd row. Ch2, *yrh and insert hook from right to left into upright thread of previous row, yrh and draw through one loop, yrh and draw through 2 loops, rep from * to end.
4th row. As 2nd row of classic Tunisian stitch.
The 3rd and 4th rows are repeated for the required length.

Eyelet Tunisian stitch

Worked over an even number of chains.
Foundation row. Yrh twice, insert hook into 3rd ch from hook, yrh, *skip 1 ch, draw through one loop, yrh, draw through 2 loops, yrh twice, insert hook into next ch, yrh and draw through one loop, yrh and draw through 2 loops, rep from * to end.
2nd row. As 2nd row classic Tunisian stitch.
3rd row. Ch2, *yrh twice, insert hook into upright thread *and* slightly sloping upright thread to right of it made in previous row, yrh and draw through one loop, yrh and draw through 2 loops, rep from * to end.
4th row. As 2nd.
The 3rd and 4th rows are repeated for the desired length.

Tunisian stockinette stitch

Worked over an even number of chains.
Foundation row. As given for classic Tunisian stitch.
2nd row. As 2nd row of classic Tunisian stitch.
3rd row. Ch1, *insert hook from front to back *between* upright threads of previous row, yrh and draw through one loop, rep from * to end.
4th row. As 2nd.
The 3rd and 4th rows are repeated for the desired length. It is important to draw through a loop that is fairly loose on the hook otherwise the work will be too tight.

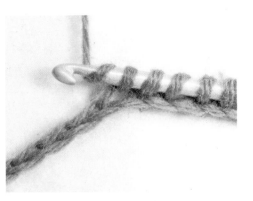

▲ *Working the first row of Tunisian crochet, from right to left*

▲ *Working the second row, from left to right, without turning the work around*

▲ *Working the third row, inserting the hook into the upright thread of previous row*

▲ *Classic Tunisian stitch*

▲ *Working double Tunisian stitch*　　▼ *Tunisian stockinette stitch*

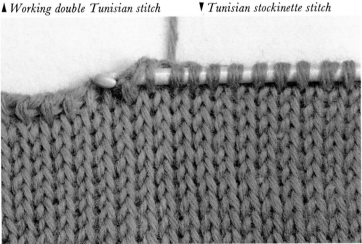

▲ *Eyelet Tunisian stitch*

▼ *Tunisian crossed stitch*

Tunisian crossed stitch

Worked over an even number of chains.
Foundation row. As given for classic Tunisian stitch.
2nd row. As 2nd row of classic Tunisian stitch.
3rd row. Ch1, *insert hook into 3rd upright thread of previous row, yrh and draw through one loop, insert hook into 2nd upright thread and draw through one loop, rep from * to end, working into 5th then 4th, 7th then 6th upright threads, etc.
4th row. As 2nd.
5th and 6th rows. As classic Tunisian stitch.
7th row. As 3rd.
8th row. As 4th.
The 5th to 8th rows are repeated for the required length.

Shaping in Tunisian crochet

▲ *Increasing one stitch at the beginning of a row*

To be able to make garments in Tunisian crochet it is necessary to understand how to increase and decrease while working the fabric. This section deals with the technique and also explains how to make buttonholes.

The method of working Tunisian crochet makes it easy to work with two yarns simultaneously, and this technique can be used with many of the stitches to achieve tweed-like textures and a thickness of fabric which is not always possible with crochet. Experiment with two different weights of yarn— a smooth with a rough for instance—for a tweedy look.

Increasing one stitch at beginning of a row

To increase one stitch at the beginning of a right side row, or the right-hand edge of the work, work 1 chain then insert the hook under the horizontal thread between the first and second upright threads, yrh and draw through one loop. Continue working into next and following upright threads in the normal way.

Increasing one stitch at end of a row

Work in the same way as given for the beginning of the row by inserting the hook under the horizontal thread between the second to last and last stitches, yrh and draw through one loop. Work the last stitch in the usual way.

Increasing two or more stitches at beginning of a row

To increase more than one stitch at the beginning of a row, work that number of chains. Into the chain work classic Tunisian stitch and continue along the row.

Increasing two or more stitches at end of a row

At the left-hand end of a right side row, put onto the hook the required number of slip stitches. Continue to work the next row in the usual way.

Decreasing one stitch at right-hand edge

Insert the hook through 2 upright threads, yrh and draw through only one loop, working to the end of the row in the normal way.

Decreasing one stitch at end of a row

Work in the same way as given for the beginning of a row by inserting the hook through the last 2 upright threads together, yrh and draw through only one loop.

Working a buttonhole

Mark the position for a buttonhole with pins on the right side of the work before beginning the right side row. Work to the beginning of the marked position. Wind yarn around the hook for the number of stitches over which the hole must stretch, skip this number of stitches and continue to the end of the row. On the next row work off each loop of yarn as if it were one stitch.

▲ *Increasing one stitch at the end of a row*
▼ *Increasing two or more stitches at the beginning of a row*

▼ *Increasing two or more stitches at the end of a row*

▲ *Decreasing one stitch at the right-hand edge*

▲ *Winding yarn around the hook for a buttonhole*
▼ *Working the 2nd row of the buttonhole*

Tunisian rib stitch

Worked over an even number of chains.

1st and 2nd rows. As given for classic Tunisian stitch (see Crochet Know-how page 230).

3rd row. Ch1, *insert hook into 3rd upright thread of previous row, yrh and draw through one loop, insert hook into 2nd upright thread, yrh and draw through one loop, continue from * in this way working in groups of 2 and crossing the threads by working the 5th then 4th, 7th then 6th, etc, ending with one st in last upright thread.

4th row. As classic Tunisian stitch.

Repeat 3rd and 4th rows as desired. If this pattern is worked over stitches which are being decreased or increased, be careful to see that the crossed stitches come immediately above the crossed stitches of the previous row, or the ribbed effect will be slightly irregular.

Tunisian diagonal rib stitch

Worked over an even number of chains.

1st and 2nd rows. Work as given for classic Tunisian stitch.

3rd and 4th rows. Work as given for rib stitch.

5th row. Ch1, work into next upright thread, yrh and draw loop through, then work one stitch into each of next 2 stitches, working the farthest away first then returning to work the skipped one, rep to end of row.

6th row. As given for 2nd row of classic Tunisian stitch.

Repeat 3rd to 6th rows as required.

Tunisian cluster stitch

This stitch can be varied to obtain different patterns.

It is worked on a ground of classic Tunisian stitch, working the clusters where required by chaining 4 or 5 before working the next stitch. The chain or cluster formed should be left on the right side of the work. Use cluster stitch spaced evenly on the surface as an all-over pattern, or grouped together in geometric designs.

▲ *Tunisian rib stitch*

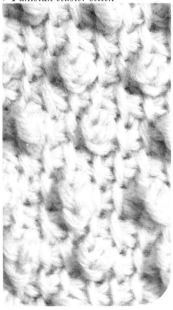

▲ *Tunisian diagonal rib stitch*
▼ *Tunisian cluster stitch*

233

Chapter 18

Crochet loops for a stole

Crochet
Know-how

Although very effective, the technique of working crochet loops is simple and quick. The stole pattern incorporates both openwork and looped fringing rows.

The technique used for looping stitches in crochet makes it possible to create openwork rows of any depth desired or, alternatively, to work rows of loops into the actual crochet to form fringing. The same fringing worked all over the fabric creates a fluffy fur-like surface.

Working openwork rows

This effect is worked by pulling a long loop the desired length out of a simple single crochet all along one row and then working the tips of the loops together on the following row with single crochet.

Several rows may then be worked before another openwork row is made or, alternatively, a very lacy fabric can be achieved by working openwork rows on every other row. To make a swatch, ch20.

1st row Work 1sc into 2nd ch from hook, *1sc into next ch, rep from * to end. Turn.

2nd row Ch1, *1sc into next st, rep from * to end.

3rd row As 2nd.

4th row Insert hook into first st, yoh and draw through 1 loop on hook, yoh and draw through both loops and drawing the new loop out to the desired length, *insert hook into next st, yoh, draw through 1 loop, yoh, draw through long loop pulling it up to the desired length, slip hook out of loop and rep from * to end of row. It may be found that it is easier to keep the loop on the hook until several are made so that it is simpler to keep them the same length.

5th row Work a number of chains the same length as the loop, insert hook into top of loop, yoh, draw through 1 loop, yoh and draw through both loops, *insert hook into next loop, yoh and draw through 1 loop, yoh and draw through both loops, rep from * along row to end.

Work several rows sc before repeating 4th row as required.

Fringing

Fringing can be worked over the fingers, but is more even when the length of loops is controlled by a piece of cardboard cut to the desired depth. Before beginning to crochet, cut a piece of cardboard, strong enough not to bend, to the desired depth and long enough to hold easily. It is not necessary to have the cardboard the full length of a row. Several loops can be worked and then the cardboard moved along.

To make a swatch, cut a piece of cardboard 1in deep and 6in long. Ch20.

Work 2 rows sc. Turn.

3rd row Hold cardboard in left hand, the base even with top of previous row. Take yarn over top of cardboard and down behind the cardboard. Insert the hook into the first st and draw yarn from the back through 1 loop, yoh and draw through both loops, rep from * to end of row. Turn. Remove the cardboard.

4th row Ch1, 1sc into each st. Work next row as 3rd row or if a shorter fringe is desired, work several rows sc before again working a loop row.

Long, dainty fringes can be worked by cutting a deep piece of cardboard and spacing the rows an inch or more apart. Short, thick, furlike fringes can be made by working over a narrow cardboard with thick yarn and working every alternate row as fringe.

Looped stole

Size

Approx 23in wide by 76in long.

Materials

Reynolds Gleneagles—9 balls
One No.F crochet hook
One piece stiff cardboard 2in deep by 8in long

Stole

Cut the cardboard to the desired depth of fringing before beginning to crochet. Ch96.

1st row Into 2nd ch from hook work 1sc, *1sc into next ch, rep from * to end. Turn.

2nd row Ch1, *1sc into next sc, rep from * to end. Turn.

3rd row As 2nd.

4th row (WS and fringe row) Ch1, *hold cardboard behind and above work, the base even with top of last row, take yarn up and over top of cardboard and down behind it, insert hook into next st and draw loop of yarn from behind base of cardboard through one st, yoh and draw through both loops, rep from * to end.

5th row As 2nd.

Rep 4th and 5th rows 10 times more.

Continue in openwork patt. Work 2 rows sc as 2nd row of fringe.

3rd row Draw loop on hook out to ½in long, *insert hook into next sc, yoh and draw through one st, yoh and draw through both loops until ½in long, leave loop on crochet hook until a few sts have been worked or slip it off and continue with next st as preferred, rep from * to last st, work ss into last st, ch4. Turn.

4th row Loop of last ch on hook, *insert hook into top of next long loop, yoh and draw through one st, yoh and draw through both loops, rep from * to end.

5th and 6th rows Work all sts in sc.

Rep 3rd, 4th, 5th and 6th rows once.

11th, 12th, 13th and 14th rows Work in sc.

Rep 3rd, 4th, 5th and 6th rows twice.

Rep last 18 rows until work measures 38in. Fasten off ends. Work a second piece in the same way. Slip stitch both pieces together.

▼ *Working the loops together after an openwork row*

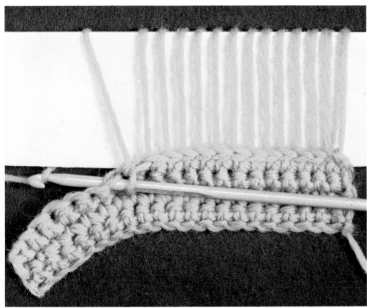

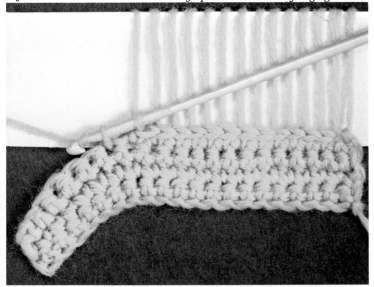

▲ *Yarn brought from back of cardboard through first stage of single crochet*
A fine stole worked in a combination of openwork rows and fringing ►

▲ *Yarn over hook ready for final stage of single crochet on fringe row*
▼ *The looped fringe when the cardboard has been removed*

Chapter 19

Introduction to hairpin crochet

Crochet Know-how

Hairpin, or fork, crochet is so called because the main tool used resembles a long hairpin or tuning fork.

Types of hairpins or forks

In the past, these were made of steel and were like a square-ended letter U. They were rigid, a little heavy, and if different widths of work were required, a selection of different hairpins had to be used to allow for the variation. Nowadays, a hairpin frame is available which consists of two lightweight rods connected at top and bottom by plastic bars. By slotting the rods into different positions on the bars, the width can be altered.

Pattern making

There are two ways in which patterns can be created. Basically, all hairpin crochet consists of long strips joined together to form the finished article. The pattern can be given great variation in the center knot between each loop and also in the way in which the completed strips are joined.

Working single crochet

Because the frame is long it is best to work with both end bars on the rods, although the illustrations show the top bar removed. Without the top bar the loops tend to pull the rods together and gauge on the finished strip will not be even. Make a slip knot in the yarn and take the top bar off until you have placed the slip knot on the right-hand rod. Replace the bar. Draw the loop out so that the knot is exactly centered between the bars. Hold the yarn behind the left rod with

236

the index finger and thumb of the left hand and turn the frame toward you from right to left until the right-hand rod has reversed to the left side. The yarn will now pass over the other rod and should be held again by the left hand behind the left-hand rod. Insert crochet hook through loop, draw a single thread through, yarn over hook, draw through loop to complete one stitch.

*Insert crochet hook through loop and draw a single thread through so that there are two loops on the crochet hook, yarn over hook and draw through both loops to complete one single crochet. Keeping loop on hook, pass the hook through to the back of the frame and turn the frame toward you from right to left as before. Repeat from *, turning the frame after each stitch. The frame is always turned the same way.

When the frame becomes full of completed loops, remove the bottom bar and slip most of the loops off the frame. Replace the bar and continue on remaining loops as before until the strip is the desired length.

To finish off, break the yarn and draw through the last single crochet.

Double single crochet

Work as for single crochet, working two single crochet instead of one by making the first into the loop as before and the second under both threads of the loop.

Single crochet on two threads

Work as for double single

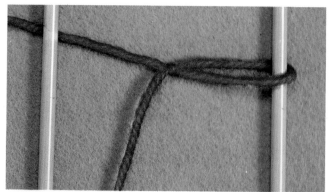

▲ The slip knot loop on the frame

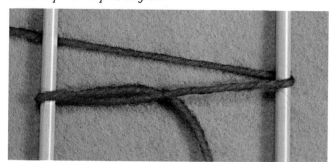

▲ The loop after turning the frame once

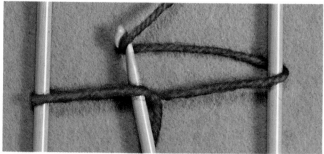

▲ Drawing the first loop through with a crochet hook

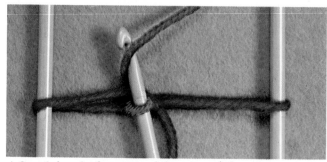

▲ Completing the first stage of the center stitch

▲ Completing the second stage of the center stitch

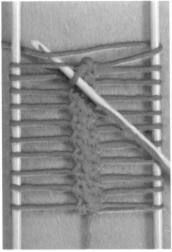

▲ *1st double single crochet stitch*

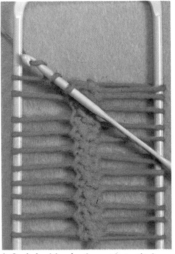

▲ *2nd double single crochet stitch*

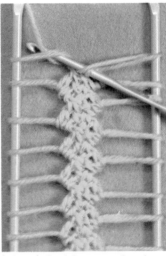

▲ *1st stitch of dc on two threads*

▲ *2nd stitch of dc on two threads*

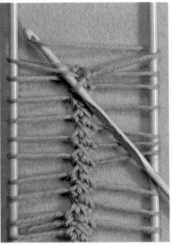

▲ *1st stitch of sc on two threads*
▼ *Joining strips with crochet hook*

▲ *2nd stitch of sc on two threads*

▲ *Stage 1 sc with dc on 2 threads*

▲ *Stage 2 sc with dc on 2 threads*
▼ *Joining strips with chain stitch*

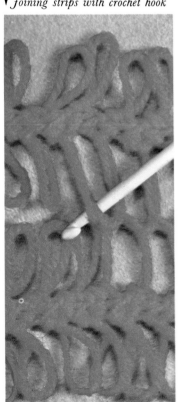

crochet but make both first and second single crochet under both threads of loop.

Double crochet on two threads

Work as for single with double crochet, making both stitches double and working them both under two threads of the loop.

Single with double crochet on two threads

Work as for double single crochet on two threads, making one single crochet under both threads of loop and then putting yarn over hook and working one double under both threads of loop.

Joining strips with a crochet hook

Place the two strips together horizontally. Using the crochet hook, lift one of the loops from the first strip and one from the second. Draw the second loop through the first then pick up the second loop of the first strip. Draw this through loop on hook then pick up second loop from second strip and draw the loop through. Continue in this way along the strips until they are joined together. Make sure that the final stitch is securely sewn to prevent it unraveling.

Joining with chain stitch

Place two strips together horizontally and work from right to left. Make a slip knot and place on crochet hook. *Insert hook through first loop of first strip and first loop of second strip, yarn over hook and draw through. Repeat from * until all the loops are joined, then finish off thread by drawing it through last stitch.

♫Hairpin crochet pillow

Once you have mastered the basic principles of hairpin crochet, you can progress to more complex groupings such as those explained in this chapter. Designs in hairpin crochet are made by joining long strips of loops together. The method used to anchor the stitches as they are made can vary, but the joining of the loop stitches is what gives each design its originality. The designs featured here are fan shaped and peacock tail.

Fan shaped grouping
Work 3 strips of hairpin crochet using sc on 2 threads (see Crochet Know-how page 236). Before joining the strips, work 1 row sc along each side as follows:
1st side *Work 1sc into group of 10 loops, work 1sc into each of next 10 loops, rep from * to end.
2nd side *Work 1sc into each of next 10 loops, work 1sc into group of next 10 loops, rep from * to end.
The strips will now be curved instead of straight and are ready to join together with crochet.
Attach yarn to first st at right side of first strip with ss. Ch5, work 1sc into 2nd st of left side of 2nd strip, *ch3, 1sc into 2nd st from last st on 1st strip, ch5, 1sc into 2nd st from last st on 2nd strip, rep from * until strips are joined together. Other strips are joined in the same way.

Peacock tail grouping
Work strips as for preceding

238

design, working the edge grouping as follows:
1st side *(Work 1sc into group of 3 loops, ch3) 3 times, twisting loops over so that they lie as shown in the illustration, work 1sc into next 9 loops twisted, ch3, rep from * to end.
Work 2nd side in same way, arranging the 9-loop groups so that they come in the center of the three 3-loop groups. When the stitches are grouped, join the strips in the same way as for Fan grouping, or slip st edges tog.

Hairpin crochet pillow

Size
About 14in diameter.

> **Gauge**
> Worked on a Hairpin Lace Frame measuring about 3in from outer edges.

Materials
Reynolds Gleneagles
2 balls color A, lilac
1 ball color B, purple
One Hairpin Lace Frame
One No.F crochet hook
One No.B crochet hook
Darning needle
Small safety pins
Foam rubber form

Front

1st strip for center
Using color A and No.B crochet hook, work strip of 66 loops at either side of center stitches worked in double single crochet (see Crochet Know-how page 236).

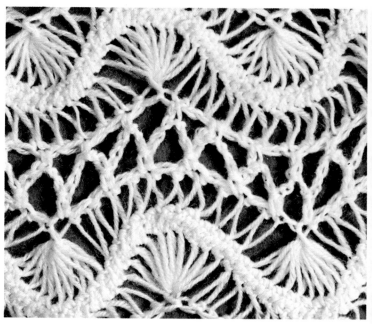

▲ *Fan shaped grouping*

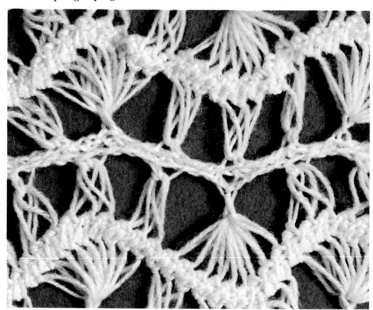

▲ *Peacock tail grouping*

Fasten off ends, joining first and last center stitches together so that strip forms a circle. Thread darning needle with short length of A and thread through the inner side loops of strip. Draw up to form center of pillow and fasten off ends securely.

2nd strip
Using B, work as for 1st strip until there are 132 loops at either side of middle stitches. Fasten off. Join first and last stitches so that strip forms circle.

Join 1st and 2nd strips
Using No.B crochet hook,

work the two strips together. Slip 2 loops from first strip onto hook, slip 4 loops from second strip onto hook and draw through first 2 loops. Slip next 2 loops from first strip onto hook and draw through loops already on hook, slip next 4 loops from second strip onto hook and draw through loops on hook. Continue in this way until all loops are joined. Thread a piece of yarn through last group and sew in place.
Leave loops on other side of 2nd strip grouped ready for next joining row. Slip 12 loops onto a safety pin. Repeat

Back

Using B and No.B crochet hook, ch7. Join into circle with ss into first ch.

1st round Ch7, (1tr into circle, ch3) 7 times. Join with a ss into 4th of first 7ch.

2nd round Ss to center of ch loop, ch7, (1tr into next ch loop, ch3, 1tr into same loop, ch3) 7 times. Join with a ss into 4th ch.

3rd round Ss to center of ch loop, ch7, (1tr into next loop, ch3, 1 tr into same loop, ch3, 1 tr into next loop, ch3) 7 times. Join with a ss into 4th ch. 21tr.

Continue in rounds in this way, working 2tr into a ch sp where an increase is required, spacing the number of increases evenly around the circle.

Work so that next round has 28tr.

5th round Has 40tr.

6th round Has 45tr.

7th round Has 48tr.

8th round Has 54tr.

9th round Has 62tr.

10th round Has 68tr.

11th round Has 74tr.

12th round Has 78tr.

13th round Has 86tr.

14th round Has 94tr.

15th round Has 98tr.

16th round Has 104tr.

17th round Has 116tr.

Fasten off.

▲ Pillow worked combining both methods of joining strips, with and without additional threads

until all loops are on pins (11 groups in all).

3rd strip
Using A, work strip as for 1st strip until there are 176 loops at either side of middle stitches. As the strip lengthens, place loops onto safety pins in groups of 16. This makes counting and joining simpler. Fasten off ends and join first and last middle stitches together, forming circle.

Join 2nd and 3rd strips
Using A and No.F crochet hook, join with 1sc to middle stitches of 2nd strip between two groups of 12 loops. 1sc into all 16 loops of first group on 3rd strip removing safety pin, *ch11, 1sc into middle sts on 3rd strip before second group of 16, 1sc into next group of 12 loops on 2nd strip removing pin, ch11, 1sc into middle sts on 2nd strip before next group, 1sc into next group of 16 loops on 3rd strip, rep from * until all loops are joined, completing circle with 1ss into first sc.

4th strip
Using B, work as for 1st strip until there are 232 loops on either side of middle sts, slipping loops off frame in groups of 8 on safety pins for next joining row. Fasten off ends, joining first and last middle sts to form circle.

Join 3rd and 4th strips
Using No.B crochet hook, slip 3 loops from 3rd strip onto hook, slip 4 loops from first safety pin of 4th strip onto hook and draw through loops already on hook, slip next 3 loops from 3rd strip onto hook and draw through loops, slip next 4 loops from 4th strip onto hook and draw through loops. Continue in this way until all loops are joined, securing last group with thread.

Joining front and back
Place back on top of front, right sides out. With back facing, insert No.B crochet hook through ch loop of back and draw through 2 loops from edge of 4th front strip, insert hook into next ch loop of back and draw through next 2 loops from 4th strip, drawing them through 2 loops already on hook. Continue in this way until three quarters of the way around pillow. Insert form and continue until all the loops are joined through the back ch loops. Fasten the last loops securely with a thread. Make a tassel with A, about 8in long, and attach to center.

239

Hairpin crochet bedspread

Many fascinating items can be assembled from strips of hairpin crochet. For a first large-scale project, try this bedspread. The illustration shows a similar hairpin crochet bedspread made in a thicker yarn.

Size

About 80in by 52in excluding fringe (length and width are easily adapted).

Gauge
Worked on a Hero Hairpin Lace Frame at full width using 3 balls of yarn together throughout.

Materials

Reynold's Angelina
36 balls
One Hero Hairpin
Lace Frame
One No.G crochet hook

Strips

Using 3 strands of yarn, make a slip loop and place on right-hand upright of frame.
Hold yarn behind left side with left hand and turn the frame toward the left (see Crochet Know-how page 236).
Insert the crochet hook into the loop in the center of the frame and draw the thread through to form a loop on the crochet hook, insert the hook under loop in center of frame and draw yarn through (2 loops on hook), yoh and draw through both loops. *Turn frame to left after passing hook and the loop on it to the back, insert hook into loop and
240

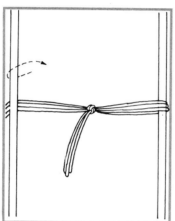
▲ *The first loop on the frame*

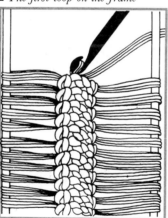
▲ *Working the center stitch*

draw thread through, insert hook under loop and draw thread through (2 loops on hook), yoh and draw through both loops. Rep from * until the frame is full, slip loops off returning the last 2 loops at each side to frame and repeating until strip measures 80in or desired length. Fasten off center thread securely and remove work from frame.
Work another 18 strips or number for width desired.

Joining

Insert crochet hook into first 2 groups of three threads at bottom right-hand side of first strip and draw first 2 groups of three threads from bottom of left-hand side of 2nd strip through. *Draw next 2 groups of three threads from first strip through loop on hook, draw next 2 groups of three threads from 2nd strip through loop on hook. Rep from * until all loops are joined. Sew last loop in place.

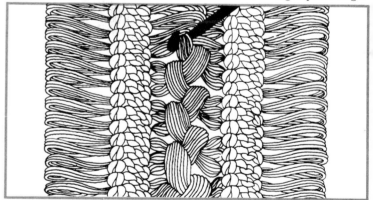
▲ *Joining the strips of hairpin crochet together*

Join other strips together in same manner.

Fringe

Cut lengths of yarn 10in long. Take 6 threads, fold in half and knot into beginning of long side. Work along edge.

Alternative edging

Work 1 length of hairpin crochet as given for the bedspread until long enough to trim the edges or to reach around bedspread as desired.

Inner edge

Using crochet hook, join double yarn to first loop on right-hand side of strip and *ch8, 1sc into next 3 loops, rep from * to end.

Outer edge

Using crochet hook, join double yarn to first loop on left-hand side, *ch6, into 4th ch from loop work 1sc, ch2, 1sc into next loop, rep from * to end forming a picot edge.

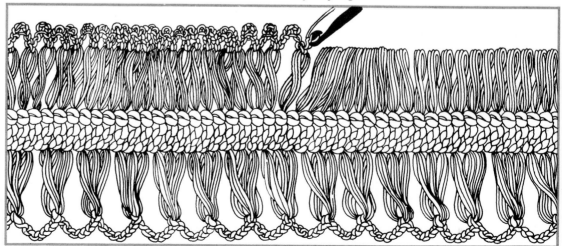
▼ *Alternative edging for bedspread which could be used instead of the fringe*

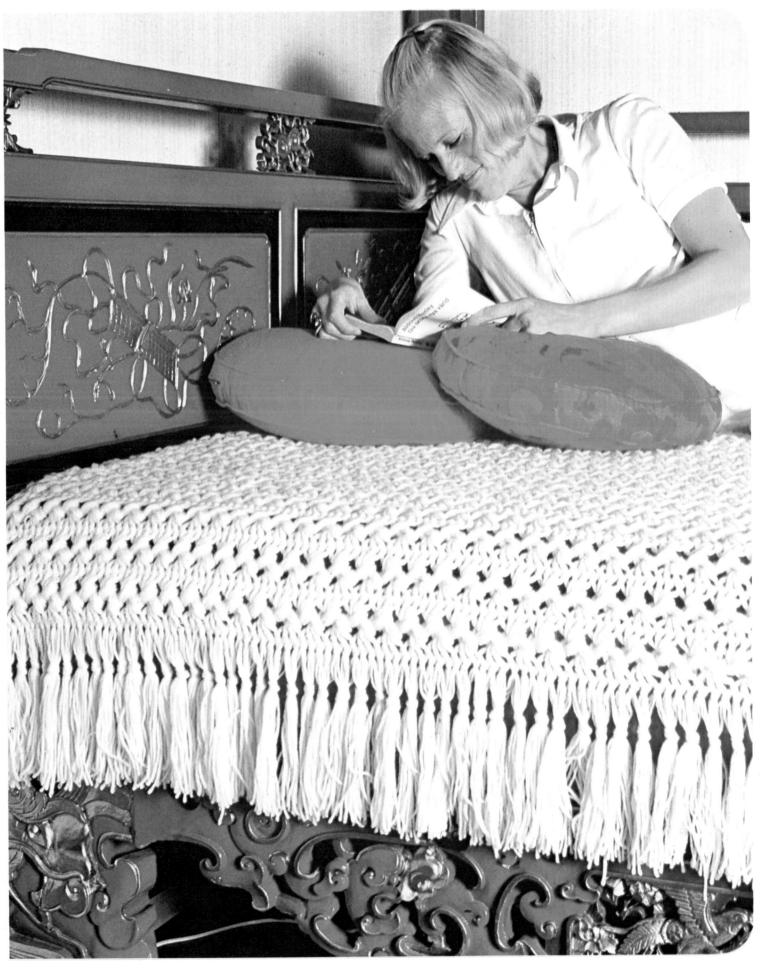

Chapter 20

Beads and sequins in crochet

This chapter tells you how to crochet beads or sequins directly into a piece of work.

Beads or sequins worked into crochet are an attractive way of giving additional interest and color.

Choice of beads and sequins

The choice of beads will depend on the thickness of the yarn to be used. Never choose large, heavy beads for a fine yarn because they will pull it out of shape. The finer or softer the yarn, the smaller the beads need to be. If the beads are to decorate a garment, make sure that they are suitable for dry cleaning.

Because they are so light, most sequins are suitable, provided they can be dry cleaned.

Threading beads or sequins

Where a bead or sequin with a large hole is to be used, it is possible to thread directly onto the yarn with a needle before working.

Most beads and sequins, however, have a small hole through which the bulk of the yarn and needle eye would not pass. In this case, cut a piece of sewing thread 8in long and thread both ends into the eye of the needle. Slide the needle halfway along the doubled thread, thus forming a loop at one end. Smooth both the ends and the loop downward. Pass the end of the yarn into the loop for several inches and then smooth the double thickness of the yarn downward.

Thread the beads or sequins onto the needle, over the sewing thread and then the yarn.

Single crochet

Although the beads lie on the right side of the fabric, they may be worked in on either a right side or a wrong side row. It is possible to leave several stitches between beads and several plain rows between bead rows.

Adding on a wrong side row. Begin a wrong side row in the usual way, working along to the bead position. Insert hook into next stitch, yoh and draw through loop, slip bead up close against the right side of the work, yoh taking the yarn from just beyond the bead and draw through both loops.

Adding on a right side row. Work to the first bead position. Insert the hook into the next stitch from back to front, slip bead up close to hook, yoh from beyond bead and draw the loop through to the back of the work, yoh and draw through all sts. Continue along the row.

Double crochet

Adding on a right side row. Work to the first bead position, yoh, slip bead up close to the hook, insert hook into next st, yoh and draw through loops, yoh and draw through two loops, yoh and draw through remaining loops.

Adding on a wrong side row. The bead is added just before the last stage of the dc. Work in dc to bead position, yoh, insert hook into next st and draw loop through, yoh and draw through two loops, slip bead up close to fabric on RS, yoh taking yarn from beyond bead and draw through remaining loops.

▲ *Slipping bead close to fabric on a wrong side single crochet row*

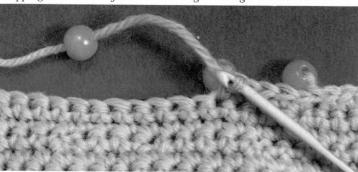

▲ *Completing the single crochet stitch after placing bead on wrong side row*

▲ *Putting yarn over hook from beyond bead on right side single crochet row*

Choker

Size

Width of choker, 1in
Length of choker, 12in, adjustable

> **Gauge**
> Center motif measures
> 1$\frac{5}{8}$in

Materials

J. & P. Coats Six Cord Mercerized No.20
1 ball
One No.B crochet hook
Two hooks and eyes
for fastening
28 pearl beads (if length is altered, fewer or more beads will be required)

Center motif

Thread 8 beads onto yarn.

1st round Wind yarn 10 times around tip of finger, remove from finger and work 32sc into ring, join with ss into first sc.

2nd round 1sc into same place as ss, *ch5, skip 3sc, 1sc into next sc, rep from * skipping 1sc at end of last rep, join with ss into first sc.

3rd round 2sc into first ch loop, insert hook into same ch loop, slip bead up to hook, yoh from beyond bead and draw loop through ch letting bead come to front of work, yoh and draw through both loops—called 1 bead sc—, ch3, 5dc into bead sc worked before ch3, ch2, 1 ss into same sc—called 1 shell—, 2sc into

▲ *Yarn over hook for first stage of double crochet on right side row*

▲ *Double crochet wrong side row*

▲ *Completing double crochet*

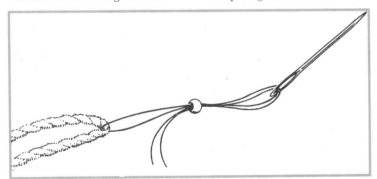

▲ *Method for threading beads or sequins onto yarn*

▲ *A pretty beaded choker which is simple to make in crochet cotton*

same ch loop, *into next ch loop work 2sc, 1 bead sc, 1 shell and 2sc, rep from * ending with ss into first sc. Fasten off.

First side of neckband
Thread 10 beads onto yarn or additional beads if length is more than 12in.
1st row Commence with *ch3, 1dc into 3rd ch from hook—called 1 ring—, rep from * 19 times more or until work measures ½in more than desired length from outer edge of center motif to center back of neck, having an even number of rings. Do not turn.
2nd row *Into next ring work 1sc, ch2, 1sc*, rep from * to * to within last ring, into next ring work 1sc, ch2, 3sc into

end of ring, ch2 and 1sc into other side, working into opposite side of rings rep from * to * to within opposite side of last ring, into last ring work 1sc, ch2 and 2sc, join with ss into first sc.
3rd row Ss into first ch loop, 1sc into same ch loop, *ch5, 1sc into next ch loop, ch3, 1sc into next ch loop, rep from * to within 3sc at end of neckband, skipping 1sc at end of last rep, skip 1sc, 1sc into next sc, **ch3, 1sc into next ch loop, rep from ** ending with ch3, skip 1sc, 1sc into next dc, ch3, join with ss into first sc.
4th row *Into next ch loop work 2sc, 1 bead sc, 1 shell and 2sc, 3sc into next ch loop, rep from * to within sc

at end of neckband, 3sc into next ch loop, 1ss into next sc, ch3, 3dc into each ch loop to within last 2 loops, ch2, 1ss into next sc, 3sc into each of next ch2 loops, join with ss into first sc. Turn.
5th row Ch1, 1sc into each of next 6sc, 3sc over next ch2 loop, 1sc into each dc, 3sc over next ch3 loop, 1sc into each of next 6sc. Turn.
6th row Ch1, 1sc into first sc, ch1, 1ss into center dc of any shell on center motif, ch1, 1ss into last sc on neckband, 1sc into each of next 7sc, ch1, 1ss into center dc of next shell on center motif, ch1, 1ss into last sc on neckband, 3sc into next sc, 1sc into each sc to within last 9sc, 3sc into next sc, 1sc into each sc to end.

Second side of neckband
Work first 5 rows as given for first side of neckband.
6th row 1sc into each of first 8sc, 3sc into next sc, 1sc into each sc to within last 9sc, 3sc into next sc, 1sc into next sc, ch1, skip 2 shells at top of center motif, 1ss into center dc of next shell, ch1, 1ss into last sc on neckband, 1sc into each of next 6sc, ch1, 1ss into center dc of next shell on center motif, ch1, 1ss into last sc on neckband, 1sc into next sc. Fasten off.

Finishing
Press under a damp cloth with a warm iron on a felt or foam pad to protect beads.
Sew hooks and eyes to ends of neckband to fasten.

Beaded accessories

Unusually pretty collar and earrings in beaded crochet.

Size

To fit average neck.
Center front depth, about 2½in.

Gauge

7hdc to 1in worked on No.B crochet hook.

Materials

Coats & Clark's O.N.T.
Pearl Cotton
One ball
One No.B crochet hook
102 beads
One button
Earring mountings

Beaded collar

Using No.B crochet hook, ch107.

1st row Into 2nd ch from hook, work 1hdc, *1hdc into next ch, rep from * to end. Turn.

2nd row Ch2, 1hdc into each of next 3hdc, *2hdc into next hdc, 1hdc into each of next 4hdc, rep from * to end. Turn.

3rd row *Ch5, skip 3hdc, 1sc into next hdc, rep from * to end. Turn.

4th row Into each ch5 loop, work 6sc ending with a ss into last st. Break off yarn.

5th row With RS facing, attach yarn to center of 3rd loop with a ss, 1sc in next sc, 1hdc into next sc, *skip first sc in next loop, work 1hdc into each of next 5sc, rep from * to 3rd loop from end, 1hdc into next sc, 1sc into next sc, ss into next sc. Break off yarn.

6th row With RS facing, attach the yarn with a ss into the center of 5th loop from end, 1sc into next st, ch3, skip 3 sts, 1sc into each of next 2

The beaded collar in champagne colored yarn with yellow beads

Matched with earrings, a beaded crocheted collar resembles jewelry ▶

sts, ch4, skip 3 sts, *1sc into each of next 2sc, ch5, skip 3 sts, rep from * 17 times more, 1sc into each of next 2 sts, ch4, skip 3 sts, 1sc into each of next 2 sts, ch3, skip next 3 sts, 1sc into next st, ss into next st. Turn.

7th row Ss into first st, work 4sc into first loop, 5sc into 2nd loop, work 7sc into each loop until 2 loops rem, 5sc into next loop, 4sc into last loop, ss into last st. Break off yarn.

8th row With RS facing, attach yarn to center of 3rd loop on preceding row with a ss, 1sc into next st, 1hdc into next st, *skip first st in next loop, work 1hdc into each of next 6 sts, rep from * to 3rd loop from end of preceding row, 1hdc into next st, 1sc into next st, ss into next st. Break off yarn.

9th row With WS facing, attach yarn to center of 5th loop on preceding row, ch4, skip 4 sts, 1sc into each of next 2 sts, ch5, skip 4 sts, 1sc into each of next 2 sts, *ch6, skip 4 sts, 1sc into each of next 2 sts, rep from * 8 times more, ch5, skip 4 sts, 1sc into each of next 2 sts, ch4, skip 4 sts, ss into next st. Turn.

10th row Into first loop work 4sc, into 2nd loop work 6sc, work 7sc into every loop until 2 rem, work 6sc into next loop and 4sc into last loop, ss into last st. Break off yarn.

11th row With RS facing, attach yarn into center of 3rd loop on preceding loop row with a ss, 1sc into next st, 1hdc into next st, *skip first sc of each loop, 1hdc into each of next 6sc, rep into each loop until 3 rem, 1hdc into next st, 1sc into next st, ss into next st. Break off yarn.

12th row With WS facing, attach yarn to center of first loop on first row of loops with a ss, ch4, ss into base of 4ch, work 5sc into loop just formed, 1sc into 4 sts to center of 2nd loop, ch5, ss into base to form loop, 6sc into loop, 1sc into 4 sts to

center of 3rd loop, ch6, ss to form loop, 10sc into loop, *1sc into each st to center of next loop, ch6, ss into base to form loop, 12sc into loop, rep from * 5 times, continue in this way working 3 loops of 7ch with 14sc in loop, then loops of 8ch with 16sc in each loop until only 12 loops rem to be worked to complete collar and dec in size to correspond to other end. Fasten off.

Finishing

Sew beads at ends of each loop arch and at base of loops on last row.
Sew button on one end, make button loop to correspond.

Earrings

Using No.B hook, begin at center, ch5. Join with a ss into first ch to form circle.
1st round Ch3, work 15dc

into circle. Join with a ss into 3rd of first 3ch.
2nd round Ch1, *1sc into next dc, ch5, ss into last sc, work 8sc into loop just formed, 1sc into next dc, rep from * to end. Join with a ss into first ch. Fasten off.

Finishing

Sew a bead at base of each loop and one in center. Stitch securely to mounting.

Basic Wardrobe Crochet

Hooded baby jacket

Crocheted in a crisp cluster stitch to make a firm yet lightweight surface, this hooded jacket is a perfect garment to keep baby warm and snug. It is designed to be suitable for a boy or a girl. The body of the jacket is made in one piece and then divided at the armhole. The hood is crocheted separately, and is attached to the completed jacket.

Sizes
Directions are for 18in chest. The figures in brackets [] refer to the 20in size only. Length, 10¾[11½]in.

Sleeve seam, 6½[7½]in.

Gauge
6 motifs and 12 rows to 4in over patt worked on No.F crochet hook
Note
One motif consists of 2 clusters worked into the same stitch.

Materials
Bernat Pompadour
4 skeins
One No.E crochet hook
One No.F crochet hook
Three buttons

▼ *Detail showing rows of cluster stitch alternating with single crochet*

Body
Using No.F crochet hook, ch87[99] loosely.
1st row Yoh, insert hook into 5th ch from hook, yoh, pull loop through, (yoh, insert hook into same ch, yoh, pull loop through) twice, yoh and pull through all 7 loops on hook to form 1 cluster—called 1cl—ch2, 1cl into same st as last 1cl, ch1, *skip 2ch, 1cl into next ch, ch2, 1cl into same ch as last 1cl, ch1, rep from * ending with 1dc into last ch. Turn. 28[32] motifs.
2nd row Ch1, *2sc into next ch2 sp, 1sc into next ch1 sp, rep from * to end. Turn.
3rd row Ch3, 1cl into 2nd sc, ch2, 1cl into same sc, ch1, *skip 2sc, 1cl into next sc, ch2, 1cl into same sc, ch1, rep from * ending with 1dc into last st. Turn.
4th row As 2nd.
Rows 3 and 4 form patt and are rep throughout.
Continue in patt until work measures 6[6½]in from beg.

Divide for armholes
1st row Work in patt over first 7[8] motifs only, 1dc into next st. Turn.
Complete right front on these sts.
Continue until work measures 8¾[9½]in from beg, ending at armhole edge.

Shape neck
Continue in patt working one motif less at neck edge every other row twice.
Fasten off.

Left front
Attach yarn to sts for left front, working 1dc into first st, then working in patt over last 7[8] motifs only.
Complete to correspond with right front.

Back
Attach yarn to center 14[16] motifs and work in patt until back measures same as fronts to shoulder. Fasten off.

Sleeves
Using No.F crochet hook,

ch30[33].
Work in pattern as given for body. 9[10] motifs.
Work 4 rows.
Continue in patt, inc 1cl at each end of next and every following 4th row until 2 motifs at each side have been inc. Continue without shaping until sleeve measures 6½[7½]in, or desired length to top of sleeve. Fasten off.

Hood
Using No.F crochet hook, ch 54[60].
Work in patt as given for body. 17[19] motifs.
Work 2 rows.
Keeping patt correct, inc 1cl at each end of every other row until there are 21[23] motifs.
Continue without shaping until hood measures 5¼[5½]in from beg.

Shape back
1st row Ss over first 7[8] motifs and continue on center 7 motifs only.
Dec 1cl at each end every other row 3 times.
Continue without shaping until hood measures 10[10¾] in from beg. Fasten off.

Finishing
Join shoulder and sleeve seams. Sew in sleeves.
Cuffs Using No.E crochet hook, work 3 rows sc along lower edge of sleeves.
Last row Without turning work, work 1 row of crab st by working from left to right, working 1sc into each sc to end. Fasten off.
Body Work as given for cuffs from center front neck edge around body to other neck edge, making 3 evenly spaced buttonholes on 3rd row, on right front for a girl and left front for a boy, by working 4ch and skipping 4sts.
Hood Work around front edge of hood as given for cuffs. Seam back of hood to side edges. Sew hood around neck edge of body. Sew on buttons.

Blue for a boy in bulky crochet ▶

Tunic suit for a toddler

If frills and ruffles aren't the style for your baby, then why not crochet this crisp and simple tunic and pant suit. Make it all in one color, or make it look extra smart with the pants and trimming worked in a contrasting color, say navy with white, or yellow with orange.

Sizes
Directions are for size 6 months.
The figures in brackets [] refer to the 1-year and 2-year sizes respectively.

Gauge
2½ "V" groups and
3 rows to 1in.

Materials
5 [6, 6] balls Spinnerin Mona 50 gram
1 No.E(4) crochet hook, or size required for gauge
4 small buttons
¾ yard elastic

Tunic front

Ch66 [70, 74] loosely.
1st row 2dc into 4th ch from hook, * skip 1 ch, 2dc into next ch. Rep from * to last ch, 1 dc into last ch. Turn.
2nd row Ch3, * 2dc into next dc, skip 1 dc, rep from * to last dc, 1 dc into 2nd ch of turning ch. Turn. 31 [33, 35] complete "V" groups.
The 2nd row forms the "V" pattern and is rep throughout.
Work 4[5, 6] rows.
Dec at each end of next row by making only 1 dc into first and last "V" of previous row. This means that in the next row, two less "Vs" are worked

248

than before the dec.
Continue patt, dec in this manner at each end of every 6th [7th, 8th] row until 28 [29, 30] rows in all have been worked. 23 [25, 29] complete "V" groups.

To shape armholes
1st row Ss over 4sts, ch3, work in patt to last 4sts. Turn.
Work 9 [10, 11] rows. 19 [21, 25] complete "V" groups.

To shape neck
Work 3 rows on 7 [8, 9] "V" groups. Finish off.
Work other shoulder in same way.

Tunic back

Work as given for front until armhole shaping row has been completed.
Next row Work across half the sts, turn, and complete one side on these sts, working as given for front.
Finish off.
Attach yarn and work other side in same way.

Sleeves

Ch32 [34, 36] loosely.
Work 3 rows in patt as given. 14 [15, 16] complete "V" groups.
Inc at each end of next row by adding 1dc to first and last "V", each of which will become a "V" in the following row, thus adding 2 "V" groups after inc.
Continue patt, inc each end of every 4th row until 18 [20, 22] rows have been worked.

Shape sleeve cap
1st row Ss over 4sts, ch3, patt to last 4sts. Turn.
Work 8 [9, 10] rows, dec at each end of every alternate row. Finish off.

Front trimming

Ch20.
Work 7 rows sc.
Work corded edge around both long sides, and one short end, as follows—
1 row sc, working from left to right instead of the usual right to left, to give an extra twist to the stitch, and inserting hook under both horizontal threads of the edge stitches.

Pants

Ch48 [52, 56] loosely.
Work in patt as given for tunic front for 23 [24, 25] rows.
22 [24, 26] complete "V" patterns.

To shape crotch
Next row Ss across 15 [17, 19] sts, ch3, work next 8 "V" groups, 1 dc. Turn.
Work 6 rows on central sts.
Next row Work to end. In place of turning ch, ch15 [17, 19] loosely.
Break off the yarn.
At the other end of same row, join yarn and ch16 [18, 20] loosely. Turn.
Work across all sts in patt.
Work 23 [24, 25] rows.
Finish off.

Finishing the tunic

Join shoulder seams. Sew in sleeves, join the sleeve and the side seams.
Back opening With right side of work facing, beg at base of left side of opening and work 1 row sc evenly up left side, around neck and down right side. Turn and work 2nd row. Mark position for 3 buttons on the left side.
3rd row Work to top of right side, level with first marker* skip 2sc, ch2.
Work in sc until next marker is reached, rep from * until

3 buttonholes have been worked, complete row. Turn.
4th row Work up right side of opening and around neck using sc. Turn.
5th row Work in corded edge st around neck to top of the opening.
Work corded edging around wrists and lower edge.
Sew tab trimming neatly to center front.
Press very lightly with a dry cloth, using a cool iron.
Sew on buttons.

Finishing the pants

Fold in half at crotch. Join side seams.
Work corded edging loosely around leg openings.
Thread elastic through waist edge, and sew ends together to form circle.
Press lightly.

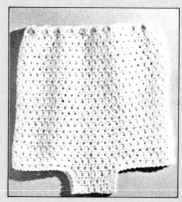

▲ The matching pants
Crocheted tunic for a toddler ►
▼ Back view of tunic

Coat and hat for a little girl

Basic Wardrobe Crochet

Light yet warm, this little unlined crocheted coat and matching hat make a charming spring outfit for two-to-three year olds.
The coat skirt is worked in a fabric stitch and the sleeves in single crochet. Use two colors or make it in one—perhaps a pastel or even navy.

Sizes
Directions are for 21in chest. The figures in brackets [] refer to the 22 and 23in sizes respectively.
Length down center back, 13¼ [14:15½]in, adjustable.
Sleeve seam, 6½[7¼:8½]in, adjustable.

Gauge
9sts and 10 rows to 2in over sc worked on No. F crochet hook.

Materials
Spinnerin Wintuk Sport (2oz skeins)
5[5:6] skeins main color A
1 skein contrast B
One No.D crochet hook
One No.F crochet hook
One No.H crochet hook
Three buttons

Back yoke
Using No.F crochet hook and A, ch53[55:57].
1st row Into 2nd ch from hook work 1sc, 1sc into each ch to end. Turn.
2nd row Ch2, 1sc into each sc to end. Turn. 52[54:56]sc including turning ch.
Work 2nd row 2[2:4] times more.
250

Shape armholes
1st row Ss over 4sts, work 1sc into each sc to last 4sts. Turn.
Work 1 row. 44[46:48]sc.
3rd row Ss over 2[2:3]sts, work 1sc into each sc to last 2[2:3]sts. Turn.
Work 19[19:21] rows on rem 40[42:42]sts.

Shape shoulders
1st row Ss over 4sts, work 1sc into each of next 11[12:12]sc. Turn.
Complete shoulder on these sts.
2nd row Ss over 2sc, 1sc into each of next 9[10:10]sc. Turn.
3rd row Ss over 3[4:4]sc, 1sc into each sc to end. Turn.
4th row Ch2, 1sc into next 5[5:5]sc. Turn.
5th row Ss over 3sc, 1sc into each sc to end. Turn.
6th row Ch2, 1sc into each of next 2sc. Pull yarn through rem loop and fasten off.
Attach yarn to last 15[16:16] sts and work other shoulder to correspond.

Left front yoke

Using No.F crochet hook and A, ch32[33:34].
1st row Into 2nd ch from hook work 1sc, 1sc into each ch to end.
Turn.
2nd row Ch2, 1sc into each sc to end. Turn. 32[33:34]sc including turning ch.
Work 2nd row 2[2:4] times more.

Shape armhole
1st row Ss over 5sts, 1sc into each sc to end. Turn.
Work 1 row.

3rd row Ss over 2[2:3] sts, 1sc into each sc to end. Turn.
Work 16[16:18]rows sc.

Shape neck
1st row Ss over 6sts, 1sc into each sc to end. Turn.
2nd row Ch2, 1sc into each of next 16[17:17]sc. Turn.
3rd row Ss over 2sts, 1sc into each sc. Turn.
4th row Ss over 4sts, 1sc into each of next 9[10:10]sc. Turn.
Work 1 row.
6th row Ss over 3[4:4] sts, 1sc into each of next 3sc. Turn.
Work 1 row.
Pull yarn through rem loop and fasten off.

Right front yoke

Work as given for left front yoke, reversing shapings and working 3 buttonholes, the first on the 3rd row and the third just below center neck edge, as follows:
Ch2, 1sc into each of next 2sc, ch2, skip 2sc, 1sc into each sc to end. Turn.
Work 1sc into each ch on the following row so that the number of sc rem the same.

Coat skirt

Join yoke side seams and shoulder seams.
Using No.F crochet hook and A, join with ss to center front edge of left front yoke.
1st row Ch2, 1sc into each sc along lower edge of left front yoke, back yoke and right front yoke. 115[119:123]sc, including turning ch.
Change to No.H crochet hook and work 1 row sc.
Continue in patt.
1st row Ch1, insert hook between next 2sc 1 row below, yoh and draw a long loop up to level of row being worked, yoh and draw through both loops on hook—called 1 long sc—*1sc into next sc, 1 long sc between 2nd and 3rd sc from previous long sc, rep from * to end, ending with 1sc into last st. Turn.
2nd row Ch1, 1sc into each sc

to end. Turn.
3rd row Ch1, *1 long sc into previous patt row, 1sc into next sc, rep from * to end. Turn.
Rep 2nd and 3rd patt rows to form patt.
Continue in patt until skirt measures 6[6½:7½]in from beg, or 2in less than required length, ending with a 2nd row.
Continue in patt, working 2 rows B and 2 rows A alternately until 3 bands of B have been worked, ending with a 3rd patt row. Work 1 row ss with B to finish edge. Break yarn and draw through rem loop and fasten off.

Right sleeve

Using No.F crochet hook and A, ch27[29:31].
Work in sc as given for yoke, inc one st at each end of 3rd row, then every 3rd [4th:4th] row until there are 39[39:43] sts. Work in sc until sleeve measures 4½[5¼: 6½]in, or 2in less than required length to underarm.

Shape cap
1st row Ss over 4sts, 1sc into each sc to last 3sc. Turn.
Work 1 row. 32[32:36]sc.
3rd row Ss over 2[2:3]sc, 1sc into each sc to last 2[2:3] sc. Turn.
Work 1 row. 28[28:30]sc.
5th row Ss over 2sc, 1sc into each sc to last 2sc. Turn.
Work 1 row.
Rep last 2 rows 1[1:2] times more. Pull yarn through rem loop and fasten off.

Left sleeve

Work as given for right sleeve reversing cap shaping.

Cuff

Using No.F crochet hook and A, join with ss to first st of lower edge, ch2, work 25[25:27]sc evenly along edge.
Change to No.H crochet hook and work 1 row sc.
Continue in 2 row patt as

given for skirt, beg with B and working until there are 3 bands of B, ending with 3rd patt row. Complete with 1 row ss using B.

Edgings

Using No.F crochet hook and B, beg at lower edge of right front and work 8sc up edge of border, attach A and continue up center front edge, working 38[42:50] sc to neck edge, 3sc into corner st, work 12[12:13]sc to shoulder seam, 13sc along back neck edge and 12[12:13] sc down other front neck, 3sc into corner st and 38[42:50]sc down left front to beg of border, complete with 8sc in B. Fasten off ends.

Collar

Using No.F crochet hook and A, with RS of work facing, work 33[33:35]sc evenly around neck, beg and ending in 4th sc from center corner sc.

Change to No.H crochet hook and work 2 rows sc, inc 8sts evenly on first row.

Change to B and patt as given for skirt, working until 3 bands of B have been worked and ending with a 3rd patt row. Complete with 1 row ss using B. Using B work 8sc along each short edge of collar. Fasten off ends.

Finishing

Press lightly.
Seam sleeves and sew in place. Sew on buttons to correspond to buttonholes.

Hat

Using No.D crochet hook and A, ch5. Join into a circle with ss into first ch.

1st round Ch1 to form first st, work 9sc into circle. Join with ss into first ch.

2nd round Ch2, 1sc into same st, *2sc into next sc, rep from * to end. Join with ss.

3rd round Ch1 to form first st, 2sc into next sc, *1sc into next sc, 2sc into next sc, rep

from * to end. Join with ss.

4th round Ch1, 1sc into each sc. Join with ss. 30 sts.

5th round Ch1, 1sc into next sc, 2sc into next sc, *1sc into next 2sc, 2sc into next sc, rep from * to end. Join with ss. 40sts.

6th and 7th rounds Ch1, 1sc into each sc to end. Join with ss.

8th round Ch1, 1sc into each of next 2sc, 2sc into next sc, *1sc into next 3sc, 2sc into next sc, rep from * to end. Join with ss. 50sts.

9th round Ch1, 1sc into each of next 3sc, 2sc into next sc, *1sc into next 4sc, 2sc into next sc, rep from * to end. Join with ss. 60sts.

10th round Ch1, 1sc into each sc to end. Join with ss.

11th round Ch1, 1sc into each of next 4sc, 2sc into next sc, *1sc into next 5sc, 2sc into next sc, rep from * to end. Join with ss. 70sts.

12th round Ch1, 1sc into each of next 5sc, 2sc into next sc, *1sc into next 6sc, 2sc into next sc, rep from * to end. Join with ss. 80sts.

Work 2 rounds without shaping.

Inc 6 sts evenly on next round. Work 1 round.

Rep last 2 rounds 1[1:2] times more. 92[92:98] sts. Continue in rounds without shaping until work measures 6[6:6½]in from center to edge.

Turn work and crochet brim. Work 1 round, inc 6sts evenly. Work 3 rounds, inc 10sts evenly in each round. Work 1 round without shaping.

Work 2 rounds, dec 10sts evenly in each round. 108 [108:114] sts. Turn work and work 1 round sc. Join with ss.

Turn work and with B work 1st patt row. Join with ss. Turn work and with B work 1 round sc. Join with ss. Turn work and with A work 3rd patt row. Join with ss. Turn work and with A work 1 round ss. Join with ss. Break yarn and fasten off ends. Press lightly.

Crocheted coat bordered in pink ▶

Lacy~sleeved dress for a little girl

Here is a pretty dress to crochet for a little girl's special occasions. It is worked in a soft, lightweight yarn in basic stitches.

Sizes

Directions are for 23in chest. The figures in brackets [] refer to the 24 and 25in sizes respectively.
Length at center back, 17¾[18½:19¼]in.
Sleeve seam, 8¾[9¼:9¾]in.

Gauge
18sc and 25 rows to 4in worked on No.E crochet hook

Materials

Bernat Pompadour
7[7:9] skeins
One No.E crochet hook
One small button

Front

Using No.E crochet hook ch70[73:76].
1st row Into 2nd ch from hook work 1sc, 1sc into each ch to end. Turn.
2nd row Ch1, *1sc into next sc, rep from * to end. Turn.
Continue in sc, dec one sc at each end of 9th and every following 10th row 5 times in all. 59[62:65]sc.
Continue without shaping until work measures 12½[13: 13½]in from beg.

Shape armholes

1st row Ss over 3sc, work in sc to last 3sc. Turn.
2nd row Work in sc to end. Turn.

Basic Wardrobe Crochet

3rd row Ss over 2sc, work in sc to last 2sc. Turn.
4th row Work in sc to end. Turn.
Rep 3rd and 4th rows once more.
Next row Ss over 1sc, work in sc to last sc. Turn. 43[46: 49]sc.
Continue without shaping until armholes measure 2¾[3: 3¼]in from beg.

Shape neck

Next row Ch1, 1sc into each of next 15[16:17]sc. Turn.
Complete left shoulder first.
Continue in sc, dec 2sc at beg of next row and 1sc at beg of every other row once.
Continue without shaping until armhole measures 4¾[5:5¼]in from beg, ending at armhole edge.

Shape shoulder

1st row Ss over 5sc, work in sc to end. Turn.
2nd row Work in sc to end. Turn.
3rd row Ss over 4sc, work in sc to end. Fasten off.
With RS of work facing, skip center 11[12:13]sc, attach yarn to last 16[17:18]sc and work right shoulder as for left shoulder, reversing shaping.

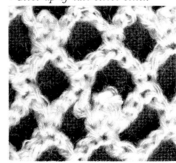
Close-up of lace sleeve stitch

Back

Using No.E crochet hook ch62[66:70].
Work as given for front, dec one st at each end of 11th and every following 12th row 4 times in all.
54[58:62]sc.
Continue without shaping until back measures same as front to underarm.

Shape armholes

1st row Ss over 2sc, work in sc to last 2sc. Turn.
2nd row Work in sc to end. Turn.
Rep 1st and 2nd rows once more.
5th row Ss over 1sc, work in sc to last sc. Turn. 44[48:52] sc.
Continue without shaping until armhole measures 1in from beg.

Divide for back opening

Next row Ch1, work 1sc into each of next 21[23:25]sc. Turn.
Complete right back first.
Continue working in sc until armhole measures same as front to shoulder, ending at armhole edge.

Shape shoulder

1st row Ss over 5sc, work in sc to end. Turn.
2nd row Work in sc to end. Turn.
3rd row Ss over 4sc, work in sc to end. Fasten off.
With RS of work facing, attach yarn to rem sts and work left back as for right back, reversing shaping.

Sleeves

Using No.E crochet hook ch23[25:27].
1st row Into 2nd ch from hook work 1sc, 1sc into each ch to end. Turn.
2nd row Ch1, *1sc into next sc, rep from * to end. Turn.
3rd row Ch3, skip 1sc, 1sc into next sc, *ch2, skip 1sc, 1sc into next sc, rep from * to end. Turn. 11[12:13] sps.
4th row *Ch5, 1sc into next ch2 sp, rep from * to end. Turn.

5th row *Ch5, 1sc into 3rd ch of ch5 sp of previous row, rep from * to end. Turn.
6th row *Ch5, 1sc into next sp, ch3, 1sc into same sp as last sc—called 1 picot—ch5, 1sc into next sp, rep from * to last 1[0:1] sp, ch5, 1 picot into last sp[0:ch5, 1 picot into last sp]. Turn.
7th row As 5th.
8th row *Ch5, 1sc into next sp, ch5, 1 picot into next sp, rep from * to last 1[0:1] sp, ch5, 1sc into last sp[0:ch5, 1sc into last sp]. Turn.
Rows 5-8 form patt and are rep throughout.
Continue in patt until sleeve measures 8¾[9¼:9¾]in from beg, or desired length to underarm.

Shape cap

Next row Keeping patt correct, ss over 2ch to center of first ch sp, 1sc into 3rd ch of ch5 loop, work in patt to last sp, 1sc into 3rd of last ch5 loop. Turn.
Rep the last row 8 times more. Fasten off.

Sleeve frill

Using No.E crochet hook and with RS of sleeve facing, work frill along lower edge.
1st row Attach yarn to first sc, *ch5, 1sc into next sc, rep from * to end. Turn.
2nd row As 5th row of sleeve patt. Fasten off.

Collar

Using No.E crochet hook ch47[49:51].
1st row Into 2nd ch from hook work 1sc, 1sc into each ch to end. Turn.
Work 2 rows sc.
4th row As 3rd of sleeve patt.
5th row As 4th of sleeve patt.
6th row As 5th of sleeve patt. Fasten off.

Finishing

Press lightly.
Join shoulder, side and sleeve seams. Sew in sleeves. Sew collar around neck edge. Work a loop buttonhole at top of back opening. Sew on button to correspond.

Fringed vests

Make these western-style vests in bright colors to delight the hearts of adventurous boys and girls.

Sizes

Directions are for 24in chest. The figures in brackets [] refer to the 26in size only. Length down center back, 10½ [11¾in].

Materials

Unger English Crepe 5[6] balls
One No.D crochet hook

All ready to round up outlaws in fringed and laced red crochet vests▶
▼ *Close-up of the main pattern stitch*

Basic Wardrobe Crochet

Back

Using No.D crochet hook, ch64[68].
1st row Into 3rd ch from hook work 1dc, work 1dc into each ch to end. Turn.
2nd row Ch2, *1dc between next 2dc of previous row, rep from * to end. Turn.
The 2nd row forms the patt and is rep throughout.
Continue in patt until work measures 4¼[5⅛]in from beg.

Shape armholes

1st row Ss over 3dc, patt to last 3dc. Turn.
2nd row Ss over 2dc, patt to last 2dc. Turn.
5 sts have now been dec at each side.
Continue dec 1dc at each end

of every row 2[3] times.
Continue without shaping until work measures 9¾[10¼]in from beg.

Shape shoulders

1st row Ss over 6[7]dc, ch1, patt to last 7[8] sts, 1sc into next st, ss in same st. Fasten off.

Left front

Using No.D crochet hook, ch33[35].
1st row Into 3rd ch from hook work 1dc, work 1dc into each ch to end. Turn.
2nd row Ch2, *1dc between next 2dc of previous row, rep from * to end. Turn.
Continue in patt until work measures 3⅝[4¼]in from beg.

Shape neck

Dec 1dc at center front edge on every row 5[3] times, 1dc on every following 2nd row 5[7] times and 1dc on every following 3rd row 2[2] times; *at the same time*, shape armhole as given for back when work measures same length as back to underarm.
Continue without shaping until work measures same as back to shoulder.
Fasten off.

Right front

Work as given for left front, reversing shaping.

Finishing

Join side and shoulder seams. Work 2 rows sc around all edges, including armholes. Make a cord for the front lacing, using 4 strands of yarn and No.D crochet hook, working a ch the required length.
Cut lengths of yarn 9½[12½]in long for the fringe. Fold 4 strands of yarn in half and pull center of folded threads through ch at lower edge to form fringe. Rep into every 2nd st along lower edge of vest. Trim ends of fringe if desired.
Thread cord through center front edges to form lacing.

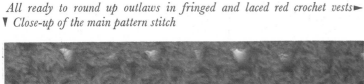

Crochet headscarf

Make this delightful, triangular crocheted headscarf to guard against playful breezes. It is worked in a simple arch stitch and buttons neatly under the chin so that it cannot slip off.

▲ *Front view and button fastening*
▼ *Back view showing edging*

Size
To fit an average head

Materials
Spinnerin Wintuk Sport
One 2oz ball
One No.C crochet hook
1 button

Headscarf

Ch6. Join into a loop by working 1sc into the first ch worked. Turn and work first row into top of this loop.
1st row Ch6, 1sc into first of 6ch, ch5, 1sc into 3rd ch of loop. Turn.

2nd row Ch6, 1sc into first of 6ch, (ch5, 1sc into 3rd ch of next loop) twice. Turn.
3rd row Ch6, 1sc into first of 6ch, (ch5, 1sc into 3rd ch of next loop) 3 times. Turn.
4th, 5th, 6th, 7th and 8th rows are worked as for 3rd row, but inc number of times sts in parentheses are worked by one rep more each row.
9th row Ch5, 1sc into 3rd ch of first ch5 loop, (ch5, 1sc into 3rd ch of next loop) 8 times. Turn.
10th row As 9th.
11th row Ch6, 1sc into first of 6ch, (ch5, 1sc into 3rd ch of next loop) 9 times. Turn. Continue in this way, inc one loop on each of 8 rows, then working 2 rows without inc. Rep until 36 rows have been worked.

Edging
Do not turn at end of last row.
1st row Work 84sc evenly along side to back point (formed by first loop), 84sc along other side to front edge, work 3sc into each loop along this front edge. Join to first sc with ss.
2nd row Work 1sc into each sc working 2sc into each of 3 sc at each corner. Join to first sc with ss.
3rd row *Ch7, 1sc into next sc, rep from * to end of 2nd side only, skipping the front edge. Finish off.

Finishing
Do not press.
Sew button to left-hand front corner using first loop at right-hand front corner as a buttonhole.

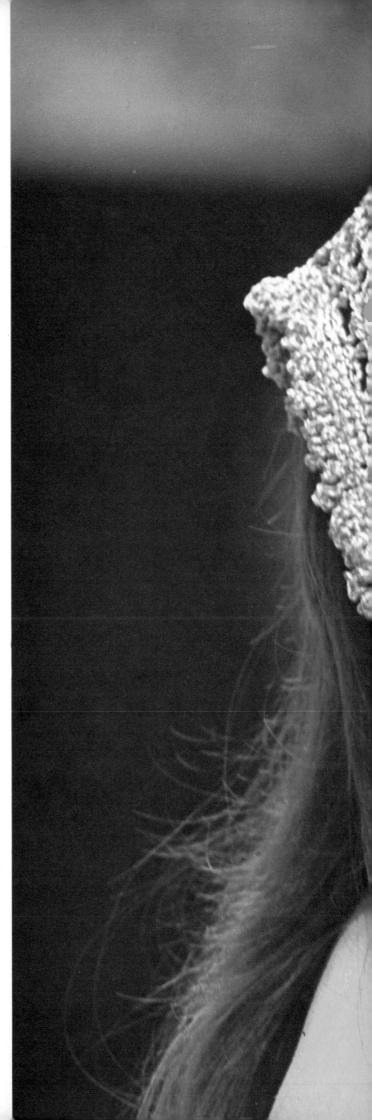

Gypsy shawl with tassel trim

This striking shawl to make in 1 color or 3 colors is a simple way to practice shaping in crochet. This chapter also tells how to make one of the most effective kinds of trimming, the large tassel.

Size
Approximately 36in from neck edge to bottom of center point.

Gauge
3dc and 1 row to 1in worked on No.J crochet hook, using 2 strands of yarn.

Materials
Spinnerin Wintuk Featherlon (2oz skeins)
One-color version
7 skeins main color A
Three-color version
3 skeins main color A
3 skeins contrast color B
1 skein contrast color C
One No.J crochet hook

Shawl

Using No.J crochet hook and 2 strands of A, ch284.
Base row Work 1dc into 3rd ch from hook, 1dc into next ch, *ch1, skip 1ch, 1dc into each of next 3ch*, rep from * to * 32 times more, ch1, skip 1ch, (1dc into each of next 3ch leaving last loop of each dc on hook, yoh and draw through 4 loops on hook, skip 1ch) twice, 1dc into each of next 3ch leaving last loop of each dc on hook, yoh and draw through 4 loops on hook, rep from * to * 34

times. Turn.
1st row Ch6, *1dc into next ch sp, ch3*, rep from * to * 33 times, skip next 3dc groups, rep from * to * 34 times, 1dc into turning ch. Turn.
2nd row Ch3, skip first ch sp, 3dc into next ch sp, *ch1, 3dc into next ch sp*, rep from * to * 30 times, ch1, (3dc into next ch sp leaving last loop of each dc on hook, yoh and draw through 4 loops on hook) 3 times—called corner group —rep from * to * 32 times, 1dc into 3rd of first 6ch. Turn.
3rd row Ch6, *1dc into next ch sp, ch3*, rep from * to * 31 times, skip corner group, rep from * to * 32 times, 1dc into turning ch. Turn.
4th row Ch3, skip first ch sp, 3dc into next ch sp, *ch1, 3dc into next ch sp*, rep from * to * 28 times, ch1, work corner group into next 3 ch sps, rep from * to * 30 times, 1dc into 3rd of first 6ch. Turn.
5th row Ch6, *1dc into next ch sp, ch3*, rep from * to * 29 times, skip corner group, rep from * to * 30 times, 1dc into turning ch. Turn.
Continue with A or break off 1 ball of A and attach 1 ball of B.
6th row Ch3, skip first ch sp, 3dc into next ch sp, *ch1, 3dc into next ch sp*, rep from * to * 26 times, ch1, work corner group in next 3 ch sps, rep from * to * 28 times, 1dc into 3rd of first 6ch. Turn.
Continue in this way, dec 1dc group at each end and on center group on every other row until 33 patt rows have been worked and

changing colors for 3-color version, as follows:
At the end of 11th row, break off 2nd ball of A and attach 2nd ball of B.
At the end of 18th row, break off 1st ball of B and attach 1st ball of C.
At the end of 26th row, break off 2nd ball of B and attach 2nd ball of C.
Complete using C only.
34th row Ch3, skip first ch sp, work corner group into next 3ch sps, 1dc into 3rd of first 6ch. Turn.
35th row Ch3. Join with a ss to top of end of corner group. Fasten off. Darn in all ends.

Edging
Using No.J crochet hook, 2 strands of A for 1-color version and 2 strands of B for 3-color version, with RS of work facing, attach yarn with a ss to end of commencing ch.
Next round *Ch1, into next ch sp work 1sc, 2dc, 1sc, rep from * along all edges, skipping 1 ch sp and working into next ch sp along neck edge. Join with a ss into same place as first ss. Fasten off. Darn in all ends.

Tassels
Make 3 tassels in A for 1-color version and 1 each in A, B and C for 3-color version. Cut 40 lengths of yarn each 24in long for 1 tassel. Fold in half and tie around securely, leaving 2 ends of yarn approximately 12in long. Bind off top of tassel securely. Insert hook through top fold loop of tassel, draw through 2 ends of yarn and ch6. Fasten off. With RS of work facing, slip 6ch through center of corner group at point and fasten off securely. Work 2 more tassels in same way.

Finishing
Press lightly on WS under a damp cloth using a warm iron.

Have a fling with several tones of one color or work in a single shade ►
▼ *Close-up of a tassel*

▼ *Shawl fabric stitch detail*

Diamond patterned shawl

Basic Wardrobe Crochet

Crochet this beautiful triangular shawl for day or evening wear. Worked in clusters, it has a pattern of alternating large and small diamonds, and is finished with a deep, looped fringe.

Size

Shawl measures about 50in from center point across center of work to straight edge, excluding fringe.

Gauge
1 large diamond measures about 3¾in across center.

Materials

Bernat Pompadour
12 1oz skeins
One No.G crochet hook
One No.D crochet hook
One piece of cardboard 8in long by 5½in deep.

Shawl

Begin at center back point and work toward longest edge.

Using No.G crochet hook, ch1.

1st row Ch3, into first ch worked (yoh, insert hook into ch, yoh and draw through loop, yoh and draw through 2 loops) 5 times, yoh and draw through all loops on hook—called 1cl—, ch2, 1cl in same st.

2nd row Ch3, 1cl into top of edge cl of previous row, ch2, 1cl between 2cl of previous row, ch2, 1cl into top of edge cl.

3rd row Ch3, 1cl into edge st (the first and last clusters are always worked into the top of

260

cl of previous row, the other cl being worked into spaces), ch5, 1cl before center cl, ch2, 1cl after center cl, ch5, 1 edge cl.

4th row Ch3, 1 edge cl, ch5, 1sc into next sp, ch5, 1 cl between 2cl, ch5, 1sc into next sp, ch5, 1 edge cl.

5th row Ch3, 1 edge cl, ch2, 1cl, ch5, 1sc into next sp, ch5, 1sc into next sp, ch5, 1cl, ch2, 1 edge cl.

6th row Ch3, 1 edge cl, (ch5, 1cl, ch5, 1sc into next sp) twice, ch5, 1cl, ch5, 1 edge cl.

7th row Ch3, 1cl, ch5, 1sc into next sp, ch5, 1sc into next sp, ch5, 1cl, ch2, 1cl, ch5, 1sc, ch5, 1sc, ch5, 1cl.

8th row Ch3, 1cl, ch2, 1cl, ch5, 1sc, ch5, 1cl, ch2, 1cl, ch2, 1cl, ch5, 1sc, ch5, 1cl, ch2, 1cl.

9th row Ch3, 1cl, (ch2, 1cl, ch5, 1sc, ch5, 1sc, ch5, 1cl) twice, ch2, 1cl.

10th row Ch3, 1cl, (ch5, 1cl, ch5, 1sc) 4 times, ch5, 1cl, ch5, 1cl.

11th row Ch3, 1cl, (ch5, 1sc, ch5, 1sc, ch5, 1cl, ch2, 1cl) twice, ch5, 1sc, ch5, 1sc, ch5, 1cl.

12th row Ch3, 1cl, (ch5, 1sc, ch5, 1cl) 6 times.

13th row Ch3, 1cl, (ch5, 1sc, ch5, 1cl, ch2, 1cl, ch5, 1sc) 3 times, ch5, 1cl.

14th row Ch3, 1cl, (ch5, 1sc, ch5, 1cl, ch2, 1cl, ch2, 1cl) 3 times, ch5, 1sc, ch5, 1cl.

15th row As 11th, rep sts in brackets 3 times.

16th row As 12th, rep sts in brackets 8 times.

17th row As 13th, rep sts in brackets 4 times.

18th row As 10th, rep sts in brackets 8 times.

Continue working in this way alternating diamonds with cl of 4 between diamonds with cl of 9.

Work until 3½ diamonds have been completed counting from point. Keeping diamond with large cluster correct, work one repeat replacing small clusters with large ones, then continue as before.

Work until there are 11 complete diamonds, then work half diamond until there are 3cl in the diamond.

Work 1 row sc around edge, working 5sc into 5ch loops and 3sc into 2ch loops.

Next row *Ch3, skip 1sc, 1sc into next sc, rep from * around all edges. Fasten off.

Complete by working fringe on 2 sides only, working loops around cardboard strip (see Crochet Know-how Chapter 18).

▼ *Detail of the shawl opposite*

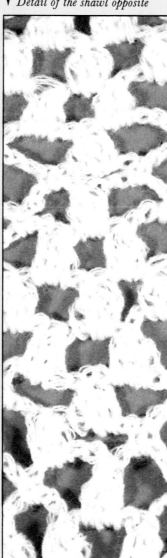

Buttoned top in Tunisian crochet

This attractive buttoned vest is an ideal project for your first attempt at making a garment in Tunisian crochet. The stitch texture combined with the rainbow yarn creates an interesting tapestry effect. The secret of success in making Tunisian crochet garments is not to pull the yarn too tightly as you work, otherwise you will find that the fabric will be on the bias.

Sizes
Directions are for 32in bust. The figures in brackets [ ] refer to the 34, 36 and 38in sizes respectively.
Side seam, 11½in.

Gauge
4½ sts and 4 rows to 1in over classic Tunisian stitch worked with No. G afghan hook

Materials
Bear Brand, Fleisher or Botany Twin-Pak Ombree Win-Knit
2 Twin-Paks (4 balls)
One No.G afghan hook
One No.F crochet hook
6 buttons
Small amount of contrasting yarn

Back

Using No.G afghan hook, ch62[66:70:74].
1st row (forward row working from right to left) Insert hook into 2nd ch from hook, yrh and draw through loops, *insert hook into next ch,
262

yrh and draw through loop, rep from * to end of ch. 62[66:70:74] loops on hook. Do not turn work.
2nd row (backward row worked from left to right without turning work) Yrh and draw through one loop, *yrh and draw through 2 loops, rep from * to end of row. One loop rems on hook. These 2 rows form one complete row.
3rd row (forward row worked from right to left) *Insert hook into first vertical or upright thread on front of work from right to left, yrh and draw through loop, rep from * into each vertical thread to end of row. 62[66:70:74] loops on hook.
4th row (backward row worked from left to right) As 2nd.
The 3rd and 4th rows form the patt and are rep throughout (see Crochet Know-how Chapter 17, classic Tunisian stitch).
Inc one st at each end of next and every following 4th row until there are 76[80:84:88] sts (see Crochet Know-how page 232 for increasing).
Work until 10in or desired length to underarm ending with one loop on hook at right-hand edge of work.

Shape armholes
1st row (forward row)
Work 1ss into next 8[9:10:11] vertical sts, patt 58[60:62:64] sts skipping last 9[10:11:12] sts.
2nd row (backward row) Work to end on 58[60:62:64] sts.
Dec one st at each end of next 6 forward rows. 46[48:50:52] sts.
Work on these sts without further shaping until armholes measure 6[6¼:6½:6¾]in ending at armhole edge with one loop on hook.

Shape shoulders
1st row Work 1ss into each of first 3 vertical threads, patt to end skipping last 4 sts.
2nd row Patt back along row. Rep last 2 rows once more. Fasten off.

Left front

Using No.G afghan hook, work 31[33:35:37] sts. Work 1st to 4th rows as given for back.
Continue in classic Tunisian stitch inc one st at beg of next and every following 4th row until there are 38[40:42:44] sts.
Work without further shaping until same length as back to underarm ending at side edge.

Shape armhole
1st row 1ss into next 8[9:10:11] vertical threads, patt 29[30:31:32] sts.
2nd row Patt back along row.
Dec one st at armhole edge on next 6 forward rows.
Work 4 rows (2 forward, 2 backward rows) ending at side edge with one loop on hook.

Shape neck
1st row Work 18 loops skipping last 5[6:7:8] sts.
2nd row Work back along row.
3rd row Work 15 loops skipping last 3 sts.
4th row Work back along row.
5th row Work 13 loops skipping last 2 sts.
6th row Work back along row.
Dec one st at neck edge on next 2 forward rows.
Work without further shaping until armhole measures same as back to shoulder, ending at

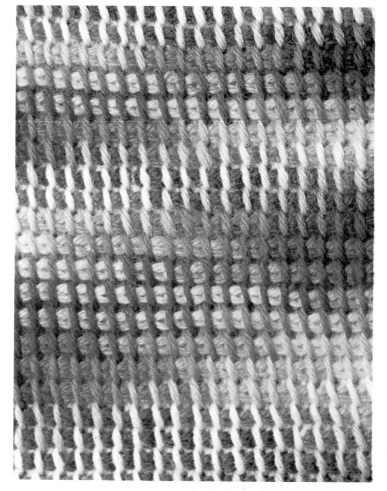

▼ *Detail of Tunisian crochet which is worked one row forward, one back*

side edge with one loop on hook.

Shape shoulder
1st row Work 1ss into each of first 3 vertical threads, patt to end.
2nd row Work back along row. Rep 1st and 2nd rows once more. Fasten off.

Right front

Work as for left front reversing all shaping.

Finishing

Join shoulder seams.

Armhole edgings
Using No.F hook, contrast wool and with RS facing, work 60[64:68:72]sc around armhole. Work 4 rows sc. Join side seams.

Lower edging
Using No.F hook, contrast wool and with RS facing, work 120[126:132:138] sts along lower edge.
Work 6 rows sc, turning at end of each row with 1ch. Fasten off.

Front edging
Using No.F hook, contrast wool and with RS facing, work 50sc along right front, 1sc into top corner, 20[21:22:23]sc up to shoulder, 24[26:28:30]sc along back neck, 20[21:22:23]sc down other side, 1sc into corner of left front and 50sc along lower edge.
Work 1 row sc working 3sc into corner sts.
Mark position for 6 buttonholes on right front and ch3 over marker skipping 3ch on next row, still working 3sc into corner sts.
Work 1 row more, working 3sc into corner sts and 1sc into each ch over buttonholes. Fasten off. Press lightly under a damp cloth using a warm iron. Sew on buttons to correspond to buttonholes.

Gay vest in Tunisian crochet ▶

Crocheted pullover with a ribbed look

The ribbed effect of this classic pullover is achieved by working from side edge to side edge on the body and sleeves. Collar, cuffs and edges are knitted in rib.

Sizes

Directions are for 34in bust. The figures in brackets [] refer to the 36, 38 and 40in sizes respectively.
Length to shoulder including lower ribbing, 22[22½:23:23½] in.
Sleeve seam including cuff, 17½in.

Gauge
15 sts and 18 rows over patt to 4 sq in worked on No.G crochet hook.

Materials

Dawn Wintuk Sports
(2oz skeins)
7[7:8:8] skeins
One No.G crochet hook
One pair No.3 needles

Back

Beg at side edge.
Using No.G crochet hook, ch56.

1st row Into 2nd ch from hook work 1sc, *1sc into next ch, rep from * to end. Turn.

2nd row Ch2, *1sc into next sc working into back loop only, rep from * to end. Turn. The 2nd row forms patt and is rep throughout.

Work 2[2:2:4] rows in patt.
Continue in patt, inc one st at end of next row.
Work 1 row.

264

Shape armhole

Next row Ch20[22:24:26]. Work in patt along ch and across rem sts.
77[79:81:83] sts.
Continue in patt, inc one st at shoulder edge on 6th[8th: 8th:8th] row and every following 6th row, counting from armhole, until there are 80[82:84:86] sts.
Work 13[13:15:15] rows without shaping.
This completes one half back. Work other half to correspond, dec instead of inc and ss over 20[22:24:26] sts for armhole. Finish off.

Front

Work as given for back.

Sleeves

Beg at side edge.
Using No.G crochet hook, ch10.

1st row 1ss into each ch to end. Turn.

2nd row Ch2, *1sc into next st working into back loop only, rep from * to end. Turn.

3rd row Ch10, 1ss into each ch, work 1sc into back loop only of each sc. Turn.

4th row As 2nd.

Continue in patt, inc 10 sts at beg of next and every other row in this way until 5 groups of 10 sts have been added to the first group of 10 sts; *at the same time* shape sleeve cap by inc one st at end of 5th and beg of 6th rows, at end of 7th and beg of 8th and continuing in this way until there are 78[80:82:84] sts in all.
Work 1 row.

Next row Ch18[18:18:20] for saddle top of sleeve, ss along ch and work in patt along rem sts.
Work 6 rows without shaping. This completes half the sleeve. Work other half to correspond, dec instead of inc and ss over groups of 10 sts for underarm seam.

Finishing

Press lightly.
Cuffs Using No.3 needles, with RS facing, pick up and K46[48:50:52] sts along lower edge of sleeve. Work 1½in K1, P1 rib. Bind off in rib.
Back lower ribbing Using No.3 needles, with RS facing, pick up and K110[114:118: 122] sts along lower edge of back. Work 1½in K1, P1 rib. Bind off in rib.
Front lower ribbing Work as given for back lower ribbing.
Join saddle top of sleeves along shoulder edge of left front and back and right front, leaving back seam open.
Collar Using No.3 needles, with RS facing, pick up and K108[108:116:116] sts evenly around neck.
Work 6in K1, P1 rib. Bind off in rib.
Join right back seam and collar. Sew in sleeves to armholes.
Join side and sleeve seams.

◄ *Detail of the ribbed effect*
Pullover with saddle top shoulder ►

Lacy pullover and pompon cap

This lacy-looking crocheted pullover, worked in a simple shell paneled stitch, is paired with a jaunty, pomponned cap worked in a cluster stitch. Although they are of dissimilar patterns, the cap and pullover, both crocheted in the same yarn, combine to make an attractive ensemble, linked by the deeper shaded edging worked on the cap, on the pullover neckline and lower edge.

Sizes
Directions are for 34in bust. The figures in brackets [] refer to the 36 and 38in sizes respectively.
Length down center back, 23½in.
Sleeve seam, 16in.

Gauge
7dc and 5 rows to 2½in worked on No.G crochet hook.

Materials
Bear Brand, Botany or Fleisher Soufflé
Pullover 6[6:7] balls main color A and 1[1:1] ball contrast color B
One No.G crochet hook
Cap 2 balls main color A
Small quantity contrast color B
One No.G crochet hook
One No.H crochet hook

Pullover back

Using No.G crochet hook and A, ch68[72:76].
1st row Into 2nd ch from hook work 1sc, *1sc into next

ch, rep from * to end. Turn.
2nd row (RS) Ch3, 1dc into each of next 7[9:11] sts, *skip 3 sts, work 4dc, ch1, 4dc all into next st to form 1 group, skip 3 sts, 1dc into each of next 8 sts, rep from * ending last rep with 8[10:12]dc. Turn.
3rd row Ch3, 1dc into each of next 7[9:11]dc, *ch3, 1sc into center of group, ch3, 1dc into each of next 8dc, rep from * ending last rep with 8[10:12]dc. Turn.
These 2 rows form patt and are repeated throughout. Continue in patt until work measures 16in from beg or desired length to underarm, ending with a 3rd patt row.

Shape raglan armholes
1st row Ss over 3[4:5] sts, patt to last 3[4:5] sts. Turn.
Continue in patt, dec one dc at each end of every row until side panel dcs have been worked off and group panel sts are reached. Then dec across groups by working ½ group less on WS rows, then continue to dec 1dc at each end of every row until 1[2:3]dc, 1 group, 8dc, 1 group, 1[2:3]dc rem. Fasten off.

Pullover front

Work as given for back shaping raglan armholes in same way until 5[6:7]dc, 1 group, 8dc, 1 group, 5[6:7]dc rem.

Shape neck
Work shoulders separately on sts outside groups on either

side of central panel, working 1dc less at armhole edge as before; *at the same time* dec 1dc at neck edge on every other row until all sts have been worked off. Fasten off.

Sleeves

Using No.G crochet hook and A, ch32[32:34].
1st row As given for back.
2nd row Ch3, 1dc into each of next 4[4:5] sts, skip 3 sts, 1 group, skip 3 sts, 1dc into each of next 8 sts, skip 3 sts, 1 group, skip 3 sts, 1dc into each of next 5[5:6] sts. Turn.
3rd row Ch3, 1dc into each of next 4[4:5] sts, ch3, 1sc into group, ch3, 8dc, ch3, 1sc into group, ch3, 5[5:6]dc. Turn.
Continue in patt, inc one dc at each end of every 4th row until there are 13[13:14]dc at either side of groups.
Continue without shaping until sleeve measures 16in from beg or desired length to underarm, ending with a 3rd patt row.

Shape raglan armhole
1st row Ss over 3[4:5] sts, patt to last 3[4:5] sts. Turn.
2nd row Ss over 2 sts, patt to last 2 sts. Turn.
Rep 2nd row 3 times more. Continue dec 1dc at each end of every row until 4[4:6]dc rem. Fasten off.

Finishing

Press lightly.
Join raglan, side and sleeve seams.
Edges Using No.G crochet hook and B, with RS of work facing, work 2 rounds sc around sleeve edges and 4 rounds sc around neck edge. Fasten off.

Cap

Using No.H crochet hook and 3 strands of A, ch3.
Join into a circle with ss into first ch.
1st round Ch2, work 5sc into circle. Join with ss into 2nd of first 2ch.
2nd round Yoh, insert hook into first st, yoh and pull up a

long st, yoh, insert hook into same st, yoh and draw up a loop, yoh and draw through all 5 loops on hook, ch1—this forms 1 cluster—work 1 cluster in same st, *2 clusters in next sc, rep from * to end. Join with ss to top of first cluster.
3rd round *1 cluster in next sp between clusters of previous row, 2 clusters in next sp, rep from * to end. Join with ss to top of first cluster.
4th round *1 cluster in each of next 2 sp, 2 clusters in next sp, rep from * to end. Join with ss to top of first cluster.
5th round *1 cluster in each of next 3 sp, 2 clusters in next sp, rep from * to end. Join with ss to top of first cluster.
6th round *1 cluster in each of next 4 sp, 2 clusters in next sp, rep from * to end. Join with ss to top of first cluster.
7th round *1 cluster in each of next 5 sp, 2 clusters in next sp, rep from * to end. Join with ss to top of first cluster.
8th round *1 cluster in next sp, rep from * to end. Join with ss to top of first cluster.
Rep 8th round 3 times more.
Change to No.G crochet hook.
12th round Ch2, *1sc into next sp, rep from * to end. Join with ss to 2nd of first 2ch.
13th round Ch2, *1sc into next sc, rep from * to end. Join with ss to 2nd of first 2ch. Break off yarn and darn in ends.

Peak

Using No.H crochet hook and 3 strands of A, ch20. Work every row sc, dec one st at beg of every row until 12sc rem. Fasten off.

Finishing

Sew peak in place. Using No.G crochet hook and 3 strands of B, work 1 row sc along all edges. Trim top with large pompon (see Crochet Know-how page 196).

Peaked cap and a lacy pullover ►

266

High-necked jacket

Basic Wardrobe Crochet

This elegant, high-buttoned, open-work crocheted cardigan has been cleverly designed in a range of sizes suitable for all figure types. Made in beige or in your favorite color, it looks stunning with skirts and pants.

Sizes

Directions are for 34in bust. The figures in brackets [ ] refer to the 36, 38, 40, 42 and 44in sizes respectively. Length down center back, 21½[21½:22:23½:24]in. Sleeve seam, 16½[17:17:17½: 17½:18]in, adjustable.

Gauge

For 34, 36 and 38in sizes, 1 motif of 3dc and 1 picot measures approximately ¾in worked on No.E crochet hook.
For 40, 42 and 44in sizes, 1 motif of 3dc and 1 picot measures approximately 1in worked on No.F crochet hook.

Materials

Bernat Pompadour 9[9:10:10:11:11] 1oz balls
One No.E crochet hook for 34, 36 and 38in sizes
One No.F crochet hook for 40, 42 and 44in sizes
Seven buttons

Back

Using No.E[E:E:F:F:F] hook, ch87[91:95:87:91:95].
1st row (WS) Into 6th ch from hook work 1sc, *ch3, 1sc into first of 3ch to form 1 picot, 1sc into next ch, ch2,

skip 2ch, 1sc into next ch, rep from * to end of row. Turn.
2nd row Ch3, 2dc into ch2 sp of previous row, *ch2, 3dc into next ch2 sp, rep from * to end of row. Turn.
3rd row Ch4, *work 1sc, 1 picot, 1sc all into next ch2 sp, ch2, rep from * ending with 1sc after 2nd last dc of previous row. Turn.
The 2nd and 3rd rows form patt and are rep throughout.
Continue without shaping until work measures 14 [14:14:15:15:15]in from beg, ending with a 2nd row.

Shape armholes

1st row 1ss into each of next 2 sts, 2sc into next sp skipping picot, patt to last sp, 2sc into sp skipping picot. Turn.
2nd row 1ss into next st, work 1sc, 1hdc, 1dc all into next sp, patt to last sp, work 1dc, 1hdc, 1sc into last sp. Turn.
3rd row As 1st.
4th row 1ss into next st, ch3, 2dc into next sp, patt to last sp, 3dc into last sp. Turn.
Continue without shaping until armholes measure 7[7:7½:8:8:8½]in from beg.

Shape shoulders

Keeping patt correct, work 2 patt less at each end of next and following alt row. Work 1 row in patt.
Work 1[1:1½:1:1:1½] patt less on next row.
Fasten off.

Left front

Using No.E[E:E:F:F:F] hook, ch47[51:59:47:51:59].
Work as given for back until

left front measures same as back to armhole, ending with a 2nd patt row.

Shape armhole

Work ½ patt less at armhole edge on next 6 rows.
Continue without shaping until armhole measures 5[5:5½:6:6:6½]in from beg.

Shape neck

Keeping patt correct, work 1 patt less at neck edge 2[3:3:2:3:3] times, then ½ patt less 1[1:2:1:1:2] times. Continue without shaping until armhole measures same as back to shoulder, ending at armhole edge.

Shape shoulder

Work 2 patt less at shoulder edge of next and following alt row. Work 1 row. Work 1[1:1½:1:1:1½] patt less on next row. Fasten off.

Right front

Work as given for left front, reversing all shaping.

Sleeves

Using No.E[E:E:F:F:F] hook, ch35[39:39:35:39:39].
Work in patt as given for back, inc one dc at each end of 6th and every following 2nd row, working the dc into patt as they are made, until there are 4 complete motifs extra at each end.
Continue without shaping until sleeve measures 16½ [17:17:17½:17½:18]in from beg, or desired length to underarm.

Shape cap

Work ½ patt less at each end of every row 13[14:14: 13:14:14] times. Fasten off.

Finishing

DO NOT PRESS.
Leave each piece flat between damp towels until dry. Join shoulder, side and sleeve seams. Sew in sleeves.
Front borders. Using No. E[E:E:F:F:F] hook, work 1 row sc up right front, around neck and down left front, working 3sc into front corner sts. Turn.
Work 3 more rows sc in same way.
5th row (buttonhole row) Mark positions for 7 buttons on left front, the first one 8 sts from the lower edge and the 7th one in the neckband with 5 more spaced evenly between. Work in sc to end, making buttonholes as markers are reached by working 3ch and skipping 3sc. Work 3sc into corner sts and dec 7sc evenly around neck edge, work in sc to end. Turn.
6th row Work in sc to end, working 3sc into ch3 sp of previous row. Turn.
Work 3 more rows sc, dec 7 times evenly around neck edge on 3rd row.
Last row Work 1 row sc, continuing along lower edge of cardigan. Fasten off.
Sleeve edges. Work 1 row sc along cuff edge of each sleeve. Fasten off.
Sew on buttons to correspond to buttonholes.

▼ *Stitch detail*   *Casually elegant coordinated with a skirt* ►

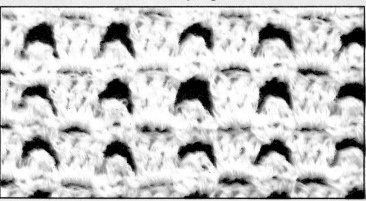

268

Buttoned coat dress

This crocheted midi-cardigan in softest cotton can be worn as a buttoned coat dress or as a tunic over pants. Make it in sparkling white with bands of lavender, light blue and navy as shown here or try French navy with scarlet and gray for the contrasting midriff panel.

Sizes
Directions are for 32in bust with 34in hips.
The figures in brackets [] refer to the 34, 36 and 38in bust sizes with 36, 38 and 40in hips, respectively.
Length to shoulder, 41[41½:41½:42]in, adjustable.

Gauge
5dc and 2½ rows to 1in worked on No.E crochet hook.

Materials
Reynolds Sonata
(50gm balls)
9[11:12:13] balls of main color A
2[2:3:3] balls of contrast B
2 balls each of contrasts C and D
One No.D crochet hook
One No.E crochet hook
Nine buttons

Bodice

Using No.E crochet hook and B, ch136[146:156:166] and work bodice in one piece to underarm.
Base row Into 2nd ch from hook work 1sc, 1sc into each ch to end. Turn. 135[145:155:165] sts.

Commence colored patt.
1st row Using B, ch2, skip first sc, 1sc into each sc to end. Turn.
2nd and 3rd rows As 1st.
4th row Using D, ch2, 1sc into first sc, *1sc into next sc, skip 1sc, 1sc into next sc, 2sc into each of next 2sc, rep from * to last 4sc, 1sc into next sc, skip 1sc, 1sc into next sc, 2sc into last sc. Turn. 162[174:186:198] sts.
5th row Using D, ch2, 1sc into first sc, *1sc into next sc, skip 2sc, 1sc into next sc, 2sc into each of next 2sc, rep from * to last 4sc, skip 2sc, 1sc into next sc, 2sc into last sc. Turn.
6th and 7th rows Using C, as 5th. Break off C.
8th row Using D, ch2, skip first sc, *1dc into next sc, 1tr into each of next 2sc, 1dc into next sc, 1sc into each of next 2sc, rep from * to last 5sc, 1dc into next sc, 1tr into each of next 2sc, 1dc into next sc, 1sc into last sc. Turn.
9th row Using C, ch2, skip first st, *1sc into next st, 2sc into each of next 2 sts, 1sc into next st, skip 2 sts, rep from * ending skip 1 st. Turn.
10th row As 9th. Break off C.
11th and 12th rows Using D, as 9th and 10th. Break off D.
13th row Using B, ch2, skip first sc, 1sc into next sc, *skip next st, 1sc into each of next 5 sts, rep from * to last 4 sts, skip next st, 1sc into each of last 3 sts. Turn. 135[145:155:165] sts.
Work rows 1-12 once more.
Change to No.D crochet hook and, using B, work 4 rows sc across all sts. 162[174:186:198] sts. Break off B.
Change to No.E crochet hook and attach A.
1st row Ch3, skip first st, *1dc into next st, rep from * to end. Turn.
Rep this row until work measures 8½in from beg or desired length to underarm, ending with a WS row.

Divide for back and fronts
1st row Work in dc across 35[38:40:43] sts. Turn.
Complete right front on these sts.
Next row Ss across first st, work in dc to end. Turn.

Shape right front neck
Next row Ss across 9[9:10:10] sts, work in dc to within 1 st of last st. Turn.
Next row Ss across first st, work in dc to within 1 st of last st. Turn. 22[25:26:29] sts.
Rep last row until 12[13:14:15] sts rem.
Continue without shaping until armhole measures 6½[7:7:7½]in from beg. Fasten off.
With RS of work facing, skip next 11[11:13:13] sts, attach yarn and work in dc across next 70[76:80:86] sts. Turn.
Complete back on these sts.
Next row Ss across first st, work in dc to within 1 st of last st. Turn.
Rep last row until 54[58:62:66] sts rem.
Continue without shaping until back measures same as right front to shoulder. Fasten off.
With RS of work facing, skip next 11[11:13:13] sts, attach yarn to rem sts and work to end.
Complete left front on these sts.
Next row Work in dc to within 1 st of last st. Turn.

Shape left front neck
Next row Ss across first st, work in dc to last 9[9:10:10] sts. Turn.
Next row Ss across first st, work in dc to within 1 st of last st. Turn.
Rep last row until 12[13:14:15] sts rem.
Complete to match right front.

Skirt

Using No.D crochet hook and A, with RS of work facing, attach yarn with ss to first st of left front.
1st row Ch3, 1dc into each of next 3[7:4:1] sts, (2dc into next st, 1dc into each of next 8[7:7:7] sts) 14[16:18:20] times, 2dc into next st, 1dc into each of next 4[8:5:2] sts. Turn. 150[162:174:186] sts.
2nd row Ch3, skip first st, *1dc into next st, rep from * to end. Turn.
Change to No.E crochet hook. Work 3 rows dc.

Shape skirt
1st inc row Ch3, 1dc into each of next 11[12:13:14] sts, (2dc into next st, 1dc into each of next 24[26:28:30] sts) 5 times, 2dc into next st, 1dc into each of last 12[13:14:15] sts. Turn. 156[168:180:192] sts.
Work 3 rows dc.
2nd inc row Ch3, 1dc into each of next 11[12:13:14] sts, (2dc into next st, 1dc into each of next 25[27:29:31] sts) 5 times, 2dc into next st, 1dc into each of last 13[14:15:16] sts. Turn. 162[174:186:198] sts.
Work 3 rows dc.
3rd inc row Ch3, 1dc into each of next 12[13:14:15] sts, (2dc into next st, 1dc into each of next 26[28:30:32] sts) 5 times, 2dc into next st, 1dc into each of last 13[14:15:16] sts. Turn. 168[180:192:204] sts.
Work 5 rows dc.
4th inc row Ch3, 1dc into each of next 12[13:14:15] sts, (2dc into next st, 1dc into each of next 27[29:31:33] sts) 5 times, 2dc into next st, 1dc into each of last 14[15:16:17] sts. Turn. 174[186:198:210] sts.
Work 5 rows dc.
5th inc row Ch3, 1dc into each of next 13[14:15:16] sts, (2dc into next st, 1dc into each of next 28[30:32:34] sts) 5 times, 2dc into next st, 1dc into each of last 14[15:16:17] sts. Turn. 180[192:204:216] sts.
Work 7 rows dc.
6th inc row Ch3, 1dc into each of next 13[14:15:16] sts, (2dc into next st, 1dc into each of next 29[31:33:35] sts) 5 times, 2dc into next st, 1dc into

each of last 15[16:17:18] sts.
Turn. 186[198:210:222] sts.
Work 7 rows dc.
7th inc row Ch3, 1dc into
each of next 14[15:16:17] sts,
(2dc into next st, 1dc into each
of next 30[32:34:36] sts) 5
times, 2dc into next st, 1dc into
each of last 15[16:17:18] sts.
Turn. 192[204:216:228] sts.
Work 7 rows dc.
8th inc row Ch3, 1dc into
each of next 14[15:16:17] sts,
(2dc into next st, 1dc into each
of next 31[33:35:37] sts) 5
times, 2dc into next st, 1dc into
each of last 16[17:18:19] sts.
Turn. 198[210:222:234] sts.
Work 9 rows dc.
9th inc row Ch3, 1dc into
each of next 15[16:17:18] sts,
(2dc into next st, 1dc into each
of next 32[34:36:38] sts) 5
times, 2dc into next st, 1dc
into each of last 16[17:18:19]
sts. Turn. 204[216:228:240]
sts.
Continue without shaping
until work measures 40½[41:
41:41½]in from top of shoulder,
or desired length less ½in.
Fasten off.

Finishing

Press on WS under a damp
cloth using a warm iron. Join
shoulder seams.
Armbands Using No.D
crochet hook and B, with RS
facing, work 1 row sc around
armhole. Turn. Work 2 more
rows sc. Fasten off.
Front borders Using No.
D crochet hook and B, with
RS facing, work in sc up
right front edge, around neck,
down left front and around
lower edge, working 3sc into
each corner st. Turn.
Next row (buttonhole row)
Work in sc, making 9
buttonholes on right front
edge, the 1st to come just
below neck shaping and rem
8, 2½in apart, by working 3ch
and skipping 3sc, and working
3sc into each corner st. Turn.
Next row Work in sc to end,
working 3sc into each ch3
buttonhole on previous row.
Fasten off.
Join armbands. Press borders.
Sew on buttons to correspond
with buttonholes.

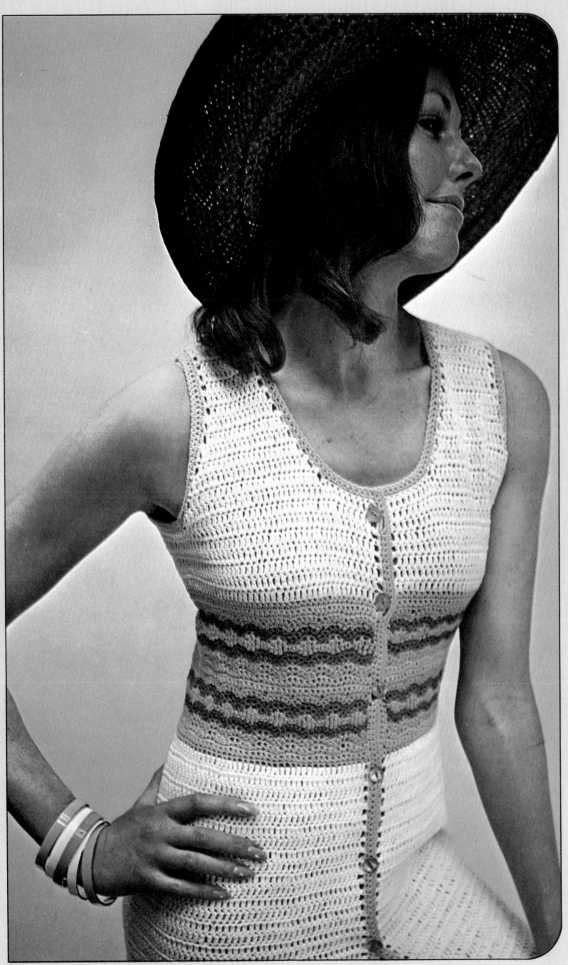

271

Charleston dress in crochet

This youthfully styled dress has the lively look of the "roaring twenties." The cleverly shaped double crochet panel insures a perfect fit and the brief patterned yoke lends a demure touch. Wear it on its own as a cool summer dress or as a dashing tunic over slim pants, or add a glittering belt for fashionable evening glamour.

Sizes

Directions are for 34in bust with 36in hips.
The figures in brackets [ ] refer to the 36 and 38in bust sizes with 38 and 40in hips, respectively.
Length down center back, 31¾in

Gauge

One patt rep of 8dc and 1 group and 7 rows to 3in over patt worked on No.D crochet hook

Materials

Dawn Wintuk Sports
7[7:8] 2oz skeins
One No.D crochet hook
One button

Back

Using No.D crochet hook, ch125[129:133].
1st row Into 2nd ch from hook work 1sc, *1sc into next ch, rep from * to end. Turn.
2nd row Ch2, 1dc into each of next 5[7:9] sts, *skip 3 sts of previous row, work 4dc, ch1, 4dc all into next st to form group, skip 3 sts of previous row, 1dc into each of next 8

sts, rep from * ending last rep with 6[8:10]dc. Turn.
3rd row Ch2, 1dc into each of next 5[7:9] sts, *ch4, 1sc into ch sp in center of dc group, ch4, 1dc into each of next 8 sts, rep from *ending last rep with 6[8:10]dc. Turn.
4th row Ch2, 1dc into each of next 5[7:9] sts, *into sc in center of group work 4dc, ch1, 4dc group, 1dc into each of next 8 sts, rep from * ending last rep with 6[8:10] dc. Turn.
Rep 3rd and 4th patt rows until work measures 4in, ending with a 4th patt row.
1st dec row Ch2, 1[2:3]dc, work next 2dc tog to dec thus: (yoh, insert hook into next st, yoh and draw loop through, yoh and draw through 2 loops) twice, yoh, draw through all 3 loops on hook, 2[3:4]dc, *ch4, 1sc into center ch of group, ch4, 1dc into each of next 3dc, dec by working 2dc tog as before, 1dc into each of next 3dc, rep from * ending last rep by working 2dc tog in center of the panel.

Continue in patt noting that there will be one dc less in each panel.
Dec one dc in the center of each panel in this way when work measures 8, 16 and 19in. There should now be 2[4:6]dc at each side and 4dc in central panels.
Work 2in without shaping. Inc one dc in center of each panel by working 2dc into one st.
Continue without shaping until work measures 25in from beg, ending with a 3rd patt row.

Shape armholes
1st row Ss to center of 1st group, ch3, 3dc into same st as base of ch, work in patt to last group, 4dc into sc. Turn.
2nd row Ch1, 1dc into each of next 5dc panel, work in patt to last half group, 1sc into last dc. Turn.
3rd row Ss to first dc, ch3, 1dc into each of next 4dc, work in patt to last dc panel, 1dc into each of 5dc. Turn.
Complete next 3rd patt row.

Divide for center back
Work 1 row dc to one st before center st, working 1dc into each dc, 3dc into ch sps and 1dc into sc. Turn. 38dc.
Work 1 row dc.
Continue in patt on these sts, beg at armhole edge.
1st row Ch2, 1dc, *skip 3 sts, work 1 group in next st, skip 3 sts, 1dc, rep from * ending with 1 group, skip 3 sts, 1dc into each of next 5dc. Turn.

2nd row Ch2, 1dc into each of next 4dc, *ch4, 1sc into center of group, ch4, 1dc into dc, rep from * ending with 2dc. Turn.
3rd row Ch2, 1dc, *1 group in sc, 1dc in dc, rep from * ending with 5dc. Turn.
Rep 2nd and 3rd rows 3 times more, then 2nd row once.

Shape neck and shoulder
Continue in patt working 1dc only at neck edge on next row and half a group less at same edge until 3 groups rem. Work next 2nd row to give straight edge. Fasten off.
Complete other side to correspond, reversing shaping.

Front

Work as given for back until 1st row of dc for yoke is completed, omitting back opening. 77dc.
Work 1 row dc, dec 1dc at each end of row.
Continue in patt as given for back yoke, beg and ending each row with 2dc.
Continue until 5 group rows have been completed. Work one 2nd row.

Shape neck
Work in patt to center 3 groups, turn.
Complete shoulder on these sts.
Continue in patt, dec 1dc at neck edge on next row only (3 groups rem), until armhole measures same as back to shoulder. Fasten off.
Attach yarn to other side of 3 central groups and work other side to correspond.

Finishing

Press lightly.
Join side and shoulder seams.
Armbands Work 2 rows sc around each armhole. Fasten off.
Neckband Work 2 rows sc around neck and edge of back opening. Make button loop at top of opening. Sew on button to other side of opening.

◄ *Close-up detail of double panel*
Simply styled and simply pretty ►

Cloaks in crochet

Once regarded as strictly an evening garment, the cloak nowadays has taken on a new importance in fashion for much more general wear and can be worn equally well over skirts, dresses and pants.

Warmly practical and yet immensely glamorous, this hooded cloak is comparatively simple to crochet using a basic square motif, plus a triangular motif to give shape to the cloak and the hood. In two colors or a single color, the instructions are for both women's and children's sizes.

Sizes

Directions are for 22-32in chest and 36-40in bust. The figures in brackets [] refer to the 36-40in size. Length down center back, 22[42]in, adjustable.

Gauge

Each square measures 3½in x 3½in worked on No.E crochet hook

Materials

Bernat Sesame
(2oz skeins)
One-color version
10[25] skeins
Two-color version
6[14] skeins of main color A
7[15] skeins of contrast B
One No.E crochet hook
One No.H crochet hook
3½[6½] yards of ½in wide velvet ribbon
2[3] frog fastenings
One spool of shirring elastic

274

Note

One 2oz skein makes approximately 10 squares in one color;
or 19 squares using A for first 3 rounds;
or completes 21 squares using B for last round.

Cape

Square motif

Using No.E crochet hook and A, ch5. Join to form a circle with a ss into first ch.
1st round Using A, ch3 and work 14dc into circle. Join with a ss into 3rd of first 3ch.
2nd round Using A, ch6, *skip 1dc, 1sc into next dc, ch4, rep from * 6 times more. Join with a ss into 2nd of first 6ch.
3rd round Using A, ch3, 2dc into first ch sp, *ch1, into next ch sp work 3dc, ch2, 3dc—called work corner —ch1, 3dc into next ch sp, rep from * twice more, ch1, work corner into next ch sp, ch1. Join with a ss into 3rd of first 3 ch, leaving 2 loops on hook.
4th round Complete using A, or break off A and attach B, pull through 2 loops on hook, ch2, 3dc into ch1 sp, ch 1, *work corner into ch2 sp between dc, (ch1, 3dc into ch1 sp) twice, ch1, rep from * twice more, work corner into ch2 sp, ch1, 3dc into last ch1 sp. Join with a ss into 2nd of first 2ch. Fasten off. Darn in all ends.
Make 66[211] more squares in the same way, allowing 15[21] squares for each row subtracted or added if you are altering the length.

Triangle motif

Using No.E crochet hook and A, ch4. Join to form a circle with a ss into first ch.
1st round Using A, ch3 and work 10dc into circle. Join with a ss into 3rd of first 3ch.
2nd round As 2nd round of square, rep from * 4 times.
3rd round As 3rd round of square, rep from * once.
4th round As 4th round of square, rep from * once.
Fasten off. Darn in all ends. Make 10[15] more triangles in same way.

Hood

Using No.E crochet hook, work 18[33] square motifs as given for cape.
Work 5[6] triangle motifs as given for cape.

Finishing

Press each motif under a damp cloth with a warm iron. Using color worked on last round, join motifs together with a darning needle or crochet hook using sc.

Cape

The points of all the triangle motifs should be placed toward neck edge.
1st row (neck edge) Beg with a square, join 1 square to 1 triangle using a total of 4[5] squares and 3[4] triangles, ending with 1

square.
2nd row Join 1[2] squares, 1 triangle, 1 square, 1 triangle, 3 squares, 1 triangle, 1 square, 1 triangle, 1[2] squares.
3rd row Join 2[3] squares, 1 triangle, 1 square, 1 triangle, 5 squares, 1 triangle, 1 square, 1 triangle, 2[3] squares.
Small size only:
4th row (arm slits) Join 2 squares and leave last edge free, join 11 squares and leave last edge free, join 2 squares.
5th and 6th rows Join 15 squares.
Large size only:
4th row Join 4 squares, 1 triangle, 1 square, 1 triangle, 7 squares, 1 triangle, 1 square, 1 triangle, 4 squares.
5th row (arm slits) Join 3 squares and leave last edge free, join 15 squares and leave last edge free, join 3 squares.
6th row As 5th.
7th-12th rows Join 21 squares. Join all rows together leaving arm slits 2[3] squares in from front edge on 4th [5th-6th] rows.

Hood

1st row (neck edge) As cape.
2nd row Join 7[9] squares. Rep 2nd row once more for large size only.
Next row (crown edge) Join 2[3] squares, 1 triangle

▼ *Stitch detail of the square motif and frog fastening*

with point to crown, 1 square, 1 triangle with point to crown, 2[3] squares.

Next row (crown) Join 2[3] squares and insert into crown edge row to close hood. Press all seams. Join neck edge of hood to neck edge of cape. With RS work facing, No.E crochet hook and color used on last round, beg at neck edge of hood and work ribbon-slot edging as follows:

Next row Ch7, *1tr into ch sp, ch3, rep from * all around edge of hood and cape, working 3tr with ch3 between into corners. Join with a ss into 4th of first 7ch. Fasten off. Thread ribbon through slots, easing fullness around face edge of hood. Sew ribbon ends together. Work edging along inside edge of arm slits in same way. Thread with ribbon. Sew down ends.

Alternative picot edging

Attach yarn as given for ribbon-slot edging.

1st row Ch1, work 1sc into each dc and ch1 sp around all edges, working 3sc into each corner sp. Join with a ss into first ch.

2nd row Ch2, work 1sc into each sc, making a picot of ch4 with ss to first ch on top of every 17th sc, and working 1sc, 1sc with picot, 1sc into each corner sc. Join with a ss into 2nd of first 2ch. Fasten off. Darn in ends. Work 2 rows along arm slits in same way.

To make frog fastening

Using No.H crochet hook and 3 strands of yarn, make button loop fastening by working 80ch. Fasten off. Darn in ends. Twist into rings and stitch together as illustrated. Make 1[2] more button loops in same way. Make 2[3] button fastenings as given for button loops, working 70ch and omitting loop for button. To work buttons see Crochet Know-how Chapter 7. Weave 2 rows shirring elastic around neck edge on WS. Sew on frog fastenings.

Elegant town coat

This slim and elegant town coat is warm enough for early spring yet, being unlined, is light enough to be indispensable to your summer wardrobe. The skirt and bodice are worked in an easy patterned stitch with simple doubles used for the yoke, sleeves, collar and pocket.

Although the photograph shows the coat worked in green crepe yarn with white trim, you can, of course, choose any color or colors you like. Directions for crocheting buttons are in Crochet Know-how Chapter 7.

Sizes

Directions are for 34in bust with 36in hips.
The figures in brackets [] refer to the 36, 38 and 40in bust sizes with 38, 40 and 42in hips.
Length from shoulder, 39 [39½: 40: 40½]in.
Sleeve seam, 17in adjustable.

> **Gauge**
> 8dc to 2in in width worked on No.F hook. 1 rep of patt to measure 3½ in in depth worked on Nos. F & G hooks.

Materials

Unger English Crepe 17[18:20:21] 1oz balls in main color A
1 ball in contrast color B
One No.F crochet hook
One No.G crochet hook
Seven buttons

Back

Using No.F crochet hook and A, ch98[102:106:110].

276

Base row Skip 2ch, work 1dc into each ch to end. Ch3 to turn. 97[101:105:109]dc.
Work 1 row dc.
Continue in patt:
1st row (right side) Using No.F crochet hook, work in dc to end. Ch2 to turn.
2nd row Using No.G crochet hook, work in sc to end. Ch2 to turn.
3rd row *Skip 1sc, 1dc into each of next 3sc, put hook in front of last 3dc and into skipped sc, yoh, draw through long loop, yoh, draw through 2 loops on hook, rep from * to last st, 1sc into last st. Ch1 to turn.
4th row Work 1sc into each st to end. Ch2 to turn.
Rep 3rd and 4th rows once more.
7th row Using No.F crochet hook, work 1dc into each st to end. Ch2 to turn.
Rep 7th row 4 times more, ending last row with ch1 to turn.
Rows 2-11 form patt.
Rep rows 2-11 once more.**
Rep 2-11 patt rows 5 times more, dec 8sts evenly across the first row of 1st, 3rd and 5th patt rep. 73[77:81:85] sts.
Rep 2-11 patt rows twice more, inc 4sts evenly across the first row of 1st and 2nd patt rep. 81[85:89:93] sts.
Continue working each row in dc only until work measures 31in from beg or required length to underarm, ending with a WS row. Skip turning ch at end of last row.

Shape armholes
Next row Ss over 9[10:11:12] sts, work in dc to last 9[10:11:

12] sts. Ch2 to turn. 63[65:67:69] sts.
Continue without shaping until armholes measure 8[8½:9:9½]in, ending with a WS row.

Shape shoulders
Next row Ss over 6[6:7:7] sts, work in dc to last 6[6:7:7] sts. Turn. Rep last row once more.
Next row Ss over 7[7:6:6] sts, work in dc to last 7 [7:6:6] sts.
Fasten off.

Right front

Using No.F crochet hook and A, ch50[54:58:62].
Work as given for back to ** 49[53:57:61] sts.
Rep 2-11 patt rows 5 times more, dec 4sts evenly across the first row of 1st, 3rd and 5th patt rep. 37[41:45:49] sts.
Rep 2-11 patt rows twice more, inc 4sts evenly across the first row of 1st patt rep. 41[45:49:53] sts.
1st and 2nd sizes only
Work 1 row dc, inc 3[1] sts across the row. 44[46] sts.
3rd and 4th sizes only
Work 1 row dc, dec 1[3] sts across the row. 48[50] sts.
All sizes
Continue working in dc until work measures same as back to underarm, ending at armhole edge.

Shape armhole
Next row Ss over 9[10:11:12] sts, work in dc to end. 35[36: 37:38] sts.
Continue without shaping until armhole measures 5 rows less than back to shoulder, ending at armhole edge.

Shape neck
Next row Work in dc to last 10sts. Turn.
Continue in dc, dec one st at neck edge on next 4 rows.

Shape shoulder
Next row Dec one st, work in dc to last 6[6:7:7] sts. Turn.
Next row Ss over 6[6:7:7] sts, work in dc to last 2sts, dec one st.
Fasten off.

Left front

Work as given for right front, reversing all shapings.

Sleeves (two alike)

Using No.F crochet hook and A, ch35[37:41:41]. Work base row as given for back, then work in dc for 2in. Continue in dc, inc one st at each end of next and every other row until there are 70[72:76:76]sts.
Continue without shaping until work measures 17in from beg, or required length to underarm. Place colored marker at each end of last row. Work 2in more for cap of sleeve, which is set into armhole. Fasten off.

Collar

Join shoulder seams.
Using No.F crochet hook and A and with WS of work facing, work in dc over center 8sts of back neck, ss over all sts to end of back neck. Ch3 to turn. Work in dc over all sts of back neck, work in dc

Sparkling white on shamrock green ►
▼ Pattern stitch and pocket detail

over 7sts of left front neck.
Ch3 to turn.
Work in dc to right shoulder,
work in dc over 7sts of right
front neck. Ch3 to turn.
Continue working in dc across
all neck sts, inc one st at each
end of every other row; *at
the same time* inc 4sts evenly
across every other row 3 times.
Fasten off.

Pocket flaps (2 alike)

Using No.F crochet hook
and A, ch12.
Work 5 rows dc.
Fasten off.
Attach yarn to side edge and
work 1 row dc around 3 sides
of pocket, working 2sts in
each corner st. Break off A
and attach B. Work 1 row dc
as before.
Fasten off.

Finishing

Press all pieces lightly on WS
under a damp cloth with a
warm iron. Sew side seams.
Sew sleeve seams as far as
markers. Sew in sleeves, sewing
cap of sleeves from markers
to bound-off sts at underarms.

Edging

Using No.F crochet hook
and A and with RS facing,
attach yarn to lower edge of
right front and work 1 row
dc along right front edge,
working 7 buttonholes evenly
spaced by skipping the length
of the button required and
working ch3, the first
buttonhole to come 9in from
lower edge and the last 8in
below neck shaping; continue
in dc around revers and collar
working twice into corners sts,
and down left front. Break
off A. Attach B and with RS
facing beg at side seam and
work 1 row dc evenly all
around edges of coat, working
twice into corner sts.
Fasten off.
Using No.F crochet hook
and B, work 1 row dc around
cuffs.
Fasten off.
Press all seams. Sew on
pocket flaps and buttons.

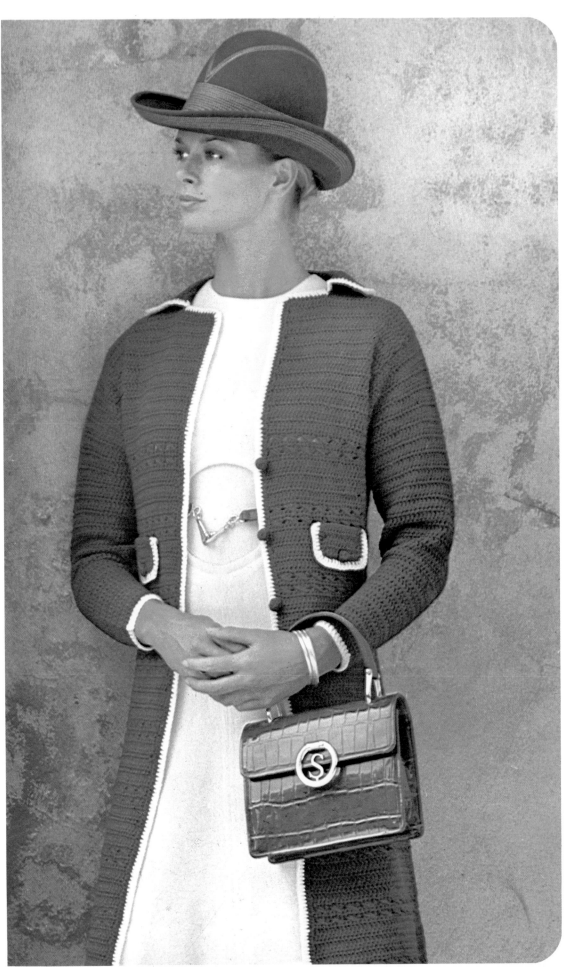

Silver evening bolero

As an example of how a simple motif design can be lifted into the couture category, this brief bolero has been worked in silver yarn. The charm of this particular design is that as each motif is worked, it is joined to the last motif completed as part of the final round of crochet, thus avoiding the necessity of sewing motifs together. This method of working also produces a lighter and more flexible fabric.

Glamorous worn on its own with a long skirt or harem pants, the bolero also looks elegant over a full-sleeved blouse or classic dress.

Size

Directions are for 34-36in bust. Length down center back, 13¾in.

Gauge

Each motif measures 4¼in sq when blocked.

Materials

Bucilla Brocade—5 balls
One No.G crochet hook
Six small buttons

1st motif

Using No.G crochet hook, ch8. Join with ss to first ch to form circle.

1st round Ch2, work 15sc into circle. Join with ss to 2nd of first 2ch.

2nd round Ch5, *skip 1sc, 1hdc into next sc, ch3, rep from * 6 times. Join with ss to 2nd of first 5ch.

3rd round Work 1sc, 1hdc, 3dc, 1hdc, 1sc into each ch sp. Join with ss to first sc (8 petals).

4th round Ch2, *ch3, 1sc into top of next petal, ch6, 1sc into top of next petal, ch3, 1hdc into sp before sc at beg of next petal, ch3, 1hdc into same sp, rep from * twice, ch3, 1sc into top of next petal, ch6, 1sc into top of next petal, ch3, 1hdc into sp before sc at beg of next petal, ch3. Join with ss to 1st of first 3ch.

5th round *Ch4, into ch6 sp work 3dc, ch3, 3dc, ch4, 1sc into hdc, 1sc into ch3 sp, 1sc into hdc, rep from * to end. Join with ss to 1st of first 4ch.

6th round *Ch5, 1dc into each of next 3dc, ch5, insert hook into 3rd ch from hook and work 1sc to form picot, ch2, 1dc into each of next 3dc, ch5, ss into next sc, ch4, insert hook into 3rd ch from hook and work 1sc to form picot, ch1, skip 1sc, ss into next sc, rep from * to end. Join with ss to 1st of first 5ch. Fasten off.

2nd motif

Work as given for 1st motif until 5th round has been completed.

6th round Ch5, 1dc into each of next 3dc, ch2, 1sc into corner picot of 1st motif, ch2, 1dc into each of next 3dc on 2nd motif, ss into 1st of 5ch after dc of 1st motif, ch4, ss into next sc of 2nd motif, ch1, 1sc into center side picot of 1st motif, ch1, skip 1sc on 2nd motif, ss into next sc, ch4, ss into ch before next 3dc on 1st motif, 1dc into each of next 3dc on 2nd motif, ch2, ss into picot at end of 1st motif, ch2. Complete this round as given for 1st motif.

Work 20 more motifs in same way, joining 8 to form first row.

On next row, join 2 motifs on 2 sides to form right front, 4 motifs to next 4 motifs for center back and 2 motifs to last 2 motifs for left front.

On next row, skip first motif of right front and join 1 motif to next motif, 4 motifs to next 4 motifs and 1 motif to next motif for left front, joining shoulder seams at same time. Fasten off. Darn in all ends.

Edging

Beg at center back of lower edge and into each ch sp and picot work 1sc, 1dc, ch3, 1dc, 1sc, around all edges, ss to first sc. Fasten off.
Darn in ends.
Work around armholes in same way and ss along underarm.
Sew on 6 buttons evenly spaced to left front to correspond with ch3 between dcs on right front.
Press lightly under a damp cloth with a warm iron.

The button fastening can be worn at either the front or the back

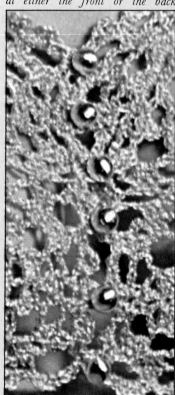

Gold & silver evening blouse

Basic Wardrobe Crochet

As a versatile addition to your evening wardrobe, try making this blouse that doubles as a lacy jacket. Wear it with your favorite skirt or over a plain sleeveless dress. Pick a thread with a lovely subtle sparkle—glowing gold, shimmering silver, gleaming bronze or lustrous copper. Combine two colors or use any one of them.

Sizes
Directions are for 34in bust. Length down center back, approx. 18½ [19:19½]in. The figures given in brackets [] refer to the 36 and 38in sizes respectively.

Gauge
3 clusters to 1in
3 rows to 1¼in.

Materials
8 [8:9] balls of Bucilla Brocade in silver
6 [7:7] balls in gold
No.E crochet hook
4 small crocheted buttons

Abbreviations
See Crochet Know-how 1

Back

Using the gold, ch102 [108: 114].
1st row Work 3dc into 3rd ch from hook leaving last loop of each dc on hook (4 loops on hook), yoh, draw through all loops to form 1 cluster (abbrev. cl). Ch 1, skip 1 ch, *1 cl into next ch, ch 1, skip 1 ch, rep from * to end working 1 dc into last ch.

280

Turn.
2nd row Using the silver, join with ss, ch2, *1 cl into next ch sp, ch 1, rep from *, ending with 1 dc.
Leave the silver.
Continue working as for 2nd row, alt using gold and silver and working from the end where the required color has been left to avoid joining.
To start a new row, work a long loop and ss into edge of last row, work 2ch and continue in patt.
Work until 11 [11¼:11½]in from start.

Shape armholes
Keeping patt correct, work 4cl less at each end of next row, and 1 cl less at each end of following row.
Work without further shaping until armholes measure 6¼ [6½:6¾]in.

Shape shoulder
Work 4cl less at armhole edges and skip 1 ch after last cl, 1 dc into next ch sp. Turn.
Next row Work 3cl, skip 1 ch after last cl, 1 dc into next ch sp.
Break yarn.
Work other shoulder in same way.

Left front

Using the gold, ch44 [48:52].
Work in patt as given for back until work measures same to armhole.

Shape armhole
Work 4cl less at side edge.
Work without shaping until center front edge measures 14¼ [14½:14¾]in.

Shape neck
1st row Work 5cl less at center front, work to end. Turn.
2nd row Patt to last ch sp, skip 1 ch after last cl, 1 dc into edge. Turn.
3rd row Work cl into first ch sp, patt to end. Turn.
4th row as 2nd row.
Continue without further shaping until armhole measures same as back to shoulder.

Shape shoulder
Work as given for back shoulder.
Finish off.

Right front

Work in same way as for left front.

Sleeves

Using the gold, ch68 [70:72].
Work in patt for 6 [7:8] rows.

Shape cap
Work 3cl less at each end of next row.
Work 1 cl less at each end of next 13 [13:14] rows.
Break yarn and finish off.

Finishing
Sew shoulder and side seams.

Border
Using the silver, work sleeve borders.
1st row *1 sc into each of next 4ch, dec in next 2ch by inserting hook into next ch, yoh and draw through ch, insert hook into next ch, yoh and draw through ch, yoh and draw through all loops, rep from * to end. Turn.
2nd row Ch2, *yoh, insert hook into next sc (yoh and draw through a long loop) 4 times in the same st, yoh and draw through all loops on hook to make 1 puff, ch 1, skip 1 ch, rep from * to end. Turn.
3rd row Ch2, 1 sc into the top of each puff and each ch to end of row. Turn.
4th row *Ch3, 1 dc into next sc, skip 1 sc, 1 sc into next sc, rep from * to end of row.

Finishing

Work other sleeve border in the same way.
Work border around jacket in same way starting at side seam and working 1 sc into each ch along lower edge, 1 sc, ch2, 1 sc into corner st, 2sc into each row up front edges, and dec twice on curves at front neck and once on either curve at back as given for sleeve. On the following row work 2ch between the puffs at the corners.
Sew sleeve seams and set in sleeves.
Sew on buttons if desired with the spaces between the puffs acting as buttonholes.

Detailed close-up of the pattern and edging of the gold and silver blouse

Glamorous evening tunic

Make this elegant long tunic, crocheted in a simple stitch which has a see-through look without being too open, for glamorous evenings of wining and dining. Wear it over trousers or as it is.

Sizes

Directions are for 34-36in bust with 36-38in hips. Length down center back, 57in. Sleeve seam, 17½in.

Gauge
6 stitches and 3 rows to one inch worked over pattern on No.E crochet hook.

Materials

Unger English Crepe
32 1oz skeins
One No.E crochet hook
6in zipper

Back

Using No.E crochet hook, ch138.

1st row 1dc into 3rd ch from hook, 1dc into each ch to end. Turn. 136 sts.

2nd row Ch5, *skip 2dc, 1dc into next dc, ch2, rep from * to end, working 1dc into turning ch. Turn.

3rd row Ch5, *1dc into next dc, (2dc into ch2 sp, 1dc into next dc) 3 times, ch2, rep from * to end, working 1dc into turning ch. Turn.

4th row Ch5, *1dc into each of next 4dc, ch2, skip 2dc, 1dc into each of next 4dc, ch2, rep from * to end, working 1dc into turning ch. Turn.

5th row Ch5, *1dc into each of next 4dc, 2dc into ch2 sp,

1dc into each of next 4dc, ch2, rep from * to end, working 1dc into turning ch. Turn.

6th row Ch5, *1dc into next dc, (ch2, skip 2dc, 1dc into next dc) 3 times, ch2, rep from * to end, working 1dc into turning ch. Turn.

Rep rows 3-6 inclusive 14 times more—62 rows in all. Work should then measure approximately 20½in from beg.

Make side slits

Next row Ch5, 1dc into 1st and 2nd of these 5ch, 1dc into turning ch dc of previous row, ch2, 1dc into next dc, patt to end.

Next row As last row. 142 sts.

Continue in patt, dec one st at each end of every 4th row until 112 sts rem.

Continue without shaping until work measures 50in from beg, or desired length to underarm.

Shape armholes

Next row Ss over first 6 sts, patt to last 6 sts, turn.

Dec one st at each end of next 6 rows. 88 sts.

Continue without shaping until armholes measure 3in from beg, ending WS row.

Divide for back opening

Next row Patt over first 43 sts, turn.

Continue in patt until armhole measures 7in from beg, ending at center edge.

Shape shoulder

Next row Patt to last 8 sts, turn.

Next row Ss over first 8 sts,

patt next 8 sts. Fasten off.

With RS of work facing, skip next 2 sts for center back, attach yarn to rem sts and patt to end. Complete to match first side.

Front

Work as given for back until armhole shaping is completed. Continue without shaping until armholes measure 5 rows less than back, ending with a WS row.

Shape neck

Next row Patt over first 35 sts, turn.

Next row Ss over first 3 sts, patt to end, turn.

Next row Patt to last 3 sts, turn.

Next row Ss over first 3 sts, patt to end, turn.

Next row Patt to last 2 sts, turn.

Next row Patt to last 8 sts, turn.

Next row Ss over first 8 sts, patt to end. Fasten off.

With RS of work facing, skip next 18 sts for center neck, attach yarn to rem sts and patt to end. Complete to match first side.

Sleeves

Using No.E crochet hook, ch54.

Work in patt as given for back (52 sts) for 6 rows.

Continue in patt, inc one st at each end of next and every following 4th row until there are 76 sts.

Continue without shaping

until sleeve measures 17½in from beg, or desired length to underarm.

Shape cap

Next row Ss over first 6 sts, patt to last 6 sts, turn.

Dec one st at each end of next 6 rows.

Next row Patt to last 4 sts, turn.

Rep last row 9 times more. Finish off.

Finishing

Press each piece under a damp cloth with a warm iron. Join shoulder and sleeve seams. Join side seams as far as side slits.

Collar. Using No.E crochet hook, ch90. Work in patt as given for back (88 sts) for 10 rows. Finish off.

Slit edges. Using No.E crochet hook and with RS of work facing, attach yarn to lower edge and work 1 row of dc to where extra sts were cast on, working 2dc into each row. Finish off.

Sew in sleeves. Sew on collar. Work 2 rows sc along sides of collar and back opening. Sew in zipper. Press seams.

Cord belt

Using No.E crochet hook and yarn double throughout, ch2. Insert hook into first ch, *yoh, draw through a loop, yoh, draw through both loops on hook*, insert hook into the left of these 2 loops and work from * to * for required length. Finish off.

▼ *Stitch detail*

Tunic with a metal link belt ▶

Plaid crochet pullover for a man

Here is an exciting pattern that you will find fun to make for someone you love— a man's sleeveless pullover in an unusual plaid effect crochet with the armbands and neckline worked in basic single crochet.

Sizes

Directions are for 38in chest. The figures in brackets [] refer to the 40 and 42in sizes respectively.

Gauge
5 vertical stripes to 2in.

Materials

Reynolds Cashmere/Lamb
8 balls brown
6 balls beige
2 balls natural
One No.G crochet hook
One No.K crochet hook

NB This garment is worked in 2 stages—the mesh background is worked first and the vertical stripes worked in afterward using yarn double throughout.

Front

Using No.G hook and single beige yarn, ch102[106: 110].

1st row Into 6th ch from hook work 1dc, *ch1, skip 1ch, 1dc into next ch, rep from * to end. Turn. 49[51:53] sp.
2nd row Ch4, skip first dc and 1ch, *1dc into next dc, ch1, skip 1ch, rep from * ending with 1dc into turning ch. The 2nd row forms the patt

and is rep throughout changing color as desired.
Work 4 rows beige and 2 rows brown throughout.
Work without shaping until 7th beige stripe is complete.

Shape armholes

1st row Skip 2 sp and join brown into next dc, ch4, patt over 45[47:49] sp, ending with 1dc and leaving 2 sp at end unworked. Turn.
2nd row Ss into 2nd dc, ch4, patt over 43[45:47] sp, ending with 1dc. Fasten off. Turn.
3rd row Skip first sp and attach beige into 2nd dc, ch4, patt over 41[43:45] sp. Turn.
This completes armhole shaping and sides are now kept straight.

Shape neck, left side

1st row Ch4, patt over 19[20: 21] sp, 1dc. Turn.
2nd row Ch4, work in patt to end. Turn.
3rd row Ch4, patt over 18[19:20] sp, ending with 1dc. Turn.
4th row Using brown, ch4, patt to end. Turn.
Continue dec 1 sp at neck edge every other row until 12 sp rem, keeping stripes correct.
Work without shaping until 2nd row of 5th beige stripe has been completed. Fasten off.

Shape neck, right side

1st row Skip 1 sp at neck edge, join beige into next dc, patt over 19[20:21] sp ending with 1 dc. Turn.
2nd row Ch4, patt over 18 [19:20] sp, ch4, skip 1ch and work 1sc into next dc.

Continue shaping in this manner until shoulder corresponds to other side. Fasten off.

Back

Work as given for front until armhole shaping is complete. Continue in patt without shaping until armholes measure same as front to shoulder, ending with 2 rows beige. Fasten off.

Work vertical stripes

Using No. K hook and double beige, begin at base of center front sp.
Make a slip loop. Holding right side of mesh ground facing, insert hook into loop and work with yarn kept at back of work (see Crochet Know-how Chapter 13). Work to up top edge keeping work to the correct measurement.
Work other stripes to side edges in the following order: *2 brown, 1 beige, 1 brown, 3 natural, 1 brown, 1 beige, 2 brown, 1 natural, rep from * to side edges.
Work back in same way.

Finishing

Darn in all ends.
Block and press each piece to correct size.

Lower edgings

Using No.G hook and single brown, work 99[103: 107]sc along lower edge of front.
1st row Ch1, *1sc into next sc, rep from * to end. Turn.
Rep 1st row until edging measures 2½in, ending with a RS row.
Fasten off.
Work back in same manner. Join shoulder seams.

Armbands

Using No.G hook and brown, with RS facing, work 118sc evenly around armhole.
Work in rows of sc as for edging for 4 rows more.
Fasten off.
Work second armhole in same manner.

Neckband

Using No.G hook and brown, with RS facing, attach yarn at left shoulder seam.
1st row Work 47sc to center front, 47sc to right shoulder seam and 43sc across back neck.
Work 6 rows sc as given for edging dec 1 st at each side of center front on every row, and 1 st at each shoulder seam on every RS row only.
Fasten off.
Join neckband seam.
Sew side seams.
Press lightly.

▼ *Detail of plaid effect stitch*

Simple yet effective plaid crochet ►

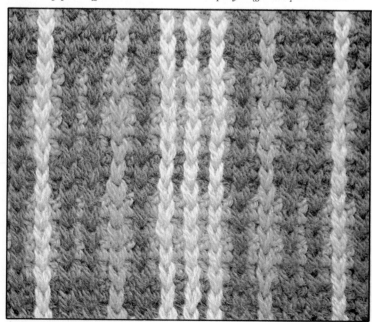

INDEX

AB